CATHOLICISM CONTENDING WITH MODERNITY
Roman Catholic Modernism and Anti-Modernism in Historical Context

This book is a case study in the ongoing struggle of Christianity to define its relationship to modernity, examining representative Roman Catholic Modernists and anti-Modernists, and exploring their relationship to their own historical context. Its aim is to counteract the tendency to lift the proposals made by the Modernists out of their setting and define them as a coherent, timeless philosophical/theological outlook which should be avoided. The book seeks to correct the proclivity of some contemporary proponents of Modernist ideas to de-contextualize those ideas and recommend their endorsement without a critical reconsideration of historical changes. It sketches the nineteenth-century background of the Modernist crisis, identifying the problems that the church was facing at the beginning of the twentieth century; and offers a fresh perspective on the Modernist crisis, a perspective arising from the pioneering work undertaken by the Roman Catholic Modernism Working Group of the American Academy of Religion.

DARRELL JODOCK is Bernhardson Professor of Lutheran Studies at Gustavus Adolphus College, St. Peter, Minnesota, and author of *The Church's Bible: Its Contemporary Authority* (1989) and editor and co-author of *Ritschl in Retrospect: History Community and Science* (1995). Until 1999 he taught at Muhlenberg College, Allentown, Pennsylvania. Founder of the Institute for Jewish-Christian Understanding at Muhlenberg, he served as the Chairman of its Board from 1989 to 1999. Since 1988 Professor Jodock has served on the steering committee of the Roman Catholic Modernism Seminar of the American Academy of Religion, as well as a variety of committees within the Evangelical Lutheran Church in America.

CATHOLICISM CONTENDING WITH MODERNITY

Roman Catholic Modernism and Anti-Modernism in Historical Context

EDITED BY

DARRELL JODOCK

CAMBRIDGE
UNIVERSITY PRESS

PUBLISHED BY THE PRESS SYNDICATE OF THE UNIVERSITY OF CAMBRIDGE
The Pitt Building, Trumpington Street, Cambridge, United Kingdom

CAMBRIDGE UNIVERSITY PRESS
The Edinburgh Building, Cambridge CB2 2RU, UK   www.cup.cam.ac.uk
40 West 20th Street, New York, NY 10011–4211, USA   www.cup.org
10 Stamford Road, Oakleigh, Melbourne 3166, Australia
Ruiz de Alarcón 13, 28014 Madrid, Spain

First published 2000

Printed in the United Kingdom at the University Press, Cambridge

Typeset in Baskerville 11/12.5pt [CE]

A catalogue record for this book is available from the British Library

Library of Congress cataloguing in publication data

Catholicism contending with modernity: Roman Catholic modernism and anti-modernism in
historical context / edited by Darrell Jodock.
p.   cm.
Includes bibliographical references and index.
ISBN 0 521 77071 8 (hardback)
1. Modernism (Christian theology) – Catholic Church – History.
I. Jodock, Darrell, 1941–.
BX1396.C39   2000
273′.9 – dc21   00–34666 CIP

ISBN 0 521 77071 8 hardback

Contents

v

Contributors

LAWRENCE BARMANN, *Professor, Departments of American Studies and Theological Studies, St. Louis University, St. Louis, Missouri.*

PETER BERNARDI, S.J., *Assistant Professor, Department of Religious Studies, Loyola University of New Orleans, New Orleans, Louisiana.*

GABRIEL DALY, O.S.A., *School of Hebrew, Biblical, and Theological Studies, Trinity College, Dublin, Ireland.*

HARVEY HILL, *Assistant Professor, Department of Religion and Philosophy, Berry College, Mount Berry, Georgia.*

DARRELL JODOCK, *Professor, Religion Department, Gustavus Adolphus College, St. Peter, Minnesota.*

PHYLLIS H. KAMINSKI, *Associate Professor, Department of Religious Studies, St. Mary's College, Notre Dame, Indiana.*

MICHAEL J. KERLIN, *Professor and Chair of the Philosophy Department, LaSalle University, Philadelphia, Pennsylvania.*

GARY LEASE, *Professor, History of Consciousness Department, University of California, Santa Cruz, California.*

ELLEN M. LEONARD, C.S.J., *Professor, Faculty of Theology, University of St. Michael's College, Toronto, Ontario, Canada.*

PAUL MISNER, *Professor, Department of Theology, Marquette University, Milwaukee, Wisconsin.*

C. J. T. TALAR, *Professor, St. Mary's Seminary and University, Baltimore, Maryland.*

GEORGE H. TAVARD, *Professor Emeritus, Methodist Theological School in Ohio, Delaware, Ohio.*

Acknowledgments

Not many things that we humans do are accomplished in isolation from others, and this collaborative project is certainly no exception. Many have contributed to it.

Most obvious are the authors of the various chapters. They have been splendid colleagues – cooperative, diligent, insightful, good-humored, and patient with their editor. Thank you.

Preliminary drafts of the papers found in this volume were reviewed and discussed at the 1994, 1995, and 1996 sessions of the American Academy of Religion Roman Catholic Modernism Seminar. Those sessions included formal respondents. Although their responses do not appear in this volume, their contributions were significant and deserve to be acknowledged with appreciation. The following persons served as respondents (listed in chronological order):

THOMAS KSELMAN, *University of Notre Dame, Indiana*

THOMAS F. O'MEARA, *University of Notre Dame, Indiana*

JAMES C. LIVINGSTON, *The College of William and Mary, Virginia*

C. J. T. TALAR, *then at Alvernia College, Pennsylvania; now at St. Mary's Seminary and University, Maryland*

WENDELL DIETRICH, *Brown University, Rhode Island*

LORETTA M. DEVOY, *St. John's University, New York*

BRIAN J. KELTY, *Australian Catholic University, Australia*

KENNETH L. PARKER, *St. Louis University, Missouri*

NADIA M. LAHUTSKY, *Texas Christian University, Texas*

JOHN A. MCGRATH, *University of Dayton, Ohio*

STEPHEN HAPPEL, *Catholic University, Washington, D.C.*

DAVID G. SCHULTENOVER, *Creighton University, Nebraska*

WILLIAM POITIER, *Mount St. Mary's College, Maryland*

The members and the steering committee of the Roman Catholic Modernism Group of the American Academy of Religion deserve a great deal of credit for initiating, supporting, and encouraging the project. They have provided the crucible within which its ideas took shape. Without the lively discussions in that Group and the considered suggestions of its members, the chapters would neither be as strong nor as interesting as they now are.

Professor George Gilmore, Spring Hill College, Alabama, handled the logistics of collecting, printing, and distributing drafts of the papers prior to the 1994, 1995, and 1996 Annual Meetings of the American Academy of Religion. It was an important, albeit unheralded, contribution.

Two members of that Group deserve special recognition for the careful advice and counsel that they gave me on several occasions regarding the design of the project: James C. Livingston of the College of William and Mary in Virginia and Paul Misner of Marquette University in Wisconsin.

Another source of good counsel has been Kevin Taylor, Senior Commissioning Editor at Cambridge University Press. During the review and the approval of the manuscript, a number of questions and dilemmas arose. I soon learned I could count on him to seek out appropriate information and to make judicious decisions. For his assistance and good judgment I am grateful.

My thanks to secretary *extraordinaire*, Mrs. Elsie Schmoyer, for the hours she spent re-formatting the essays. As always, she worked with care and good humor and kindly brought to my attention things that I had missed.

And last, but certainly not least, my profound thanks to Muhlenberg College for providing me with the setting and the support to undertake the task and to Gustavus Adolphus College for providing a new setting in which to complete it.

Gustavus Adolphus College, St. Peter, Minnesota　　　DARRELL JODOCK

Abbreviations

For works cited in more than one chapter

Barmann, *Baron*	Lawrence F. Barmann. *Baron Friedrich von Hügel and the Modernist Crisis in England.* Cambridge: Cambridge University Press, 1972.
Blondel, *Action*	Maurice Blondel. *Action: Essay on a Critique of Life and a Science of Practice.* Translated by Oliva Blanchetti. Notre Dame, Indiana: University of Notre Dame Press, 1984. English translation of *L'Action: essai d'une critique de la vie et d'une science de la pratique,* 1893. Most recently published in Maurice Blondel, *Œuvres complètes,* vol. I: *1893 Les Deux Thèses.* Paris: Presses Universitaires de France, 1995.
Blondel, *Letter*	A. Dru and I. Trethowan (eds.). *Maurice Blondel: The Letter on Apologetics and History and Dogma.* London: Harvill Press, 1964. Reprinted: Grand Rapids, Michigan: William B. Eerdmans Publishing Co., 1994. English translation of Maurice Blondel, *Lettre sur les exigences de la pensée contemporaine en matière d'apologétique* (1896) in *Les Premiers Ecrits de Maurice Blondel.* Vol. II. Paris: Presses Universitaires de France, 1956.
Blondel, *LSS*	Maurice Blondel. *La Semaine sociale de Bordeaux et le monophorisme.* Paris: Bloud &

Gay, 1910. Reprint of a series of articles published between October 1909 and May 1910 under the pseudonym of "Testis" in the *Annales de philosophie chrétienne* 159 (October 1909), 5–22; (November) 162–184; (December) 245–278; (January 1910) 372–392; (February) 449–472; (March), 561–592; and 160 (May 1910), 127–162.

Chadwick, *Secularization* Owen Chadwick. *The Secularization of the European Mind in the Nineteenth Century.* Cambridge: Cambridge University Press, 1975.

Daly, *Transcendence* Gabriel Daly. *Transcendence and Immanence: A Study in Catholic Modernism and Integralism.* Oxford: Oxford University Press, 1980.

Fitzer (ed.), *Romance* Joseph Fitzer (ed.). *Romance and the Rock: Nineteenth-Century Catholics on Faith and Reason.* Minneapolis: Fortress Press, 1989.

Jenkins (ed.), *Newman* Arthur H. Jenkins (ed.). *John Henry Newman and Modernism.* Sigmaringendorf: Glock und Lutz, 1990. Special issue of *Internationale Cardinal-Newman-Studien.*

Keylor, *Academy* William R. Keylor. *Academy and Community: The Foundation of the French Historical Profession.* Cambridge, Massachusetts: Harvard University Press, 1975.

Komonchak, "Modernity" Joseph A. Komonchak. "Modernity and the Construction of Roman Catholicism." *Modernism as a Social Construct.* Papers of the American Academy of Religion Working Group on Roman Catholic Modernism. Mobile, Alabama: Spring Hill College, 1991. Pp. 11–41.

Kurtz, *Politics* Lester R. Kurtz. *The Politics of Heresy: The Modernist Crisis in Roman Catholicism.* Berkeley, California: The University of California Press, 1986.

Loisy, *Autour*	Alfred Loisy. *Autour d'un petit livre.* Paris: Alphonse Picard et Fils, 1903.
Loisy, *Duel*	Alfred Loisy. *My Duel with the Vatican.* Translated by Richard Wilson Boynton. New York: E. P. Dutton & Company, 1924. Reprinted: New York: Greenwood Press, 1968. English translation of *Choses passées.* Paris: Nourry, 1913.
Loisy, *Gospel*	Alfred Loisy. *The Gospel and the Church.* New edition with a prefatory memoir by the Rev. G. Tyrrell. Translated by Christopher Home. London: Pitman & Sons, 1908. Reprinted: Philadelphia: Fortress Press, 1976. English translation of *L'Evangile et l'Eglise.* Paris: Alphonse Picard et Fils, 1902.
Loisy, *Histoire*	Alfred Loisy. *Histoire du canon d'Ancien Testament.* Paris: Letouzey, 1890. Reprinted: Frankfurt: Minerva G.M.B.H., 1971.
Loisy, *Mémoires*	Alfred Loisy. *Mémoires pour servir à l'histoire religieuse de notre temps.* Paris: Nourry, 1930–31. 3 vols.
Loome, *Liberal*	Thomas M. Loome. *Liberal Catholicism, Reform Catholicism, Modernism: A Contribution to a New Orientation in Modernist Research.* Mainz: Grünewald, 1979.
McCool, *Catholic*	Gerald A. McCool. *Catholic Theology in the Nineteenth Century: The Quest for a Unitary Method.* New York: Seabury Press, 1977. Republished as *Nineteenth-Century Scholasticism.* New York: Fordham University Press, 1989.
Misner, *Social*	Paul Misner. *Social Catholicism in Europe: From the Onset of Industrialization to the First World War.* New York: Crossroad, 1991.
O'Connell, *Critics*	Marvin R. O'Connell. *Critics on Trial: An Introduction to the Catholic Modernist Crisis.* Washington, D.C.: Catholic University Press of America, 1994.

Petre, *Life*   Maude D. Petre. *Autobiography and Life of George Tyrrell*. London: Arnold, 1912. 2 vols.

Poulat, *Histoire*   Emile Poulat. *Histoire, dogme et critique dans la crise moderniste*. Second edition. Paris: Casterman, 1979.

Schultenover, *View*   David Schultenover. *A View from Rome*. New York: Fordham University Press, 1993.

Tyrrell, *Medievalism*   George Tyrrell. *Medievalism: A Reply to Cardinal Mercier*. New York: Longmans, Green and Co., 1909. Reprinted: Tunbridge Wells: Burns & Oates, 1994, with a foreword by Gabriel Daly.

Tyrrell, *Scylla*   George Tyrrell. *Through Scylla and Charybdis; or, The Old Theology and the New*. London: Longmans, Green and Co., 1907.

Vidler, *Variety*   Alec. R. Vidler. *A Variety of Catholic Modernists*. Cambridge: Cambridge University Press, 1970.

Virgoulay, *Blondel*   René Virgoulay. *Blondel et le Modernisme: la philosophie de l'action et les sciences religieuses (1896–1913)*. Paris: Editions du Cerf, 1980.

Von Hügel, *Eternal*   Baron Friedrich von Hügel. *Eternal Life: A Study of Its Implications and Applications*. Edinburgh: T. & T. Clark, 1912.

Von Hügel, *Letters*   Bernard Holland (ed.). *Baron Friedrich von Hügel: Selected Letters, 1896–1924*. London: Dent, 1928.

Von Hügel, *Mystical*   Baron Friedrich von Hügel. *The Mystical Element of Religion as Studied in Saint Catherine of Genoa and Her Friends*. Second edition. London: Dent, 1923. 2 vols.

Weisz, *Emergence*   George Weisz. *The Emergence of Modern Universities in France, 1863–1914*. Princeton, New Jersey: Princeton University Press, 1983.

Note on the text

Chapter 8, 'The Modernist as mystic' by Lawrence Barmann, was published in substantially the same form in the October 1997 issue of the *Zeitschrift für Neuere Theologiegeschichte / Journal for the History of Modern Theology* (Walter de Gruyter, Berlin).

Introduction I: the Modernist crisis

Darrell Jodock

On 8 September 1907 Pope Pius X issued *Pascendi dominici gregis*, an encyclical in which he condemned "Modernism" as the "synthesis of all heresies."[1] The Modernists, he said, "lay the axe not to the branches and shoots, but to the very root, that is, to the faith and its deepest fires . . . so that there is no part of Catholic truth from which they hold their hand, none that they do not strive to corrupt."[2] In the pope's mind the Modernists posed a threat to the church that was all the more dangerous because "the partisans of error are to be sought not only among the Church's open enemies; they lie hid, a thing to be deeply deplored and feared, in her very bosom and heart."[3] In *Pascendi* this "Modernism" was defined in such an encompassing way, those labeled "Modernists" were condemned with such vehemence, and the measures prescribed to prevent its growth were so stringent that it virtually slammed the door on any historical study of the Bible, on theological creativity, and on church reform. The door would remain closed for the next three decades. Its consequences were serious and far-reaching.

What kind of perceived threat elicited this response? Who were the Modernists and what did they advocate? And what was the origin of the anti-Modernism that reached full expression in this encyclical? These questions, and others like them, will occupy this entire volume. Its chapters will explore the various personal, social, political, ecclesiastical, and theological backgrounds that influenced the major actors in this "Modernist crisis," as the episode has come to be called. Rather than offering exhaustive answers, the task of this introduction is more modest: first, to set the scene and give some

---

[1] One translation of *Pascendi* can be found in *The Papal Encyclicals*, vol. III: *1903–1939*, ed. Claudia Carlen (Raleigh, North Carolina: McGrath Publishing Company, 1981), pp. 71–98. The phrase cited appears on p. 89, §39.
[2] Ibid., p. 72, §3.   [3] Ibid., p. 71, §2.

preliminary indication of the issues and persons involved and, then, to explain the purpose of the volume and the significance of the topic.

An initial observation must be made: if Modernism is defined as a coherent system of thought, no such thing existed prior to the encyclical. Alfred Loisy, Friedrich von Hügel, and George Tyrrell, all among those regularly considered to be Modernists, each objected to the accuracy of the portrait drawn by the encyclical. As Bernard Reardon points out, "Loisy, himself the most distinguished of them [the Modernists], refused to accept any description of the move-ment's adherents as 'a homogeneous and united group'" and called "the pope's exposition of their doctrines 'a fantasy of the theological imagination.'"[4] The encyclical itself admits as much (in a passage which also reveals its low opinion of the Modernists):

since the Modernists (as they are commonly and rightly called) employ a very clever artifice, namely, to present their doctrines without order and systematic arrangement into one whole, scattered and disjointed one from another, so as to appear to be in doubt and uncertainty, while they are in reality firm and steadfast, it will be of advantage . . . to bring their teachings together here into one group, and to point out the connexion between them.[5]

Pascendi proceeds to organize and define the system of thought; then its author goes on to claim that he has shown "that their system does not consist in scattered and unconnected theories, but in a perfectly organised body, all the parts of which are solidly joined so that it is *not possible to admit one without admitting all.*"[6] The lasting power of the encyclical resided partly in this claim, because, during the years to follow, a person who espoused any idea associated with the system it had erected was presumed to be guilty of endorsing the complete compilation of "all heresies." That person became a target for the full opprobrium of the anti-Modernists.

Pascendi did not name any names or condemn any particular individuals. However, several who are identified below were among those under suspicion. These Modernists did not constitute a unified school of thought; they were not the followers of a single charismatic or intellectual leader, nor were they very numerous. A handful of people, each of whom had priorities and areas of interest somewhat

---

[4] Bernard M. G. Reardon, "Introduction" to *Roman Catholic Modernism* (Stanford, California: Stanford University Press, 1970), p. 10.
[5] *Pascendi*, p. 72, §4.   [6] Ibid., p. 89, §39. Emphasis added.

different from the others, were engaged in what can best be described as tentative explorations. Their commonality came primarily from what they were seeking to avoid. In the face of the rigidities of neo-scholastic versions of Catholicism and its resistance to notions of historical development and change, these Catholics were seeking an alternative way of interpreting the faith. What if some of the same tools that were being used by non-Catholic theologians could be used to interpret Catholicism? What if historical criticism of the Bible could be incorporated into a Catholic understanding of Christian origins? What if doctrinal development could be understood in a positive way? What if the church could be selective, accepting some features of modernity (e.g., its democracy) while rejecting others (e.g., its individualism)?

Not only were the Modernists united by the neo-scholasticism they sought to avoid, another similarity was that each person's program issued in a call for reform.[7] Their approaches and priorities differed, and the specific proposals for updating the structure and theology of the church varied from one Modernist to another, but they agreed that change was needed in order for the church to respond effectively to the challenges of modernity. Yet another similarity was that their call for reform issued from a deeply held conviction that Catholicism could and should play a part in transforming European society. They were motivated by hope and by a dedication to Catholicism and its ideals (as they understood them).

PIUS X'S VIEW OF MODERNISM

Without naming names, *Pascendi* declared persons conducting such explorations to be enemies of the church. Again and again, the encyclical called into question the motives and integrity of the Modernists. Not only do the Modernists advocate doctrines that are contrary to each other, it said, they "display a certain contempt for Catholic doctrines."[8] They employ "a thousand noxious arts," "disdain all authority . . . and relying upon a false conscience, they

---

[7] In this regard, the Modernists moved beyond the "liberal Catholics" of previous decades who advocated freedom of scholarly inquiry. The Modernists shared with the earlier liberal Catholics a concern about relating contemporary knowledge to Catholicism, but liberal Catholics did not call for the kind of theological and ecclesiastical reform envisioned by the Modernists.

[8] *Pascendi*, p. 78, §18.

attempt to ascribe to a love of truth that which is in reality the result of pride and obstinacy."[9] Their ideas stem from ignorance, unregulated curiosity, and pride. Pride "puffs them up with that vainglory which allows them to regard themselves as the sole possessors of knowledge, and . . . rouses in them the spirit of disobedience."[10] They do not seem to recognize that "their system means the destruction not of the Catholic religion alone but of all religion."[11] One cannot help but wonder why the pope portrayed persons who posed no organized threat as such insidious enemies and such dangerous traitors of the church. To this question various chapters in the book will return.

Pascendi assumes the validity of a specific philosophical/theological point of view. The encyclical operates with a distinction between nature and supernature – each in its own realm, each with its own way of being known. Closely related to this distinction is another: between reason and revelation. Unaided reason can understand nature and discern the existence of God. Revelation is supernatural, objectively given, and knowable. It was bestowed on humans via a "deposit of faith" that can be found in the Bible and in the immutable dogmas of the church. The church had been authorized to define and defend the faith. If one operates out of these assumptions, *Pascendi*'s critique of the system it calls Modernism makes sense. If one does not, its critique seems almost entirely external.

The basic philosophical errors that *Pascendi* claims to discern in Modernism are agnosticism and immanentism. Agnosticism is the teaching that "human reason is confined entirely within the field of *phenomena*, that is to say, to things that are perceptible to the senses, and in the manner in which they are perceptible; it has no right and no power to transgress these limits." "Given these premises, all will readily perceive what becomes of *Natural Theology*, of the *motives of credibility*, of *external revelation*. The Modernists simply make away with them altogether."[12] Agnosticism is thus a negative position; immanentism is its positive correlate. Because the Modernists cannot appeal to external revelation to explain religion, they seek its source instead "in man," in "a movement of the heart" which is called a "sentiment." "Hence the principle of *religious immanence* is formulated."[13] Modernism wrongly asserts, according to *Pascendi*, that

9 Ibid., p. 72, §3.   10 Ibid., pp. 90–91, quotation from p. 90, §40.
11 Ibid., p. 89, §39.   12 Ibid., p. 72, §6.   13 Ibid., p. 73, §7.

religion arises out of the human subconscious and that faith has no basis outside this internal religious sentiment. Modernism falls into fideism; that is, it bases everything on a willed faith for which no reasons can be given. For the Modernists, revelation is likewise to be found within the religious experience of humans. It is "at the same time *of* God and *from* God." From this "springs that ridiculous proposition of the Modernists, that every religion, according to the different aspect under which it is viewed, must be considered as both natural and supernatural. Hence it is that they make consciousness and revelation synonymous."[14]

Pascendi accuses the Modernists of reserving no special place for the truth of Catholic Christianity, because all religions spring from this religious sense: "Nor is the Catholic religion an exception; it is quite on a level with the rest; for it was engendered, by the process of *vital immanence.*"[15] Having denied the distinctiveness of Catholic revelation, the Modernists, *Pascendi* charges, go on to deny the immutability of dogma. For them the human intellect uses words merely to give expression to the faith that arises from the experience of immanence. On the basis of religious sentiment, the intellect creates formulas, and from these come dogma.

Consequently, the formulae too, which we call dogma, must be subject to these vicissitudes, and are, therefore, liable to change. Thus the way is open to the intrinsic *evolution* of dogma. An immense collection of sophisms this, that ruins and destroys all religion. Dogma is not only able, but ought to evolve and to be changed.[16]

This then is one of the specific things to which *Pascendi* stands opposed – any notion that dogma may have evolved or that it may need to change again.

Pascendi also objects to the historical criticism of the Bible. Over against those Modernists who claimed that historical investigations of the Bible were objective and independent undertakings, it asserts that the Modernists' "history and their criticism are saturated with their philosophy, and that their historico-critical conclusions are the natural fruit of their philosophical principles."[17] Their judgments regarding what is/is not historical are made on the basis of *subjective* standards. The Modernists often adopt the view that the books of the Bible evolved and were not written by the persons whose names

---

[14] Ibid., p. 74, §8.   [15] Ibid., p. 74, §10.   [16] Ibid., p. 75, §13.
[17] Ibid., p. 84, §30.

they bear. Hence "it is quite clear that the criticism We [Pius X] are concerned with is an *agnostic, immanentist, and evolutionist* criticism. Hence anybody who embraces it and employs it, makes profession thereby of the errors contained in it and places himself in opposition to Catholic faith."[18]

Pascendi acknowledges that the Modernists affirm the reality of the divine, but it rejects what it claims to be their basis for that affirmation – namely, "the *experience of the individual*."[19] Other theological notions to which it objects are Modernist views of faith and science, of dogma and the sacraments, of the inspiration of Scripture, of the church, and of church–state relations. On the path to "the annihilation of all religion" the first step "was taken by Protestantism; the second is made by Modernism; the next will plunge headlong into atheism."[20] For *Pascendi*, Modernism is clearly on the wrong road; it attempts to travel on a "slippery slope" that can only end in atheism.

As we have already indicated, one of the several reasons for the long-term impact of *Pascendi* was the anti-Modernist measures that it established. More specifically, it

(1) ordained (that is, reaffirmed what Leo XIII had already ordained) "that scholastic philosophy be made the basis of the sacred sciences";

(2) mandated that anyone "imbued with Modernism" be "excluded without compunction" from becoming or remaining a director or a professor of a seminary or a Catholic university;

(3) required bishops to "prevent writings infected with Modernism or favourable to it from being read when they have been published, and to hinder their publication when they have not";

(4) insisted that bishops "use the utmost severity in granting permission to print"; they must maintain a strict process for granting the *Imprimatur* and the *Nihil obstat*;

(5) prohibited congresses of priests except on very rare occasions and even then only "on condition that matters appertaining to the Bishops or the Apostolic See be not treated in them, and that no motions or postulates be allowed that would imply a usurpation of sacred authority, and that no mention be made in them of Modernism, presbyterianism, or laicism";

(6) established "Councils of Vigilance" in each diocese to "watch

---

[18] Ibid., p. 86, §34.   [19] Ibid., p. 76, §14.   [20] Ibid., p. 90, §39.

most carefully for every trace and sign of Modernism both in publications and in teaching." In order to preserve "the clergy and the young" from Modernism, these Councils of Vigilance "shall take all prudent, prompt and efficacious measures";

(7) required that bishops and generals of religious orders report to the Vatican every third year concerning the things mandated by the encyclical.[21]

In 1910 Pius X took an additional step. He required that all clerics and other officeholders take an oath against Modernism. That oath included a pledge to "reject the heretical theory of the evolution of dogmas" and to hold as certain "that faith is not a blind religious sense welling up from the recesses of the *subconscious* under the impulse of the heart and at the begging of a morally-informed will, but a genuine assent of the intellect to a truth received extrinsically by hearing, by an assent, namely, based on the authority of an all-truthful God."[22] The person taking the oath likewise promised to "submit and adhere whole-heartedly to the condemnations, declarations, and all the prescriptions which are contained in the encyclical letter 'Pascendi' and in the decree 'Lamentabili' [which in 1907 had condemned 65 propositions considered to be Modernist errors] especially those which bear on what is called history of dogma." The oath goes on to repudiate any view that a person can hold historical conclusions independent of belief so long as they do not deny it directly, to repudiate any interpreting of the Bible that discounts the church's tradition in favor of rationalistic procedures, to reject any view that "the teacher or writer in the field of historical theology must from the start set aside all preconceived ideas, whether about the supernatural origin of Catholic tradition, or about the promise of divine help in the enduring preservation of each revealed truth," and to condemn any view that the church fathers can be examined with the same "freedom of enquiry with which any profane document is normally examined." Finally, the oath required an expression of "vehement opposition to the error of the *modernists* who hold that there is nothing of divine character to be found in sacred tradition" and required an affirmation of the faith of the fathers as preserved by episcopal succession, "so that not what might seem better suited to the culture of each age should be held, [but] rather

---

[21] Ibid., pp. 92–97, §§44–56.
[22] The oath appears in appendix 2 of Daly, *Transcendence*, pp. 235–236. Subsequent quotations are from p. 236.

that the absolute and immutable truth first preached by the Apostles *should never be believed* or understood *in a different manner.*" Because the contents of this oath were considered to be part of church teaching, it proved to be an effective tool for transmitting anti-Modernism to subsequent generations of priests and officeholders.

These stringent measures not only stifled Modernism but also placed the full weight of the institution against historical investigations of church doctrine and the Scriptures, to say nothing of any suggestion of theological reform that was not recognizably neo-Thomist.

THE MODERNISTS

We return to the question, "Who were the Modernists?" In retrospect, it seems clear that there was no easily identifiable (to say nothing of an organized) group who could be so designated. Only a handful of scholars are usually included (although a relatively small number of priests and young Catholic intellectuals may also have been sympathetic to their ideas). Among these scholars some were concerned primarily with the freedom to pursue the historical study of the Bible and to take seriously its implications for theology; others focused primarily on developing a philosophical outlook that provided an alternative to neo-scholasticism. Some were critical of authoritarian uses of papal authority and resisted openly; others trimmed their sails to avoid confrontation. Some were pragmatists, others mystics. Some were saintly, others cantankerous. The Modernists often were openly critical of each other; they formed no uniform group.

Several individual Modernists will be identified in "Introduction II: the Modernists and the anti-Modernists."

THE ANTI-MODERNISTS

Historians have also asked, "Why were the Modernists regarded to be such a threat as to elicit the heavy-handed response found in *Pascendi?*" In order to answer that question, attention has turned to the anti-Modernists. The anti-Modernists measured every theological proposal according to the paired standards of neo-scholastic teachings and of unquestioning submission to papal authority. According to neo-scholasticism, a "perennial philosophy" existed that had been expressed most adequately by the thirteenth-century scholastics, among whom Thomas Aquinas was the leading authority. This philosophy assumed that the world was essentially static, not dynamic or developing. Historical changes did not affect the essential nature of persons or institutions, and consequently historical investigations, which detailed those unimportant changes, held little authority. Students normally encountered neo-scholasticism in manuals of theology whose formulations retained none of the vigor of healthy theological thinking, whether of the sort found in the thirteenth century or the late nineteenth. These manuals organized and disseminated conclusions rather than promoting theological inquiry.

Already by the 1850s the neo-Thomists had decided that the modern theologies of the first half of the nineteenth century were all "intrinsically unsatisfactory." According to Gerald McCool, "The adverb was all important. For, if the systems were *intrinsically* unsatisfactory, they could not be corrected from within, they would have to be replaced."[23] Their deficiency stemmed from their theory of knowledge. Only by abandoning their epistemological assumptions and adopting those of St. Thomas could a scientific theology be constructed. What is interesting to note, of course, is that *Pascendi* applied to Modernism the same criticism that the neo-Thomists of fifty years earlier had used against their opponents: the Modernists had a defective theory of knowledge. Anti-Modernism was following a well-known script, employing familiar ideas found in the teaching already ascendant in the seminaries.

Neo-scholasticism held that there are two realms of knowledge: the natural and the supernatural. The former can be known by unaided natural reason. Included in it was knowledge of the existence of God. The supernatural is known only when God chooses to reveal it. This realm contains information beyond the grasp of natural reason but, once given by God, it can be largely, although never completely, understood by reason. Access comes through the assent of faith. This faith, however, involves no "blind leap"; its assent can be aided and encouraged by rational arguments, including those drawing evidence from the "supernatural facts" of prophecy and miracle. It was very important, the neo-scholastics argued, to distinguish nature from supernature, the truths of reason

---

[23] McCool, *Catholic*, p. 138.

from the truths of revelation, and philosophy from theology, but this did not mean that they could be in conflict, because the God who was the author of nature and what could be known by reason was also the author of revelation and what could be known by faith.

As already indicated, the world-view employed by the neo-scholastics was static. Historical study was unimportant because it did not deal with the essence of the matter; it only traced the incidental changes experienced by humans and other temporal beings. The "nature" that the neo-scholastics claimed could be known by reason was a metaphysical reality not subject to the vicissitudes of temporal change. Moreover, the source of the super-natural was beyond history. It disclosed eternal truths that likewise were not subject to change. These truths could be found in the Bible, which the neo-scholastics interpreted as a handbook of theological axioms, and in tradition. On the inerrancy of biblical and doctrinal statements the whole theological system was built. The authority of the Bible was simply assumed; the neo-scholastics put their energy into building and refining the theological edifice rather than exam-ining its historical foundations. More attention was given to ex-plaining and defending the philosophical and theological system than to the historical study of the Bible. The definitive interpretation of the Bible and tradition was a task that had been bestowed on the church, particularly as embodied in the supremacy and infallibility of the papacy. The church's magisterium was to protect the faith from unwarranted changes brought about by new cultural pressures. For the anti-Modernists a neo-scholastic formulation of the faith and the faith itself were so identified that they could hardly be separated; to reject the formulation was to reject the faith itself.

In response to his own question why church authorities bothered with the Modernists, Lester Kurtz has observed:

In part, it may have been because the authorities were not cognizant of the consequences of their actions. More importantly, however, the existence of the modernist movement was not only a threat but a source of strength as well. The modernists were a symbolic focus for the hierarchy's attack on subversive forces, which it held responsible for the church's many problems.[24]

The Modernists enabled the anti-Modernists to redefine the bound-aries of belief. Excluded from those boundaries were not only the

[24] Kurtz, *Politics*, p. 17.

philosophical/theological explorations of the Modernists but also what came to be labeled "social modernism" – that is, favoring policies too accommodating of any non-hierarchical social arrangements, such as Sangnier's democratic *Sillon*, and of any labor unions outside of church control.

Several anti-Modernists will be identified in "Introduction II: the Modernists and the anti-Modernists."

MODERNISM AND ANTI-MODERNISM IN CONTEXT

The condemnation by Pius X automatically de-historicized Modernism. Without any reference to the persons who held those condemned thoughts or the circumstances under which they had been formulated, his encyclical defined Modernism as a coherent system of thought with a clear, albeit deliberately camouflaged, agenda. In a real sense, his encyclical created the organized pattern of thought to which it ascribed the label of "Modernism." Anyone who today uses the term "Modernism" in the way Pius X and his successors did has de-historicized and de-contextualized it. So used, the term refers to an abstraction rather than to a concrete historical phenomenon. For some very specific, carefully delimited purposes such an abstraction may be a useful form of shorthand but, as a historical designation, it is not. As Gabriel Daly observes in chapter three, it cannot serve as the basis upon which to interpret or to understand the Modernists.

However, many who have been inspired by the reformist tendencies of the Modernists have also de-historicized Modernism. If the Vatican made them villains, more recent reform-oriented theologians have sometimes made them heroes and claimed their legacy for positions on issues quite different from the ones they themselves addressed. There is nothing wrong, of course, with regarding them as heroes and claiming to follow in their tradition, but a definite risk is involved: appealing to the Modernists in this way tends also to de-historicize them. For a fuller and more nuanced understanding, the Modernists and the positions they advocated need to be viewed in their own historical context.

If one wants to draw accurate parallels, careful distinctions are important. For example, some observers see in recent developments the triumph of Modernism. It is true that part of what the Modernists stood for has been adopted. In 1943, in an encyclical entitled *Divino afflante spiritu*, Pope Pius XII sanctioned the use of historical-

critical methods in scriptural studies, thereby permitting the kind of
scholarly investigations that Loisy and von Hügel wanted to see.
Pope John XXIII (1958–1963) announced a policy of *aggiornamento*
which "opened the windows" to the modern world, thereby de-
sanctioning the "circle-the-wagons" mentality of the anti-Modernists. And the documents formulated by the Second Vatican Council
(1962–1965) did move away from neo-scholasticism and utilize a
more developmentalist view of Catholic history. However, when the
Modernist movement was condemned, it was only in an embryonic
stage. Those identified as Modernists were still exploring options;
diverse possibilities were under consideration. Without a coherent
agenda, no blanket statement can be made regarding the accom-
plishment of its goals. Moreover, the recent ideas that resemble those
favored by the Modernists have now been "domesticated." They
have been reworked in such a way that they are less threatening to
institutional authority. In the light of such reworking, can one still
say that the views of the Modernists actually triumphed? Moreover,
no one theological outlook prevails today. To the degree that
Modernist ideas have been accepted, they form a part of a "broad-
church" outlook that encompasses a variety of theological options.
Even if their ideas are no longer anathema, the Modernists have
hardly "triumphed."

Likewise, some observers draw parallels between the anti-
Modernists and the outlook of a Cardinal Ratzinger or parallels
between the condemnation of the Modernists and more recent
Vatican rulings that Hans Küng and Charles Curran are no longer
Catholic theologians. It is true that papal authority is still an issue,
and perceived challenges to that authority have affected these more
recent decisions as much as they did the condemnation of the
Modernists, but the context of such decisions has changed. For one
thing, neo-scholasticism is no longer as pervasive or as officially
sanctioned as it was in 1900. For another, by 1988 two-thirds of the
bishops were from places other than Europe and North America.
The attention of church officials is more and more frequently drawn
to developments in Africa, Asia, South America, and elsewhere.
However defensive the actions of the Vatican may sometimes be, it is
reacting against forces other than those found in the theological
conflicts and the church–state struggles occurring in turn-of-the-
century Europe. In other words, differences in the church's context
mean that discontinuities as well as continuities must be identified if

anti-Modernism is not to be lifted out of its own historical context to become another abstraction.

The present volume is an attempt to understand the Modernists and the anti-Modernists more deeply and more fully by placing them both in their historical context(s). It attempts to identify the multiple motives of the persons involved in the Modernist crisis. As the following essays will show, some Modernists were concerned about public education and about finding a place for the study of religion within the secular university. Other Modernists were concerned about reviving those traditions in Catholicism, such as mysticism, not emphasized by the neo-scholastics with their attention focused on rational understanding and on faith as intellectual assent. Meanwhile, the anti-Modernists often focused their attention as much on political developments as on theological issues. They felt that their own program for preventing the dechristianizing of Europe – a program that included neo-scholastic theology and tighter church authority – was jeopardized by the Modernists. As Paul Misner points out in chapter two, the anti-Modernists were there first; they already had a well-developed theological position that preceded Modernism and to which the Modernists were reacting. In order to reflect this reality, it would perhaps be better to re-label the parties as, say, the integralists (as some anti-Modernists came to be known) and the anti-integralists. However, this volume does not take that step; it retains the conventional labels.

BACKGROUND AND PURPOSE OF THIS VOLUME

As already indicated, the present volume seeks to explore the historical settings in which the Modernists and anti-Modernists worked. It asks: what issues, influences, and historical developments helped prompt each Modernist and each anti-Modernist to adopt the position that he/she did?

Its chapters emerge out of the investigations conducted by a group of theologians, historians, and philosophers who have since 1976 gathered at each Annual Meeting of the American Academy of Religion. This "Roman Catholic Modernism Group" began by investigating archival resources, the lives of individuals involved in the controversy, and the issues at stake between Modernists and anti-Modernists. Its members then decided that they needed to know more about the broader historical setting of the figures they were discussing. One important stimulus was an essay by Gary Lease, entitled "Modernism and 'Modernism': Christianity as Product of its Culture," which was presented in 1986 and subsequently published in the *Journal for the Study of Religion*.[25] Lease suggested that Roman Catholic Modernism needed to be understood within the context of a more general cultural upheaval occurring at the end of the nineteenth century: namely, cultural modernism. This upheaval undermined certainty regarding what was traditional, fixed, and eternal, and focused attention on the *perception* of reality. Developments in historical narrative, painting, music, politics, literature, and philosophy all give evidence of this "modernism and its problematic of representation."[26] Religion was not exempt. It "was profoundly shocked and sent reeling with the culture-wide recognition that our human attempts to *represent* reality were not that reality itself."[27] Although Lease acknowledged that this recognition was not entirely new, by the end of the nineteenth century, he claimed, it had permeated European culture and society to a degree not seen before.

Lease recommended that Roman Catholic Modernism and anti-Modernism should both be understood against the backdrop of cultural modernism. He did not mean to say, thereby, that the Modernists *endorsed* cultural modernism. They were critical of it while at the same time also being critical of "the institutional barrenness of their church."[28] However, they can be considered " 'modernists' in the sense that any sensitive, reflective and concerned European was at the turn of the century." They "recognized the moment of change in which they were situated, understood the nature of that change, if only partially, and participated in it, attempting to be full members of a culture and society only beginning to take form. To be a [Roman Catholic] Modernist, therefore, was to be a [cultural] 'modernist' first."[29] These "protagonists of Roman ecclesiastical reform can not be understood in any useful fashion without setting them within the broader framework of their culture's modernism."[30]

---

[25] *Journal for the Study of Religion* 1 (September 1988), 3–23. It also appeared in *"Odd Fellows" in the Politics of Religion: Modernism, National Socialism, and German Judaism* (Berlin and New York: Mouton de Gruyter, 1995), chapter 6, pp. 110–127.

[26] Ibid., p. 17.   [27] Ibid., p. 4.

[28] From sentences added by Lease in 1994. Unpublished working paper, Roman Catholic Modernism Seminar, American Academy of Religion, 1994, p. 5.

[29] Ibid., p. 19.   [30] Also from sentences added in 1994, p. 5.

In its subsequent discussions Lease's specific claims regarding the continuities between cultural modernism and Roman Catholic Modernism were not always endorsed by the Group – in fact some of his formulations engendered more disagreement than agreement – but his paper served as an important stimulus. He successfully challenged the Group to explore the impact of the larger cultural context with more intensity than it had before. In due time its members decided that their discoveries constituted contributions to an understanding of the Modernist crisis important enough that they should be made available to a wider audience. One possibility was to select essays that had already been presented within the Group. For a variety of reasons that plan was abandoned in favor of a proposal to solicit new essays. Over a three-year period, initial drafts of these new essays were prepared. With one exception (the paper by Peter Bernardi), each was discussed by the Group. All were subsequently revised, taking into account the suggestions received during those discussions.

It was originally envisioned that the volume would have two parts. Part I would contain essays that sketched the general background of Modernism and anti-Modernism. One essay would trace the ecclesial background, a second sketch the philosophical and theological antecedents, a third focus on the socio-political setting, and a fourth explore the regional differences influencing and separating Catholics in France, England, and Italy. Part II would contain essays that explored specific influences on the thinking and behavior of individual Modernists or anti-Modernists. As things turned out, the essay by David Schultenover exploring regional differences could not be included for reasons of length, and Gary Lease's discussion of Vatican diplomacy fit better into part I than part II. Moreover, the assembled chapters do not reflect quite as clear a distinction as was originally envisioned. The opening essays are expressly about the general background, and the later essays do focus on specific individuals or movements, but specifics are not absent from some of the essays in part I, nor are general developments untouched in the essays devoted to particular individuals. Although the specific chapters have changed, the purpose of part I remains the same. I have chosen to subdivide the second part, so that the remainder of the volume now contains the following three parts: Maurice Blondel and Alfred Loisy in France (part II), Friedrich von Hügel and Maude

Petre in England (part III), and social modernism and anti-Modernism in France (part IV).

When the Roman Catholic Modernism Group was contemplating this project, the initial suggestion was that the collection seek to be comprehensive, including as many major figures as possible and covering developments in Italy, Germany, and the United States, as well as those in France and England. In order to produce a volume of manageable length, that plan was also abandoned. The present collection makes no claim to be comprehensive. It does not discuss the question of Modernism in Germany[31] and gives virtually no attention to an important cluster of Modernists in Italy.[32] Instead of seeking to be comprehensive, the collection intends to exhibit the importance of a kind of investigation: one that explores the context of the major figures, understands them in terms of their other concerns and involvements, and identifies the historical forces under whose influence they worked.

The work of the Roman Catholic Modernism Group has certainly been pioneering. It has generated a wide variety of fresh insights, and the essays in this volume are the direct result of its pioneering work. One would like to claim that these chapters provide a "revisionist" view of Modernism and anti-Modernism but, since other interpreters have also begun to pay attention to the historical and cultural setting of the dispute, a more modest claim is probably in order. What can be said is that these essays clearly do intensify and extend that investigation. Their primary purpose is to exhibit the kind of insights that this approach can generate. The essays also reflect a shared conviction that there is still more to be learned about the complex interaction between various aspects of the historical setting and the contrasting responses of the Modernists and the anti-

---

[31] See Otto Weiss, *Der Modernismus in Deutschland: Ein Beitrag zur Theologiegeschichte* (Regensburg: F. Pustet, 1995).

[32] For a brief overview of Italian Modernism, see Roger Aubert et al., *The Church in a Secularised Society* (volume v of *The Christian Centuries*; New York: Paulist Press, 1978), pp. 194–197. Comparing the Italian Modernists with the French, Aubert writes: "The aim of the Italians was not so much to grapple with Protestant and rationalist science but rather to deepen the religious culture of the average Catholic, conscious as they were of its deficiencies, which were attributable to the so easily superficial character of the Catholic faith among Italian Catholics" (pp. 195–196). However, Italy lacked church officials who could interpret the Modernists. Thus "the panic in Italy was even greater [than in France] and, as invariably happens in such cases, the reaction soon raged indiscriminately against all who strayed, even by an inch, from the traditional path" (p. 197). In addition to Aubert, see also Maurilio Guasco, *Modernismo: i fatti, le idee, i personaggi* (Milan [Cinisello]: Edizioni Paoline, 1995).

Modernists. If this volume not only provides access to the insights already generated by such investigations but also stimulates yet further work on those topics, it will be successful.

THE SIGNIFICANCE OF THE MODERNIST CRISIS

The Modernist crisis was, in one sense, a part of a larger story during the nineteenth and twentieth centuries: the ongoing struggle within Christian theology to decide simultaneously how much of post-Kantian modern thought it could endorse and how much of the inherited theological tradition it should revise. Unlike what had prevailed in Europe amid the earlier pattern of Christendom, modern culture, though a product of the Western tradition, became an independent force. Bearing its own assumptions and its own values and priorities, it was not under Christian control. Theologians had to decide how alien or how congenial it was to Christianity. The anti-Modernists emphasized its alien character, tried to draw a sharp line between modernity and Christianity, and adopted an aggressive stance over against anything they identified with modernity. In this regard (although not in others) they were similar to the Fundamentalists who emerged in the United States during the same decades (1890–1910). Conversely, the Modernists sought to use historical study to help fashion discriminating judgments which could distinguish the developing, Spirit-led community of faith from those historical expressions that could be changed, and they sought to make discriminating judgments regarding the value of various aspects of modern culture. In this regard their task was not unlike that of liberal-to-moderate mainline Protestant theologians who were heirs of the tradition known since Schleiermacher as "modern theology."

In another sense, however, Roman Catholic Modernism is distinctive. For one thing, at the same time that it was dealing with the issues already mentioned, it also sought to formulate an alternative to the liberal Protestant outlook. Loisy's attention to Harnack in *The Gospel and the Church* and Tyrrell's extended critique of liberal Protestantism in *Christianity at the Cross-Roads* are illustrative.[33] Though themselves influenced by liberal Protestantism, the Modernists did not find its views congenial. To identify but one issue, liberal

---

[33] George Tyrrell, *Christianity at the Cross-Roads* (London: Longmans, Green and Co., 1909).

Protestantism was, in the eyes of the Modernists, too individualistic to capture the corporate, churchly character of Catholicism. Secondly, for Catholic Modernism issues of church authority were more front and center, and the centrality of these concerns distinguished it from similar movements in Protestantism. Thirdly, Roman Catholic Modernism faced a defensive posture toward modernity that had already been formulated before the Modernists came on the scene. This "circle-the-wagons" mentality had been constructed by Pius IX and his successors.[34] Some of the significant steps in its creation were the longevity of Pius IX (who, while in office from 1846 to 1878, became an icon of defiance for Catholics throughout the world), the Syllabus of Errors in 1864 with its sweeping rejection of modernity, the First Vatican Council with its endorsement of papal authority (thereby strengthening the internal cohesion of the church as it faced a hostile external environment), Leo XIII's insistence on the authoritative role of scholastic philosophy and theology, specifically that of Thomas Aquinas, as mandated in his 1879 encyclical *Aeterni Patris*, Leo XIII's rejection of scientific biblical criticism in his *Providentissimus Deus* (1893), his condemnation in 1899 of Americanism, and the creation of the Pontifical Biblical Commission in 1902.[35] The theological dispute between Modernists and anti-Modernists occurred after nearly a century of reaction against the socio-political implications of the French Revolution and after more than half a century of a deliberately defensive reaction to modern culture. Within Protestantism, the defensive, fundamentalist reactions generally followed (rather than preceded) the work of "liberal" biblical scholars and/or modernizing movements of social action. In Catholicism the order was reversed: anti-Modernism came first.

The distinctiveness of Roman Catholic Modernism must be acknowledged so that parallels to similar movements can be sorted out carefully. However, its distinctiveness does not hinder the broader purpose of this volume, whose intention is not merely to

[34] In this regard Leo XIII differed in strategy but not in purpose. The change in strategy gave mixed signals. On the one hand, he encouraged theological study and allowed scholars a little more latitude in their investigations. Some interpreted this to offer encouragement to the kinds of endeavors undertaken by the Modernists. On the other hand, he also endorsed one particular theological approach, neo-Thomism. While his endorsement did encourage some serious theological endeavors, it also sanctioned lesser lights, codifiers of propositions, to content themselves with formulas and to repudiate all who deviated from those formulas.
[35] See chapter two for a fuller exposition of these developments.

understand more fully the Roman Catholic version of Christianity's encounter with modernity, but to illumine the dynamics at work in all those encounters.

If postmodernity is but a continuation of modernity, as some argue, then Christianity needs to continue to assess its relationship to the values and priorities of modern culture. The job is not over, because the issues remain essentially the same. Conversely, if, as others argue, modernity is being replaced by something different, by something genuinely *post*-modern, then the need for careful assessment is not lessened because Christianity has to decide what aspects of the culture of the last two hundred years to perpetuate and what dimensions to abandon or – as Schleiermacher would have said – to relegate to the past for safe-keeping. The purpose of this book is to illumine the issues faced by the Modernists and anti-Modernists in such ways as to inform the theological judgments that must still be made in our own day about the relationship of modernity and the Christian faith.

Introduction II: The Modernists and the anti-Modernists

Darrell Jodock

Who were the Modernists, and who were the anti-Modernists? Several persons who are usually included on each side of the controversy will be identified below. Our purpose is not to offer a comprehensive directory but to illustrate the variety of Modernist and anti-Modernist concerns and to introduce some of the persons discussed in the chapters that follow.

Readers already familiar with the *dramatis personae* may want to skip to chapter one.

THE MODERNISTS

The following are among those persons usually considered to be Modernists:

MAURICE BLONDEL (1861–1949), a French philosopher. He is sometimes considered a precursor of Modernism and at other times included as a Modernist. His disagreements with Loisy regarding the relationship between biblical criticism and dogma, his readiness to arrive at orthodox conclusions, and the failure of his thinking to advance beyond its early formulations incline some to see him as a precursor. His sense of vocation and his quest for an understanding of humanity that was "open" to the divine rather than closed off from it – one that did not employ the rigid nature/supernature distinction of the neo-scholastics – incline some to see him as a Modernist. In any case, his thought influenced other Catholics with more explicit Modernist sympathies.

He is best known for his doctoral thesis, published in 1893, *L'Action: essai d'une critique de la vie et d'une science de la pratique* (*Action: Essay on a Critique of Life and a Science of Practice*) and his *Lettre sur les exigences de la pensée contemporaine en matière d'apologétique* (*Letter on Apologetics*) in 1896. His basic argument is that human action is not

20

closed off but open to transcendence. Thus a philosophy which
analyzes human action (including thinking, all of human behavior,
and all the conditions that give rise to a free action) can be fully
rational while at the same time being open to religion and the
possibility of sharing in an infinite life, the gift of a supernatural
destiny. His differences with Loisy surfaced in *Histoire et dogme: les
lacunes philosophiques de l'éxégèse moderne*, published in 1904. There he
objects to "historicism" (associated with Loisy), where history
determines the interpretation of dogma, while at the same time
objecting to the "extrinsicism" of the neo-scholastics, where dogma
determines the interpretation of history.

Blondel came under suspicion during the Modernist crisis but was
never excommunicated, in part, perhaps, because he was a layman.
He remained an active Catholic but from the appearance of *Pascendi*
in 1907 until 1934 refrained from publishing anything on the
relationship of philosophy and Christianity. Only after 1934 did
several new and revised volumes appear. His philosophical reflections about the relationship between the natural and the supernatural influenced the "new theology" which developed in France
during the 1930s and 1940s and included such figures as Henri De
Lubac, S.J., and Yves Marie-Joseph Congar, O.P.

ALFRED LOISY (1857–1940), a French priest and biblical scholar.
During the earlier years of his career, he endeavored to incorporate
the results of historical study into a revised Catholic theology. In
1902, in his most famous work, *L'Evangile et l'Eglise* (*The Gospel and the
Church*), he sought to defend a Catholic understanding of the church
and its organic connection to the gospel against the liberal Protestant
perspective of Adolf von Harnack. The latter claimed that a purely
historical analysis uncovered a simple gospel regarding the father-
hood of God and the infinite value of each individual human being,
a gospel which stood in opposition to dogmas "about Jesus" and in
opposition to the institutional church. Loisy's image of the church
included organic, historical development, but this meant, of course,
that its institutions evolved rather than remain unchanged, as the
neo-scholastics asserted. Loisy likewise rejected the traditional view
that Jesus himself had instituted the dogmas and traditions of the
church but affirmed instead, against Harnack, that Jesus had
founded the community that grew into the church. In the area of
biblical studies, Loisy argued against any attempt to have dogma
determine the outcome of historical investigation. More than other

Modernists, he defended the independence of historical investigation
from the realm of theology. In 1903 five of his books, including *The
Gospel and the Church* and his *Autour d'un petit livre* (1903) in which he
clarified and defended the former volume, were placed on the Index
of Forbidden Books. After his excommunication in 1908, Loisy
abandoned his quest for a reformed Catholic theology and became a
scholar of the history of religions who taught at the Collège de
France. He professed a religion of humanity and worked outside the
boundaries of the church.

FRIEDRICH VON HÜGEL (1852–1925), a lay theologian of aristocratic social standing and international connections. Born in Italy of
an Austrian father and a Scottish mother, von Hügel moved to
London in 1871. He became the "nerve center" of the fledgling
Modernist movement. He read widely, traveled extensively, and
corresponded with a large number of persons, relaying to them what
he had learned on his travels, discussing with them the latest books,
encouraging their intellectual pursuits, and introducing them to each
other. He was particularly interested in questions of historical and
biblical study and somewhat less ready than some other Modernists
to endorse modern philosophical ideas; he emphasized transcendence more than they did, and expressed himself more cautiously
than (say) George Tyrrell. In 1908 his major (two-volume) work
appeared: *The Mystical Element of Religion as Studied in Saint Catherine of
Genoa and Her Friends*. Although under suspicion, von Hügel, as a
layman, was not disciplined.

GEORGE TYRRELL, S.J. (1861–1909), a priest in England. Born in
Ireland, he converted to Catholicism after moving to England in
1879. At first an adherent of Thomism, he met von Hügel in 1897
and, at his suggestion, read Blondel, Laberthonnière, and others
who had abandoned the scholastic tradition. As a result, he moved
relatively quickly from Thomism to his own version of Modernism.
In 1899 he published an article, "The Relation of Theology to
Devotion," that would later be renamed "Lex Orandi, Lex Credendi." There he asserted that theology must constantly be informed
by and corrected by devotion – that is, by the lived faith of believers.
In 1899, he published a second article, "A Perverted Devotion," in
which he recommended caution regarding the endorsement of
traditional teachings, because they cannot contain the full mystery of
the spiritual life. The main thrust of his ideas was that doctrines
were a guide to life; their practical value must be understood and

appreciated. Theology "has to be reminded that, like science, its hypotheses, theories, and explanations, must square with the facts – the facts here being the Christian religion as lived by its consistent professors."[1] In *The Church and the Future* (1907) he contrasts "official" Catholicism (which teaches that every aspect of the church and its teachings was present in an original "deposit of faith") with a modified version that he endorses – one that recognizes that the creative life of the Spirit introduces changes. Always courageously (some would say recklessly) outspoken, Tyrrell was dismissed from the Jesuit order in 1905 and, after publishing two articles in *The Times* attacking *Pascendi*, was excommunicated in October of 1907. He continued to publish. A collection of essays, *Through Scylla and Charybdis; or, The Old Theology and the New*, came out in 1907; *Medievalism* appeared in 1908, and *Christianity at the Cross-Roads* in 1909. In the last, Tyrrell affirms his conviction that Catholicism is the only authentic version of Christianity and the best expression of the spiritual needs of human beings. By the time this last book appeared, Tyrrell, never deviating from his loyalty to Catholicism, had died. He was denied Catholic burial, and a French priest, Henri Bremond, was suspended for saying prayers over Tyrrell's grave.

EDOUARD LE ROY (1870–1954), French mathematician and philosopher. His 1905 article, "Qu'est-ce qu'un dogme," became the nucleus of a book entitled *Dogme et critique*, which appeared in 1907. It argued that dogmas were not to be understood primarily as intellectual truths but instead as practical guides to religious and moral life. *Dogme et critique* was placed on the Index in 1907, but Le Roy went on with his work without altering his position.

LUCIEN LABERTHONNIÈRE (1860–1932), French priest, philosopher, and from 1905 to 1913 the editor of the *Annales de philosophie chrétienne*. He was attracted to Blondel's philosophy, and the two men became friends, but differences between them eventually ended that friendship. Laberthonnière rejected the use of Thomas Aquinas and scholasticism in theology and was critical of papal authority whenever it was used to suppress rather than to educate. He saw Christianity as a way of life, a "metaphysic of charity." Although he regarded the critical approach to the Bible to be helpful, his concerns were primarily theological/philosophical rather than historical/biblical. His *Essais de philosophie religieuse* and *Le Réalisme*

---

[1] Tyrrell, *Scylla*, p. 104.

chrétien et l'idéalisme grec were put on the Index in 1906 and the *Annales de philosophie chrétienne* met a similar fate in 1913. That same year he was forbidden to publish. He submitted to authority but did not abandon his views; he continued to write, with instructions that his writings be published either after the papal ban was lifted or after his death.

GIOVANNI SEMERIA (1867–1931), Italian biblical scholar, who published *Dogma, gerarchia e culto nella chiesa primitiva* in 1902. Semeria, together with SALVATORE MINOCCHI (1869–1943), whose reviews had introduced the works of Loisy, Tyrrell, and Blondel to Italian readers, and ANTONIO FOGAZZARO, the author of the Modernist novel, *Il Santo*, founded the review *Il Rinnovamento*. It began publication in January 1907, and was suppressed in November 1909.

ERNESTO BUONAIUTI (1881–1946), Italian writer. Reputedly the author of *Il programma dei modernisti* (1907), a reply to *Pascendi*, which argued that the purpose of Modernism was to reconcile Catholicism with the results of recent biblical and historical criticism. It was translated into English by Tyrrell (*The Programme of Modernism*) and placed on the Index in 1908. From 1905 until 1910 Buonaiuti was the editor of *Rivista storico-critica delle scienze teologiche*, a journal devoted to church history and the history of dogma. It too was placed on the Index in 1910. He was excommunicated in 1925.

MAUDE PETRE (1863–1942), an English author. A descendant of a long-standing English Roman Catholic family, she was a close associate of George Tyrrell and Friedrich von Hügel and the biographer of Father Tyrrell. In 1890 she joined the Filles de Marie (the "Daughters of Mary") and later became the superior of the English and Irish provinces of that order. Under suspicion for her sympathies and her associations, she was denied the sacrament in her home diocese of Southwark but received it daily in Kensington and escaped further reprisals because she was not a member of the clergy and (after 1908 when she did not renew her vows) no longer a member of a religious order. She remained loyal to Modernism and to Catholicism.

The persons named above have sometimes been designated "philosophical" and "doctrinal Modernists." Another group to come under suspicion were the "social modernists." Whether they should be counted as part of the Modernist movement is a matter of dispute, but one thing is clear: there was no direct correspondence between theological Modernism and social modernism. For one thing, with only an exception or two, the theological Modernists were not involved in the movements usually associated with social modernism. For another, these movements of social reform included Catholics representing a variety of theological positions. They were lumped together by their adversaries who accused them of advocating autonomy and being impatient with authority. One group accused of social modernism was the *Sillon* (the "Furrow"). Begun by Marc Sangnier and others in 1894 for the religious purpose of applying faith to daily life, this lay movement organized study groups among young workers and (unlike other similar Catholic movements) entrusted the leadership of individual groups to the workers themselves. The study groups discussed various social problems, and the movement cultivated good relations with the papacy. Comfortable neither with the monarchist right nor the anticlerical left, the movement after 1906 became increasingly involved in politics. They continued to support democracy and to advocate social reform, but now they also welcomed non-Catholics who supported their aims, started a newspaper, and supported candidates for office. Increasingly they confronted opposition from bishops who thought the *Sillon* did not defer sufficiently to their authority. Accused by those loyal to *Pascendi* of flirting with Protestantism, trying to democratize the church, and undermining ecclesiastical authority, the movement was condemned by Pius X in 1910. The letter of condemnation instructed the *Sillon* to form in each diocese a separate group that would function under the authority of the local bishop.

THE ANTI-MODERNISTS

Among the leaders of the anti-Modernist forces were the following:

PIUS X (Giuseppe Sarto), pope from 1903 to 1914. Of humble birth, he was primarily a parish priest and bishop, not an aristocrat skilled in diplomacy (as had been Leo XIII) nor a scholar/theologian. Already while bishop of Mantua in 1887 one of his pastoral letters warned against the tendencies he later called Modernism; another pastoral letter called for unquestioning obedience to the pope. Once in that office, he operated with an acute sense of crisis; in his mind the church faced enemies all around. In response he did all he could to increase the authority of the papacy, oppose historical study of the Bible, support neo-scholasticism, and resist any erosion of the church's influence. In 1906 he condemned the French law, passed the previous year, which revoked the Concordat of 1801, separated church and state, and transferred the church's property to lay associations. In July of 1907, *Lamentabili sane exitu* condemned 65 propositions regarded to be errors of the Modernists.[2] Several of the 65 statements paraphrased and pulled out of context positions taken by Loisy. In September, Pius X issued *Pascendi*. In November, he decreed that all Catholics were bound to submit to the decisions of the Pontifical Biblical Commission (which in 1906 had affirmed the Mosaic authorship of the Pentateuch and rejected other positions commonly endorsed by progressive biblical scholars). In 1910 he required that all clerics take an oath against Modernism, in which they had to pledge submission to the teachings of *Pascendi* and *Lamentabili*. That same year he also condemned the *Sillon*. Clearly Pius X was a most active, powerful, and effective anti-Modernist.

RAPHAEL MERRY DEL VAL (1865–1930), cardinal and secretary of state under Pius X. Merry del Val had been in the papal diplomatic service since 1888. He became the chief counselor to Pius X. Although more capable of diplomacy than Pius X, he was equally uncompromising in his anti-Modernism.

LOUIS BILLOT, S.J. (1846–1931), Professor of Dogmatic Theology at the Gregorian University from 1885 until 1911, when he was appointed a cardinal. He came to the Gregorian as one of several Thomists assembled by Leo XIII to carry out the instructions laid down in his *Aeterni Patris*, namely to make the philosophy and theology of Thomas Aquinas normative for Catholic teaching. Billot was probably the most able philosopher/theologian of that group; however, he lacked not only historical training but also any appreciation for the importance of historical study. In 1904 he published *De sacra traditione contra novam haeresim evolutionismi*, in which he argued that dogmatic propositions must be unchanging, since truth cannot change. More specifically, he objected to Laberthonnière's view that the philosophy of Aristotle had been allowed too much influence in theology. He criticized Blondel's philosophy of action and Loisy's view of revelation which he thought completely undermined Catholic faith. In all of these cases he objected to any notion of relative truth, any distinction between truth in religion and truth outside

---

[2] For the 65 condemned statements, see for example, Bernard M. G. Reardon, *Roman Catholic Modernism* (Stanford, California: Stanford University Press, 1970), pp. 242–248.

religion, and any appeal to an act of willing that, he thought, usurped the role of the intellect in discerning religious truth.

JOSEPH LEMIUS, O.M.I. (1860–1923), Procurator General of the Oblates of Mary Immaculate. Not well known in his own day, scholars today usually credit him with producing the original draft of the doctrinal sections of *Pascendi*. He considered Loisy to be an "intellectual atheist" whose methods excluded in advance the possibility of the transcendent manifesting itself in history. Only a combination of Aristotelian philosophy and Thomistic theology, Lemius believed, could safeguard Catholic teaching from the dangers and errors which were in his day threatening to destroy dogma. Thomism was for him a perfectly coherent and unified system; he was thus an "integralist" in the sense of believing that no part of this unified system could be modified without endangering the whole. (Interestingly, Modernism for him was a mirror image; he presented it as an equally coherent system of thought.)

RÉGINALD GARRIGOU-LAGRANGE, O.P. (1877–1964), French theologian and philosopher and from 1909 to 1960 Professor in Rome. A proponent of the teachings of Thomas Aquinas, he wrote a work critical of the evolution of dogma. Over against the Modernists, he asserted that dogma itself is immutable, although its formulation may change. That work appeared in 1909 as *Le Sens commun, la philosophie de l'être et les formules dogmatiques.*

SODALITIUM PIANUM or SAPINIÈRE, a secret group founded in 1909 by an Italian journalist, seminary teacher, and undersecretary of state during the papacy of Pius X, Umberto Benigni, to carry out *Pascendi*'s call for vigilance against doctrinal deviation. Benigni's group enjoyed the support of Pius X, although Merry del Val, himself more cautious than the impetuous Benigni, sometimes endeavored to restrain him. Unfortunately the Sapinière made anonymous attacks against persons suspected of Modernism, often extracting passages out of context to discredit them, and in the process ruined the reputation of a number of Catholic scholars. Especially active in France, their attacks were disseminated through various Catholic newspapers and periodicals in various parts of Europe. Most active during the papacy of Pius X, the group lost credit after Benedict XV became pope in 1914 and was suppressed in 1921.

PART I

The late nineteenth-century setting of Modernism and anti-Modernism

CHAPTER I

Vatican foreign policy and the origins of Modernism

Gary Lease

Consalvi, Antonelli, Rampolla: one could write a fascinating and rich history of nineteenth-century Europe through the eyes, and above all the work, of the Vatican's secretaries of state. These ministers helped form foreign policy throughout Europe's various governments, made decisions based on information and the artful gauging of the future's likely course, and worked together with the foreign ministers of secular states to forge a common political course, where possible, to ensure not only peace but above all survival and political stability.

The twentieth century, however, standing in the shadow of 1870 and the demise of the Church State as a meaningful political base for the Vatican's policies, has not been so productive. A history of the Roman Catholic Church in this century, making use of its secretaries of state as a point of departure, would be a thin story indeed. Merry del Val, Gasparri, Pacelli, Casaroli: compared to their counterparts in the preceding century, the achievements are few, if any, the embarrassments many, and the lack of an effective, respected *policy*, or set of policies, noteworthy. Rather than cooperatively forming the basic guidelines for actual political decisions, and thus events, in Europe and elsewhere, these now almost faceless ministers found themselves trapped by the lack of any stable political power base: the disappearance of the Church State in 1870 led to the bloodletting of the "war" with Bismarck, the draining struggle with France, and the internecine battle over Modernism; in turn, these moments led to this century's straitjacket of the Lateran Treaties and surrender of the German concordat. As Rilke noted in this century's first decade, who speaks these days of victory? Survival is everything.[1]

---

[1] "Wer spricht von Siegen? Überstehn ist alles." From Rainer Maria Rilke, "Requiem für

That may be an adequate, even comforting existential stance but it certainly does not meet the needs of modern states and their societies. Foreign relations are not only the products of themes that concern their partners, but also produce their own themes. These concerns, in turn, "form patterns of activity that reflect enduring interests and actions on the part of government, that is, policy."[2] Applied to the Roman Church, this analytic principle reveals that the Napoleonic upheaval at the beginning of the nineteenth century created a policy vacuum for the Roman Church which it sought unsuccessfully to fill throughout the nineteenth and early twentieth centuries. The church's leaders, the popes and their secretaries of state, attempted to freeze their policy in relational forms that were no longer possible. As that struggle became more and more impossible, there occurred a retreat from all effective foreign policy and a concentration upon the inner forum: the minds, hearts, wills and consciences of the institution's members. A review of the Vatican's foreign ministers and their policies during the nineteenth and early twentieth centuries will reveal that the anti-Modernist spasm at the turn of the century represents the final stage of a failed foreign policy program of almost a century's duration.[3]

A quick glance at the bibliographic resources available for such an investigation reveals how the Vatican's foreign policy during the past two centuries has to a large extent been ignored. Recent and noted historical handbooks on the one hand, and respected historical analyses on the other, make precious little mention of studies associated with the Church State's foreign policy.[4] There are, of course, some studies, but to no one's amazement, they deal mainly with World War II, the Jewish Holocaust, and post-World War II

Wolf Graf von Kalckreuth," *Gesammelte Gedichte* (Frankfurt: Insel-Verlag, 1962), p. 420. Though Rilke penned these lines in the night of 4 and 5 November 1908, it is certain that he did not have in mind the fate of the Roman Catholic Church, locked in its anti-Modernism.

[2] Bruce B. Williams, "Archaeology and Egyptian Foreign Policy," *American Research Center in Egypt Program and Abstracts* (47th Annual Meeting, 12–14 April 1996), pp. 72–73.

[3] That is, since the Congress of Vienna in 1815.

[4] For the former, see the respected *Guide to Historical Literature* now in a new third edition (Oxford and New York: Oxford University Press, 1995). Apart from chiefly medieval studies, its two very full volumes contain practically nothing related to the Vatican's foreign adventures; what mention there is remains relegated to themes and categories dominated by the world's states themselves. For the latter, let me cite Henry Kissinger's *Diplomacy* (New York: Simon & Schuster, 1994). Surprisingly, in such a broad-ranging study of European foreign policy development, not a single pope or secretary of state is mentioned, nor is the role of the Vatican in the nineteenth century's foreign relations ever raised.

events.[5] The nineteenth century and its turbulent foreign policy entanglements are all too often reduced to mentioning the *Kulturkampf* ("who won?" is the question that is always answered, though seldom analyzed) and the formation of the new Italian national state with the consequent elimination of a Church State centered in Rome ("was that good or bad?" is usually the query put to the reader here).

We are even more stingily informed when it comes to the actual actors, the Vatican's several secretaries of state throughout the nineteenth and twentieth centuries. One slim volume, now over thirty years old, has made the attempt to gather some data on these now almost forgotten personages, while biographies, that exegetical staple in the historian's larder, are few and far between, and when available usually of questionable dependability.[6]

Ercole Consalvi (1757–1824), the key advisor of Pius VII, left us, of course, his memoirs, and there have been several attempts to evaluate his accomplishments during and after the era of Napoleon.[7] But a full-blown study that places Consalvi in the complex and complicated currents of the nineteenth century's first two decades is

---

[5] Robert Graham's *Vatican Diplomacy: A Study of Church and State on the International Plane* (Princeton, New Jersey: Princeton University Press, 1959) is perhaps the single study devoted to a broad-based attempt to unravel Vatican foreign policy prior to the twentieth century. For the twentieth century Hyginus Cardinale has attempted the same breadth in *The Holy See and the International Order* (Gerrards Cross, England: Smythe, 1976). Humphrey Johnson investigates the Vatican's efforts to broker a peace agreement during World War I, in his *Vatican Diplomacy in the World War* (Oxford: Blackwell, 1933). *Ireland and the Vatican: The Politics and Diplomacy of Church–State Relations, 1922–1960* by Dermot Keogh (Cork: Cork University Press, 1995) seeks to untangle the foreign policy implications of this century's new Irish state. The central focus of work, however, has been on the question of the Jewish Holocaust and the Vatican's response on the diplomatic as well as active front; John Morley's study, *Vatican Diplomacy and the Jews during the Holocaust, 1939–1943* (New York: Ktav Publishing House, 1980) is an excellent place to start, along with the ongoing source publications from both German and Vatican archives. Good background is offered by Stewart Stehlin, *Weimar and the Vatican, 1919–1933* (Princeton, New Jersey: Princeton University Press, 1986). George Irani's *The Papacy and the Middle East: The Role of the Holy See in the Arab–Israeli Conflict, 1962–1984* (Notre Dame, Indiana: University of Notre Dame Press, 1986) brings us up to date on the continuing fall-out of the Holocaust for current foreign relations. A parallel study of Vatican diplomatic efforts in Eastern Europe is provided by Hansjakob Stehle in *Die Ostpolitik des Vaticans, 1917–1975* (Munich: Piper, 1975). Eric Hanson's *The Catholic Church in World Politics* (Princeton, New Jersey: Princeton University Press, 1987) is an attempt to assess the contemporary extent of the Vatican's foreign policy efforts.

[6] See Wilhelm Sandfuchs (ed.), *Die Außenminister der Päpste* (Munich: G. Olzog Verlag, 1962).

[7] See Ercole Consalvi, *Mémoires*, ed. J. Cretinaux-Joly (Paris: Plon, 1866). For an older analysis, cf. Fritz Fleiner, "Cardinal Consalvi," *Ausgewählte Schriften und Reden* (Zurich: Polygraphischer Verlag, 1941), pp. 375–395. Richard Wichterlich hit the nail on the head with his study entitled *Sein Schicksal war Napoleon* (Heidelberg: Kerle, 1951). The most recent life is John M. Robinson, *Cardinal Consalvi* (London: Bodley Head, 1987).

still to be written. For Tommaso Bernetti (1779–1852), secretary of state under two popes (Leo XII and Gregory XVI), there are only slim pickings, while Luigi Lambruschini (1776–1854), who served the final decade under Gregory XVI, has received but one major study.[8] Surprisingly, we are not much better off when it comes to Giacomo Antonelli (1806–1876), the right-hand man of Pius IX. Though Europe was awash with supermarket publications following his death, it is only now that Antonelli has received anything approaching a balanced evaluation based on broad archival study.[9] One might think that with Mariano Rampolla (1843–1913), the close partner of Leo XIII, we would find a new and flourishing field of investigation. Sadly, nothing of note has appeared since the 1920s![10] Much the same can be said for Raphael Merry del Val (1865–1930), the intimate advisor of Pius X. Some of his correspondences have been published but, in the main, isolated studies and hagiographical "biographies" make up the body of writing devoted to his life and work.[11] Perhaps this is not surprising, given the fact that his cause

[8] For the former see the eulogy delivered at the first anniversary of his death: *Elogio funebre del Cardinale Tommaso Bernetti, recitato il giorno anniversario della sua morte nella Metropolitana di Fermo li 17 Marzo 1853* (Loreto: Brothers Rossi, 1853); the eulogy itself covers some 26 pages, but 13 pages of notes contain the skeleton of a future biography. Lambruschini penned a well-known *Polemical Treatise on the Immaculate Conception of the Blessed Virgin* (New York: Sadlier, 1855; original Italian edition from 1842), and published his spiritual meditations, *Operette spirituali delle Cardinale L. Lambruschini* (Rome: F. Bourlie, 1833). More in tune with his role as Vatican diplomat are his memoirs as papal nuncio to France: *La mia nunziatura di Francia*, ed. Pietro Pirri (Bologna: N. Zanichelli, 1934). An early and very sketchy biography, based on his funeral eulogy, was done by Giovanni Piantoni, *Biografia del Cardinale Luigi Lambruschini della Congregazione de' Barnabiti* (no date, 1859?; this is a separate publication from the author's article, "Il Cardinale Luigi Lambruschini," in *Annali delle Scienze Religiose* 13 [1854], 128–153). The most recent, and most substantial treatment is from Luigi Manzini, *Il Cardinale Luigi Lambruschini* (Vatican City: Vatican Library, 1960), containing over 100 pages of documents and appendices.

[9] For an example of the "yellow journalism" that flourished in the 1880s and later, see Leon Nordberg, *Die Tochter Antonellis. Bearbeitet nach historischen Daten und den stenographischen Acten aus dem Prozesse der Gräfin Lambertini contra Card. Antonellis Erben in Rom* (Vienna: 1878). It is Frank Coppa's achievement to have provided us with the first useful biography of Antonelli yet to appear: *Cardinal Giacomo Antonelli and Papal Politics in European Affairs* (Albany, New York: SUNY Press, 1990). See also Christoph Weber's sober assessment in his magisterial two-volume *Kardinäle und Prälaten in den letzten Jahrzehnten des Kirchenstaates* (Stuttgart: Hiersemann, 1978), here vol. I, pp. 266–284.

[10] The single biography of any value is G. Pietro Sinopoli di Giunta's *Il Cardinale Mariano Rampolla del Tindaro* (Rome: Vatican Press, 1923). For archival source materials see also Crispolto Crispolti and Guido Aureli, *La politica di Leone XIII da Luigi Galimberti a Mariano Rampolla su documenti inediti* (Rome: Bontempelli e Invernizzi, 1923).

[11] See, for example, Gary Lease, "Merry del Val and Tyrrell: A Modernist Struggle," *"Odd Fellows" in the Politics of Religion: Modernism, National Socialism, and German Judaism* (Berlin and New York: Mouton de Gruyter, 1995), pp. 55–76. Among the biographies, the best is from

for beatification was introduced in the early 1950s, though at the moment all is quiet on that front.[12] In other words, the vital field of the Vatican's foreign relations has been left, particularly in the excited nineteenth and twentieth centuries, without the attention to its main actors that they so richly deserve.

The title and office of a "secretary of state" to the pope emerged much earlier, at the end of the sixteenth century; by 1605 it was an official position, though the function itself had been present for at least a century. The establishment of a complex system of nuncios, or papal representatives, at Europe's various courts demanded someone who would read and analyze their frequent reports. This meant, of course, that the office of secretary of state took on almost immediately a grave importance. Such a person controlled the information regarding foreign relations, and many other matters also, that reached the pope. In other words, popes quickly became dependent upon the occupant of that office. Since 1644 the holder of the secretariat has always been a cardinal; a century later (1721) the secretary of state had become ex officio both the prime minister of the Papal States and the controller of foreign policy information channelled through the various nuncios. By the beginning of the nineteenth century and Consalvi's service to Pius VII, the secretary of state was clearly an "alter ego" to the pope, with the consequence that this official was necessarily close to the pope's point of view on all major issues, indeed enjoyed a personal relationship with the pope second to none among Vatican officials.[13] When Modernism breaks on the scene at the end of the nineteenth century, it quickly finds its counterpart in Rome's institutional anti-Modernism, an

Pio Cenci, *Il Cardinale Merry del Val* (Turin: Berruti, 1933). Besides his published defense of papal infallibility (*The Truth of Papal Claims: A Reply to the Validity of Papal Claims by F. Nutcombe Oxenham, English Chaplain in Rome* [London: Sands, 1902]), Merry del Val also left behind reminiscences of his service under Pius X, published posthumously (*Memories of Pope Pius X* [Westminster, Maryland: Newman Press, 1951]).

12 *Romana Beatificationis et Canonizationis Servi Dei Raphaelis Card. Merry del Val Secretarii Status Sancti Pii Papae X. Informatio-Tabella Testium-Summarium Litterae Postulatoriae super causae Introductione et Summarium ex Officio super Scriptis* (Vatican City: Vatican Press, 1957).

13 For the development of the office see Owen Chadwick, *The Popes and European Revolution* (Oxford: Oxford University Press, 1981), pp. 298–301; also Klaus Mörsdorf, "Der Kardinalstaatssekretär-Aufgabe und Werdegang seines Amtes," in Sandfuchs (ed.), *Außenminister*, pp. 11–25: the relationship of trust between pontiff and secretary is key to the success of the office; recall that the secretary of state is the one Vatican official whose office and living quarters are next to the pope's, and that his office ends with the death of the pope. This intimacy in personal relationship is also emphasized by Wilhelm Sandfuchs (ed.), "Vorwort," *Außenminister*, pp. 7–10.

appearance that owes a great deal to the foreign policy dealings of
previous papal secretaries of state throughout the preceding decades.
Modernism and anti-Modernism are, in other words, not without
their antecedents, and many of the most important of these roots are
to be found in the Church State's foreign relations rather than
exclusively in doctrinal distinctions and debates.

AN ERA OF RECOVERY (= DENIAL AND DECLINE), OR: THE AGE OF CONSALVI

As Chadwick trenchantly observes, prior to the French Revolution
there were three Catholic powers in Europe (Austria, France, Spain)
and but one Protestant (Britain); after the Revolution that ratio had
turned completely around: Britain, Prussia, and Russia were the
Protestant or non-Catholic powers, while only Austria remained
Catholic. This situation was clearly the result of Napoleon's attempt
to bring all of Europe under his unified rule. While the seventeenth-
century wars of religion had left a rough balance in Europe,
Napoleon's wars overthrew this, leaving Europe with a Protestant
political ascendancy over Catholics, and the popes with far less
weight in the political arena than, say, Berlin or Moscow.[14]

The suppression of revolution in Italy and the Papal States after
the Congress of Vienna was designed to restore imperial power to
Austria, Prussia, and Russia – it did not have as its goal the
restoration of religion. In contrast, Catholics and, above all, their
popes wanted to reconstruct a more Christian society; this inevitably
meant a shift to the political right and cooperation with the anti-
democratic and against the constitutional movements opposed by
the three empires. The only reason Metternich supported the
restoration of the Roman Church and its Papal State was because he
saw it as a "glue," if you will, to hold together a political order; for
him "Catholic religion was the surest defence of a State against
anarchy."[15]

Thus the goal of the post-1815 Roman Church was to salvage
what rights and independence it could in the face of an expansion of
state power and influence. To this end, Consalvi was convinced that
only when the papacy had firm control of its traditional territories
would it be able to guarantee its independence from the other

---

[14] Chadwick, *Popes and Revolution*, pp. 535–537.   [15] Ibid., pp. 537, 610.

European powers, and thus ensure the essential condition of its ecclesiastical effectiveness.[16] His goal was to have the papacy accepted once again by the European powers as an equal; all his efforts to weave a web of concordats were expended to this end. The ironic conclusion, however, is that most of these attempted relationships by treaty ended in failure and in an increase in state control. All along the line Consalvi had to concede key points if he was to gain the aid needed to rebuild a devastated church: it was a steep price to pay (episcopal appointments, lost lands, etc.). In South America, revolutions moved from one country to another while he lacked any ability to stem the tide; in Spain the Inquisition was reinstituted and Ferdinand VII chased from the throne by a coup (1820), only to be restored three years later by force, leading eventually to civil war in 1833. Where the church wished to survive, religion became identified with the politically conservative goals of the imperial states.[17]

The French Revolution had demonstrated just how fragile faith is, just how uncertain the social structure of the church is, and just how much religion is, in the end, conformity. This experience, the key marker of the Roman Church's entry into the modern age, was already the hallmark of its foreign policies prior to the mid nineteenth century. "Consalvi failed," judges Chadwick, "because the problems were insoluble, not because he lacked wisdom."[18] With the restoration of the Papal States there was now a single government that one might blame, rather than foreign buffers onto which one could shunt disgruntlement. In his flexibility and desire to see the Papal States once again in place, Consalvi ended up baptizing the Napoleonic system, giving up the pre-revolutionary rights of the cardinals and Roman nobility. The result was a harbinger of things to come. Though the Congress of Vienna (1815) had restored the Papal States in order to limit Austrian power, all that was achieved was chaos. The popes were unable to rule the territories effectively but felt called to do so anyway. This was a sure recipe for disaster. It marked the Roman Church's entry into the nineteenth century, while at the same time it affected the papacy's attitude toward the democratic and constitutional character of the emerging modern

---

[16] Fleiner, "Consalvi," p. 386.
[17] See E. L. Woodward, *Three Studies in European Conservatism: Metternich, Guizot, the Catholic Church in the 19th Century* (London: Constable, 1929).
[18] Chadwick, *Popes and Revolution*, p. 554; see also pp. 539–566.

√√ world. Long before the Modernist crisis, the pope was seen as a
"supreme spiritual court," but certainly not a political one; in other
words, the decline of political and state power on the part of the
pope was compensated by "feeling" rather than by law and a
political role.[19]

With Austria in complete control of the Italian peninsula, Metternich and the Austrian armies became a prop to the Papal States.
France was on the outside, looking in, and the Russian move to gain
influence in Rome was effectively blocked.[20] Shortly after Gregory
XVI's election in 1831, a revolt broke out in the Papal States. The
pope's new secretary of state, Bernetti, was opposed to Austrian
support, but the pope had little choice. Once again, France was
trumped by Austria, though it did not cease to work for entry into
the Italian political scene. A multi-state conference, called in the late
spring of that year to consider the "Roman Question," failed
because Bernetti allowed it to. His policy was to play Austria off
against France, hoping that the resulting turmoil would allow the
papacy to control the Church State. Even though the Austrians
withdrew some of their troops at the pope's request, Gregory soon
replaced Bernetti with Lambruschini, who lavishly made use of
Austrian support in maintaining internal control of the Papal
State.[21]

By the election of Pius IX in 1846, however, Austrian power in
Italy was beginning to break down. With revolt breaking out in
Naples (January 1848), it was time for the Austrians to cut their
losses: while Austria now no longer tried to keep France out of Italy,
France was no longer trying to throw them out. The result was that
the Vienna solution of 1815 had finally ceased to function; the Holy
Alliance (Austria, Prussia, Russia) was unable to guarantee any
longer Metternich's grand goal of overall supremacy in Italy.
√ Nationalism, liberalism, and economic change were all working to
undermine the previous order. Papal strivings were now directed
toward the dubious aim of recovering this lost structure of apparent
stability; in the best of scenarios the Papal States would be at the
center of such a "new" or recovered Italian order, at the worst at

---

[19] Ibid., p. 570.
[20] Paul Schroeder, *The Transformation of European Politics 1763–1848* (Oxford: Oxford University
Press, 1994), pp. 568–570.
[21] Ibid., pp. 692–695.

least a viable one.[22] A new chapter in Vatican foreign relations had begun.

AN ERA OF DOUBT (= DEPENDENCY), OR: THE AGE
OF ANTONELLI

Despite the restoration of a Church State by Consalvi and Metternich in 1815, Napoleon's imposed example of Italian unity continued to entice Italian political hopes. In 1831–32 the Papal States were rocked by revolts; dissatisfaction with the practice of jurisprudence and the overall administration of the Church State had led to rebellion in the northern sectors, and only the presence of Austrian troops helped to put it down. The presence of foreign powers over many years, however, simply increased the disquiet. By refusing to join the Piedmontese uprising against the Austrians in April 1848, Pius IX undermined the good will that his steps toward a democratic constitutional state had created; on 15 November 1848 the papal prime minister Rossi was assassinated in parliament. Revolution had finally overtaken Rome itself.

The last cardinal to be created without sacerdotal orders – he received the diaconate in 1841 but never sought priestly ordination – Antonelli helped plan the flight of the pope from Rome, and five days later was named secretary of state, an office he held for the next 28 years. Working tirelessly for the pope's return to Rome, he was able to persuade Austria, France, and Naples to retake Rome (May 1849), and in April 1850 Antonelli accompanied Pius IX on his return to Rome. Though he won the pope's trust and confidence, Antonelli found opposition not only among the liberal factions of the Church State and college of cardinals, but also among the antiprogressives led by the former secretary of state for Gregory XVI, Lambruschini. The reasons were not hard to find: Antonelli was a political realist, not an ideologue; he was bound to encourage enemies from all directions on the ideological compass. Nevertheless he was able to remove the entire Church State deficit within nine years, and along the way found avenues for supporting industry, trade, and business. The result was that by the end of the 1850s the average citizen in the Papal State paid less than half the taxes of the average French citizen!

---

[22] Ibid., p. 803.

However, Antonelli was swimming against the tide. His most formidable opponent was Cavour, president of the Kingdom of Piedmont (1852) and indefatigable proponent of a united Italy without a separate Church State. In 1859 Piedmont and France joined in a war designed to drive the Austrians out of Italy; the consequence was that Austria's influence on the peninsula came to an end. An unexpected result was that the areas left vacant by the Austrian withdrawal were turned into revolutionary hotbeds (e.g. Bologna, Umbria, the Marches). The Romagna was lost to Piedmont, as Napoleon III expressed a desire to withdraw French troops from Rome; Cavour's plan to found an Italian federation with France's aid was moving closer to realization. In response, Pius IX, against the advice of Antonelli, called for a volunteer army to be formed from Catholics all over Europe. A year later Cavour attacked and overran this Vatican force as 15,000 French troops sat idly by. Antonelli's only hope was to play Turin (Piedmont) off against Paris (France), while in the process gaining support from Spain and Austria. This was clearly a strategy doomed to failure, and Antonelli knew it.[23]

After the declaration of the dogma of the Immaculate Conception in 1854, Antonelli had hoped for restraint in injecting religious belief and practice into foreign policy. But Pius disappointed him. Just as public, certainly more scandalous, and more of a problem for the Vatican's foreign relations, was the case of Edgar Mortara, similar in the scope of its European uproar to the Dreyfus Affair some decades later. Pius had, of course, kept Rome's Jewish community restricted to its traditional ghetto, but his treatment of the respected, and well-off Jewish family of Mortara from Bologna overstepped all bounds. Young Edgar Mortara, born in 1851, had been babysat from birth by a teenage Christian girl from Bologna. During his first year he had become quite sick; worried that he might die still an infidel Jew, the young nurse, Anna Morisi, baptized him while the parents were absent. The boy survived the illness and several years elapsed. In 1858, however, Edgar's younger brother also became ill and then died before Anna could baptize him, as she had Edgar. The ensuing guilt made her worry about Edgar's fate: unlike his younger brother he had been delivered from the danger of dying without salvation, yet he did not even know it! Conversations with neighbors made

[23] Walter Brandmüller, "Antonelli," in Sandfuchs (ed.), *Außenminister*, pp. 43–57.

their way to the local priest; from there it was a hop and a skip to the archbishop of Bologna. Despite careful investigation and several court actions, it is still unclear who said what to whom; but on 24 June 1858 the police, under order of the Inquisition, came to the Mortara household, took young Edgar, and disappeared with him. By the next morning he was on his way to Rome.[24]

The European and North American publics were outraged. Appeals were made from throughout the two continents to the Vatican, but Pius IX made it clear that this was a spiritual case outside his temporal jurisdiction. He was bound, he maintained, by an earlier ruling from Benedict XIV (1740–1758) according to which Jewish children, even if illicitly baptized, are to be separated from their families and educated as Christians.[25] In any case, conflicting reports very soon circulated: one had him crying for his parents and family, begging for a *mezuzzah*, while others had him adopting his new faith with warmth, adapting easily to his new residence in the Roman Home for Catechumens. While declining to take any action to release the child to his parents, Pius did make young Edgar his personal ward![26]

Finally, in 1861, the Mortara family did bring the Italian government to demand that at least the nurse be prosecuted for kidnapping. Pius IX replied that this was impossible since the young woman in question had already entered a nunnery. Indeed during the traditional New Year's audience granted by the pope to the Jewish

---

24 See first the older, unsigned account in the *Encyclopaedia Britannica* (11th edition; New York: Encyclopaedia Britannica, 1910), vol. XVIII, p. 877. Bertram Wallace Korn offers judicious corrections of both the event itself and its public aftermaths in his *The American Reaction to the Mortara Case: 1858–1859* (Cincinnati, Ohio: American Jewish Archives, 1957); mention is also made in San Waagenaar's *The Pope's Jews* (LaSalle, Illinois: Open Court, 1974), pp. 208–213. Many of the contemporary relevant documents are to be found in the pamphlet *Roma e la opinione pubblica d'europa nel fatta Mortara* (Turin: Union Press, 1859). For the official church file, see the Vatican secret archives, secretariat of state, rubric 66 (= Jews, Schismatics, non-Catholics), year 1864 (= 1858–1864: Posizione relativa al neofito fanciullo Edgardo Mortara. Battesimo).

25 In his rule "On Baptism of Hebrews, Children and Adults" from 1747. Benedict XIV (Lambertini), a famous canon lawyer, based his opinion on the well-known canon 60 from the Council of Toledo held in 633. It is worth noting that throughout the nineteenth century the old *Corpus Iuris Canonici* remained in force; thus "Sicut Iudeis" (*Decretals*, bk. 5, tit. 6) specifically prohibited the forced baptism of Jews. Lambertini certainly recognized this, as did also Pius IX; the rub was, of course, the status of a forced baptism (and thus illicit) after it had occurred. And here the situation was clear to Pius: illicit or not, it was still valid.

26 For the first see the report in the *New York Times* (27 November 1858), 2, repeating a story from the Genoese *Corriere Mercantile*. The opposite view can be found in the *New York Tablet* (20 November 1858), 3, carrying an article from the Turin *Armonia*.

community, the Mortara family appeared and appealed to the pope for the release of their son. Pius replied that he had no intention of paying attention to the general uproar caused by his actions and praised the Mortaras for having given Europe such a wonderful example of obedience to higher authority(!). Two years later young Edgar was presented to the Jewish community in the robes of a seminarian.[27] Antonelli knew that such intransigent intrusion of religious persuasions into the conduct of foreign relations could cause great harm to the goals set by the Vatican. At the very least Napoleon III was angered, and that, in turn, placed very much in doubt the support of French troops in propping up an already shaky Church State.[28]

By 1864, Napoleon III was ready to act, promising Piedmont that he would withdraw French troops from Rome within two years. In fact, he kept that promise but then turned around and hindered Garibaldi in occupying the city of Rome itself, though the rest of the Church State fell to his army of Italian unity. When the Germans and French came to war just four years later in 1870, Napoleon no longer had the luxury of trying to keep both Cavour and Pius happy: the French troops left Rome for good, and the tiny papal army was quite unable to resist the Italian onslaught. On 20 September 1870 the city was bombarded and then taken. A new "Roman Question" was thus created, very much the result of the first Roman Question forty years previously. While Pius had striven repeatedly to empha- size his spiritual power and authority, first by a papal dogmatic definition (Immaculate Conception, 1854), followed by a religiously dictated kidnapping (Mortara affair, 1858), then by a papal condem- nation (Syllabus of Errors, 1864), and finally by orchestrating a conciliar dogmatic definition of his own infallibility (First Vatican Council, 1870), it was now clear that the only action left to Vatican diplomacy was protest. Anywhere in the world that an attack was perceived to be made against the Roman Church, Antonelli was

---

[27] See August Bernhard Hasler, *Wie der Papst unfehlbar wurde. Macht und Ohnmacht eines Dogmas* (Frankfurt am Main: Ullstein, 1981), pp. 251–252. Upon the fall of Rome in 1870, Mortara was given the chance to revert to Judaism, but he chose instead to remain a Catholic and entered the Augustinian order, studying at waystations in Brixen (Tyrol) and Poitiers (France), where he was ordained a priest in 1873. He worked hard in support of the poor, achieving an excellent reputation as a preacher in the many countries in which he served (Italy, Austria, Belgium, France, Spain, England, America). Mortara died almost unnoticed at the age of 88 in 1940.

[28] Coppa, *Antonelli*, pp. 98–99.

quick to arrange a response. The ironic result of Antonelli's faithful execution of his master's wishes, and his skillful manipulation of competing powers in order to keep the Church State propped up as long as possible, was that he missed the notable opportunity to free the Roman Church of the ballast of political government. Instead, the Papal States ceased to exist and a new era in Vatican foreign relations began.

AN ERA OF ACCOMMODATION (= DETENTE), OR: THE AGE OF RAMPOLLA

In the first nine years of his pontificate, Leo XIII ran through three different secretaries of state, before finally settling on Mariano Rampolla for the last sixteen years of his reign.[29] With his appointment the "Spanish connection" to the development of the Vatican's foreign policies begins to bear fruit: Giovanni Simeoni, Pius IX's last secretary of state and the successor to Antonelli, had been plucked from his position as nuncio in Madrid to head the entire foreign policy operation (1875–1876); Franchi, Leo XIII's first secretary of state, had served three years as the nuncio in Madrid (1868–1871); Rampolla himself had served first as the secretary to the Spanish nuncio (1875–1877) and then had been the nuncio for five years before moving up to the papal secretary of state (1882–1887); and the secretary to Rampolla in Madrid had been Giacomo della Chiesa, later to become pope as Benedict XV; finally, Raphael Merry del Val, Rampolla's successor as secretary of state under Pius X, was the son of a well-known Spanish diplomat. In sum, from 1876 to 1922, Vatican foreign policy was formed by secretaries of state and a pope who either had worked in the Spanish nunciature or had a direct connection to Spanish diplomacy.[30]

It was Donoso Cortés who provided substance to this Spanish connection. Though his life as an influential theoretician of Spanish, and indeed European conservatism, was brief (1809–1853), he nevertheless bequeathed to his political and ecclesiastical successors a fundamental insight into the likely development of the nineteenth century, for it was Cortés who recognized that the religious and

---

[29] Two of Rampolla's predecessors died in office, the first, Alessandro Franchi, after only five months in his new position!

[30] Prior to that string, the secretaries had been marked by service in Paris, St. Petersburg, and Vienna (Bernetti, Lambruschini).

national conservative powers in Europe – Catholic royalty in its Romance form, the dynastic character of evangelical Prussia, and the partnership of Russian orthodoxy with czarism – were doomed: they would never, in his judgment, be able to achieve the same homogeneous unity that marked for him the movement of "international" revolution. In view of this overwhelmingly likely development, Cortés was convinced that there was only one avenue of escape: dictatorship.[31]

The Roman Church had, of course, already experienced the power and force of the nineteenth century's liberal and democratic demands: by 1870 the Papal States had disappeared as a political entity. That event, in turn, threatened to erode the even more essential spiritual obedience to Catholic faith as an objective complex of norms. Certainly one of the chief moments in the definition of papal infallibility at the First Vatican Council was the attempt to centralize the administration of belief and to protect the church against all democratic influences. By proclaiming legal principles (infallible interpreter of belief, universal jurisdiction) in the form of articles of faith, these elements of law were effectively removed from future debate.[32] With this reaction to the collapse of the Church State in place, in complete harmony with Cortés' predictions, the Spanish connection in the Vatican's foreign policy machinery was fully prepared to mount an anti-Modernist campaign against any who questioned these legal principles even before the so-called Modernist crisis came on stage. From the vantage point of a papal secretary of state, the Modernist crisis had already arrived.

The chief ideologue of the anti-Modernist party, long before any actual "Modernists" were in view, was a Spanish prelate, Dr. Felix Sardà y Salvany (1844–1916). His influential and widely circulated pamphlet, *Liberalism is a sin!*, provided a blueprint for an anti-Modernist program twenty years before there was a Modernist crisis.[33] Sounding a theme from the later papal pronouncement, *Lamentabili*, Sardà y Salvany sees the real danger in liberalism to be

[31] See Carl Schmitt, *Donoso Cortes in gesamteuropäischer Interpretation* (Cologne: Greven, 1950), pp. 65–66.
[32] See Fritz Fleiner, "Geistliches Weltrecht und weltliches Staatsrecht," *Ausgewählte Schriften und Reden* (Zurich: Polygraphischer Verlag, 1941), p. 263.
[33] *El liberalismo es pecado* (Barcelona: Libreria catolica, 1884). By 1885, just one year later, the pamphlet was in its third edition! The German translation made its appearance in 1889 as *Der Liberalismus als Sünde*, trs. from the seventh Spanish edition by Ulrich Lampert with an introduction by Josef Scheicher (Salzburg: Mittermüller, 1889).

its uniting of all errors in a synthesis: it is a sin because it includes "all heresies and errors in itself"; it is thus a system just as the Catholic Church is. This "social atheism" has led to devastating practical results: the church has lost its temporal power and possessions.[34] "A person, an organization, a book or a government," maintains Sardà y Salvany, "for whom the Catholic Church is not the single, exclusive and only measure in matters of faith and morals, is liberal." This is so because metaphysically religion and politics are one; the latter is contained in the former, just like a limb on a tree. Politics, or the *art* of ruling people, is morally nothing more than the application of the great principles of religion to the organization, ordering, and governing of society. "The Catholic thesis," he continues, "is the power that belongs to God and His gospel, namely to rule exclusively in the social sphere, and the duty, namely to force all classes in this sphere to subject themselves to God and His gospel."[35] The burden left behind by Antonelli and Pius IX was thus the collapse of a Church State coupled with an unbending persuasion that it must be restored if the church is to rule over the minds and hearts of its members as it should.

Rampolla worked closely with Leo XIII, perhaps as intimately as Merry del Val and Pius X were to collaborate later. For Leo, and thus also for Rampolla, the Church State issue was paramount, taking precedence over the matter of church politics. Thus Rampolla's style of directing the Vatican's foreign relations resurrects an earlier model, striving to achieve a balance of power by helping to build groups that play off against each other, just as his great counterpart, Bismarck, also did. While Leo gave Rampolla his marching order at the time of his appointment – to protect the church against revolution and impiety – how he was to achieve that goal was often his own design.[36]

Conditions, of course, had changed radically for a Vatican foreign policy. Two new states, Italy and Germany, had been added to the European constellation, and these had, in turn, changed the landscape of alliances. The Triple Alliance had begun with Germany

---

[34] *Liberalismus*, pp. 3, 9, 58, 13, 8 (all citations are from the German translation). Scheicher adds in his introduction the note that liberalism is the foundation of all opposition to the Catholic Church.

[35] Ibid., pp. 41, 136, 147.

[36] See Leo XIII's famous letter of instruction from 15 June 1887, encompassing some eleven pages, in Sinopoli di Giunta, *Rampolla*, pp. 85–96, here p. 85.

and Austro-Hungary in 1879; Italy joined in 1882. Almost immediately this group was expanded by the addition of Serbia (1882) and Rumania (1883). Initially Leo, and also Rampolla, hoped that their chief goal of a restoration of the Church State could be achieved through the help of this Alliance. Bismarck, however, wanted to wait, and slowly Rampolla began to see the Vatican's best chances lay with France. Though he was not an enemy of Germany by any stretch of the imagination, he never forgave Austria's alignment with Germany *and* Italy. At the same time Austria was most unhappy with Rampolla's policy of support for Slavic liturgies in the Austro-Hungarian Empire, thus endangering, in Vienna's view, German hegemony in the Danube monarchies. Since, therefore, the Triple Alliance was unlikely to help the return of the Papal States, thereby solving the "Roman Question," Rampolla shifted his attention to France. It is possible that he also was thinking of a counterweight, together with Russia, against the "German" grouping (including England).[37]

In any case, the *Ralliement*, or reconciliation of the Vatican with France, had as its goal a Catholic presence in the French government without deciding whether the form of state should be monarchical or republican. At the same time, Rampolla worked tirelessly to gain as well the emerging French–Russian alliance in support of a restored Church State.[38] As things turned out, both France and Russia took advantage of the Vatican: the former to control increasingly unruly French Catholics, the latter to keep Polish Catholics under control. And all the while Rampolla nurtured his (and Leo's) persuasion that

[37] See Rudolf Graber, "Rampolla," in Sandfuchs (ed.), *Außenminister*, pp. 58–72. George Kennan also mentions initial Vatican opposition to Russian Orthodox advances in Catholic Poland, in his *The Decline of Bismarck's European Order* (Princeton, New Jersey: Princeton University Press, 1979), p. 62. But in the second volume of his study, Kennan acknowledges that the Vatican began, in 1890, to realize the necessity of a reconciliation between the church and Republican France; *The Fateful Alliance* (New York: Pantheon, 1984), pp. 3–4, 195. Of note, too, was Rampolla's well-known zeal for the conversion of Russia; the successful reestablishment of a Catholic hierarchy in England (1850) certainly spurred him in this direction as did the 1896 decision against the validity of Anglican orders: if one can move against schismatics in one place, why not another? Cf. Sinopoli di Giunta, *Rampolla*, pp. 154–166.

[38] It was Leo's and Rampolla's policy to support the formation of conservative Catholic political parties that would systematically insert themselves into the democratic and parliamentary European states (except for Italy, of course!); the goal was to influence the legislative and administrative processes along Catholic lines: Fleiner, "Weltrecht," pp. 274–275.

a Church State was absolutely essential for Christian civilization to flourish and for Europe to enjoy tranquillity.

To this end Rampolla sought to bolster the pope's standing by encouraging his role as an international arbiter, thus enhancing the pope's legitimacy as a source of universal moral judgment. Already a participant through the Madrid nunciature in the Caroline Islands arbitration, Rampolla was the chief tool for the reinsertion of the pope into international politics. At the same time he was the beneficiary of the end to the *Kulturkampf,* in which Leo, and also Rampolla, helped Bismarck put this hindrance behind him, while in the same moment undercutting Windhorst and the Catholic Center Party. Bismarck had, in fact, "gone a long way toward Canossa, but not all the way," and Bismarck only had to revise, but not do away with the hated May Laws.[39]

Rampolla's end came with the death of Leo in 1903, though much attention is directed to the dramatic conclave that elected Pius X. The Austrian veto could have been ignored if the college of cardinals had wished; in fact, Rampolla's vote count went up on the next two scrutinies after Puzyna's announcement of the veto. But secretaries of state rarely follow themselves, either in that office or as pope (Gasparri and Pacelli are the exceptions), and the usual desire to see a change of direction manifested itself here.[40] In any event, Rampolla's policies had ultimately failed: there was no new Church State at Leo's death. In addition, Austria's veto against his election as pope was based on the Vatican move toward France; there seems little doubt that Berlin and Vienna coordinated the veto for the same reason. However, the French policy was doomed anyway: in 1905 under Combes, the complete separation of church and state in France was proclaimed.[41] And in perhaps the chief irony of Rampolla's long tenure as secretary of state, working hard at arranging an

---

[39] Otto Pflanze, *Bismarck and the Development of Germany,* vol. II (Princeton, New Jersey: Princeton University Press, 1990), pp. 219, 197. Ultimately Bismarck had made some important advances in separating church and state in the German Empire; what he had to give up, as Windhorst immediately recognized, was far less.

[40] Ludwig Pastor reports a conversation with Merry del Val from 29 December 1920, in which Pius' former secretary of state maintained that Rampolla never had a chance at papal election; a block of at least forty cardinals were opposed to his election from the very beginning because they felt a change in the system was needed; Rampolla was never able to garner more than thirty votes from the 63 cardinals in conclave: *Tagebücher, Briefe, Erinnerungen* (Heidelberg: Kerle, 1950).

[41] Michael Sutton, *Nationalism, Positivism, and Catholicism: the Politics of Charles Maurras and French Catholics, 1890–1914* (New York: Cambridge University Press, 1982).

edifice of foreign policies for the Vatican that would hold off the
onslaught of a liberal modern world responsible for the elimination
of the Church State, Pius X, the successor to Rampolla's Leo,
delivered himself of the judgment, just weeks before his death, that
Rampolla had been allied with the Modernists![42]

AN ERA OF STRUGGLE (= WAR), OR: THE AGE OF MERRY DEL VAL

Like Consalvi a century before, Raphael Merry del Val was plucked
from his role as secretary of the papal conclave to be secretary of
state by the new pope, Pius X. Consecrated bishop just three years
before by Cardinal Rampolla (his predecessor in office), Merry del
Val was marked by the same uncompromising intransigence that
had been characteristic of the English Cardinals Manning and
Vaughan. And that style fit his new pope perfectly. While Leo XIII
had been a "political" pope who sought influence for the church in
world affairs, mainly through diplomatic and political avenues, Pius
X sought the same goal but chiefly through "purely" religious and
spiritual ways. And that strategy fit his new secretary of state
perfectly. For Merry del Val had set pastoral care, as he understood
it, as the criterion of his actions: "Bring me souls" was his motto.
Alberto Canestri, an early biographer, once called him a "missionary
in scarlet," hitting the nail on the head.[43] This was a fundamental
characteristic of Merry del Val, and thus of his conduct of the
Vatican's foreign policy. As late as 1909 Count Széczen von Temerin,
the Austrian ambassador to the Vatican, observed that the pope was
even less well informed about diplomatic practices than his secretary
of state – and this, after six years of on-the-job training! And like a
missionary, Merry del Val and, consequently, his foreign policy were
extremely focused. In the controversy in Germany over confessionally mixed versus confessionally limited labor unions, he observed
that the former (the so-called Cologne model) were as bad as mixed
marriages (the Berlin model)![44] In other words, both Pius and Merry
del Val saw politics and foreign policy as the practice of proceeding
always down the right path, not as the art of compromise.

[42] Pastor, *Tagebücher*, entry for 30 May 1914.
[43] Cf. Josef Oswald, "Merry del Val," in Sandfuchs (ed.), *Außenminister*, pp. 73–93, here p. 85.
[44] Ibid., pp. 84–85. The Count added that Merry del Val pushed his *Kampfeslust* a bit too far
in order to be a successful diplomat.

Unlike Rampolla and Leo, Merry del Val was convinced that a restored Church State, one that involved political control over parts of Italy, was not desirable. Rather, he sought a new and different Church State, one independent of Italy; in contrast to Pius, therefore, he opposed any reconciliation with Italy. Toward this end he advanced the notion of an international treaty that would confirm the independence of the Holy See; the only role for Italy would be the protection of the Vatican in the name of the European powers. Though this scheme was discussed at high levels in Vienna, it never achieved large scale agreement. At the same time, however, and in concert with Pius, Merry del Val encouraged the participation of Italian Catholics in public life, just as Rampolla and Leo had done in France and Germany. This step may well have preserved Italy and the Vatican from a full-scale *Kulturkampf*.[45]

Such a battle was not avoided with France, however. Merry del Val and Pius shelved Rampolla's program of a *Ralliement* and fought fiercely against a laicization of the French state. This struggle, begun almost immediately in 1903, culminated in the formal and final break in 1905. The results were a complete separation of church and state in France and the end of the concordat. At the same time Spain broke off its relations to the Vatican, while Portugal implemented a separation of church and state modelled after the French example.

Such unwillingness to face the necessity of compromise came naturally to Merry del Val. Born into and raised in a Catholic Church in England that felt itself to be a distinct minority and one under implied, if not always open, attack from the anti-Roman Anglican majority, he was from the beginning a thorough-going ultramontane. However cosmopolitan Merry del Val may have become by exposure to the diplomatic life of Europe through the agency of his father as well as his service as secretary of state, he remained subject always to the quasi-paranoia which permeated the English Catholic Church at the end of the nineteenth and in the early twentieth centuries.

The fundamental inheritance of this church was its strict adherence to a papally endowed hierarchy of authority. As is usual for cases of cognitive dissonance, this view of Catholicism saw itself under siege and strove to achieve survival by dependence upon an

[45] One danger he perceived in any possible reconciliation with Italy was an Italianization of the curia; this is why he remained until the very end opposed to the Lateran Treaties of 1929. For a discussion of these themes, ibid., pp. 90–91.

external authority which could not and would not be questioned. This position, buttressed by the definition of papal authority at the First Vatican Council just thirty years before, was ready-made to capture the allegiance of a minority Catholic Church such as was found in England; Merry del Val's early theological training hammered this principle home. All through his life one can find him describing a current situation in military and combative terms; he is constantly under attack and therefore constantly in need of defending himself, that is, the church. Equipped with a penetrating but narrow intellect, perceptive but inflexible, Merry del Val treasured the virtues of obedience and loyalty. While such hallmarks saw him through his most difficult times, they were also the virtues least able to deal with the rising forces demanding change in the face of the age's intellectual advances.

Since his involvement in the commission to investigate the validity of Anglican orders (1896), Merry del Val had identified closely with the exercise of papal authority. His appointment as president of the Academy of Ecclesiastical Nobility in 1900, followed so quickly by his elevation to both the secretariat of state and the red hat just four years later, bolstered this persuasion that no representative of central authority may be criticized or called into question without also calling into question that central, issuing authority itself. This principle remains a key to understanding Merry del Val's strategies, tactics, and operations as the Vatican's secretary of state, a role that helped determine in a substantive way the next fifty years of the Roman Church's presence on the world stage.

As a result of these persuasions and tendencies, Merry del Val, under the direction of Pius X, abandoned any attempt to achieve reconciliation or accommodation with the new political constellations in Europe, North and South America, and the East. Instead, their reaction to the collapse of a Church State and the resultant decline in the political power and role of the Vatican was to refocus the church's attention and energies upon the so-called inner forum, namely the consciences of the faithful. If one cannot control the actions and policies of other countries and their governments, then one can at least control what their populations believe.[46] In concert with the infallibility and jurisdiction definitions of the First Vatican

---

[46] Fleiner, "Weltrecht," pp. 262–263. By maintaining the old rule from the Decretals, namely that all matters involving sin belong before the forum of the church (taken over by the 1917 Codex, c. 1553), the Vatican sought to retain control over its members.

Council, Merry del Val and Pius strove to substitute control over what its members believed for direct influence on the legislation and administration of countries now outside its power. "Foreign" policy under Merry del Val became an anti-Modernist campaign to protect the substance of faith. Under his secretariat, the collapse of the Church State in 1870, a product of the previous seventy years, became no longer an interlude but an accepted state of affairs. For the sake of an anti-Modernist program that had been under preparation for half a century, if not longer, Merry del Val went to war over a Modernist "crisis" of which he was at least one of the authors, if not the chief motivator.[47]

POSTSCRIPT: AN ERA OF SURVIVAL, OR: THE REST OF THE STORY

This story of the Vatican's foreign ministers and their policies throughout the nineteenth and early twentieth centuries provides us with solid and useful points of departure for understanding better not only the emergence of the Modernist movement, but above all the genesis and development of the Vatican-directed anti-Modernist campaign. In the long-lasting struggle of the Roman Catholic ✓ Church's governing organs to sustain or restore a politically viable state parallel to Europe's nation states we should seek the chief, but by no means only, sources of the anti-Modernist program. We can, in turn, also learn that the Roman Catholic Modernist movement was frequently and fundamentally misunderstood in its motivations, its program, and its goals. Rather than viewed as an inner-commun- ity effort to aid the Roman Church to become as vibrant and successful as possible in what was clearly a new "modern" world, the Modernists were condemned broadly as traitors to the continued existence of the Church of Rome as a "nation" state equipped with all the political power and authority accruing to late nineteenth-century European nation states. How that misassignment of motives and goals came about is at least partially or, I have argued here, to a great degree explained by the Vatican's foreign policy history throughout the nineteenth and early twentieth centuries. Yet this story does not end cleanly and completely with the forceful

---

[47] Cf. Lease, "Merry del Val."

suppression of the Modernists in 1907. The same energies that fueled anti-Modernism have continued to shape Vatican policy.

For almost an entire century since *Pascendi* the Vatican has heroically tried, in the face of the past failures outlined here, to redefine its role on the world's political stage. This redefinition, however, has not worked; the Vatican has been involved in a seemingly never-ending attempt to establish, or better, re-establish a formative presence in Europe, Africa, North and South America, the Near East. But the burden of the nineteenth century and its anti-Modernist program goes far in understanding why and how the Vatican has gained the dreary and almost hopeless position which it now occupies in the world's diplomatic fields. To analyze critically this development would at the same time be an ideological and historical critique of the role which religious institutions play in the political lives of contemporary Western societies, and those other of the world's societies controlled, or at least manipulated by them. Such a critique would involve several major issues.

Abundant contradictions reveal a two-handed game of so-called Vatican diplomacy. On the one hand, the Vatican has steadfastly insisted on imposing on other states the distinction between religion and political action, but at the same time has claimed that very distinction for its own. On the other hand, and this is key, the Vatican designers of ecclesiastical policy have failed to see, much less acknowledge, that their own actions and attempts at "mediation" represent primarily *political* undertakings! The "fundamental" goals of Vatican diplomacy are frequently portrayed as the preservation of the faith (= in Christian communities), the fostering of peace, and moral guidance.[48] Yet at the same time dark warnings are sounded that failure in these areas might well mean a blow to the "prestige of the Papacy"! What prestige? As a "religious" institution?! Since when, to echo Newman's critique of papal infallibility, does "prestige" become a vital note for a religious community instead of a devotional luxury? In fact, prestige can only be effective on a political stage, where the Vatican struggles schizophrenically with its identity as a "state" and as a religious institution. The political weight of an institution cannot be based on its "religious mission," as the anti-Modernist campaign of Merry del Val and Pius X would have it.

---

[48] Irani, *The Papacy*, p. 2.

Indeed, the cat is let out of the bag when critics still use the term "Holy See," from canon 7 of the now superseded *Codex* of 1917. Here we find that the main difference – as if it were one only of accident and not of substance! – between the monarchical constitution of the church and the government of a state, is the fact that the church's government (= Vatican) is of "divine origin" and thus not subject to change. As a direct reflection of the anti-Modernist program, Cardinal Ottaviani's hoary yet resilient double standard is still to apply: in societies where Roman Christians are in the majority, the Vatican must support "the idea of the confessional State with the duty of exclusive protection of the Catholic religion"; in a society, however, where Romans are not in the majority, the Holy See must claim "the right to tolerance or to the outright equality of the sects."[49]

This position is not only the basic key to Vatican foreign policy as an outgrowth of the anti-Modernism of the nineteenth and early twentieth centuries, it is also the heart and soul of real colonialism, such as Christianity has supported and practiced for centuries, from the extirpation of Jewish Christians in the second and third centuries to the "moral guidance" which it still seeks to impose on non-European cultures and societies.[50] "Religion," as defined in the West, is assumed to stand apart from "politics," and thus is capable of supporting and guiding, but not being part of, diplomatic efforts to shape other countries' internal and foreign policy. Take, for example, the supposition that the Vatican could, historically or otherwise, determine Jerusalem's political or religious function and fate! That city has never functioned as the source or location of Christianity; at the very most it was, for a few brief moments, the headquarters of a Jesuanic movement which quickly moved its power base out of Palestine – and for good reason. To claim now a

---

[49] Cardinal Ottaviani, in a lecture at the Lateran Seminary on church and state, 2 March 1953; in Gerald Fogarty, *The Vatican and the American Hierarchy from 1870 to 1965* (Stuttgart: Hiersemann, 1982). Ottaviani offered as support for his stance the fact that "two weights and two measures are to be applied: one for truth, the other for error. Men who feel in the secure possession of the truth and of justice do not compromise. They demand the full respect of their rights. On the other hand, how can those who do not feel sure of possessing the truth demand that they alone hold the field without sharing it with him who claims respect for his own rights on the basis of principles?" Ottaviani, it should be recalled, was the author of one of the Vatican's most important textbooks for its diplomatic school. The heritage obviously continues.

[50] Most useful and clearest example available: T. Todorov, *The Conquest of America* (New York: Harper & Row, 1984).

right to "determine" the future of that city is to manifest in all its raw tones the colonialist understanding of power: the right and ability to enforce a definition of what may count as "truly" religious, or culturally acceptable, or politically expedient, and so on. This attempt to claim religious justification for political policies is anti-Modernism in full bloom!

The end result is an ever increasing powerlessness on the part of Vatican diplomacy and thus increasingly an illusionary meaningfulness which can only be seen as meaninglessness.[51] Dedicated to the memory of a Vatican State which has long since disappeared and that State's anti-Modernist ideology, the Vatican's diplomacy has yet to take seriously what it means to practice diplomacy without an adequate power base. Stalin's purported remark on how many divisions the pope has at his disposal strikes the nail on its proverbial head. Bismarck knew that every state which attempted to operate outside the sphere of its own particular interests exercised a politics of power rather than of policy. And he also recognized that the formation and execution of political policy is not a logical and exact science, but rather the art of selecting in each changing moment of a particular situation the position or action which will provoke the least damage or which is the most useful.[52] He saw, that is, what the Vatican failed to see throughout the nineteenth century and throughout the Modernist crisis, and what it still fails to see, that to lay down a "personal" morality as the basis for political policy formation is doomed to a moribund fate. From the Roman Church's foreign policy tribulations of the last century and the resultant anti-Modernist program we can learn that, if the Vatican wishes to contribute effectively to the resolution of the terrible problems confronting our contemporary world, then it must pay heed to Bismarck's sage advice.

These are serious matters indeed. The transition of Western culture from the nineteenth to the twentieth century was as fragile as our contemporary shift from the twentieth to the twenty-first century is proving to be. None of that culture's institutions were exempt, nor are they currently exempt, from the widespread failure of broadly shared values and persuasions. Momentous events rocked the

[51] Stehlin, *Weimar*, and Graham, *Diplomacy*.
[52] Otto von Bismarck, *Gesammelte Werke*, vol. xiii, p. 335, from a speech before the Reichstag, 6 February 1888; p. 468, from a speech to a delegation from the University of Jena, 30 July 1892.

Roman Church from the collapse of its political independence as a result of the Italian revolution in 1870, through the great scientific and historical upheavals of the end of the nineteenth century and the final demise of European stability in World War I, to the establishment of a new relationship between the Vatican and Western societies, culminating in the Lateran Treaty of 1929. This sixty-year period, roughly encompassing the era of Modernism and anti-Modernism, also witnessed successful challenges to fundamental assumptions about the presence of institutional Christianity in the Western world, and in particular in Europe; it saw, too, the disengagement of such ecclesiastical institutions from a previous intimacy with the political, cultural, and intellectual workings of Western societies, in some instances taken for granted since before the Reformation. In many ways the Modernist/anti-Modernist period from 1870 to 1930 was a time of revolutionary transition for the Roman Church from one world and mode of existence to another, and the repercussions of that transition are still being felt today. Modernism and anti-Modernism remain markers for this passage from a secure and absolute persuasion of the role and function which institutionalized Christianity should and must play in the furtherance of Western culture and society to a most uncertain position which, in effect, made both the function and the value of such an institutionalized Christianity at best relative to all other societal constructions, and at worst dubious and highly questionable in any future society. It is precisely these consequences that make reflection upon the Vatican's foreign policy, its diplomatic machinations, and their several authors during the Modernist/anti-Modernist era so valuable today.

CHAPTER 2

Catholic anti-Modernism: the ecclesial setting

Paul Misner

Of the various settings or contexts that shaped the Modernist crisis in Roman Catholicism a century ago, none was closer to the bone of the protagonists than church life itself. The Modernists were, after all, engaged in what they saw as a necessary church reform movement. Their concern was with the intellectual vigor of Catholicism in the modern world. The most conspicuous element in their immediate church context was the "obscurantism" (Wilfrid Ward) that they ran up against in influential circles. The degree to which it gained the upper hand, making a crisis out of a controversy, requires explanation.

After all, the Modernists' pursuits were predominantly "academic." They scarcely touched upon the burning issues of church and state that preoccupied bishops and curial officials. Moreover, Pope Leo XIII (pope from 1878 to 1903) was calling for a renewal of ecclesiastical studies to bring them up to par with the challenges of the modern world. In these circumstances, reform-minded scholars who were ecclesiastics could well have expected some elbowroom for revising conventional positions. The mobilization of anti-Modernism was so effective, nevertheless, that a full battery of papal condemnations was loosed upon them in the pontificate of Pius X (1903–1914), especially from 1907 onwards. Where did this anti-Modernism come from? What were its sources of strength within the Catholic communion?

It is my contention that the anti-Modernist forces that stifled the Modernist movement in the Roman Catholic Church pre-existed Modernism and the Modernists (Alfred Loisy, George Tyrrell, Ernesto Buonaiuti, Umberto Fracassini, Giovanni Semeria, Giovanni Genocchi, Friedrich von Hügel, Maurice Blondel, and Lucien Laberthonnière being among the more notable). The anachronistic "medievalism" that George Tyrrell decried in 1908 was itself a modern, largely nineteenth-century, development, but it pre-dated and set the stage for the Roman Catholic Modernist controversy. As Roger Aubert has remarked of the disturbances around Jansenism in the seventeenth century, it is unfortunate that a term in "anti," as in "anti-Modernist," makes one think that the "Modernism" in question must have existed first, whereas it may well be the other way round.[1]

I conceive my task in this essay to be twofold: firstly, to look into the stages of development of the ultramontanism that had become so strong by the time of the Modernist controversy. The relationship of the Catholic Church with modern culture, already broken in key respects in the seventeenth century, did not heal at all during the Enlightenment. Emerging from the shock of the French Revolution, Catholicism rebounded in successive phases, each of which was more emphatically marked by ultramontane ecclesiology (or view of church pivoting on papal authority) than any pan-church movement since the Gregorian Reform in the eleventh century. In the nineteenth century, however, ultramontanism became a form of traditionalism, fueled in large part by resentment against, or at least opposition to, various aspects or consequences of modernity.

The second question has to do with the period just prior to the Modernist controversy. Should one think of the Leonine pontificate (1878–1903) as an opening to the modern world in the age of liberalism? Did it effect a softening of the intransigent attitude of previous ultramontanism? Or should it be regarded as the first fully effective ultramontane pontificate, once papal authority had been established beyond any question through the Vatican Council? How effectively ultramontane traditionalism operated in Leo's time, quite apart from Blondel, Loisy, and Tyrrell, will be examined in three sectors of ecclesiastical life: the political, the socio-economic, and the religio-cultural.

A brief concluding section will document its continued force during the time-span of the sharpest anti-Modernist measures, the pontificate of Pope Pius X (1903–1914).

---

[1] Aubert in a response (p. 20) to Lucien Ceyssens, "Pour une histoire plus poussée et plus explicite de l'antijansénisme," *Actes du colloque sur le jansénisme* (Bibliothèque de la Revue d'histoire ecclésiastique, fasc. 64; Louvain: Nauwelaerts, 1977), pp. 1–22.

THE LONG MARCH OF ULTRAMONTANE ECCLESIOLOGY[2]

Revolution (1789–1815) and Restoration (1815–1848)

✓ The mystique of church unity by way of authority may well go back
to Ignatius of Antioch in the early second century. It received,
however, a powerful new generalization and formulation in the early
nineteenth century at the hands of Joseph de Maistre (1753–1821),
aided and abetted by Louis de Bonald (1754–1840) and Félicité de la
Mennais (1782–1854). The last, opposed primarily to the subordination of the church to the state, picked up de Maistre's almost purely
external, "political" angle on what the church was good for: namely,
establishing and preserving the order of human society. Lamennais
(as he called himself after his break with the papacy) was enormously
influential not only in France, but in Germany and Italy as well; his
advocacy was decisive in getting the ultramontane ball rolling.
Backed by his prestige and by a strong tide of disappointment over
the benefits of the Restoration for Christian civilization, more and
more clergy took the following typical chain of reasoning as
"proved" by tradition and the experience of the modern society:

    no public morality or national character without religion;
    no religion in Europe without Christianity;
    no Christianity without Catholicism;
    no Catholicism without the pope;
    no pope without the supremacy that is his due.[3]

✦ In fact, what de Maistre had done was to take the early modern
absolutist notion of "sovereignty" to extremes; he rounded out his
system of political science by extending it into the realm of the
church as the theoretically necessary all-encompassing and supra-
national authority.[4] The notion of national sovereignty, developed
and located in the monarch by Jean Bodin (1530–1596), was
common coin in political discourse (think of Hobbes and Rousseau);
de Maistre intensified its necessity as an ultimate guarantor of order.
For de Maistre and those influenced by him, sovereignty and

---

[2] On the development up to 1868, see Klaus Schatz, *Vaticanum I 1869–1870*, 3 vols.
(Paderborn: Schöningh, 1992–1994), vol. I, pp. 1–34.
[3] Yves Congar, *L'Eglise de saint Augustin à l'époque moderne* (Paris: Editions du Cerf, 1970), p. 416;
citing de la Mennais, *De la religion* (3rd edition; 1826), p. 181.
[4] Hermann Josef Pottmeyer, *Unfehlbarkeit und Souveränität: Die päpstliche Unfehlbarkeit im System der
ultramontanen Ekklesiologie des 19. Jahrhunderts* (Mainz: Grünewald, 1975), pp. 61–73.

infallibility were identical; "infallibility" was simply the property by which a given decision of authority was the last word, against which there was no appeal; that is, what Lamennais called "supremacy."

An Italian monk named Mauro Cappellari had made a move like de Maistre's, in a 1799 book that was little noticed at the time, entitled (in defiance of the Zeitgeist) *The Triumph of the Holy See*.[5] As pope of the Restoration, he, Gregory XVI (1831–46), would be so opposed to any reform that smacked of liberalism that even Metternich thought he should be more flexible, at least in the administration of the Papal States themselves. Gregory XVI's book indicated a hardening of ecclesiological fronts even in traditionally ultramontane Italy. Previously, ultramontane ecclesiologists retained some concern with the authority of bishops as well as of popes, even though the pope's primacy and infallibility were given priority. Now there set in "an exaltation of authority, intact only if personal and absolute."[6]

That such a one-sided approach could carry conviction at some levels of the church is only understandable against the background of the destructive revolutionary storm that had swept across Europe since 1789. It left ecclesial structures a shambles. In France, the Revolution had turned to violence on a then unprecedented scale.[7] Not just high nobility and their cousins in church office were hunted down in the name of the nation, but ordinary priests and lay Catholics who would not support their persecution as well. Church institutions were secularized, that is, disbanded, and their property confiscated. The churches in the Holy Roman (German) Empire and in Italy were affected just as deeply. Their organizational structure and institutions, from temporal prince-bishoprics to seminaries and parishes, were thoroughly disrupted.[8]

In France, ecclesiastical order could be restored on the basis of the Concordat with Napoleon of 1801, but chaos reigned much longer elsewhere. The first great "secularization" of the nineteenth century occurred with the final act of the Holy Roman Empire in 1803: all

---

[5] Ibid., pp. 46–47.
[6] Giuseppe Alberigo as cited by Pottmeyer, ibid., p. 47. It seems, however, that a predecessor of Cappellari, Pietro Ballerini, had reached virtually the same point in 1760; see Richard F. Costigan, "The Consensus of the Church: Differing Classical Views," *Theological Studies* 51 (1990), 25–48, here 39–46.
[7] Ralph Gibson, *A Social History of French Catholicism 1789–1914* (London and New York: Routledge, 1989), pp. 51–55.
[8] Rudolf Lill in *History of the Church*, ed. Hubert Jedin, 10 vols. (New York: Crossroad, 1980), vol. VII, pp. 132–142, together with Aubert, ibid., vol. I, pp. 85–132.

the prince-bishops and ruling abbots had to give up their dominions to compensate the secular princes who lost their territories on the left bank of the Rhine. As with the confiscation of church lands in France during the earlier years of the Revolution, these expropriations, though compensated in some sort by salaries for the clergy, proved irreversible. They were confirmed by the Concordat of 1801 and by the post-Napoleonic settlements at the Congress of Vienna. Of all the bishops of Europe, only the pope's temporal power over his states in central Italy was ever restored, from 1801 to 1809 and from 1815 to 1870.

Unburdening the bishops and abbots from the responsibilities of civil government was of course a blessing in the long term, but a heavily disguised one. It made millions of Catholics in German lands subject to authoritarian Protestant princes and hence threw them into a kind of second-class citizenship until at least 1848. Without the old state boundaries, one often did not even know who was in charge, ecclesiastically; bishoprics often remained unfilled for years until the boundaries could be redrawn and bishops appointed who were acceptable to the new rulers. Pope Pius VII (1800–1823) and his secretary of state, Cardinal Ercole Consalvi, rose to the occasion by negotiating concordats in the years following the Congress of Vienna. Concerned Catholics appreciated the papacy as never before for the chance that it gave them to build up basic church institutions once more.

The Concordat of 1801 with Napoleon had unforeseen consequences for the future development of ultramontanism in France.[9] Ultramontane apologists such as Lamennais could point out the fact that Napoleon did not attempt to redraw the ecclesiastical map of France on his own authority, or convoke a national council of bishops to do it; instead he had to deal with the pope, who alone had the power to make such necessary surgical interventions upon the ecclesial body. What remained, if only on paper, of the diocesan structure of the Gallican church was wiped away; bishops were forced to resign, and a new set of bishoprics was erected, with bishops appointed by the pope upon the nomination by the government. The inner-church checks and balances to papal power called for by Gallican ecclesiology were simply disregarded. Ultramontanes

---

[9] Austin Gough, *Paris and Rome: The Gallican Church and the Ultramontane Campaign 1848–1853* (Oxford: Clarendon, 1986).

took this development to be fully in accord with the structure of authority given to the church by its founder and not merely to be a makeshift provision in extraordinary circumstances.

While Louis Philippe reigned in France (1830–48) and Pope Gregory XVI in Rome, the church of France reached a rather cool and distant, even strained relationship with the government, but not one that led to thoughts of seriously revising or abandoning the Concordat. Ecclesially, the pope and the French episcopate were mutually supportive, in line with the traditional Gallican ideas of communion. Gregory XVI did not give up the extreme ultramontane convictions that he had expressed at the depth of the Revolution. They now constituted an acknowledged theological position in the whole Catholic world, shared by some in France and Germany as well as south of the Alps. Though perhaps not yet quite respectable, neo-ultramontanism put itself forward more and more as the only serious alternative to "parliamentary Gallicanism" or state control of the church in France.

On the accession of Pius IX in 1846, it seemed for a brief period as if the time had come for the realization of Lamennais's ultramontane but "liberal Catholic" or *L'Avenir* program of 1830. The two causes, the freedom of the peoples and the freedom of the pope, seemed to be forming a more than tactical alliance. However, the revolutions of 1848 ended by frightening people and making them take refuge in the camp of law and order, averse to revolutionary slogans and aspirations. They also convinced observers of the incompatibility of the standard liberalism and the standard Catholicism of the time. Mediating positions were formulated, but with diminished status on each side.

Aggressive ultramontanism (1848–1868)

Aubert emphasizes that around 1850, Rome moved from a cautious policy, merely welcoming signs of spontaneous ultramontanism, to an actively interventionist stance of undermining Gallican or national-church customs defended even by bishops. In France, this culminated in an encyclical in 1853, *Inter multiplices*, which indicated in no uncertain terms that seminary textbooks still bearing traces of episcopal Gallicanism were to be replaced. The Roman stance found considerable support among the rural clergy influenced by the grassroots ultramontane movement since the 1820s. The bishops complied, even though they and their Sulpician advisers were of a different opinion.

Outside France as well, the governments that signed concordats continued to behave as if the *ancien-régime* prerogatives of absolute monarchs were still in force, even or especially when liberal cabinets de facto set policy. They insisted on a measure of freedom and self-determination for parliamentary political forces, but not for the church(es). As recognized public bodies, these were expected to toe the line drawn for them by the sovereign parliamentary majority. Thus, in many countries, the state-church phenomenon known variously as Erastianism, regalism, Josephism, or (in Italian at least) "jurisdictionalism," displayed a striking continuity in the passage from monarchical to constitutional government. Church people came in ever greater numbers to think that, unless they bestirred themselves in an ultramontane sense, all the disadvantages and none of the advantages of absolutist rule would be carried over and intensified, if only for Catholics, in the age of liberalism.

As the Papal States were threatened and then reduced by the national unity movement in Italy, the papal reaction to the modern world intensified. It reached a climax, perhaps more sensational than was intended, in the Syllabus of Errors in 1864. Owen Chadwick notes that "historians of the twentieth century have minimized or neglected" this papal act, as concerning only "the doctrine of authority in a particular church," as if it were "a matter only of theology and not of European politics."

Europe saw the Pope condemn liberalism – whatever that was, the Pope condemned it. And without precisely defining liberalism, or defining it in diverse ways, Europe saw that this was the irresistible force of the age. The Pope sat on his throne like Canute amid the incoming tide. But the pope looked not merely ridiculous. Ethical ideals were associated with the slogans of liberalism, words like liberty and fraternity, freedom of conscience, tolerance, justice in the way of equality before the law. Many western Europeans had the sensation, not just that the Pope was wrong, but that he was morally wrong.[10]

---

[10] Chadwick, *Secularization*, pp. 111–112. See also the nuanced restatement by Peter Steinfels, "The Failed Encounter: The Catholic Church and Liberalism in the Nineteenth Century," in *Catholicism and Liberalism: Contributions to American Public Philosophy*, ed. R. Bruce Douglass and David Hollenbach (Cambridge: Cambridge University Press, 1994), pp. 19–44.

The First Vatican Council (1869–1870)

The Council was also all about authority. Under dispute was the better way to strengthen authority in church and society. The majority tended toward a catastrophic reading of current relations between Christian tradition and modern culture. The minority saw those relations as certainly tense and problematic but not yet hopeless; were the Council to set the church on a collision course with modern aspirations, however, they foresaw an irreparable breach. Those who saw the prevailing situation as unsustainable, whether from a utopian (as with Henry Edward Manning, archbishop of Westminster) or an apocalyptic (Pio Nono) perspective, formed the heart and soul of the majority and seized the initiative. As the most recent historian of the First Vatican Council, Klaus Schatz, finds, the basic issue of the whole event was how to deal with a world that was denying religion its accustomed place in Western society.[11]

The role of two influential daily newspapers in France helped popularize and perpetuate the Maistrian reaction that would seem to have outlived its time. The ascendancy achieved first by the *Univers* under the editorship of Louis Veuillot in the French Second Empire (Pius IX's time) and then by *La Croix* in the Third Republic (Leo XIII's time) goes a long way toward explaining the prevalence of a strident traditionalism in Catholic public opinion. *Der Katholik* of Mainz, and later, the Center Party press headed by *Germania* of Berlin, represented a less lopsided version of anti-liberal opinion among Catholics in Germany. The most authoritative journalism in Catholicism was that of the Roman Jesuit periodical, the *Civiltà Cattolica*, which offered ultramontanism of the purest water.

Louis Veuillot was "a son of the people" (of a cooper, actually), who through favorable circumstances was able to overcome his lack of higher education and become a provincial journalist. He was converted to Catholicism in 1838 on a visit to Rome and became editor of the *Univers* in 1843. Soon he built up the circulation of the struggling daily to 8,000 (temporarily – its more usual circulation was 5,000 or less). Most of the subscribers were country clergy, the very ones who suffered from their educational inferiority in

---

[11] Schatz, *Vaticanum I*, vol. III, pp. 305–306; cf. Komonchak, "Modernity," pp. 11–41; Komonchak documents further sources and studies in abundance.

comparison with *universitaires*. Veuillot assured them that a modern university education was worthless; he taught them everything they had never heard in the seminary about papal prerogatives as the source of church vitality. Veuillot "in effect re-educated the parish clergy, giving them a daily course in simplified theology and political doctrine, supported by a highly tendentious précis of church history . . . The complex ideas of Maistre's *Du Pape* and Lamennais's *Essai sur l'indifférence* became clear as crystal."[12]

Veuillot's devotion to the pope was boundless, and Pius IX reciprocated. The supreme test came in 1860, when the pope asked Veuillot to publish an encyclical, *Nullis certe*, protesting Louis Napoleon's actions in regard to the defense of the Papal States. Fully expecting that this would be the last issue of the *Univers*, Veuillot published the encyclical.[13] Napoleon III suppressed the paper the next day, 29 January 1860; Veuillot turned to writing books. The *Univers* was permitted to resume publication in 1867. In combination with the *Civiltà Cattolica*, it would again be a mainstay of ultramontane propaganda as the First Vatican Council was prepared and held.

Given the wealth of data that Pottmeyer has assembled on the reception of the idea of infallibility as a necessary perfection of all true sovereignty, it is far from fanciful to conclude that de Maistre's (and Cappellari's) assimilation of the idea of absolutist sovereignty was present in the conciliar majority's notion of what they were defining. A minute and thorough study of the issue of infallibility at the First Vatican Council[14] concludes that the key point in defining papal infallibility was to see to it that the primatial authority of the pope extended also to matters of truth or doctrine and that no appeal would be possible from the pope's solemn decisions – precisely de Maistre's goal in the context of rolling back the French Revolution!

On the day the final amendments to the infallibility decree were approved, the last words to the fathers of the First Vatican Council by Vincent Gasser, bishop of Brixen and relator of the Deputatio de

---

[12] Gough, *Paris and Rome*, pp. 94–96.
[13] Marvin L. Brown, *Louis Veuillot: French Ultramontane Catholic Journalist and Layman, 1813–1883* (Durham, North Carolina: Moore, 1977), p. 262. See also Pierre Pierrard, *Louis Veuillot* (Paris: Beauchesne, 1998).
[14] Anton Houtepen, *Onfeilbaarheid en hermeneutiek: De betekenis von het infallibilitas-concept op Vaticanum I* (Bruges: Emmaüs, 1973).

Fide, lauded papal infallibility not just as the guarantee of unity in the Roman Catholic Church, but in particular as an example to civil society, whose last foundations were tottering.

No remedy for this woeful condition [of society] exists except in the church of God, in which an infallible authority has been divinely instituted in the whole body of the teaching church as well as in its head. I am convinced it is God's purpose in having the doctrine of papal infallibility placed before the Vatican Council in these days, that the eyes of all should look to this rock of faith, which the gates of hell cannot overcome.[15]

Chadwick overstates the matter, but only by a hair, when he declares:

The first Vatican Council of 1869–70 was afterwards seen to be concerned with the theology of faith and ecclesiastical certitude. That was not what was believed at the time, not even perhaps by the Pope. At the time it was believed to be concerned with the question of questions, whether liberalism and Catholicism could be reconciled.[16]

From the perspective of the *Civiltà Cattolica* and the *Univers*, the answer was clear – never! Is it possible to see in Bishop Gasser's words the outline of a subtly different tack along the lines that Pope Leo XIII would take: that liberal institutions such as constitutions, parliaments, political parties, and newspapers could and should be reconciled with Catholicism? All they had to do was to change their ways and they would find a hand stretched out from the barque of Peter to grasp theirs. Let them merely drop their anticlericalism, recognize (and subsidize) the civilizing, moralizing, and charitable role that only the Catholic Church can play in society, crack down on Freemasonry and other secret societies, and in general come to their senses and refrain from pursuing the utopia of a society beneficently liberated from religious influence. This less forbidding view of how the relations of the church and European society could go forward was predicated on an assessment of modern society no less negative than the one held by Manning and Pius. The ills and stresses afflicting secular society were so manifest that it would be forced sooner or later to have recourse to the church that alone could state with authority what was God's will.

---

[15] J. D. Mansi, *Sacrorum conciliorum nova et amplissima collectio*, ed. L. Petit and J. B. Martin (Paris: H. Welter, 1899–1927), vol. LII, p. 1317; cf. Schatz, *Vaticanum I*, vol. III, p. 158.

[16] Chadwick, *Secularization*, p. 113.

The curtain falls

Meanwhile, however, the "Roman Question" (Rome as papal city
vs. Rome as capital of united Italy) was settled by the royal Italian
army on 20 September 1870. Pope Pius IX would not accept the *fait
accompli.* Seeing no acceptable way to deal with the problem, he
became "the prisoner of the Vatican." His many denunciations of
the situation before sympathetic audiences, faithfully reported in the
Catholic press, only reinforced this reading of the modern world as
desperately misguided, indeed, in apocalyptic throes.

Public opinion, welcoming the fall of papal Rome, rejected an
ideal of the relationship between church and society, an ideal that
official church statements and unofficial gestures nevertheless were
intent on maintaining. Giuseppe Martina explains:

> The taking of Rome did not mean only the annexation of the city to the
> Kingdom of Italy and the crowning of Cavour's vision of the unity of Italy,
> nor only the end of the Popes' temporal power; it also meant the
> disappearance of a political and social structure anchored in models of the

> *ancien régime*, with its tight connection between civil and religious life.
> Without a deeper analysis, we recall some of its typical elements: the official
> recognition of Catholicism as the state-religion, religious unity as the
> foundation of political unity, the resulting confessional discrimination and
> religious intolerance, the relevance of the norms of canon law for civil
> legislation, the traditional ecclesiastical immunities, the Church's monopoly
> in education and in charitable works, the broad support of the secular arm,
> [and] psychological pressures more or less energetically exercised upon the
> faithful for the fulfilment of their religious duties.[17]

In connection with the survival of this Christendom paradigm,
Komonchak comments: "Right down to the Second Vatican
Council, such an arrangement was considered the ideal, the 'thesis;'
at best (or worst) in conditions of the 'hypothesis,' the Church might
have to bear with another arrangement in order to prevent a greater
evil."

The Paris Commune of 1871 rising up from below and the
Kulturkampf that broke out from on high in Germany soon thereafter
only reinforced the lesson (or: aggravated the psychology). The spirit
of revolution that seemed to be the most prominent feature of the
modern world was a metaphysical evil. One read de Maistre again
and shuddered at his insight into the satanic character of the French

---

[17] Komonchak, "Modernity."

Revolution: "elle est satanique dans son essence."[18] Attempts to find
common ground with this monster were rejected out of hand.[19]

The future Modernists who were growing up in these times would
pick up the baton from the small band of "liberal Catholics."[20]
From the 1860s on, these liberal Catholics were increasingly hard
pressed, as the prospects for a conciliation or synthesis between
modern culture and Catholicism became so bleak. Would Pope Leo
XIII revive those prospects?

THE CHURCH IN THE MODERN WORLD UNDER LEO XIII

The defiant anti-liberalism of Pius IX's reign, with the Syllabus and
the Vatican Council, had led public opinion to surmise that the pope
elected in 1878 in the Vatican compound – no longer a state – would
be the last. In the modern world, there was scarcely room for such a
relic of the past. One index of the work Leo accomplished or
permitted is that since his time the world has again been keenly
interested in papal elections. And yet it would be a mistake to
suppose that Leo's achievements came because he deviated even
slightly from the fundamental position adopted by ultramontane
Catholicism. Such an impression was and is easy to come by. After
all, instead of harping on the illegitimacy of the Third French
Republic, Leo XIII asserted himself diplomatically, culminating in a
much noted but ill-fated attempt in the 1890s to get monarchists to
cooperate with the Republic and to work within its framework. This
Ralliement is misunderstood if seen as a departure from the basic
posture of opposition to nineteenth-century liberalism that the
papacy had assumed all along.

In his latest attempt to characterize the relationship of Leo XIII to
modern society, Roger Aubert lines up aspects of continuity between
Pius IX and Leo XIII alongside the new departures of the latter.[21]
He notes strong continuity in the reaction of both popes against

---

[18] Cited by Pottmeyer, *Unfehlbarkeit*, p. 73.
[19] Komonchak, "Modernity," p. 39, n. 69. See Thomas A. Kselman, *Miracles and Prophecies in Nineteenth-Century France* (New Brunswick, New Jersey: Rutgers University Press, 1983), p. 137, on the renewed vitality of an apocalyptic view of history and its consequences for political intransigence in the Third French Republic.
[20] On whom see Steinfels, "Failed Encounter," pp. 30–37.
[21] Aubert in *La Chiesa e la società industriale (1878–1922)*, ed. Elio Guerriero and Annibale Zambarbieri, 2 vols. (Turin: Edizioni Paoline, 1990), vol. I, pp. 74–86. See now also Marcel Launay, *La Papauté à l'aube du XXe siècle: Léon XIII et Pie X* (Paris: Editions du Cerf, 1997).

rationalism and secularization, in their intransigence on the Roman Question, and in pursuing increased centralization of church affairs in the Vatican. Under the second heading, he identifies changes in the style of dealing with governments and in the attention paid to the labor question, the unity of Christians, and the activation of the laity. Aubert also includes under the changes "the initiation of a dialogue with modern society," but here the emphasis must rest on "the initiation," rather than "a dialogue." He allows that "Leo was no enthusiast for modernity" and cites Emile Poulat's 1977 statement that "Leo XIII was at least as antimodern as Pius IX before him and Pius X afterwards."[22] So there can be no question of his warming up to the distinctively "modern" aspects of contemporary society. True, the diehards in the church kept making odious comparisons between him and his predecessor for coming to terms with liberal Catholicism, but their criticism stemmed from a completely mistaken judgment on his real position. And Aubert cites Pietro Scoppola's distinction from 1957 between Leo's attitude and that typical of liberal Catholics. On the one hand, the liberal Catholics

tended towards a rethinking from a Christian perspective of the principles of liberalism, a weighing and sifting that would free certain claims that they thought were essentially consonant with the Christian spirit from irreligious accompaniments or deviant cultural expressions. Leo XIII's approach to the modern world, on the other hand, started from a different inspiration: availing himself of new means, he wished to recreate the situation that was compromised by the progressive secularization of government, restoring to the Church the full exercise of that office of guidance and direction that it had constantly exercised in previous centuries.

That this anti-liberal, and in this sense anti-modern, orientation of Leonine Catholicism set the stage for the integrist reaction against Catholic Modernism, can be seen in three respects. Whether in the political order, in the socio-economic arena, or in the cultural realm, ultramontane Catholicism refused to relegate itself to the private sphere alone. For most of us, I think, basic human rights now include the freedom of people, Catholics and others, clergy and laity, to state a case in the public square. Anticlerical liberals, for their part, did not respect this right when it came to priests or even "clerical" laypeople; the latter were suspected of being under some spell of psychological or moral dependence. On the other hand,

---

[22] See Emile Poulat, *Eglise contre bourgeoisie* (Tournai: Casterman, 1977), p. 175.

ultramontane Catholics during Leo's pontificate, or for a long time afterwards, did not consider mere permission to try to persuade the public to be an adequate platform for their message. They could not see how the church's mission could be adequately carried out in the long run without societal recognition of the "social reign of Christ," as authoritatively interpreted by the church and hence by the papacy.

Modern political circumstances and the church

Martin Marty has located the "modern schism" of secularization in several countries around 1870, the year of the Franco-Prussian War of 1870 with its defeat of "Catholic" France at the hands of "Protestant" Germany.[23] In its wake, nationalism and liberalism were the dominant political forces, without which electoral success was impossible. Socialism and the First International were increasingly serious threats on the left. By tradition, but also as a defense against socialist influence, liberals in general (as distinct from radicals) were not "democratic" but conservative: they preferred a limited suffrage, tied to property ownership and education; they were not committed to tolerating the freedom of social choice of those who disagreed with them; and considering organized religion a danger to societal maturity and civil self-development, as they did, they sought at the very least to wrest the education of children from the control of the clergy and the religious. Hence education was a frequent bone of contention between Catholics and liberals. The former thought it was the job of the church to educate the young, whereas the liberals sought to gain control of the future and ameliorate it by universal education. What Kipling called "the white man's burden" was, domestically, the liberals' burden. In many places, this struggle had been going on since early in the century, and it was not over yet.

In combination with the defensiveness of Catholic clergy and people, the mistakes and excesses of liberal parliamentary majorities in the "culture wars" of the latter third of the nineteenth century clearly contributed to the longevity of Catholic anti-Modernism. Many liberals were anticlericals, driven by a passion to replace Catholicism with a secular religion of enlightenment surcharged

---

[23] Martin Marty, *The Modern Schism: Three Paths to the Secular* (New York: Harper & Row, 1969).

with positivism and nationalism. They could not understand why liberal society failed to thrive as expected. In lieu of realistic analyses, they attributed its failure to a conspiracy organized by the Jesuits.[24] Ultramontanes, from the pope down, harbored a mirroring myth about a vast conspiracy of Freemasons and secret societies pulling the strings of modern society. Perhaps this myth had more foundation in fact than the "Jesuit conspiracy" theory, but it tipped over into pure delusion, as with the fraudulent "revelations" of one "Leo Taxil."[25]

Pope Leo XIII did introduce several nuances into his rejection of liberalism. Of these the most important was the thesis of the church's indifference regarding various forms of government. He backed away from his predecessors' insistence on monarchy, where once established, and stated that, in principle, any of the three classically distinguished types of regimen (monarchy, aristocracy, or democracy) was in principle equally compatible with the church's public role as a perfect society alongside the state. (Perhaps his brief diplomatic posting in constitutional Belgium, along with his neo-Thomism, had something to do with this timely adjustment.) Yet he left no room for pluralism or religious freedom, except on the "hypothesis" of avoiding a still greater evil. Like his predecessors and several of his successors, he continued to pursue a Christendom model of church and state long after the social and cultural underpinnings for such a relationship had been knocked away. For real-world democracy, therefore, Leo XIII had no endorsement.

Pope Leo XIII's political and diplomatic initiatives were not, on the whole, very successful. To his credit, he was able to provide Otto von Bismarck with a way to call off his own unfortunate church–state engagement, the *Kulturkampf*. But Leo himself must have concluded that his strategy of allying the papacy with so-called conservative or reactionary forces and regimes was not working. Consequently he launched the *Ralliement* with the French Third Republic, which foundered on reactionary Catholic opposition and, of course, the Dreyfus affair. His new style of church–state relations

---

[24] Geoffrey Cubitt, *The Jesuit Myth: Conspiracy Theory and Politics in Nineteenth-Century France* (New York and Oxford: Oxford University Press, 1993); cf. Gibson, *Social History of French Catholicism*, p. 111.

[25] Oskar Köhler in Jedin (ed.), *History of the Church*, vol. IX, pp. 216–218; cf. Eugen Weber, *Satan franc-maçon: la mystification de Léo Taxil* (Paris: Gallimard, 1964) and Kselman, *Miracles and Prophecies*, pp. 134–140. For an analysis of this mentality, see in particular Schultenover, *View*.

produced results no better than his predecessor could boast. The ascendancy of political liberalism left the papacy with a weak diplomatic hand to play. Does the picture look different if we broaden our view to the social and the cultural sectors?

The church and socio-economic life

Catholicism's rebuilding of itself after the trauma of 1789 proceeded not only on hierarchical lines, but very vigorously at the level of lay associations and organizations. By a series of pragmatic responses to challenges and opportunities, Catholicism in many countries had assumed or given itself a new shape by the end of the nineteenth century.[26] Sometimes such a reshaped Catholicism had a political party or grouping as its most conspicuous public feature ("political Catholicism");[27] sometimes a Catholic labor movement in rivalry with socialist unions would attain notable strength, with backing from Catholic politicians and clergy ("social Catholicism"). Where such organizations of laity were prominent (particularly in Germany, northern Italy, and Belgium), they were a prime example of the leading paradox of ultramontane Catholicism. Traditionalist in ideology, they nevertheless represented typically "modern" adaptations to post-Enlightenment, post-revolutionary society. The public role that law or custom previously accorded bishops or papal diplomats in Catholic countries had faded, but these "modern" associations exercised a public role in different arenas and in new ways. Perhaps nowhere is this paradox more obvious than in the social Catholicism that Leo's *Rerum Novarum* so powerfully abetted.

From early on, Catholic apologists accounted for laissez-faire or economic liberalism largely in terms of the secularization of public life, or *la Révolution* tout court – the modern apostasy and its attendant moral decay: individualistic selfishness and greed. This diagnosis was natural enough, but had its regrettable aspects all the same. The intransigent or neo-ultramontane mentality interpreted secularization as a failure of the will and the imagination, the result of bad ideas gaining currency in twisted minds (what may be called

---

[26] For the most encompassing presentation of this First Vatican Council Catholicism in a short space, see the oft-cited Komonchak, "Modernity."

[27] Jean-Marie Mayeur, *Des partis catholiques à la démocratie chrétienne XIXe–XXe siècle* (Paris: Colin, 1980); Karl-Egon Lönne, *Politischer Katholizismus im 19. und 20. Jahrhundert* (Frankfurt: Suhrkamp, 1986).

an "intellectualist" fallacy, placing the ultimate blame for all unfavorable phenomena on modern "rationalism"); whereas in large
measure it was the outcome of population growth, the rise of mass
markets and industry (gradually displacing agriculture from its
position as virtually the only source of wealth), and economic strains
that sharpened social inequality in the contemporary world. These
factors at least deserved much more sustained attention than they
received.

By 1880, it became a common reproach among socially minded
intransigent Catholics that the French Revolution had absolutized
private property as an inviolable right (in the Declaration of the
Rights of Man, Art. 17). On the other hand, revolutionary legislation
had also severely curtailed the right to association in the economic
realm with the *Loi Le Chapelier* of 1791. This law abolished the guilds
and artisans' "corporations" of the *ancien régime* and forbade any
similar combinations in restraint of trade. A provision of the
Napoleonic Code (1804) forbade any and all associations of workers;
it remained in effect in France until 1868 and in Belgium until 1883.

Inasmuch as these measures of the Revolution turned all control
of economic production over to those who had the capital and
denied any say to those who only provided the labor, they were
injurious to the interests not of the clergy directly, but of workers.
According to a perspective arrived at independently by many nineteenth-century social Catholics, including Bishop Wilhelm Emmanuel von Ketteler (1811–1877) of Mainz, the congenital defect of the
post-revolutionary disorder was the exaggerated individualism of
bourgeois liberals. They were careless about, if not downright
destructive of, all community ties and duties (except those freely
entered into by particular, legally enforceable contracts). This outgrowth of Protestantism and the Enlightenment then called forth the
opposite but equally mistaken extremes: anarchism or, more typically, the collectivism and regimentation of the socialists. What was
needed, in the words of a cardinals' commission in 1852, was a
middle way vindicating "the *freedom* of association" (against socialist
legislative proposals, but also against the harmful monopolies of the
old guilds), in tandem with the encouragement of "free *association*,"
against the atomizing tendencies of liberalism.[28]

These last propositions are no longer considered particularly

---

[28] On all this, see Misner, *Social*, index; on the early Roman position of 1852, p. 128.

reactionary or anti-modern – in the interim they have been largely accepted in Western societies – but in the heyday of classic liberalism, they were a challenge to its congenital individualism and anti-traditionalism. This challenge was enough to establish the link between the renewed counter-revolutionary fury of Catholic "knights of the Syllabus" and their program of social reform and social justice.[29]

We perhaps need to remind ourselves that even Leo XIII's pioneering social encyclical, *Rerum Novarum*, only left the door open to, while not actually endorsing, autonomous labor unions; it was recommending workers' pious associations under the direction of the clergy. Here again the pivotal prescription for the modern world in the papal pharmacopoeia was clearly recourse to hierarchical and ultimately papal *authority* – not the medicine that moderns as such were eager to take.

Leo XIII was cautious enough not to lay down the law on matters of economic science. However, his emphasis on the role the church was to play in solving the social question indicates that he was by no means willing to allow modern principles of autonomy to confine religion to the private life. Just as the pope must guide and judge the rulers of nations (be they kings or parliaments or voters), so it was his charge to remind economic agents of their duties, the foremost of which was heeding the voice of the church.

We approach the subject with confidence, and in the exercise of rights which manifestly appertain to Us, for no practical solution of [the social] question will be found apart from the intervention of religion and of the Church. It is We who are the chief guardian of religion and the chief dispenser of what pertains to the Church; and by keeping silent we would seem to neglect the duty incumbent on us.[30]

Clergy and social class

As a rule, laboring people lost touch with the church when they migrated from their native regions to the new cities and conurbations in search of work. Even in cases where urban working-class boys remained or became churchgoers, few if any would learn Latin

[29] E.g., Maurice Maignen (1822–1890), Albert de Mun (1841–1914), and René de La Tour du Pin (1834–1924), for whom see Misner, ibid.
[30] *Rerum Novarum*, no. 16, in *The Papal Encyclicals*, vol. II: *1878–1903*, ed. Claudia Carlen (Wilmington, North Carolina: McGrath Publishing Company, 1981), pp. 241–257.

from the parish priest and enter a minor seminary at a tender age, as was customary in village parishes. Hence virtually no priests came from industrial working-class milieus. Did that leave only peasant sons as the bulk of the priesthood? In eighteenth-century France, they had been a minority, Gibson informs us, whereas in the nineteenth century they did make up the majority of the parish clergy, but not an overwhelming majority.[31] A large number still came from the towns, mostly from the modest but not poverty-stricken strata of artisans, shopkeepers, and the like. In Germany, where the formation of a working "class" was not as advanced, priestly recruitment probably mirrored the Catholic population more fully, which meant the priests were still predominantly from modest family backgrounds.

The Napoleonic Concordat provided for a seminary in each of the fifty (later eighty) dioceses, to no one's advantage. The multiplication of small schools produced a poorly educated country clergy. Not even anticlerical liberals really benefited by this, especially after Veuillot turned their alumni into an anti-liberal fighting force. The Concordat also made the creation of new parishes and missions dependent upon the state budget. In ballooning centers such as Paris or the burgeoning industrial towns, this proved to be a great obstacle to founding parishes to follow population movements. Paris, for instance, made do with a few huge city parishes catering to the small percentage of the bourgeoisie and aristocracy who cared to attend. The Concordat also made every priest more unilaterally accountable to his bishop, who in turn was responsible for their politically prudent behavior to the prefect and the state religion ministry.[32]

Among the European bourgeoisie, practicing Catholic families were in a distinctly minority situation.[33] There was a noticeable attraction to Catholicism among French bourgeois in the 1850s, and again at the end of the century, especially among some intellectuals disenchanted with positivism. The recruitment of clergy waxed and waned with the attitude of governments, but never sank to the levels

---

[31] Gibson, *A Social History of French Catholicism*, pp. 62–69.
[32] Ibid., pp. 39–63; Aubert in Jedin (ed.), *History of the Church*, vol. VIII, pp. 14–16.
[33] These were the breeding grounds of many Modernists, members of the cultured laity of the relatively monied classes such as Friedrich von Hügel, Maude Petre, Tommaso Gallarati Scotti, and Maurice Blondel. Modernist priests, mostly from more modest backgrounds, could function in these circles as teachers and writers.

of the Revolutionary and immediately post-Revolutionary era at the beginning of the century.

Given this situation, a close relationship between pastor and parishioners was class-dependent. Where a better-educated priest from the bourgeois or aristocratic class had similar people in his parish, the conditions for mutual understanding were present. Where a rural pastor dealt with farmers' families like his own, there could also be a bond. One problem, however, was that he had spent so many formative years being trained in a clerical way of life that this bond was weakened; another was that even a rural parish might count among its members a local aristocratic landowner, perhaps a prosperous farmer or two with education, and, as the education system developed, also a liberal, university-trained teacher. The education the priest had received in the typical diocesan seminary stamped him as no gentleman and deprived him of the resources necessary to hold his own with the local elite.

Perhaps more important, however, was the attitude instilled by the clergy's seminary training. The older ideal was to keep aloof from the world and society, and hence even from one's parishioners apart from religious ministrations. Settled habits did not change simply because the pope endorsed a challenge to get "out of the sacristy." However, in the wake of *Rerum Novarum* in 1891, a number of new-style *abbés démocrates* did emerge.

The Catholic press

The freedom of the press championed by liberals was often hedged in by serious restrictions. Nevertheless the rise and proliferation of Catholic periodicals and newspapers were conspicuous features of nineteenth-century Catholicism both early and late.[34] Although the earlier Catholic journalists freely admitted that freedom of the press was corruptive of good order, it was, for committed Catholics, a necessary evil. One had to engage in journalism for the good of the church, deprived as she was of more suitable (authoritarian) defenses.

La Croix was the success story par excellence of a Catholic opposition press, attaining a national circulation of 180,000, or, with

---

[34] Aubert in Jedin (ed.), *History of the Church*, vol. viii, pp. 53–55, and Köhler, ibid., vol. ix, pp. 215–216.

its hundred local (weekly) editions, up to 700,000 by 1897.[35] It was
part of the press agglomeration of the Assumptionist Fathers, who
were a target of anticlerical legislation in 1900–1901. Rivaling the
anticlerical press in the vehemence of its language, it prominently
added Jews to the list of modern conspirators against a Christian
France and thereby secured for itself an infamous reputation in the
history of the Dreyfus case. After the encyclical *Rerum Novarum*, it
looked favorably upon the beginnings of Christian democracy, as a
Christian alternative to liberalism and socialism; but when the trend
toward worker autonomy in the management of labor unions
became apparent, it detected their anti-authoritarian direction and
joined the integrist attack on the Christian labor movement.[36]

The Mennaisian, Maistrian, counter-revolutionary rhetoric of the
Univers lived on in *La Croix*, along with the coarseness of personal
attacks, which almost seemed to be of the essence of journalism to
these practitioners (also "a necessary evil" or "a dirty business" in
their eyes?). Faced with the satanic revolution, de Maistre had
written in a letter in 1817, attacks on persons were the only effective
way to oppose ideas.[37] Catholic daily papers and other periodicals
were also well established in Germany, Belgium, and the Netherlands. On the whole, their editors conducted themselves more civilly
than *La Croix*'s did. In Italy, the development of modern Catholic
newspapers was to go on until the advent of fascism, but Don
Davide Albertario in Milan matched the Assumptionists in France in
pugnacity if not in circulation or national scope. It was also the case
in Italy that "Modernist" writers could develop a fairly broad
readership, as Romolo Murri and Antonio Fogazzaro did (below).

Church and culture

Education, conceived of as capturing the loyalties of the next
generation, was a prominent public issue in the age of liberalism.
This had always been the mission of the church, and now anticlerical
liberals were passionately promoting a rival "civilizing mission,"
that of the "nation." France is the exemplary type of this develop-

---

[35] Bellanger, Claude et al., *Histoire générale de la presse française* (Paris: PUF, 1969–76), vol. III,
pp. 333–338; Köhler in Jedin (ed.), *History of the Church*, vol. IX, p. 216.

[36] Misner, *Social*, p. 314.

[37] Joseph de Maistre, *Du Pape* of 1819/21, ed. Jacques Lovie and Joannès Chetail (Geneva:
Droz, 1966), p. xi.

ment, leading to the notion of the two French nations, *les deux France*. We shall see that education was at the heart of the developments that would lead to the end of the concordatory relationship of church and state.

For higher education and research, the idea of a Catholic university was abroad in ultramontane circles. Belgium's unique compromise between liberals and Catholics permitted a university worthy of the name to be erected and maintained at Louvain. Because of the strength of the Catholic Party in Belgium, the church was allowed to run schools and other public institutions for its own flock, an approach dubbed "subsidized freedom." The advantages this conferred on Belgian Catholicism were considerable, but these did not stop some Catholics from waging a persistent crusade against liberalism. Since Catholic leaders shrank from undermining the parliamentary system that had assured Catholic institutions a share of public funds, the Belgian situation never developed into a full-scale life-or-death conflict between just two sides. Still, the immediate result was more the development of a vigorous Catholic "pillar" than a fruitful dialogue with liberal society.[38] Nor was the Belgian solution regarded as anything to be imitated, any more than American arrangements were; at best, it passed as a tolerable exception on the "hypothesis" of an entrenched liberal regime.

In the 1890s, it seemed to some whom we now call Modernists as if the forces of intellectual modernization in the church had a chance of making a difference. Thus, for example, in Fribourg in 1897, before an International Catholic Scientific Congress, Marie-Joseph Lagrange, O.P. (1855–1938) and Friedrich von Hügel were able to deliver critical analyses of the then burning question of the Mosaic authorship of the Pentateuch. And this was done in full awareness of the recent (1893) papal encyclical on biblical studies, the first of its kind, *Providentissimus Deus*. Lagrange went on to publish his essay at the head of the 1898 volume of the new *Revue biblique*, which he edited in Jerusalem.[39] He did this only after much soul-searching

---

[38] "Pillars" and "pillarization" are designations applied to a model of comprehensive subcultures existing side by side without a strict domination on the part of one "establishment." The prime example is the Netherlands.

[39] See Bernard Montagnes, *Le Père Lagrange 1855–1938: l'exégèse catholique dans la crise moderniste* (Paris: Editions du Cerf, 1995) pp. 78–87; cf. Christoph Theobald, "Le Père Lagrange et le modernisme," in *Naissance de la méthode critique* (Colloque du centenaire de l'Ecole biblique et archéologique française de Jérusalem; Paris: Editions du Cerf, 1992).

and correspondence with his religious superior in Rome, in the conviction that "only critical study can combat critical study."[40] The essay, innovative in its probing of the concept of scriptural inspiration, would come in for severe criticism but also earned the newly founded Ecole biblique in Jerusalem much respect in Catholic scholarly circles. His reading of *Providentissimus Deus* and other signals out of Rome, to which he was extremely sensitive, permitted him and some other Modernists to hope that the restrictive understanding of historical criticism endorsed by the encyclical was not the last word; it would be up to scholars like himself to show the necessity and permissibility of abandoning certain positions whose weaknesses were becoming apparent.

In the last years of Leo XIII's reign, there were some signs that a favorable attitude toward biblical criticism was developing; these followed other contrary signals. Leo XIII's leading collaborator and secretary of state, Cardinal Mariano Rampolla (1843–1913), set up a Biblical Commission of which he became head in 1902. The Commission even made the *Revue biblique* its official organ of communication! In this atmosphere, Lagrange treated the book of Genesis in a series of lectures in Toulouse as an example of what "historical method" could offer: nothing innovative or provocative as in his 1897 Fribourg paper, just the standard procedure of Bible scholars as it had been practiced at the Ecole biblique in the decade or so since its founding. *The Historical Method* had a greater impact than was expected, four or five thousand being printed before its sale was stopped by Rome.[41] The time was now 1904; *The Historical Method*, delivered before but published just a few months after Alfred Loisy's *The Gospel and the Church*, had appeared in March 1903; and Pope Pius X had succeeded Leo XIII in August, 1903. The Biblical Commission underwent a change of character and personnel, going so far as to insist on the Mosaic authorship of the Pentateuch by June of 1906. Looking back from the ordeals of the Modernist crisis, scholars have seen an era of positive Leonine latitude, even "liberalism." What was the substance of this evaluation?

---

[40] *Revue biblique* 12 (1903), 299.
[41] Marie-Joseph Lagrange, *La Méthode historique, surtout à propos de l'Ancien Testament* (Paris: Lecoffre, 1903).

Leo's grand design and neo-Thomism

According to the founders of *Civiltà Cattolica* in mid century, and in Leo XIII's own grand strategy, Thomistic philosophy was to play a key role in the Catholic revival.[42] An index of its importance in Leo's overall plan was the early attention and careful follow-up he gave to his encyclical on the subject, *Aeterni Patris* of 1879, only a year after his inaugural encyclical. Just as it does not detract from the intrinsic significance of *Rerum Novarum* to see it as part of Leo's overall ambition of reconstructing a Christian society, so it does not detract from neo-Thomism as a philosophical movement to note that the pope's insistence on its importance in forming the minds of educated Catholics was motivated by the need, as he saw it, for a consistent intellectual approach to the problems of modern society.

Knowledgeable commentators on Leo XIII speak repeatedly of his "grand design," a design described by James Hennesey as one "of philosophical renewal that would lead to social and political renewal."[43] Ultimately he saw his mission as enabling the *world*, no less, to accept a cure for the social and political disruptions that were plunging it into a state of deep moral resignation.[44] He turned the heartfelt, but vague, intuition of Bishop Gasser at the end of the Vatican Council into something almost resembling a plan of operations. The passage of time has revealed his project to have been utopian, but it nevertheless provided an intellectual rallying-point for the Catholicisms of the first half of the twentieth century and helped them thrive as vigorous sub-groups within secularizing societies.

Leo's grand design of societal reconstruction had three main focal points, each with one or more major encyclicals dedicated to it, but with clear cross-references to the other two and the overall "cause."[45] *Aeterni Patris* sprang from the conviction that it would be useless to dream of a comprehensive renewal of modern society, a Christian social order, without the common coin of a social philosophy. This

[42] Aubert in Guerriero and Zambarbieri (eds.), *La Chiesa e la società industriale*, vol. II, pp. 203–207; Komonchak, "Modernity," pp. 31–33, with further references.

[43] James Hennesey, "Leo XIII's Thomistic Revival: A Political and Philosophical Event," *Celebrating the Medieval Heritage: A Colloquy on the Thought of Aquinas and Bonaventure*, ed. David Tracy = *The Journal of Religion* 58 (1978) S185–S197, here S195. Note that the pope aimed at *philosophical* renewal, not at theological renewal.

[44] Köhler in Jedin (ed.), *History of the Church*, vol. IX, p. 21.

[45] Emile Poulat, *L'Eglise, c'est un monde: l'ecclésiosphère* (Paris: Editions du Cerf, 1986), p. 221.

philosophy would have to be a restored Thomism, an Aristotelian
philosophical instrument that neo-Thomistic pioneers had reduced
to a system.[46] Neo-Thomists such as Leo regarded it as a fully
adequate alternative to Kantian subjectivism, one capable of coordi-
nating a hylemorphic metaphysics and a realistic epistemology with
a communitarian social and political philosophy. In the second
place, then, it would be necessary to recall and, if necessary, refine
the proper notion of public authority and the relationships of church
and state. This was the task especially of *Immortale Dei* (1885) and
Libertas praestantissimum (1888). Thirdly, the changes that industrial-
ization had brought to economic life required its readjustment to the
requirements of the Christian social order (*Rerum Novarum*, 1891).
For the neo-Thomists, the root problem was "one grand system of
rationalism gradually displaying itself first in theology and then,
successively and cumulatively, in philosophy, politics, and society."[47]
The remedy, therefore, had to be an equally grand and unitary
system upending that rationalism. Leo XIII's *Aeterni Patris* echoed
this analysis by tracing "the troubles that now vex public and private
life" to "false conclusions concerning divine and human things,
which originated in the schools of philosophy, have now crept into
all the orders of the State and have been accepted by the common
consent of the masses."[48]

Ultimately, the success of this grandiose undertaking would hinge
on whether the Catholic vision of papal religious authority, as set
forth in the First Vatican Council, would set in motion a vast wave of
conversions from liberalism. This wave would eventually lead the
church to a position of leadership in the contemporary world
paralleling that of Innocent III in the Middle Ages. That this did not
take place was a disappointment not only to Leo, but to many other
Catholics (though some of them had always wondered whether the
reliance on Thomistic thought was not excessive). On the whole,
however, Catholics, including intellectuals, were more confident of
their position vis-à-vis the modern world after the Leonine revival
than before.

The Modernists comprised those Catholics whose ideas of reform
did not set much stock in updating medieval Thomistic thought. For
Blondel, it was one tradition of Catholic thought among others and

[46] McCool, *Catholic*.
[47] Komonchak, "Modernity," p. 15; see also p. 31.
[48] *Aeterni Patris*, no. 2, in Carlen (ed.), *The Papal Encyclicals*, vol. ii, pp. 17–18.

did not really meet the legitimate requirements of contemporary criticism. For Loisy, it was a hopelessly unreal and ahistorical culture that mummified the Christian tradition. Von Hügel concurred. They could not take altogether seriously what Leo XIII proposed in all earnestness and what was becoming normative among the Catholic intelligentsia (for example, Désiré Mercier at Louvain). In the social setting of *fin-de-siècle* Catholicism, set as it was against prevailing anti-traditional trends, there would be little tolerance for deviant reform programs.

Anti-Modernism before the outbreak of the Modernist crisis

Nevertheless, modernity was exacting its tribute. Despite explicit opposition to the Enlightenment, modern Catholicism (as distinguished from Catholic Modernism) was taking, in significant respects, exactly the route that modern liberal society since the Enlightenment had assigned to "religion." Two related principles of modernity are autonomy and social differentiation. "Social differentiation implies the concentration of Christianity in the church, as it meant the concentration of governance in the state, of the economy in capitalism, and of intimacy in the family."[49] By the time of the Modernist crisis, the Roman Catholic Church was well along in its own process of modernization in this sociological sense, while protesting vehemently against the need to do so. Something almost like a state within a state eventuated, a "complete society" (*societas perfecta*) alongside of or within civil societies. Perhaps the resulting construction is best termed a counter-society or, more neutrally, a *subculture*.[50] It was a *modus vivendi* at once forced on Catholicism by circumstances, and taken energetically in hand by lay and clerical church leaders, so that the initiative would not remain solely in the hands of others, of representatives of "liberalism."

In the conditions of modern scholarship, the church's battle-ready stance against liberalism in all its manifestations, the emphasis on internal solidarity, loyalty, and attentiveness to authority, and the suspicion of reform and of all that came from the modern outlook,

---

[49] Karl Gabriel, "Die neuzeitliche Gesellschaftsentwicklung und der Katholizismus als Sozialform der Christentumsgeschichte," in *Zur Soziologie des Katholizismus*, ed. Karl Gabriel and F. X. Kaufmann (Mainz: Grünewald, 1980), p. 205, as cited in Komonchak, "Modernity," pp. 34–40, here p. 37.

[50] Komonchak, "Modernity," pp. 34–40.

coupled with a distinct underdevelopment of any self-critical sense, all combined to put the future Modernists in a disadvantageous position within the church. In particular, the bad reputation that already attached to subjectivity in philosophy, and to rationalist historical investigation in studies of the Bible and tradition, would predispose the official church (*ecclesia docens*) to fear certain prominent features of modern scholarship, no matter how effective the apologetics of the Modernists against Protestant and secular adversaries might be.

Both the Modernists and the anti-Modernists in the Roman Catholic Church of the turn of the century could agree that a purely private religiosity was not Catholic Christianity. They agreed further on the liberty of the church to fulfill its public mission. If the Modernists ran the risk of being too "civil," too deferential to liberal sensibilities, the anti-Modernists could not shake off their propensity to overshoot the mark in the opposite direction. For them, the modern freedoms were irreconcilable with the liberty of the church, meaning authoritarian direction from the church's teaching office.[51]

THE INTEGRALIST INTENSIFICATION UNDER PIUS X
(1903–1914)

The Modernist crisis occurred during the pontificate of Leo's successor, as the Roman center of world Catholicism determined to rid the church of those elements that pursued a line of conduct at variance with its own. Partly in response to outside forces and partly in response to the perceived danger of Modernism within the church, the stance known as "integralism" gained respectability and influence in the highest echelons of church power. Clerics and other Catholics schooled in the Vatican claims to virtually unlimited religious authority found it hard to refute integralist logic, even when their Christian common sense told them that it was not the answer. The basic Catholic integralist position held that all areas of human behavior are subject to judgment by church authority and therefore to papal authority.[52]

[51] See Schultenover, *View,* p. 33.
[52] See Maurizio Tagliaferri, *L'Unità Cattolica: studio di una mentalità* (Rome: Gregorian University Press, 1993). From this perspective, the very idea of a "rightful autonomy" (*justa autonomia*) of earthly affairs (to cite the Second Vatican Council's highly pertinent *Gaudium et Spes* [1965], no. 36) was anathema.

Catholics perceived the growing threat of socialism, which was just as anticlerical as its predecessor and progenitor, liberalism. Their response was hampered by acrimony between the democratic and the integralist strains in the Catholic response to the challenges of the times. I shall mention just two important political developments in Italy and in France that preoccupied Pius X, but the same dynamic played itself out all over Catholic Europe.[53]

In Italy, Pope Pius X[54] was quite willing to have Catholics enter into electoral pacts with liberal conservatives who would forgo further anticlerical measures in return for needed support from the Catholics against the socialists. The restoration of papal rule over central Italy was no longer a seriously sought aim. The rule against Catholics voting in the elections for the Italian parliament remained in place, but it was increasingly riddled with exceptions in the interest of keeping socialists out of office – even if the endeavor meant becoming political eunuchs for the liberal conservatives.[55] This behavior may serve to show that Pius X was not immune from modernizing adjustments, if it appeared that they could be kept under papal control.

The event overshadowing all else in relations between France and its Catholics was the Law of Separation of 1905. Laws were passed against religious congregations in 1901, especially the ⟨teaching⟩ orders, and these laws led to their suppression. The Assumptionists of *La Croix* were exiled, along with Jesuits and Lagrange's Dominican confreres. By 1905, under tensions resembling those of the earlier *Kulturkampf* in Germany, French republicans found themselves rather precipitately abrogating the Napoleonic Concordat and cutting all ties between the French state and the churches. This move seemed scarcely less traumatic than the French Revolution itself, at least in Rome and in integralist circles in France. Although the French bishops were prepared to negotiate with the government to ease the

---

[53] See Wolfgang Ockenfels (ed.), *Katholizismus und Sozialismus in Deutschland im 19. und 20. Jahrhundert* (Paderborn: Schöningh, 1992). See now also Hubert Wolf (ed.), *Antimodernismus und Modernismus in der katholischen Kirche* (Paderborn: Schöningh, 1998).

[54] See Gianpaolo Romanato, *Pio X: la vita de papa Sarto* (Milan: Rusconi, 1992), who devotes only one of forty numbered sections of the biography to the anti-Modernist efforts of Pius X, but notes that these were what most powerfully motivated Pius XII to canonize this predecessor under whom he served as a young priest. See now also Owen Chadwick, *A History of the Popes 1830–1914* (Oxford: Oxford University Press, 1998).

[55] On the papal policy against Catholics in parliamentary elections, see the article, "non expedit," in the *Dictionary of Modern Italian History*, ed. Frank J. Coppa (Westport, Connecticut: Greenwood Press, 1985), p. 296.

abrupt transition, Pius X and his secretary of state, Cardinal Merry del Val, refused to lend any appearance of legitimacy to the matter.[56] In regard to economic justice, too, the French "social weeks" or *Semaines sociales* that encouraged and clarified options for democratically oriented Catholic social undertakings became objects of suspicious surveillance, with censure following from on high. Maurice Blondel, in fact, came closest to being officially branded as an unreliable Catholic, not for his modern philosophy, but because he came to the defense of the *Semaine sociale* leadership in a pseudonymous article critiquing "monophorisme" or one-way thinking, his coinage for the integralist approach.[57]

In Italy itself, the form which "Modernism" assumed in Pope Pius X's mind was determined most vividly by the figure of Romolo Murri (1870–1944), a neo-Thomist cleric and pioneering Christian Democratic organizer. He deployed a prodigious energy in making propaganda for a Christian social movement in and alongside the *Opera dei Congressi*, the non-political association of Italian Catholic forces in the newly unified, liberal Kingdom of Italy. Murri had crossed swords with the pope when the latter was still Cardinal Giuseppe Sarto, patriarch of Venice, in 1902.[58] In the years following, Murri cultivated contacts with Modernists, aiming for a common front of scholars and social activists who were chaffing under hierarchical control. This fed into the suspicion, only too alive among integralists, that the essence of Modernism was the common denominator of these troublesome reformers, autonomy and intolerance for authority. Hence the classification of Murri with the Modernists, despite his lack of sympathy, as a Thomist, with the concrete aims of the post-Thomistic scholarly Modernists.[59] Hence also the condemnation of Antonio Fogazzaro's best-

---

[56] Thomas A. Kselman, "Separation of Church and State," *Historical Dictionary of the Third French Republic, 1870–1940*, ed. Patrick H. Hutton (Westport, Connecticut: Greenwood Press, 1986), pp. 927–928.

[57] Blondel, *LSS*. Cf. Misner, *Social*, pp. 296–298 with pp. 306–318 for context.

[58] Misner, *Social*, p. 253.

[59] This hypothesis was already suggested by Pietro Scoppola, *Crisi modernista e rinnovamento cattolico in Italia* (Bologna: Il Mulino, 1961), p. 158; now it has been confirmed by a new study that places Italian Modernism more firmly in the setting of the international phenomenon and underlines its specific originality more explicitly, namely Maurilio Guasco, *Modernismo: i fatti, le idee, i personaggi* (Turin: Edizioni Paoline, 1995), here pp. 140–141.

selling novel, *Il Santo* (1905), which fictionally combined the social, scholarly, and church reform movements.[60]

Though frequent condemnations emanated from the Vatican from the beginning of Pius X's reign, they turned into a flood from 1907 onwards, with the crystallization of the image of "the Modernist" in the integralist mind. The defiant attitude taken by the pope facing the separation of church and state in France turned into something "bordering on panic"[61] among his close associates, the cardinals Gaetano De Laï (1853–1928), Louis Billot (1846–1931), and Raphael Merry del Val (1865–1930). To these may be added the clandestine delations of Msgr. Umberto Benigni (1862–1934) and his "spies" in the so-called *Sodalitium Pianum*.[62] Although Pius X kept himself informed of Benigni's activities and helped him out financially, his group was not nearly as numerous or otherwise well-connected as rumor had it for several decades.

The case of Marie-Joseph Lagrange, O.P., is instructive. Among the targets of the integralist attacks, no one has been so thoroughly and unequivocally vindicated. And yet the damage and delay caused by anti-Modernist measures against his work were great. His critical work in Old Testament studies came to an end; he was never allowed to publish the commentary on Genesis that he completed in 1906. His work was in fact finally disavowed officially by Cardinal De Laï's Consistorial Congregation in 1912,[63] whereupon Lagrange abandoned all work in scriptural exegesis. Although Pius X personally allowed him to return to Jerusalem the following year, and encouraged him and the *Ecole* and the *Revue biblique* to resume their labors, the prohibition against the use of his works in seminaries was not revoked.

---

[60] See O'Connell, *Critics*, pp. 323–325.

[61] Jacques Gadille, "La Lutte antimoderniste. Le Courant 'intégriste'," in *Libéralisme, industrialisation, expansion européenne (1830–1914)*, ed. Jacques Gadille and Jean-Marie Mayeur (= Histoire du christianisme, vol. xi; Paris: Desclée, 1995), p. 460. Two of the three strongest condemnations date from 1907, the erroneous propositions listed in *Lamentabili sane exitu* of 3 July and the encyclical, *Pascendi dominici gregis* of 8 September. The third would be the Motu proprio, *Sacrorum antistitum*, of 1 September 1910, setting forth an "anti-Modernist oath" to be sworn by all officeholders in the church.

[62] Emile Poulat, *Intégrisme et catholicisme intégral. Un réseau secret international antimoderniste: la "Sapinière" (1909–1921)* (Paris, Tournai: Casterman, 1969). A compilation of the various measures taken to squelch Modernism is found in Silvio Tramontin, "La repressione del modernismo," in Guerriero and Zambarbieri (eds.), *La Chiesa e la società industriale*, vol. ii, pp. 283–291.

[63] Decree of 29 June 1912 of the Consistorial Congregation, in *Acta Apostolicae Sedis* 4 (1912), 530.

The reasons that moved the Consistorial Congregation to inter-
dict Lagrange's works reveal the integralist mindset of these years.
According to the Congregation the *Revue biblique* had to be censured
for the calamitous effect its reading had on seminarians; it was
glaringly evident to the reader how backward Roman Catholic
scripture scholarship was. The works Lagrange found important
enough to review and to utilize in the *Revue*'s articles were predominantly from Protestant or unbelieving university circles, whereas the
works of traditionalist Catholic authors were treated with a kind of
disdain. The Congregation also found fault with the hermeneutical
procedures that Père Lagrange taught and practiced, in that they
rested on a theory of inspiration that relativized the truth of the
scriptural word and even admitted the existence of errors in secular
matters. The way narratives were treated would reduce or even
suppress their historical truth, for example in the story of Lot's wife
being changed into a pillar of salt. Lagrange's theory of the biblical
books' composition envisaged the existence of pre-scriptural written
sources, thus disturbing the traditional dating and contesting the
authorship of Moses and other biblical authors.[64] In the interest of
protecting the authority of the church, which seemed to be bound up
with conventional but uncritical positions on biblical questions,
Cardinal De Laï was ready to employ that same authority to strike
out at all who disagreed, no matter how loyal they might be.

CONCLUSION

In the view of Paul Ricœur, no civilization other than the European
has been able to mediate the tensions between critical study and the
authority of a revealed word. Charles Taylor suggests that this has
been possible only because of the "break-out" of modern Western
civilization from its symbiosis with Christian culture during "the
ages of faith."[65] Christian catholicity – tradition – being greater
than any given culture can encompass, express, or incarnate adequately, it took a break-out from the embrace of the medieval

---

[64] Montagnes, *Le Père Lagrange*, pp. 148–149.
[65] Paul Ricœur, as cited in Montagnes, *Le Père Lagrange*, p. 227: "One of Europe's greatest
achievements is the successful cohabitation of Christianity and critical thought; this joining
of revealed word and critical reflection does not exist elsewhere, neither in Islam nor in the
Far East." Charles Taylor, *A Catholic Modernity?* (Marianist Lecture, University of Dayton,
1996), p. 11.

synthesis to allow certain dimensions of the gospel space for development. Unfortunately, however, modernity's more prominent feature is a loss of transcendence, the "death of God."

Stark choices faced the Roman Catholic Church in the nineteenth century. They rendered all the more difficult the task of recognizing sprouts from gospel seeds amidst all the "foreign" modern growth. The First Vatican Council met at one of the low points in this struggle for European Catholics. It confirmed the church on a course in opposition to the modernization of society under the unquestioned authority of the pope. Pope Leo XIII responded with determination, resourcefulness, and flexibility. That combination allowed Modernist hopes to arise, but guaranteed that their new departures would not be welcomed by those more in tune with papal policies. When historical contingencies intervened, such as the choice of a new pope and the deteriorating relations of Catholics and republicans in France after the Dreyfus affair, the conditions were created in which writers proposing a quite different apostolic strategy, even though not widely known before their condemnations, would become the scapegoats in a full-scale ecclesiastical inquisition.

The anti-Modernist campaign did not succeed in definitively breaking the ties between scholarship and faith in the Roman Catholic communion. Given the odds against such ties, that is a quite remarkable outcome. It is due, as Ricœur and Taylor jointly suggest, to "Europe," or theologically speaking, to a humanly bewildering providence, and not just to the internal resources entrusted specifically to the Roman Catholic Church.

CHAPTER 3

Theological and philosophical Modernism

Gabriel Daly, O.S.A.

"In a higher world it is otherwise; but here below to live is to change, and to be perfect is to have changed often."[1] John Henry Newman's celebrated dictum still has the power to startle, coming as it does from a dedicated opponent of liberal Christianity. Newman's conception of Christianity as a "great idea" enabled him to contemplate its interaction with history as a living thing, constantly changing in order to retain its identity. The daring model of Christianity as an "idea," that is, an impression made upon the *imagination*, proved incomprehensible to the neo-scholastic mind, which treated the imagination as vastly inferior to the discursive intellect and which saw no reason at all to wrestle with the seemingly intractable problem of how doctrine could preserve its identity as it passed through the cultural vagaries of historical existence. Neo-scholastic ultramontanism saw itself as charged with the custodianship of a fixed and unchangeable deposit; it described the philosophy on which it drew for cognitive self-expression as *perennis* – that is, valid in and applicable to all ages. The conflict between the concept of Christian doctrines as immutable and perennially valid, on the one hand, and, on the other, as culturally limited expressions of truths which are antecedent to their formulation constitutes the theological core of the Modernist crisis which occurred in the Roman Catholic Church between *c.* 1890 and 1914.

DEFINING MODERNISM

Theological commentators on modernism need to give careful consideration to the inescapable problem of defining their topic

---

[1] John H. Newman, *An Essay on the Development of Christian Doctrine*, 1845 edition, ed. J. M. Cameron (London: Penguin Books, 1974), p. 100.

before they discuss it. Defining Modernism is a political act, in that it commits one, if not to a position, at least to a perspective from which to launch one's investigations. Attempts at historical objectivity are as commendable as claims to have achieved it are illusory.

There has been a suggestion that "the most manageable description of Modernism is to be found in the document which condemns it."[2] It is well to reflect on what this piece of advice would entail. *Pascendi*'s definition of Modernism is notorious: "And now, with Our eyes fixed upon the whole system, no one will be surprised that We [*scil.* Pius X] should define it to be the synthesis of all [the] heresies."[3] The condemnation of modernism cannot be allowed to set the agenda, for the very good reason that it is itself a major part of the problem to be resolved. Rome did much to create the monster it slew. Allowing *Pascendi* to define Modernism leads to the intrinsically ridiculous business of deciding who was and who was not a Modernist by reference to an artificial criterion: there is a considerable measure of agreement among scholars that no single Modernist conforms to the systematic profile depicted in *Pascendi*.

Any worthwhile definition of Catholic Modernism will incorporate a value judgment. Part of the problem stems from the instability of the term itself. Friedrich von Hügel, writing to Maude Petre in 1918, distinguished between two "modernisms." The first modernism is the never-ending attempt to interpret the old faith "according to what appears the best and the most abiding elements in the philosophy and the scholarship and science of the later and latest times." The second Modernism is "a strictly circumscribed affair . . . that is really over and done," namely, that which took place during the pontificate of Pius X.[4] Von Hügel's distinction is of course open to being seen as a not altogether creditable attempt to distance himself from "those terrible years." From the perspective of today's postmodernity his distinction appears more plausible than it seemed to Maude Petre or would have seemed to George Tyrrell.

Although the term "Modernism" was first used by its Roman opponents, Tyrrell had no problem accepting and working with it as

[2] Fitzer (ed.), *Romance*, p. 347. This view had already been expressed by J. J. Heaney: "Any definition of Modernism must be drawn mainly from *Pascendi*, the most solemn Church condemnation," *The Modernist Crisis: Von Hügel* (London: Chapman, 1969), p. 232.

[3] *Encyclical Letter ("Pascendi Gregis") of Our Most Holy Lord Pius X by Divine Providence Pope on the Doctrines of the Modernists* (London: Burns & Oates, 1907), p. 48.

[4] Von Hügel, *Letters*, p. 248.

a label for the conviction that Catholic faith is compatible with modern culture. In chapter 16 of *Medievalism* he writes: "Medievalism is an absolute, Modernism a relative term. The former will always stand for the same ideas and institutions; the meaning of the latter slides on with the times."[5] On this evidence Tyrrell would not have cared much for our contemporary term "post-modern." As Malcolm Bull has put it, "Contrary to Tyrrell's expectations, modernity proved unable to keep up with itself, and modernism has now become as much an absolute as medievalism."[6] That does not affect Tyrrell's argument, since cultural relevance is what he is seeking, whether or not one calls it modernity. His protest is not against medieval theology as such but only against its imposition upon the modern church as a timeless absolute. He delighted in the thought that St. Thomas Aquinas was a thirteenth-century modernist.

There would seem to be little point in trying to relate theological Modernism to modernism in the arts. In spite of the fact that, as Malcolm Bull has observed, modernism in the arts and Modernism in theology came to prominence in the same time and place – Paris at the beginning of the twentieth century – "the two are rarely discussed in the same context,"[7] arguably with good reason. Bull suggests that they were "out of synch" and that their interests were even in some respects opposed.

MODERNISM AND MODERNITY

A more important and productive question is how to relate Catholic Modernism to liberal Protestantism. In this connection it is advisable to distinguish between modernity and Modernism. What Rome condemned as "Modernism" – and it should never be forgotten that it was Rome which gave the term its *theological* currency – was a belated attempt by some Catholic scholars to respond to the challenge of modernity. Protestant theologians had already begun to make this response more than a century earlier.

---

[5] Tyrrell, *Medievalism*, p. 133.
[6] Malcolm Bull, "Who was the First to Make a Pact with the Devil?" *London Review of Books* (14 May 1992), 22. This short review-article raises a number of thought-provoking ideas on the relationship (or absence of it) between modernity and postmodernity in the arts and in theology.
[7] Ibid., pp. 23–24.

For convenience of reference, and all too briefly, I shall rehearse here some well-known features of intellectual history which are crucial for an understanding of Modernism. The challenge offered by modernity to Western Christianity and its belief system was complex and cumulative. Broadly speaking it came in three thrusts: (1) the scientific revolution; (2) the revolution in critical, philosophical, and historical thought centered in the Enlightenment; and (3) the French Revolution, the overthrowing of the *ancien régime* with which the Catholic Church was identified, and the proliferation of "liberal" ideas which could be politically related to the loss of the Papal States. Each of these thrusts was perceived as constituting a threat to religious authority.

Copernicus's nervous critique of geocentricism issued eventually in Galileo's defiant assault on the Aristotelian philosophers and his clash with the Holy Office. Galileo's telescope powerfully symbolizes the move from unverifiable *a priori* theories about the universe to careful observation and measurement. Mathematical and empirical questions about space, time, and velocity replaced metaphysical questions about essence and purpose. Church censure of Galileo in 1616 had the effect not only of implying a conflict between science and religion but also of raising radical questions about authority, its use, and its scope. There were philosophical questions implicit in the scientific revolution which seemed to challenge the supernaturalist assumption of the existence of a smooth and uninterrupted continuum between the transcendent and the historical. Science increasingly gave very earthly answers to questions which had formerly seemed religious, at least in principle. In addition its arguments were inductive where the arguments of theology were deductive.

Philosophy was prompt to respond to the scientific revolution. Descartes' methodological doubting of everything so that he might find an indisputable foundation for human thinking led to an affirmation of subjectivity coupled with a sharp dichotomy between thought (or rather the thinking subject), on the one hand, and material existence, including the body, on the other. Cartesian rationalism set the agenda for much subsequent philosophy. Although Descartes expressed reverence for Christian revelation, in practice it was reason that was for him the ultimate arbiter.

British empiricism, beginning with John Locke's rejection of innate ideas together with his total reliance on experience and sense data, culminated in David Hume's assault on causality. Hume took empiricism to its ultimate conclusion, affirming that what we identify as causal connection is merely the result of our observation of constant conjunction. We perceive that B constantly follows A, and so we conclude to a necessary causal connection between them, which is an adequate guide to everyday life but is vulnerable to rigorous philosophical analysis. Hume was mordantly dismissive of miracles as evidence for divine presence and action. The chief casualty of his attack was the fashionably rationalist "natural religion" of the eighteenth century which gave prominence to the argument from design. All of this awoke Immanuel Kant from his dogmatic slumbers and led him to accept much of Hume's critique of rationalism. However, he believed that Hume had gone too far in his assault on causality and had consequently "driven his ship aground." Kant proposed to refloat the ship and give it a pilot.

Immanuel Kant's critique of metaphysics is, from the standpoint of religion and theology, perhaps the most powerful factor in bringing about the modern world. It is particularly important for an appreciation of the theoretical attack which Rome made on the Modernists. Even a cursory examination of the anti-Modernist literature reveals a deep-seated and obsessive preoccupation with the effect of Kant's critique on Catholic fundamental theology, with its heavy reliance on miracles as evidence for the truth of Christianity.

Kant, it will be remembered, responded to Hume by restoring the philosophical universality and necessity of causality, but at the cost of proclaiming it to be an *a priori* form, a category of the mind, to which all experience of phenomena must conform. Of the noumenal world, the world as it is in itself as distinct from the world as it is for knowledge, he maintained that we can know nothing. Kantian "agnosticism" about reality was deemed by *Pascendi* to be the basic negative element in what the encyclical construed as the Modernist "system."

One can hardly deny that the Kantian critique, if accepted as valid, had devastating implications for traditional dogmatic and fundamental theology and for the natural theology which had been cultivated in the eighteenth century. It allowed no communication between God and human beings, except indirectly through the slender filament of moral experience. Recourse to moral experience as the only link between the divine and the human constituted what Karl Barth was to describe as the "terms for peace" which Kant offered to Christian theology.[8] It was Protestant theologians in the main who appreciated the gravamen of Kant's critique of metaphysics and his turn to the subject. Friedrich Schleiermacher sought peace between science and religion by withdrawing religion from the arena of science and by concentrating his theological attention on human religious experience rather than on a metaphysical order lying beyond the senses. Schleiermacher rejected Kantian moralism while accepting the validity of Kant's attack on doctrine as a true statement of how things are about God and about God's relationship with the world. Schleiermacher is rightly described as the father of modern theology, largely because it was principally he who taught theologians that the point of departure for the doing of critical theology is human experience. (Karl Barth was later to accuse him of turning theology into anthropology.)

In the important Second Speech from his book, *On Religion*, Schleiermacher argues that religion, or piety, manifests itself as a sense of the infinite, a feeling of absolute dependence; it is a specific "affection," which is to be distinguished from *both* doctrine *and* morality.[9] In his later book, *The Christian Faith*, he turns to the relationship between religion and doctrinal statement. "Christian doctrines are accounts of the Christian religious affections set forth in speech."[10] Commenting on this famous dictum, Wayne Proudfoot writes: "The subject matter of theology [for Schleiermacher] is neither God nor evidence of divine creation and governance in the world but the self-consciousness of the religious believer in the context of his or her community."[11] Thus Schleiermacher, while accepting Kant's terms for peace, replaces Kant's bleak moralism with pious self-awareness before God. The authors of *Pascendi* seem convinced, without any supporting evidence, that the Catholic Modernists held much the same view.

Schleiermacher's mysticism (or, if one prefers, his romanticism or pietism) was not allowed to go unchallenged within liberal Protestantism. Albrecht Ritschl regarded Schleiermacher as his

---

[8] Karl Barth, *Protestant Theology in the Nineteenth Century: Its Background and History* (London: SCM Press, 1972), p. 278.

[9] Friedrich Schleiermacher, *On Religion: Speeches to Its Cultured Despisers*, trs. Richard Crouter (Cambridge: Cambridge University Press, 1988), pp. 96–140. The chapter concludes: "To be one with the infinite in the midst of the finite and to be eternal in a moment, that is the immortality of religion" (p. 140).

[10] Friedrich Schleiermacher, *The Christian Faith* (Edinburgh: T. & T. Clark, 1928), p. 76.

[11] Wayne Proudfoot, *Religious Experience* (Berkeley: University of California Press, 1985), p. 16.

predecessor and accepted Schleiermacher's contention that the essence of religion is experience. He differed from Schleiermacher, however, in holding that it is practical, or moral, experience which mediates divine revelation. Ritschl rejected Schleiermacher's mysticism and summoned liberal Protestant theology "back to Kant" – a phrase which became a slogan – and away from both metaphysics and a preoccupation with subjective states of piety. Ritschl and his followers were fundamentally historians who looked back to the origins of Christianity for their religious inspiration. In those origins they discovered not piety but a moral imperative. Adolf von Harnack, recognised by Paul Tillich as the greatest of the Ritschlians,[12] observed that just as Plato is the philosopher of Eastern Orthodoxy, and Aristotle the philosopher of Catholicism, Kant is the philosopher of (liberal) Protestantism.

There is a good deal of truth in this generalization, at least in respect of the years between the two Vatican Councils. However, the Aristotle of Catholic theology and philosophy was Aristotle at a remove, that is, as interpreted first by Thomas Aquinas, who in turn was interpreted by the commentators of the sixteenth and seventeenth centuries and by the neo-Thomists of the nineteenth century. With the eventual triumph of neo-Thomism Kant became the *bête noire* of neo-scholastic orthodoxy. He retained this role throughout the Modernist period and beyond.

In the early nineteenth century there were three different Catholic reactions to the perceived threat of eighteenth-century rationalism.[13] The first was French Traditionalism which declared unambiguously that reason was simply incompetent in matters of revelation and faith. Joseph de Maistre, Louis de Bonald, and Félicité de Lamennais appealed to divine revelation as the only trustworthy source of religious and moral beliefs.

A second way of engaging with rationalism was, first, to recognize that Kant and the Idealists had issued a challenge which theology could ill afford to ignore, and then to borrow from idealism some of its characteristic methods of approach to metaphysical reality and to the mind's ability to register that reality. The Catholic theologians of Tübingen University were prominent among those who pursued this second stratagem. Their founder, Johann Sebastian von Drey,

[12] Paul Tillich, *Perspectives on 19th and 20th Century Protestant Theology* (London: SCM Press, 1967), p. 219.
[13] McCool, *Catholic*, pp. 18–19.

responded in a measured way to Kant's challenge, appreciated the importance of history for the proper study of theology, and was aware of Schleiermacher's attempt to commend religion to its cultured despisers. George Hermes in Germany, Anton Günther in Austria, and Louis Bautain in France utilized Jacobi's distinction between intuitive reason (*Vernunft*) and discursive reason (*Verstand*) as a way of responding to Kant without capitulating to fideism. Discursive reason was declared incompetent to deal with metaphysics and revealed truth. Aristotelian philosophy, according to Günther, operated through discursive reason.

It was discursive reason, however, which the third group, the neo-Thomists, believed to be indispensable in every stage of Catholic theology. They rejected modern philosophy out of hand and called instead for a wholehearted return to Aristotelian metaphysics and epistemology as the only reliable partners for orthodox Catholic theology.

In the subsequent battle for the soul of Catholic theology and philosophy, Roman authority weighed in on the side of the neo-Thomists, who were rapidly making their presence felt, especially in Italy. A stream of Vatican condemnations in the 1850s and 1860s made it very clear that the Roman authorities were declaring war on modernity and using neo-Thomism as an ideology to support its war program. Because the Papal States were now under continuous political and military threat, politics and theology were inseparable in the minds of the popes and their advisors. All "liberals" were deemed to be enemies of the church. The *Syllabus of Errors* of 1864 amounted to the proclamation of a crusade against modernity in all its forms. The effects of that crusade were felt more painfully within than outside the church. Neo-Thomism, now left with no serious rivals, prospered to the point of becoming not merely a favored system within Catholic theology and philosophy, but was finally declared to be the *only* system fully in accord with Catholic orthodoxy. *This declaration became a defining feature of anti-Modernism.* From Pius IX to Pius XII, Rome interpreted opposition to the scholastic method as a symptom of failure in orthodox faith.

In 1879 the new pope, Leo XIII, in an encyclical letter, *Aeterni Patris*, imposed Thomism on the church at large.[14] This was a serious blow to the mild pluralism which had traditionally been

---

[14] On *Aeterni Patris* see McCool, pp. 226–240.

permitted to exist in Catholic theology. Indeed it broke with a long-established convention that the Roman teaching body does not interfere in disputes between the various schools of theology and philosophy. It was a particularly severe blow to the Augustinian-Franciscan school of thought which laid emphasis on the role of the will, of the affections (to use St. Augustine's term), and of feelings in general in matters of faith. Alexander of Hales, St. Bonaventure's teacher, had written that theology is not a science in Aristotle's sense; theology is "affective, moral, experimental, and religious."[15] The Modernists would have applauded, but the neo-Thomist manuals which dominated Catholic theology after *Aeterni Patris* saw to it that such ideas would not be allowed to sully the purity of neo-Thomistic intellectualism. The condemnation of Modernism was later to stigmatize the word "experience" as subjective, unstable, and totally unfitted to express the perennial, objective truths of Christian revelation. Faith was presented as intellectual assent to divine truths revealed by God and guaranteed by external signs, namely, miracles and fulfilled prophecies. Theology was scarcely more than a series of logical deductions made from the premises extrinsically revealed by God. History, positivistically understood, supplied the proofs. Lucien Laberthonnière, Blondel's friend and collaborator, would later say of both liberal Protestantism and Catholic Modernism: "With the liberal Protestants it was faith without belief: here [with neo-Scholasticism] it is belief without faith."[16]

LIBERAL PROTESTANTISM AND CATHOLIC MODERNISM

It is easy to understand why the neo-Thomists singled out Kant as their principal philosophical opponent. It is equally easy to account for the hostility of the Modernists toward the scholastic system which Rome made the touchstone of orthodoxy. It is less easy to account for the hostility of Loisy and Tyrrell toward liberal Protestantism. Loisy and Tyrrell went out of their way to discriminate between themselves and liberal Protestants like Auguste Sabatier and Adolf von Harnack. Three points are worth noting in the not always convincing case that they made against liberal Protestantism.

[15] Yves Congar, *A History of Theology*, (New York: Doubleday, 1968), p. 11.
[16] Lucien Laberthonnière, "Dogme et théologie," *Annales de philosophie chrétienne* 5 (1908), 511.

(1) They rejected the liberal Protestant quest for an essence of Christianity which would be purged of the effects of its association with later church history and dogma. In its place they affirmed a necessary continuity between the gospel and the church. (2) Both Loisy and Tyrrell accused liberal Protestantism of being heavily individualistic, and Tyrrell reproved it for naive optimism about human progress. (3) They complained that liberal Protestantism ignored the eschatological and apocalyptic elements in the gospel and simply projected its nineteenth-century liberal ideals back to the time of Jesus.

The third point is particularly important. Johannes Weiss's book, *Jesus' Proclamation of the Kingdom of God* (1892)[17] had seriously disturbed Tyrrell by shaking him out of his easy acceptance of the kingdom as a present and interior reality.[18] For Weiss the kingdom is an external, future, and apocalyptic event which will burst into history. Loisy, though he accepted the broad thrust of Weiss's thesis, softened the impact of his apocalyptic by combining it with the present social reality of life in the church: "Jesus proclaimed the Kingdom, and it was the church that came." Tyrrell was grateful for this partial relief from the painful angularities of consistent eschatology expressed in apocalyptic images, even though he firmly renounced "the hope of smoothing away the friction between Christianity and the present age."[19] Acceptance of the apocalyptic perspective of Jesus' teaching pointed Tyrrell in the direction of symbolism and the hermeneutics of symbols. As Sagovsky has noted, Tyrrell puts his finger on a major feature of twentieth-century theology when he writes, "What each age has to do is to interpret the apocalyptic symbolism into terms of its own symbolism."[20]

In spite of the discriminations made by the Modernists between their own positions and that of liberal Protestantism, it is clear that liberal Protestantism had an important influence on their thought – a fact which both Loisy and Tyrrell were prepared on occasion to admit. The general Modernist appeal to experience as a religious datum marks a logical and epistemological break with neo-scholastic

[17] Trs. Richard H. Hiers and D. Larrimore Holland (Philadelphia: Fortress Press, 1971). Original title: *Die Predigt Jesu vom Reiche Gottes*.
[18] See David Schultenover, *George Tyrrell: In Search of Catholicism* (Shepherdstown, West Virginia: The Patmos Press, 1981), pp. 263–279.
[19] Cited in Nicholas Sagovsky "*On God's Side*": *A Life of George Tyrrell* (Oxford: Clarendon Press, 1990), p. 256.
[20] Ibid.

deductive methodology. This move from deduction to induction probably played a more important part than is usually recognized in prompting the neo-scholastic establishment to describe the Modernists as crypto-Protestants. Catholic integralism depended heavily on essentialism in its metaphysics and deductive argument in its logic and epistemology. It is an interesting, if purely speculative, exercise to wonder whether, if openness of inquiry and freedom of communication had not been suppressed in the Roman Catholic Church, something both modern and distinctively Catholic might have emerged from the Modernist enterprise.[21]

As things turned out, the question was whether nineteenth-century Roman Catholicism had *anything* to say to the modern world, or whether its self-understanding and its formulas of faith were so artificially tied to medieval culture that membership of the Catholic Church in intellectual terms necessarily entailed total rejection of modern culture and the substitution for it of the intellectual values of the thirteenth century. H. Richard Niebuhr has pointed out that when Leo XIII imposed Thomism on the whole church in 1879, he could not hope to replicate Aquinas's synthesis between faith and culture, for the very good reason that the success of such an enterprise depends upon its being a synthesis between faith and *present* culture.[22]

The contrast with Protestant scholarship is striking. Academic Protestantism faced into the chill winds of modernity with remarkable courage, integrity, and intellectual virtuosity. Its theologians liked to argue that it was precisely their Protestantism which made their liberalism possible. (For entirely negative and unecumenical reasons integralist Catholics would have concurred heartily with this contention.) Time and again Catholic critics of Modernism claimed that the Modernists had succumbed not merely to the spirit of the age but also to the principles of the Reformation. Jean Réville, himself a liberal Protestant, argued that "the chief characteristic of Liberal Protestants is that they are independent of the authority of tradition in their respective Churches,"[23] and that this attitude is

---

[21] I have tentatively explored this issue "Catholicism and Modernity," *Journal of the American Academy of Religion* 53 (Summer, 1985), 784–791; reprinted in Ray L. Hart (ed.), *Trajectories in the Study of Religion: Addresses at the Seventy Fifth Anniversary of the American Academy of Religion* (Atlanta, Georgia: Scholars Press, 1987), pp. 240–247.

[22] H. Richard Niebuhr, *Christ and Culture* (New York: Harper & Row, 1975), p. 138.

[23] Cited in Bernard M. G. Reardon, *Liberal Protestantism* (London: A. & C. Black, 1968), p. 191.

implicit in the *sola scriptura* principle. Further reflection has, he claims, shown that freedom of inquiry and Luther's appeal to the individual conscience are warrants for the liberal Protestant's struggle against both Catholic and Protestant orthodoxy.[24] Liberal Protestantism proclaims, not the authority of the Reformers, but "the principles which were the *raison d'être* of their work."[25]

Paul Tillich refines this argument into his doctrine of "the Protestant principle."[26] It was, says Tillich, the Protestant principle that gave liberal theology a good conscience when it applied the critical methods of historical research to the Bible.

It was the Protestant principle that enabled liberal theology to realize that Christianity cannot be considered in isolation from the general religious and cultural, psychological and sociological, development of humanity . . . It was the Protestant principle that destroyed the supra-naturalism of the Roman Catholic system, the dualism between nature and grace, which is ultimately rooted in a metaphysical devaluation of the natural as such.[27]

Tillich's judgment, in spite of its somewhat triumphalistic rhetoric, is just: Protestant theology, especially in Germany, *did* shoulder its responsibilities toward modernity, while Catholic theology fought a stubborn rear-guard action against it. In general, Catholic theologians who attempted to fulfil their responsibilities toward modernity were assailed by the authorities of their church.

CATHOLICISM AND MODERNITY

In the hundred years before the Second Vatican Council there were three such major attempts: the first in the 1860s (Reform Catholicism), the last in the 1940s (*Nouvelle théologie*). Between these two there occurred the attempt which was named and condemned by Rome under the term "Modernism." The Vatican created the myth of a modernizing movement which was allegedly threatening the very existence of the church. It has been suggested[28] that the decision to attack the Modernists stemmed from Rome's general hostility to post-Enlightenment developments outside the Catholic Church. The sociologist, Lester R. Kurtz, argues that the Modernists were an asset to the Vatican in that they "served as the negative model for the church's stance towards the modern world."[29] In short, Rome,

[24] Ibid., pp. 194–195.   [25] Ibid., p. 202.
[26] Paul Tillich, *The Protestant Era* (Chicago: University of Chicago Press, 1948), *passim*.
[27] Ibid., p. xxiii.   [28] For example by Kurtz, *Politics*.   [29] Ibid., p. 179.

which found itself powerless against the modern world, could bring all its might to bear successfully on its own dissidents, thereby revitalizing the Catholic will to resist modernity and – far more significantly – to do so on Rome's terms. Loisy, in *The Gospel and the Church*, had opposed some central tenets of liberal Protestantism, but his description of *The Gospel and the Church* as "a very Catholic book" was both plausible and disingenuous. John Kent applies much the same sort of argument to the church of both Pius IX and Pius X, which, he claims, "was being ruled by a counter-revolution which constantly presented itself as the victim."[30]

In 1863 the German Catholic historian Ignaz von Döllinger, while professing loyalty to papal authority, made a vigorous attack on the scholasticism of his age, accusing it of sacrificing historical scholarship to sterile speculation. He went on to contrast the brilliance of German thought with the decadence of theological thought in the Latin countries. Pius IX replied in a letter, *Tuas libenter*, to the archbishop of Munich-Freising which not only proclaimed the authority of the Roman Pontifical Congregations but condemned the existence in Germany of a movement against the "Old School" and its doctors, who have served the church so well down the ages.[31] *Tuas libenter* laid down the pattern of things to come. The *Syllabus of Errors* (1864) reinforced what was contained in *Tuas libenter*.

This raises the question of how Modernism is to be related to liberal Catholicism, especially the liberal Catholicism (or, "Reform Catholicism") of the 1860s. Tyrrell used the terms "liberal Catholic" and "Modernist" interchangeably, once the latter term had become current[32] and saw the ultramontane ecclesiology of *Tuas libenter* as the direct antecedent of Pius X's church. Edmund Bishop, the leading Catholic liturgical scholar in Britain, who was happy to describe himself in private as a Modernist, believed that the Munich Brief (*Tuas libenter*) was the decisive event in Rome's stand against modernity. All that followed was, in Bishop's opinion, simply the application of its principles: clericalism, papal pretence to unrestrained control over all scholarship, and affirmation of scholasticism as the language of that control. In 1909 Bishop wrote to von Hügel

[30] John Kent, "Newman and Lilley" in Jenkins (ed.), *Newman*, p. 164.
[31] *Acta Sanctae Sedis* 8 (1874), pp. 436–442.
[32] George Tyrrell, *Christianity at the Cross-Roads* (London: Longmans, Green and Co., 1909), p. 1.

that *Pascendi* was "a *conclusive* act, giving out to the world the whole force and meaning of the *Munich Brief of 1863*."[33]

"In the second half of the nineteenth century a militant and successful neoscholasticism brought energy and formal clarity to Catholic theology; it also brought limitations, controversy, and intolerance."[34] T. F. O'Meara's judgment is a useful reminder of the dual character of Rome's campaign against modernity. The growth of papal power in the church found ideological support in a refurbished scholasticism. Each fed the other in a remarkable example of institutional symbiosis. Scholastic essentialism provided the Vatican with a language well suited to the articulation of its immobilist position on doctrine, while the Vatican in turn used its authority to make neo-scholasticism the exclusive language of its conception of orthodoxy. It is no coincidence that *Tuas libenter* not merely commended the "old theology" over the new but also employed the term "ordinary magisterium" for the first time in an official Roman document.[35]

The link between the 1860s and the Modernist period is mainly an ecclesiological one. Edmund Bishop's view of *Pascendi* as an application of *Tuas libenter* oversimplifies matters somewhat and ignores the topics of agnosticism and immanentism, neither of which was at issue in 1863. Nevertheless, as Tyrrell was to argue, there is a close theological connection between the absence of an immanent dimension in the concept of God and an ecclesiology which is patriarchical and authoritarian: a distant God needs to delegate power to human representatives.

It was Leo XIII who gave final focus to the anti-modern movement which proclaimed and defended the exclusivity of the "old school." In 1879 Leo published his encyclical letter, *Aeterni Patris*, which made Thomism, as a philosophico-theological system, mandatory for the whole church. It is important to note that it was Thomism, and not simply scholasticism, which the pope imposed. In an unprecedented act – Rome normally kept out of disputes between the schools – Leo wrote to the General of the Franciscans informing

---

[33] Cited in Loome, *Liberal*, p. 73.
[34] Thomas F. O'Meara, *Church and Culture: German Catholic Theology, 1860–1914* (Notre Dame, Indiana: University of Notre Dame Press, 1991), p. 25.
[35] See J. P. Boyle, "The 'Ordinary Magisterium': History of the Concept," parts 1 and 2, *The Heythrop Journal* 20 (October 1979), 380–398; 21 (January 1980), 14–29.

him that the Order was not free to follow St. Bonaventure and
Scotus, if it meant departing from the mind of St. Thomas.[36]

To return finally to the problem of definition, in the context of
Aeterni Patris Catholic Modernism may be defined as follows.
"Modernism" was the term employed by Pius X and his curial
advisers in their attempt to describe and condemn certain liberal,
anti-scholastic, and historico-critical forms of thought occurring in
the Roman Catholic Church between *c.* 1890 and 1914. I am
therefore contending that, although Catholic Modernism was a
belated attempt to respond to the challenge of modernity, it cannot
be defined merely in terms of its responsiveness to modernity but
must be related to the scholastic lineaments of Rome's understanding
of orthodoxy. On the basis of this contention one can reasonably
take Maurice Blondel's *L'Action*[37] as the point of departure of
Catholic philosophico-theological Modernism.

MAURICE BLONDEL

Blondel was a lay philosopher from Dijon whose doctoral thesis for
the Sorbonne was on the topic of "action," by which he meant the
whole dynamic thrust of human life, including mind, will, affections,
and aspirations. Blondel was heir to a tradition of personalism in
French philosophy which went back to Maine de Biran (1766–1824),
who expressed a deep antipathy to what he saw as a scholastic
rationalism which paid no attention to interior dispositions. This
school was as opposed to scientism as it was to rationalism. Thus
Emile Boutroux (1845–1921), who was the *raporteur* of Blondel's
doctoral thesis, *L'Action*, took a lively interest in science and in the
philosophical limitations of scientific method. Another of Blondel's
teachers, Léon Ollé-Laprune (1839–98), rejecting what Blondel
would later describe as the "extrinsicism" of scholastic apologetics,
identifies a vital role for the will in the recognition of moral and
religious truth. According to Maine de Biran the human spirit
"always aspires to the absolute and the unconditional."[38] Blondel
based his central thesis, with its "method of immanence," upon this

---

[36] Barmann, *Baron*, p. 140 note. As von Hügel observed to Wilfrid Ward, this extraordinary
prohibition was quickly ignored.
[37] Blondel, *Action*.
[38] Cited in Frederick C. Copleston, *A History of Philosophy*, vol. IX, *Maine de Biran to Sartre*
(London: Search Press, 1975), p. 29.

contention of Maine de Biran and expanded it into a large-scale philosophical system.

Blondel's thesis anticipates the later existentialist critique of essentialism as an inauthentic exercise in disengaged theory. Analysis of human dynamism shows, he claimed, that we are faced with the need to make an inexhaustible stream of choices, none of which ever fully satisfies us. This deficiency in satisfaction he describes as a "sickness" which drives us to ask basic questions about the meaning of life and about the possibility that God may be offering an answer through revelation. Blondel's *L'Action* was an attempt to construct a philosophical argument for revelation which was not vulnerable to the Kantian critique of metaphysics. Blondel remarked to a friend that in *L'Action* he was trying to do for Catholic religious thought what Germany had done for the Protestant form.[39]

In 1896 Blondel published his *Letter on Apologetics*, which gave explicit expression to certain implications contained in *L'Action*. Prevailing Catholic apologetics, he argued, relied on extrinsic arguments which totally lacked any interior resonance. "If the revelatory fact is to be accepted by our minds and even imposed upon our reason, an interior need, and, as it were, an ineluctable appetite must prepare us for it."[40] Neo-scholastic reliance on miracle and fulfilled prophecy as proofs of divine presence and communication is inept. Miracles exist "only for those who are already prepared to recognise the divine action in the most usual events."[41] We do not encounter the transcendent merely by registering miraculous events and allowing them to authenticate an *externally* delivered revelation. In 1904 Blondel, in his long article, *Histoire et dogme*, coined the term "extrinsicism" to describe the fundamental theology which then prevailed in the Catholic Church and which he accused of lacking an interior dimension or immanent preparation for responding to divine revelation: "The Bible is guaranteed as a complete unit, not by what it contains, but by an external divine seal: why, then, bother to verify the detail? It is full of absolute knowledge, fixed in its eternal truth: why bother to search for its human conditions and its relative sense?"[42]

Blondel's friend and colleague, Lucien Laberthonnière, an Oratorian priest who survived the first shots of the anti-Modernist

[39] Maurice Blondel, *Lettres philosophiques* (Paris: Aubier, 1961), p. 34.
[40] Blondel, *Letter.*   [41] Ibid., p. 135. (*Les Premiers Ecrits*, vol. II, p. 14.)
[42] Ibid., p. 229. (*Les Premiers Ecrits*, vol. II, pp. 158–159.)

campaign but in 1913 was forbidden to publish, was an ardent advocate of interiority and an impassioned opponent of scholastic positivism. Laberthonnière is even more Augustinian than Blondel in his espousal of the inner dynamic of unsatisfied aspiration as a preparation for receiving the gospel.

Blondel's "method of immanence" took the Kantian critique of metaphysics with a seriousness and readiness to make concessions which was quite foreign to the scholastics but which would exercise a significant influence on the transcendental Thomists. The integralist attack on Blondel and Laberthonnière focused on their alleged "Kantian" denial of (a) the competence of the intellect in religious questions, (b) the apologetical value of miracles, and (c) the gratuitous character of the supernatural order. These considerations were, in the event, overshadowed by Alfred Loisy's contribution to the Modernist crisis.

ALFRED LOISY

Although in 1897, after the publication of the *Letter on Apologetics*, Alfred Loisy wrote to Maurice Blondel suggesting that Blondel's philosophy might complement his (Loisy's) biblical exegesis, he was at that time working out a religious philosophy of his own which is contained in an unpublished manuscript entitled "Essais d'histoire et de philosophie religieuses (*1898–99*)."[43] Loisy quarried extensively from this manuscript for a series of articles he wrote under the pseudonym "Firmin" in the *Révue du clergé français* and for his centrally important book, *The Gospel and the Church*.[44] In his *Mémoires* Loisy remarks that there were only two people who might be said to have had a philosophical influence on *The Gospel and the Church*, namely, Ernest Renan and John Henry Newman.[45] It was Renan who introduced him to textual criticism of the Old Testament and gave him a method for approaching all such work.[46] Initially Loisy hoped to be able to take on Renan with Renan's own weapons. What happened, however, was that he became increasingly convinced that scientific biblical criticism was bringing him into inevitable conflict with the ideas on biblical inspiration and inerrancy

[43] The work is preserved among the Loisy papers in the Bibliothèque nationale in Paris.
[44] Loisy, *Gospel*. The French original, *L'Evangile et l'Eglise*, was published in 1902.
[45] Loisy, *Mémoires*, vol. II, pp. 56of.   [46] *Mémoires*, vol. I, p. 117.

which then prevailed in the Catholic Church.[47] The Catholic integralist system depended on a pre-critical reading of the Bible in general and of the Gospels in particular. Biblical criticism undermined the methodological foundations of the entire system as well as challenging accepted ideas on such topics as the resurrection, the virginal conception, and the self-consciousness of Jesus.

In the late 1890s Loisy was still under the influence of John Henry Newman and still believed that Catholicism could speak with force and relevance to the modern world, but that to do so it would have to abandon its intransigent immobility and its preoccupation with the immutability of doctrine. Tyrrell remarked shrewdly that "as Luther would have burned Harnack, so Newman would have burned Loisy. But so far as 'Newmanism' means, not his scope & motive, but his method, Newman is the father of Modernists."[48] The distinction is an important one. Newman's *method* is palpably non-scholastic, but his substantive theology is pre-modern. However, as Tyrrell recognized, Newman's method lent itself to use by later theologians whose theology was eminently liberal. In describing what had to be opposed in current Catholic theology Loisy took over Archbishop Mignot's lapidary phrase "an immobile church in possession of an immutable dogma."[49] What appealed to Loisy above all in Newman was the latter's basic model of doctrinal development as a living process which presupposes a dynamic relationship between the gospel message and the church to which it was committed and within which it has to be newly understood and articulated in every age.

Loisy directed his program against two disparate positions: Catholic "immobilism" and Protestant "individualism." This program was soon to become a general Modernist one. The occasion was the publication in 1900 of a series of popular lectures on the essence of Christianity given by Adolf von Harnack for the academic year 1899–1900.[50] Harnack was the foremost authority of his time on the history of dogma. He was a "Culture-Protestant" who had a very uneasy relationship with the German Evangelical Church, which tended to regard him as a heretic. In common with other Ritschlians

[47] Ibid., vol. I, p. 142.
[48] Letter to Houtin, December 1907, cited in Loome, *Liberal*, p. 39.
[49] Cited in Nicholas Lash, "Newman and 'A. Firmin,' " in Jenkins (ed.), *Newman*, p. 70.
[50] Adolf Harnack, *What is Christianity?*, trs. Thomas B. Saunders (5th edition; London: Ernest Benn, 1958).

he disliked mysticism and metaphysics, saw dogmas as corruptions of Christian simplicity, and blamed Hellenism for their appearance in Christian thought. The gospel has to do with God the Father rather than with Jesus the Son. It is the gospel *of* Jesus not the gospel *about* Jesus which matters.

In early 1902 Loisy began *The Gospel and the Church*, a reply to Harnack's book, and it was aimed at least as much at Roman neo-scholastic orthodoxy as it was at Harnack (who always claimed that he could not understand the point of Loisy's attack on him). In attacking Harnack's liberal Protestantism, Loisy put forward a version of Catholicism which the church authorities of the time rejected. Whereas, however, Harnack regarded dogmas as corruptions of faith, Loisy saw them as necessary for the proclamation and defense of the faith. For Loisy the church and its doctrines are the means whereby the gospel perpetuates itself and speaks to every age. He also saw doctrines as *relative* to their age and replaceable by later formulations. Loisy rejects the kernel/husk metaphor and employs the image of the growth of a living thing.

The basic thesis of *The Gospel and the Church* is that "the Church is the Gospel continued" and is as necessary to the gospel as the gospel is to it. The following words are famous.

Jesus foretold the kingdom, and it was the Church that came; she came, enlarging the form of the gospel, which it was impossible to preserve as it was, as soon as the Passion closed the ministry of Jesus. There is no institution on the earth or in history whose status and value may not be questioned if the principle is established that nothing may exist except in its original form. Such a principle is contrary to the law of life, which is movement and a continual effort of adaptation to conditions always new and perpetually changing. Christianity has not escaped this law, and cannot be reproached for submission to it. It could not do otherwise than it has done.[51]

The double target of Loisy's book, namely, liberal Protestantism and neo-scholastic Catholicism, clouds Loisy's purpose and gives his argument a disturbing ambiguity. His case against Harnack committed him to a view of dogma which his Catholic enemies construed as pure relativism. They certainly did not share his view that it was "a very Catholic book,"[52] and they were fiercely opposed to his interpretation of dogma.

[51] Loisy, *Gospel*, pp. 166–167.   [52] Loisy, *Autour*, p. 208.

The conceptions that the Church presents as revealed dogmas are not truths fallen from heaven, and preserved by religious tradition in the precise form in which they first appeared. The historian sees in them the interpretation of religious facts, acquired by a laborious effort of theological thought. Though the dogmas may be Divine in origin and substance, they are human in structure and composition.[53]

Loisy brought the neo-scholastic conception of dogma as immutable propositions to the bar of history by his claim that "the creeds and dogmatic definitions should be related to the state of general human knowledge in the time and under the circumstances when they were constituted."[54] Dogmas, then, are symbolic expressions which, being products of their age, are secondary to the revealed truths that exist pre-conceptually behind them.

The epistemology which underlies this approach to doctrine, though shared by nearly all the Modernists, is vulnerable to later post-structuralist attack. Within the confines of Christian theology itself it has been famously challenged by George Lindbeck's cultural-linguistic critique of experiential-expressivism. The cultural-linguistic theory of doctrine is based on the psychological *and epistemological* contention that "it is necessary to have the means for expressing an experience in order to have it, and the richer our expressive or linguistic system, the more subtle, varied, and differentiated can be our experience."[55] It might be plausibly argued that of all the Modernists Edouard Le Roy comes nearest to Lindbeck's intratextual theory when he claims that "a dogma has principally a *practical* meaning. It states first and foremost *a prescription of the practical order.*"[56]

Friedrich von Hügel placed careful emphasis on pre-reflective experience, which he regarded as the meeting place between the infinite God and the finite, contingent beings that men and women are. Von Hügel was less concerned than the other Modernists to interpret primary religious experience as pre-linguistic. He was more interested in the pre-*reflective*, "dim," unfocused character of religious experience and the response to it which he described as the "mystical element" of religion.[57] Von Hügel's greatest fear (Loisy

---

[53] *Gospel*, pp. 210–211.   [54] Ibid., p. 215.

[55] George A. Lindbeck, *The Nature of Doctrine: Religion and Theology in a Postliberal Age* (London: SPCK, 1984), p. 37.

[56] Edouard Le Roy, *Dogme et critique* (Paris: Bloud, 1907), p. 25. However, even Le Roy refers to the truth which underlies the formula, ibid., p. 3 note.

[57] See von Hügel, *Mystical*.

called it his nightmare) was the doctrine and philosophy of pure
divine immanence which would collapse divinity into human
consciousness of itself as a higher self. He is always careful to
emphasize that this primary meeting, in dim experience, is between
human beings as contingent and God as absolute and transcendent.

In their reaction against the dogmatic positivism which then
prevailed in official Catholic theology, the Modernists in their
different ways appealed to a pre-linguistic form of truth which
constituted the primary source of revelation and of which historically
controlled formulas were the symbolic and variable expressions. The
polemical literature of the period, including the Roman condemnation of Modernism, makes it quite plain that this alleged pre-
linguistic substratum of dogmatic truth lies at the heart of the matter.
By definition as pre-linguistic it is beyond church control: only the
formal doctrinal statement can be an instrument of control. That is
why Rome fought so relentlessly to make formally expressed doctrine
the criterion of truth and orthodoxy and condemned as "agnostic"
any appeal away from it to a deeper pre-dogmatic level of revealed
truth. No Modernist appreciated this more than George Tyrrell,
who quite correctly saw that the crucial theological issue was that of
revelation.

GEORGE TYRRELL

In 1899 Tyrrell published an article entitled "The Relation of
Theology to Devotion."[58] This article is an important early Modernist text. Tyrrell recognized it as a turning-point in his own theological development and as a compendium of his thought on
revelation.[59] He initially spoke in terms of the relationship between
devotion and theology, and he depicted the relationship as similar to
that between art and art-criticism. Later he exchanged the word
"devotion" for the word "experience." Revelation occurs as part of
a wider experience: and he expressly intended "experience" to
embrace not only knowledge but also feeling and will. His deepest
concern was to reject with passion the notion that revelation is
statement.

Lucien Laberthonnière, with his theory of *dogmatisme moral* (moral

[58] Most conveniently available under the title "Lex Orandi, Lex Credendi," in Tyrrell, *Scylla*,
pp. 85–105.
[59] Ibid., p. 85.

affirmation), was saying much the same thing when he claimed that ideas are a "simplified substitute for our inner experience."[60] Indeed Laberthonnière's "critical mysticism" led him to hold that facts have an interior reality[61] which has to be discerned in the act of interpreting them. Scholastic extrinsicism ignored all this in its apologetical scheme of externally authenticated truths proposed to the intellect to be assented to in an act of mental obedience dissociated from the content of what is to be believed. The Modernists condemned this approach as morally and religiously empty.

Tyrrell articulated the ecclesiological implications of extrinsicism with tighter focus than the other Modernists did, and his argument may strike many Roman Catholics today as impressively relevant to their own situation. He saw democratic attitudes and procedures as instruments of the Holy Spirit present in the whole church and not merely in its leaders. His opposition to papal hegemony was not merely ecclesiological; it arose out of his conviction that the sort of centralization which gave the pope virtually absolute power while identifying the papacy with one narrow theological party and denying a hearing to all others, obstructed the channels through which the Holy Spirit communicated with the church. Tyrrell held that the absence of an immanent dimension in the scholastic doctrine of God leads directly to "sacerdotalism" (or patriarchy, as we might say today) in that church authority becomes "the delegate of a purely transcendent, not of an also immanent God."[62] As a corrective to this "deistic" approach to God Tyrrell proposes that church authority be accountable "to God immanent in the collective mind and conscience of the community."[63] This was, and remains, the deepest and most compelling theological reason for greater democratization in the Catholic Church then as today.

Long before collegiality had become an important issue in the twentieth-century Catholic Church Tyrrell was protesting against the notion that bishops are papal delegates, priests episcopal delegates, and laity passive recipients of clerical instruction. In *Medievalism* he argues that the tendency to confuse theology and faith, long present in the church, was deliberately intensified after the First

---

[60] Lucien Laberthonnière, *Le Réalisme chrétien: précédé de Essais de philosophie religieuse*, ed. C. Tresmontant (Paris: Editions du Seuil, 1966), p. 60.

[61] "Les faits ont aussi un dedans." Ibid., p. 263.

[62] Tyrrell, *Scylla*, p. 364.   [63] Ibid., p. 371.

Vatican Council in an effort to promote uniformity through verbal orthodoxy.

The conflict between Modernism and the Vatican was, in the last analysis, a hermeneutical one. Roman neo-scholastic orthodoxy fulfilled many of the criteria which today are recognized as characterizing fundamentalism: integralism, historical positivism, and naive epistemological realism. Fundamentalism of any sort makes little if any allowance for the interpretative process which necessarily takes place in the act of understanding and professing a faith, especially an historically based faith such as Christianity. Tyrrell grasped this point and, in a letter to von Hügel, remarked that the difference between the Modernists and their Roman critics was not "about this or that article of the creed . . . ; we accept it all; but it is the word *credo*; the sense of 'true' as applied to dogma; the whole value of revelation that is at stake."[64]

The grim story of the condemnation of Modernism need not be told here.[65] The documents *Lamentabili* (July 1907), *Pascendi dominici gregis* (September 1907), and *Sacrorum antistitum* (September 1910), with its prescription of an oath to be taken by teachers and office-holders in the church, intensified the program for a continued Catholic withdrawal from engagement with modernity. Draconian measures were prescribed to extirpate Modernism root and branch from the church. Scholastic philosophy was to be the basis of the sacred sciences, and anyone criticizing it was to be removed from whatever office he held. Publications were to be censored in every diocese throughout the church.

The theoretical portion of *Pascendi* has a perverse brilliance about it. It takes disparate elements from contemporary non-scholastic theology, Protestant as well as Catholic,[66] and weaves them into a systematic presentation which could in principle be comprehended by the scholastic mind. It finds agnosticism and immanentism to be the two errors which founded the entire Modernist "system." Tyrrell responded that whereas *Pascendi* "tries to show the Modernist that he

---

[64] Cited in E. Duffy, "George Tyrrell and Liberal Protestantism," *King's Theological Review* 2 (1979), 17.

[65] See Daly, *Transcendence*, pp. 190–217.

[66] Joseph Lemius, the principal draftsman of the theoretical part of *Pascendi*, makes it evident in his notes that he was familiar with the writings of Auguste Sabatier and that he drew upon them for the construction of the system which the encyclical condemned.

is no Catholic, it mostly succeeds only in showing him that he is no scholastic."[67]

The condemnation of Modernism shaped the course of subsequent mainline Catholic theology down to the Second Vatican Council. Theology, almost exclusively a clerical pursuit at that time, was to be done in an atmosphere of extreme repression on the part of the guardians of orthodoxy and consequent circumspection on the part of authors and teachers.

Fundamental theology was integralist, in that it viewed revelation as a package of truths disclosed by God, taught by Christ, and committed to the Catholic Church to be proclaimed and defended as a unit, no part of which could be detached from the rest without damage to the whole. It was extrinsicist, in that the system it proclaimed was defended by arguments based, not on the intrinsic compulsion of the message, but on the allegedly probative force of miracles and prophecies.

Above all, the notion of experience was banished from orthodox Catholic theology. Any theological appeal to experience was judged to be "agnostic" in that it appeared to put human subjectivity before objective truth objectively taught by God through divinely appointed legates. The appeal to history was regarded as suspect at the best of times and dangerous to faith when brought to bear on church dogmas.

There were of course scholars working discreetly at the fringes of this command theology. They were called into the center of the church during the Second Vatican Council and became primary instruments in the dismantling of scholastic fundamentalism. Mandatory Thomism, the central plank of the anti-Modernist program, collapsed without resistance in the 1960s. Released from the artificial enclosure of a walled village, Catholic theologians have entered the surrounding jungle not merely of the modernity from which they were sheltered, but also of the postmodernity which, for reasons extraneous to religion and theology, is busily undermining so many of the ideas that were cherished and promoted under the title of modernity. Freed from the restraints of a command theology, Catholic theologians can now dialogue openly with their Protestant colleagues and be as cognitively miserable (in Peter Berger's nice phrase) as any post-Enlightenment Protestant theologian. There are

---

[67] Petre, *Life*, vol. II, p. 336.

signs in some contemporary theology today of a disposition to invoke postmodernism as warrant for a wholesale rejection of modern theology from Schleiermacher onwards. Thus Diogenes Allen can claim that "in a postmodern world Christianity is intellectually relevant"; Linell E. Cady is surely right to observe that such a claim is "a bit too convenient."[68] It is all too easy to invoke postmodern intratextuality as an excuse for promoting sophisticated forms of fideism. Fundamentalism is, of course, a reality in the postmodern age, but it is mostly unconcerned with the obscure subtleties of intratextuality.

Thus we end on a note of irony. The postmodern critique of the Enlightenment project relativizes much of what the Modernists strove for. They fought for the turn to the subject and the theological significance of experience. The turn to the subject has now been challenged by the turn to language and a widespread dissatisfaction with the appeal to pre-linguistic experience, religious or otherwise. In spite of these developments, it remains reasonable to contend that most of the issues debated during the Modernist period are as alive today as they were then. They always will be for anyone who is stirred by the great questions of who God is and how God can be thought of as present and active in the world. Attempts to answer these awesome questions must "slide on with the times," as Tyrrell put it. Today's usage, however, no longer permits us to employ the term "modern" as a moveable constant. Presumably the same fate will eventually befall "postmodern." Fashionable nomenclature, however, will do nothing to rebut John Henry Newman's conviction that perfection is the fruit of constant change. Historical faiths such as Christianity will always have to face the task of reconciling the imperative of cultural change with the need to preserve an identity born into history and enshrined in a tradition.

---

[68] Linell Cady, "Resisting the Postmodern Turn: Theology and Contextualization," in *Theology at the End of Modernity*, ed. S. Greeve Davaney (Philadelphia: Trinity Press International, 1991), pp. 88–89.

PART II

Maurice Blondel and Alfred Loisy in France

CHAPTER 4

Seeking transcendence in the modern world

Phyllis H. Kaminski

In France, and to a lesser degree in Germany and Italy, philosopher Maurice Blondel (1861–1949) is considered a major figure in the revitalization within Roman Catholicism at the beginning of this century.[1] An intellectual deeply committed to his faith, Blondel was convinced that contemporary experience demanded a rethinking of the problem of God. He found the prevailing patterns of rationalist philosophy indifferent to ultimate human destiny. He also regarded the static understanding which characterized the dominant Catholic theology of his day to be less well suited for expressing God's presence to human destiny than the historical character of life and thought, brought out by modern philosophy, psychology, and intellectual experience. Blondel's approach to transcendence in the modern world through his monumental study of action marked a significant shift in Catholic responses to modernity.

His ideas on the openness of the human person to a supernatural destiny, many of which bore fruit in the Second Vatican Council, are no longer considered radical. In fact his influence within the Catholic world has been quietly unobtrusive. Yet as it engages the tension between philosophical reason and Catholic faith, Blondel's thought retains a certain boldness. This essay explores how the multiple contexts within which Blondel labored shed light on his contribution to modernity. They perhaps also illumine tensions among late twentieth-century Catholic Christians, as the church still struggles with the questions he raised.[2]

---

[1] See Kenneth L Schmitz, foreword, pp. 6–8, and preface, p. 9, in Blondel, *Letter.* This reissue of two of Blondel's most significant texts in translation, with its sketch of his historical and biographical background, provides an excellent introduction to Blondel for English-speaking readers.

[2] Henri Bouillard, *Blondel and Christianity,* trs. James M. Somerville (Washington, D.C.: Corpus Books, 1969), p. 4; *Blondel et le christianisme* (Paris: Editions du Seuil, 1961), p. 2; Gregory Baum, *The Credibility of the Church Today: A Reply to Charles Davis* (New York: Herder and

To understand Blondel fully, it is not sufficient to focus on the Modernist/anti-Modernist struggle within Catholic circles. The cultural context of late nineteenth-, early twentieth-century France played a major role in shaping the thinker and his project. Blondel belongs to a highly creative generation of modern French intellectuals. He is roughly contemporary with Bergson and Brunschvicg, Ravel and Debussy, Matisse and Rouault, Barres, Gide, Proust, Péguy, and Claudel. By studying Blondel, therefore, we can perceive not only some unique texture and detail of the Catholic Modernist landscape, but also glimpse the breadth and depth of the transformation of consciousness taking place at the turn of the century.

In this essay, I will argue that Blondel was deeply aware of that transformation and perceived the scientific and cultural developments of modernity largely in a positive light. He viewed them, moreover, from his unique standpoint as a philosopher and a practicing Catholic. This two-fold perspective prompted him to look to the limits of modernity and to its effects on the individual, social, moral, and religious dimensions of human life. I will explore how Blondel's desire to pursue these larger questions within the French academic philosophical community drew him into the apologetic and ecclesiastical controversy considered by Roman Catholic authorities as the "Modernist crisis." Blondel positioned himself at a strategic border, considering it his Christian vocation to struggle against scientific, rationalist, positivist historicism with its immanent boundaries on the one side and against neo-scholastic extrinsicism[3] with its imposition of answers from above on the other side. Blondel hoped to overcome the deficiencies of such lines of vision by disclosing the "fixed point" that could reconcile these apparently incompatible tendencies. The critical convergence of historical and cultural influences, public professional aspirations, and personal religious convictions, I suggest, illumines the unique ardor underlying Blondel's philosophical project.

Reading the "Letter on Apologetics" and "Principe élémentaire

---

Herder, 1968), pp. 13–15. In *Man Becoming: God in Secular Experience* (New York: Seabury Press, 1970), Baum develops the "Blondelian shift." See also Gustavo Gutiérrez, *A Theology of Liberation: History, Politics and Salvation*, trs. and ed. Sister Caridad Inda and John Eagleston (Maryknoll, New York: Orbis Books, 1973), p. 9; and John Paul II, "On the Centenary of Blondel's *L'Action,*" *Communio* 20 (Winter, 1993), 721–723.

[3] In a general sense, this term characterizes the lack of historical perspective in the dominant Catholic theology of Blondel's era.

d'une logique de la vie morale"[4] in this light, I further submit that
Blondel's method of immanence and logic of action are key
contributions to the reconciliation of ~~Catholic doctrine~~ with historical and cultural change. They are Blondel's way of saying that
only in the action of the finite subject does "a principle of
transcendent truth become immanent" and only "in the transcendence of immanent thought and action" does philosophy find an
internal principle of absolute judgment.[5] For Blondel, human
destiny is tied up, not with specific dogmas or this or that specific
gift of God, but with *"the very form and fact of the gift."*[6] Blondel's
personal reflections reveal, however, how deeply his own life is
centered in a specific understanding of the love of the God
incarnate.

Blondel's own diaries and recent scholarship on his family relations provide access to Blondel's spirituality. I conclude, therefore, by
looking briefly at this personal context and suggest that, while
Blondel's methodological quest for traces of transcendence broaden
and positively influence Catholic approaches to modernity, his
personal piety colors his perceptions and delimits the reception of his
project.

This study thus introduces fundamental themes in Blondelian
thought, as it situates Blondel in the multiple interrelated contexts
which formed the horizon of his larger project. I take as an overarching image what Blondel himself wrote about perception at the
horizons. In his first published article, when he was a twenty-seven-
year-old philosophy student, Blondel studied the complex process of
the perception of stars on the horizon. He anticipated Kuhn's
paradigms as he identified the influence of an unconscious logic on
the genesis of sensation itself. Perception, he suggested, is always
affected by this logic. Errors arise more often from these *a priori*

---

[4] Blondel, *Letter* (page numbers refer first to the English translation, then to the *PE* edition [see next entry]); "Principe élémentaire d'une logique de la vie morale," *Bibliothèque du Congrès International de Philosophie* (Paris: Colin, 1903), vol. II, pp. 51–85. Reprinted in *Les Premiers Ecrits de M. Blondel* (1956), pp. 123–47 (Hereafter *PE*). See Jean Lacroix, *Maurice Blondel: An Introduction to the Man and His Philosophy*, trs. John C. Guinness (New York: Sheed & Ward, 1968), pp. 120–125, for an excerpt in translation.

[5] "Une des sources de la pensée moderne: l'évolution du Spinozisme," *Annales de philosophie chrétienne* 128 (June and July 1894); reprinted in M. Blondel, *Dialogues avec les philosophes* (Paris: Aubier, 1966), p. 36; *Letter*, p. 183 (67–68).

[6] Christophe Theobald, "Attempts at Reconciling Modernity and Religion in Catholic and Protestant Theology," in *The Debate on Modernity*, ed. Claude Geffré and Jean-Pierre Jossua, *Concilium* 1992/6 (London: SCM Press, 1992), p. 31.

filters than from astronomical or physical miscalculation.[7] In sketching Blondel, I strive to represent accurately his own perceptions of his cultural, philosophical, and religious horizons and the filters that influenced his discernment. I also acknowledge that my perceptions of Blondel and the Modernist landscape are filtered through a judgment which values the unity of Blondel's work but prefers Blondel's 1893 thesis *L'Action* to his later elaboration in the 1930s Trilogy (*La Pensée, L'Etre et les êtres, L'Action*).[8]

PRESENTING BLONDEL: A FIGURE AT THE CROSSROADS

Maurice Blondel viewed the twentieth century from a highly privileged vantage point. Born in Dijon to an old Burgundian family, Blondel's immediate world was characterized by remarkable unity and stability. Family wealth protected him from financial cares. Both family and friends encouraged his strong beliefs and his creative independent thought.[9]

Shy and sensitive, Blondel developed perceptions that were at once realistic, attuned to nature, and highly symbolic. Fascinated as a child by insects and their metamorphoses, he frequently pondered the action of the grasshopper "who jumped headlong with all its being." This love of concrete dynamic symbols never left Blondel. As an adult he made the cicada and the grasshopper, along with the Mediterranean olive branch, the visual symbols of his personally designed book plates.[10]

Early diaries disclose the profound conviction Blondel had about his career and what he considered his vocation to be a philosopher. Deeply pious, with a special devotion to the Eucharist, Blondel maintained "the restlessness of the seeker beneath the serenity of the believer."[11] From his first entry, "I will. Let my whole life respond

---

[7] Maurice Blondel, "Une association inséparable: l'agrandissement des astres à l'horizon," *Revue philosophique de la France et de l'étranger* 26 (November 1888), 489–497.

[8] Blondel, *Action*. Maurice Blondel, *Œuvres complètes*, vol. I: *1893 Les Deux Thèses* (Paris: Presses Universitaires de France, 1995) reprints *Action* and Blondel's Latin thesis with the complete documentation of his controversial dissertation defense. For information on the Trilogy, as well as works by and about Blondel, consult René Virgoulay and Claude Troisfontaines, *Maurice Blondel: bibliographie analytique et critique* (Louvain: Editions Peeters, 1975, 1976), 2 vols.

[9] Lacroix, *Blondel*, pp. 11–24.

[10] *Carnets intimes* II *(1894–1949)* (Paris: Editions du Cerf, 1966), pp. 190–194.

[11] *Carnets intimes* I *(1883–1894)* (Paris: Editions du Cerf, 1961), p. 557 (cf. p. 332) (hereafter, *CI* I). For a published translation of this text see "A recollection sent to a priest of Saint Sulpice, 9 September 1893," trs. John Lyon, in *Communio* 20/4 (Winter, 1993), 708–720;

and define: I will,"[12] Blondel reveals his commitment to the action of reflection. Even as a young student, he perceived the gap between his provincial, Catholic world and the secular French university milieu. Although he feared its possible danger to his faith, Blondel was drawn to this modern expansive world and wanted to understand it on its own terms.[13]

In later years, Blondel recalled life during his thesis days as a crossroads in French history. He lived and wrote within

a milieu in which one oscillated from dilettantism to scientism, where Russian neo-christianism clashed with the rigorous virtuosity of radical German idealism; where in art and literature, as in philosophy not to say in religious pedagogy itself, the notional, the formal, even the unreal seemed to triumph; where the very efforts that one made to reopen the sources of a profound life and of a fresh art ended only in symbolism, without succeeding in rehabilitating the concrete, the direct, the singular, the incarnate, the living letter which takes the whole human composite, a sacramental practice which introduces into our veins a spirit more spiritual than our spirit, a popular common sense and Catholic realism.[14]

Blondel instinctively saw the need "to take up the underpinnings," to stand directly and freely "in the face of the current conflicts." His goal was to satisfy "the total exigencies of criticism and the permanent calls of human destiny."[15]

In his doctoral thesis, *Action: Essay on a Critique of Life and a Science of Practice*, therefore, Blondel engaged in an internal critique of modern culture. He took its questions about religion seriously, but he wanted to raise the question of religion in a different way, through a philosophical study of action. According to Blondel, the reconciliation of religion and modernity presupposed that one renounce neither the specific demands of the Catholic conception of revelation nor the legitimate rights of reason: "If it is true that the demands of revelation are well founded, one cannot say that we are completely

---

citation here from p. 719. In addition to the *Carnets*, Blondel's correspondence speaks of the depth of his piety and its nourishment in Scripture and authors such as Augustine, Bernard, Ignatius, and Rodriguez.

[12] *CI* 1, p. 17.

[13] *CI* 1, p. 546 and Emile Poulat, "La Pensée Blondélienne dans le cadre de la crise moderniste," in *Maurice Blondel: une dramatique de la modernité (Actes du colloque Maurice Blondel. Aix-en-Provence, mars 1989)*, ed. Dominique Folscheid (Paris: Presses Universitaires de France, 1990), p. 20.

[14] *L'Itinéraire philosophique de Maurice Blondel*, collection by Frédéric Lefèvre (Paris: Aubier Montaigne, 1966), pp. 35–36.

[15] Ibid., p. 18.

at home with ourselves; and there must be a trace of this insufficiency, this impotence, this demand in man purely as man, and an
echo in the most autonomous philosophy."[16]

Blondel held that the task of philosophy, philosophy of religion in
particular, was to decipher the traces of transcendence in human
beings and society. Philosophy does not exceed its bounds in
pursuing this task, but rather by formally studying human action it
comes to acknowledge its insufficiency. In his thesis Blondel would
do just that. He demonstrated that, in following the dialectical
movement of our concrete choices and our deepest desires, we
discover an incompleteness, a natural inachievability that cannot be
filled without going beyond ourselves.

Not surprisingly, such a thesis was highly controversial. Blondel
passed his defense but was barred from teaching. M. Liard, Director
of Higher Education, refused to consider his application, because he
saw Blondel's understanding of the philosophical and moral problem
as "destructive of the method and conception whose dignity the
Director of Higher Education had the obligation to protect." It took
almost a year, but thanks to Blondel's mentor Emile Boutroux and
an intervention of Lucien Poincaré with his brother Raymond,
Minister of Public Instruction, he obtained a post at Lille.[17]

Having had a difficult reception as a doctoral thesis, *Action*
provoked even stronger reactions at its publication. Rationalist
philosophers such as Léon Brunschvicg respected the subtle Blondelian dialectic and the thoroughness of his method. However
Brunschvicg estimated that Blondel's affirmation of the necessity of a
revelation went against philosophy's principle of immanence. It
made of *Action* a disguised apology for Christianity. Partisans of the
scholastic renewal regretted the concessions that Blondel made to
the problematic of Kantian critical philosophy, yet lauded his
Christian spirit.[18] Other Catholics, such as Fonsegrive and Abbé
Denis, even as they rejoiced to see a return to the Christian idea,
made the error of reading *Action* as a psychological apologetic.
Certain authors insinuated that Blondel established too strict a line
between the natural aspirations of the human will and the gratuitous
gift of God. Others accused him of doing the exact opposite, of
becoming immanentist in his approach, and of making religious

---

[16] *Letter*, p. 155 (37). This translation is my own.   [17] *CI* i, p. 487, note; p. 501.
[18] Virgoulay, "Lignes de force de la critique blondélienne," *Bibliographie* ii, p. 8. See entries
nos. 1, 8, 9, 14, 15, for summaries of early Catholic reviews of *Action*.

faith the mere prolongation of human aspirations.[19] Even the popular Catholic community that Blondel so loved was not more receptive than the academy. One clever homilist even condemned the young scholar in verse from the pulpit: "L'Eglise vous crie; Pélagie et hérésie!" (The Church cries out: Pelagius and heresy!)[20]

Blondel was not unaffected by the contradictory comments. He suffered from the lack of comprehension which greeted him on both sides. Before his rationalist critics, the young philosopher defended the philosophical rigor of his thesis. To his Catholic opponents, he asserted that he had preserved the gratuity of grace. By distinguishing the reality of the transcendent from the immanent affirmation of the transcendent, Blondel maintained that he was within the legitimate bounds of a philosophical approach to the religious question.

These misunderstandings, for all the pain they caused Blondel, only deepened his central conviction that action constructs and defines the individual in relation to others, to God, and to the world. From 1896–1913,[21] Blondel stood his ground in the academy and in the church. The voluminous correspondence, exchange of articles, and the literature analyzing the debates provide ample evidence of the energy expended during these critical years. Even initial exposure to Blondel's thought indicates how ardently his eyes gazed at the philosophical horizon, desiring the reconciliation of the modern mind and Christian truth.

THE TRANSCENDENCE OF ACTION AND THE RELIGIOUS QUESTION

The Catholic theological community, which by and large accepted Blondel's conclusions, continued to question his method. His thesis had shown that openness to the truths of faith corresponds to a fundamental human aspiration. Approaching the necessity of a

---

[19] Ibid., no. 4, Le Querdec (Fonsegrive); no. 21 G. Fonsegrives; no. 22, Ch. Denis; no. 12 P. de Broglie. See also Daly, *Transcendence*, p. 35; and Dru, "Introduction," in Blondel, *Letter*, p. 56, for the misrepresentations and party spirit that characterized the Catholic opposition.

[20] Maurice Blondel and Auguste Valensin, *Correspondance* vols. I and II: *1899–1912* (Paris: Aubier, 1957), vol. I, p. 322 (hereafter, *BV* I and *BV* II).

[21] These dates delineate the *Letter* and the end of the *Annales de philosophie chrétienne* with the condemnation of Laberthonnière and the outbreak of World War I. Principal texts from this period include the *Letter*, *History and Dogma*, and *LSS*.

supernatural fulfillment from the dialectic of the will in action made Christian faith meaningful from a strictly secular point of view. Yet strong convictions about the autonomy of philosophy prompted Blondel to remind his theological adversaries that apologetic philosophy is not "philosophical apologetics."[22]

It is in the context of these discussions with Catholic theology that the *Letter on the Requirements of Contemporary Thought in Matters of Apologetics and on the Method of Philosophy in the Study of the Religious Problem* must be situated. Published in 1896 in six issues of the *Annales de philosophie chrétienne*,[23] the *Letter* is closely linked to *Action* and presupposes a knowledge of this prior work.

A striking example of Blondel's systematic thought, the *Letter* specifies the truly philosophical basis of the religious problem and the most rational and legitimate method of approaching it. It discusses the mutual renewal of philosophy and religion by the development of modern critical thought. What is significant is that Blondel strengthens his position on the interdependence of the problem of knowledge and the question of the supernatural, when considered from the point of view of the human subject in action. He addressed the *Letter* to the philosophical community to show how his method applied philosophy to religion without distorting one or the other. Although Blondel saw himself as a modern apostle of Catholic Christianity, he strongly criticized the insufficiency of theological methods in the first part of the *Letter*. However, by so doing, Blondel inadvertently provoked the formation of a "scholastic front,"[24] because many theologians saw the *Letter* as an outright demolition of classical apologetics. From a neo-scholastic viewpoint it destroyed the rational foundations of faith and allowed an illegitimate intrusion of philosophy into the domain of revelation.[25]

As early as 1886, Blondel had intuited that these negative reactions represented a dying logic:

[22] Virgoulay, *Blondel*, pp. 37–38.
[23] Virgoulay, *Blondel* gives the specific issues and pages.
[24] Cf. Daly, *Transcendence*, pp. 36–43; Virgoulay, *Blondel*, pp. 30, 56. See Virgoulay, *Blondel*, pp. 56–58, 65–92, for the violent neo-scholastic reactions to the *Letter* during the years that followed. See *Lettres philosophiques* (Paris: Editions Montaigne, 1961), pp. 87–89, for Blondel's intentions vis-à-vis the theological community.
[25] For the full text of the accusations, see the articles by M. B. Schwalm who accuses Blondel of subjectivism and fideism, "Les Illusions de l'idéalisme et leurs dangers pour la foi," *Revue Thomiste* (September 1896), 413–441, and H. Gayraud, who finds Blondel guilty of naturalism, "Une nouvelle apologétique chrétienne," *Annales de philosophie chrétienne* (December 1896; January 1897), 257–273; 400–408.

I want to speak of the contemporary state of mind. A great renewal is taking place at the present time: it will be apparent that it is a question of adopting a whole moral attitude, that it is not only in the domain of thought that our salvation is decided, but above all in the secret recesses of the heart . . . The old logic, no doubt, was very narrow and it has burst. Truth is no longer an equivalency of object and understanding (*adequatio rei et intellectus*). No one lives on 'clear ideas' any longer. But truth remains, and the truth which remains is living and active; it is an equivalency of understanding and life (*adequatio mentis et vitae*).[26]

Even the most vehement attacks convinced Blondel that his philosophical project had profound implications for the future of Christianity. When he set out to discuss the concrete point of the encounter between the natural order and the supernatural, he felt he was at the heart of the "great renewal" taking place in the modern thought of his day. That his Catholic opponents did not see Blondel's approach as supportive troubled him; yet he did not back down from his argument. He was looking to the wider phenomena and realized with many of his contemporaries that a new age of human consciousness was dawning, one which called for "a new and mutual adaptation of man [*sic*] and of Christianity."[27]

Blondel argued that in order to speak to modern thinkers, a discussion of the religious question had to start, not by supposing the presence of some gratuitous divine gift, but by supposing its absence.[28] *Action* had shown that fidelity to human autonomy and authentic human growth leads to an ultimate option for or against the fulfillment that cannot come from us. The logic of such fidelity implies openness toward an eventual gift of God. Since fidelity to conscience is all that most people have to resolve the problem of existence, Blondel does not want to impose recognition of the Catholic faith as the criterion of the authenticity of action.[29]

Blondel specifies, therefore, that his approach to the religious dimension of human destiny does not prejudge the question by beginning with an answer. Nor does he adopt the critical stance which makes human subjectivism into an absolute. Rather he asserts that before we can pronounce on the significance of what we are thinking, we must decide what in fact we are thinking. We do this, from within action, by going over the whole series of our inevitable

---

[26] *CI* i, p. 86.   [27] Poulat, *Histoire*, p. 11.   [28] *Letter*, p. 140 (21).

[29] Claude Troisfontaines, *Le Christ "Lien Substantiel" dans les premiers écrits de Maurice Blondel* (Dissertation, Universitas Gregorianum Romae, 1965), p. 91.

ideas and the conceptions that depend on them. It is important to critique carefully the apparent distortions and partial restrictions of our reflected decisions, which may, when they superficially intervene, short-circuit the process of human realization.

Blondel now precisely defines the dialectic of *Action* as a philosophical method:

The method of immanence, then, can consist in nothing else than in trying to equate, in our own consciousness, what we appear to think and will and do with what we do and will and think in actual fact – so that, in the factitious negations and ends which are not genuinely willed, our innermost affirmations and the irrepressible needs which they imply may be discovered.[30]

Because he wants to preserve both the gratuity of grace and human autonomy, Blondel explicitly excludes from his method a doctrine of radical immanence. He emphasizes that "the immanent affirmation of the transcendent (even of the supernatural)" does not prejudge the transcendent reality of the immanent affirmation. Moreover, his method of immanence prevents any premature spiritualization of human existence. By focusing on action and the genesis of our ideas of revelation, the method determines the conditions necessary "if what we think and will is to *exist*," even as it shows that we are incapable of making it exist on our own. Blondel maintains that in order to find God we have to see ourselves as both lacking something indispensable and looking for it. We are lost if we give up the quest prematurely or settle for only what is found thus far. What we truly will is in conformity to our idea of it, only if we acknowledge it as beyond our grasp.[31] When we follow action to its limits, we arrive at a critical juncture. We must continue to act, but our action opens to an action that transcends us.

I want to draw out two overarching implications from this Blondelian dialectic of unrest, search, crisis, and decision. First, Blondel's method shows that we arrive at questions of faith and salvation from within human existence in all its concrete psychological, social, political, and cultural reality. His point is that only truth which has a prior point of contact within us can form the basis of a summons. It is not up to us to decide under what concrete form that summons will come. Blondel's thesis had demonstrated that human action is not completed in the natural order. The immanent dialectic of freedom in the *Letter* "establishes in each one of us, that which

---

[30] *Letter*, p. 157 (39).   [31] *Letter*, pp. 178–179 (62); 160–161(42–43).

judges each one of us. Everyone is a law unto himself (*Ipse quisque sibi lex*)."[32] At the same time Blondel's method of immanence preserves ~ Bʀᴜ the gratuity of grace. What is truly in conformity with the profound movement of human freedom and the original (*primitif*) aspiration of the human heart transcends our grasp. In response to the "inner" fact of the stirrings and restlessness of the human will, the philosopher posits an act of natural faith that would opt for a transcendent answer to the question of the meaning of human life. In terms more properly Christian, one remains open to the "outer" fact of revelation should it be offered.

However, since the reality of what is proposed as necessary cannot be produced by us, there is a second correlative implication of Blondel's method of immanence: we do not save ourselves. Without reducing the supernatural order to the determinism of human finitude, Blondel shows that the fulfillment of our deepest desire (the "adequation" of the two-fold will) is accessible only from within a free human option: "Only practical action, the effective action of our lives, will settle for each one of us, in secret, the questions of the relations between the soul and God."[33] The actual choices we make, whether or not we are conscious of their ultimate meaning, lead us to recognize the necessity of something more. Authentic action gives us the aptitude, not to produce or define the gift, but to recognize and to receive it. By a sort of "thoughtful grace" it offers us "that baptism of desire, which presupposing God's secret touch, is always accessible and necessary apart from any explicit revelation, and which even when revelation is known, is, as it were, the human sacrament immanent in the divine operation."[34]

These two implications work reciprocally to substantiate the nuance of Blondel's position within the context of his culture. As an academic philosopher, he wanted to meet unbelievers and even adversaries of Christianity on their terms. As a committed believer, Blondel also saw the need to distance himself from the misguided zeal of fellow Catholics who sought certitude in definition, denunciation, defense of orthodoxy, and rejection of the unbeliever.[35] To make sense to modern seekers, religious faith incarnate in action

---

[32] *Letter*, p. 194 (80). Cf. Rom 2:14.   [33] *Letter*, p. 164 (45).

[34] *Letter*, pp. 162–3 (44). Dru translates *grâce prévenante* as "prevenient grace." Even if Blondel used the term in the Augustinian sense of the word, I believe that because of the nature of the *Letter*, it is possible to use a translation with a broader meaning.

[35] *CI* I, pp. 258, 248.

must offer something positively human. Blondel was convinced that it did, but he was equally convinced that religion did not provide easy answers and that it should not be used as a weapon in its own defense. To neo-scholastic apologists, he repeated his deeply held spiritual conviction: "It is first of all ourselves whom we should interrogate when we inquire into the nature of conversion and of the obstacles to conversion."[36] Writing to his friend Abbé Wehrlé on the dangers of "ideological idolatry" within the church, Blondel confided his vision of modern apologetics: "the true apologetic is founded on the fruitfulness of the inner life; it makes the atmosphere healthy for understanding, shows Christianity living and attractive, and counts on the social power of lived Catholicism, on the goodness and truth of Christ perpetuated and manifested in the faithful."[37]

THE LOGIC OF ACTION AND THE MORAL LIFE

Following publication of the *Letter*, Blondel wrote in response to the polemical discussions of his work within Catholicism while he continued to address the larger questions of modernity. In "L'Illusion idéaliste" and "Le Point de départ de la recherche philosophique," he developed the epistemological dimensions of action and used them to refine further his approach to the religious question.[38] In 1905 he bought the *Annales de philosophie chrétienne*, a journal that represented a non-neo-scholastic Christian philosophy and held itself open for critical discussion with all currents of the time. In order to be able to continue seeking new ways of thinking and responding to the questions at hand, he handed over the editorship to his friend Lucien Laberthonnière.[39]

One trajectory at this point would be to follow Blondel's movements within ecclesial discussions through the *Annales*, through his pseudonymous articles, and through his correspondence. This path would wind through Blondel's response to historical-critical questions through his correspondence with Alfred Loisy, Baron Friedrich

---

[36] *Letter*, p. 196 (83).

[37] Maurice Blondel and Joannès Wehrlé, *Correspondance* I, II (*Extraits*), annotation by Henri de Lubac, S.J. (Paris: Aubier Montaigne, 1969), 12 and 15 December 1902, pp. 72, 73.

[38] "L'Illusion idéaliste," *Revue de métaphysique et de morale*, 6 (1898), pp. 727–746, reprinted in *PE* pp. 97–122; "Le Point de départ de la recherche philosophique," *Annales de philosophie chrétienne* 151 (1905), 337–360; *Annales de philosophie chrétienne* 152 (1906), 225–250.

[39] Peter Henrici, "Blondel and Loisy in the Modernist Crisis," *Communio* 14 (Winter, 1987), pp. 366–367.

von Hügel, Lucien Laberthonnière, and others. It would highlight Blondel's contributions to Catholic thought in *History and Dogma* (1904), where Blondel continues his stance at the frontier. Here he criticizes the dangers of historicism (but purposely does not name Loisy) and pursues his longstanding debate with neo-scholastic apologists, arguing against the extrinsicism of their methods. Both historicism and extrinsicism Blondel deems insufficient because their one-sided approaches place historical facts and dogmatic truth in unmediated juxtaposition.[40]

I, however, want to take another direction regarding Blondel and the Modernist context. This path explores Blondel's intentional relationship with wider cultural currents. Recent studies of the sources of Blondel's thesis have unearthed not only the philosophical partners with whom he was in dialogue, but also his study of the developing psychological and sociological sciences in Wilhelm Wundt, Frédéric Le Play, and Emile Durkheim.[41] An avid reader of literature, Blondel made repeated, though unnamed references to Paul Bourget's *Le Disciple* in *Action*'s section on education.[42] Also, writing in 1898 to Henri Brémond about works that influenced his thought, Blondel confesses that he often borrowed from the novels of George Eliot. He especially noted her presentation of moral decisions and the logic of action.[43] In fact her popular approach to moral choices and their consequences would spur his philosophical development.

During the ferment of the apologetic debates, Blondel looked beyond the Catholic community and began to work on a general set of canons for the logic of life.[44] In 1900, he presented a paper to the first International Congress of Philosophy in which he addressed the logic of action so frequently referred to in his thesis.

The elaboration of a logic of the moral life represents one of the

---

[40] Ibid., p. 356; also Poulat, *Histoire*, pp. 513–620; Michael J. Kerlin, "Blondel and von Hügel: The Debate about History and Dogma," *American Benedictine Review* 28/2 (1977), 210–225; John Sullivan, "Blondel and Apologetics," *Downside Review* 105 (1987), 1–11.

[41] See Peter Henrici, "Les Structures de *L'Action* et la pensée française," in Folscheid (ed.), *Maurice Blondel: une dramatique de la modernité*, pp. 32–43; and "De l'Action à la critique du monophorisme," *Bulletin de la société des amis de Maurice Blondel*, n.s. 3 (December 1991), 9–28.

[42] Henrici, "De l'Action," p. 12.

[43] Henri Bremond and Maurice Blondel, *Correspondance* 1 (Paris: Aubier Montaigne, 1970), p. 83.

[44] "Ebauche de logique générale: essai de canonique générale," 10 February 1894. Published in *Revue de métaphysique et de morale* 65 (1960), 7–18.

most original aspects of Blondelian thought and constitutes the keystone of his dialectical method.[45] Blondel respected modernity's attention to the human subject, but he refused to separate individual freedom from its communal, historical context. In Blondel's scheme, action, even in its most personal manifestations, is fundamentally moral and social. The value of his science of practice is that it points to the transcendence inherent in the very dynamism of life. In the unfolding of action, there is a logic of freedom, an interior norm that is present and ratified in one way or another by an option as free as it is inevitable. The question of human destiny is decided in deed, in action.

While Blondel's ultimate philosophical aim is to demonstrate the metaphysical and religious foundation of human action as a whole, he considers ethics a necessary stage in the unfolding of the dialectic of the will. In "Elementary Principle of a Logic of the Moral Life" (1903), Blondel establishes the link between human destiny and ethical responsibility. Attuned to popular culture, he specifically cites the novels of George Eliot for their attentiveness to historical contingencies and the organic complexities of reality. Blondel credits Eliot with having "skillfully portrayed the consequences of acts sown by the will as they develop in human consciences and in the world."[46] He then acknowledges his debt to Leibniz, as he draws out the basic principles of action in a way which includes freedom and necessity without sacrificing one to the other. In keeping with his larger project, he will explore the moral logic so well expressed in Eliot's novels.

Two key points from this technical article merit explanation, because they highlight Blondel's understanding of the ontological implications of modern philosophy's concern to "explain the becoming which constitutes our role as human beings and our moral destiny."[47] First is the principle of contradiction as Blondel moves it from its formal use in Aristotelian logic to its operation in real life. Second is Blondel's use of the notion of *steresis* (privation), because it provides the logical foundation for what he calls "privative knowledge" and for the absolute value of human choices.

---

[45] René Virgoulay, *L'Action de Maurice Blondel – 1893: relecture pour un centenaire* (Paris: Beauchesne, 1992), p. 21.
[46] *PE*, p. 123.   [47] Blondel, "Une des sources," in *Dialogues*, p. 24.

The principle of contradiction

To describe the logic of moral action, it is impossible to remain on the level of language and thought as does Aristotelian formal logic. While the formally logical fact is rational, structural, abstract, capable of excluding what does not fit its scheme, the moral act exists only in real life. In human history, concrete choices are always, at one and the same time, idea and body, spirit and nature. Even the purest intention that can be conceived does not remain in the air. As soon as it is incarnate in action, intention is caught in the mechanism of events with their physical and psychological forces.[48] It is shaped by them, as the beach is shaped by the waves. Moral logic, however, does not exclude human freedom. Blondel suggests that to the Aristotelian framework, constituted entirely from the point of view of negation (*apophasis*) or contradiction (*antiphasis*), it is necessary to propose a logic constituted methodically from the point of view of privation (*steresis*).

In formal logic, affirmations and negations remain on the level of language. Abstract thought can proceed by a complete inclusion or exclusion of the idea. On this level, the contradictory that is excluded ceases to have any relevance or exercise any influence. Therefore Aristotle may correctly hold that the contradictory never exists. Errors of perception and judgment which contradict the actual state of affairs, do not introduce contradiction into the real order. In the Blondelian scheme, contradictories occur, but the principle of contradiction operates somewhat differently. Action frequently includes motives which are contradictory in thought. In reflection on the dialectic of human action, we come to the awareness that the diverse phenomena, the opposing motives, the conflicting energies which enter into the action of reflection, can be held in tension. When a choice is made, it excludes others. Yet it also includes them because in a sense it sums them up:

The diverse phenomena (which enter into reflective consciousness only by attaching themselves to motives or to something that moves them from outside), the multiple sources of action, which urge us, form spontaneously before reflection a systematized whole: each lends its intrinsic power to the idea of a whole which embraces them all and organizes them as into mutually opposing syntheses. When one is realized by choice, it is thus at

---

[48] *PE*, pp. 125–126.

the same time as if it is opposed to others and as if it embodies and uses to its advantage the living force of them all.[49]

According to Blondel, the reflected and selected act gives the relative data of this particular choice "a fixity, an independence (an *autoarcheia*) which makes of them the resistant foundation of logical oppositions." This resistant foundation of completed action he calls "the principle of *antitypie*." Not easily translatable, the principle means that our act is irreplaceable and exclusive, because we place ourselves absolutely in what we have chosen, willed, and done.[50]

Simply expressed, the Blondelian notion of contradiction does not refer to the future. It comes from the irreparability of the past. However, it does not apply to the past, as it is thought, known, possible, or conceivable; it applies to the past only "as it is acted, constituted in the real, consecrated by the activity which willed it or which submitted to it."[51] To demonstrate this irreparability, Blondel gives the example of the child who breaks a straw while playing. It is impossible to unbreak it. An example from adult life can be found in his notes on *Adam Bede*: "Is this the same Arthur . . . the one who could not envision a real evil as able to create others? The same, but changed, changed by his conduct and circumstances. – Our actions have an effect on us as much as we have an effect on our actions."[52]

To realize that a thing might be otherwise, Blondel suggests, we must be conscious of our action as double-edged. The principle of contradiction is thus grounded in the experience of freedom. On the level of life, every deliberate choice implies its contradictory. The alternative, which may be excluded in fact and in concept, is not eliminated dynamically. Indeed, in the real order, every application of the principle of contradiction derives its force from our experience of it in the moral order. In other words, because of the "solidarity" of levels of reality, beneath all the seemingly contingent and arbitrary forms of action, there is an indomitable logic, an inexorable

[49] *PE*, p. 130. Blondel refers his readers to *Action*, pp. 109–149 (103–149) for a detailed explanation of this psychological dynamism which hinges on Blondel's distinction between *motives* (*motifs*: prospective forces which on the level of reflection provide us with a vision of the end of action) and what moves us (*mobiles*: projective forces that can be regarded as instrumental or efficient causes).

[50] *PE*, pp. 130–131. M. Franck, *Dictionnaire des sciences, philosophiques* (2nd edition; Paris: Hachette, 1875) defines *antitypie* as "an essential characteristic of matter equivalent at the same time to resistance and impenetrability."

[51] *PE*, p. 132. Cf. James M. Somerville, *Total Commitment: Blondel's l'Action*, (Washington, D.C.: Corpus Books, 1968), pp. 345–346.

[52] Archives Blondel, MSS L 12200, Notes on Adam Bede.

necessity. To understand the meaning of that logic, it is necessary that, at least confusedly from within the conflict of our tendencies and of the requirements of our destiny, we find ourselves faced with an option which affects our very being. Since no one escapes this option, Blondel suggests, the norm of action is transcendent but immanent to action itself. In short, action bears within itself its own sanction.

Privative knowledge and the inevitable transcendence of action

The logic of action thus serves as a fulcrum for radical decisions of the will. The intellect can perceive relations, but it cannot perform its judicial role without the cooperation of the will. Because action always moves us as a whole, all free decisions have a moral dimension and a certain absoluteness. Each concrete action, which, in Blondel's terms is both "precarious and solid," becomes a spring-board for further choices which engage human destiny up to the absolute alternative, that of our final end. At any stage, our option may become decisive; it need not be a consciously dramatic moment: "expressing symbolically the final necessity of an absolute option, the principle of contradiction, by its artificial applications, supposes in some fashion that the passage to the limit is perpetually operated and that this supreme option can, at any moment and with reference to anything, be decided here and now."[53]

This option is what Blondel calls the "auto-ontological" alternative. Because we are free, we determine the direction of our actions. Because we are oriented to the transcendent order, the difference between our affirmation or negation of that order is definitive. In moral choices the act which is excluded leaves its trace. Every voluntary and reflected decision decides future possibilities and fixes them in the being of an act. In the final option, the will retains within it the presence of the term it excludes. Once the deed is done, it cannot be undone. Conversely, if it is not done here and now, it becomes forever impossible. The irreplaceable deed makes an absolute difference. This difference is inevitably moral, because action is a synthesis of what we do and also of what we do not do but should have done:

[53] *PE*, p. 137.

The original and real meaning of the principle of contradiction is to establish that what could have been and what could have been incorporated through what we do, into what we are (*exis*) is forever excluded (*steresis*) without what is thus excluded ceasing to be used to think distinctly what has been chosen and done, to nourish the effort of knowledge and of performance, and to determine morally the realized act and the agent himself.[54]

Faced with the great alternative that will determine the meaning of life and destiny, humans are free to opt against the "*one thing necessary.*" What has been rejected does not cease to exist. The lack of adequation between our deepest will and the deliberate willed act makes the contradiction real. Privation for Blondel is thus not simply an absence. It is a living synthesis and a kind of knowledge, albeit privative knowledge:

While *negation (apophasis) suppresses the concept denied without leaving a trace of it, privation (steresis) leaves in the power which was able to realize it the mark (le stigmate) of the excising act.* And the state of being (*exis*) which follows is not identical to the being (*exis*) which preceded privation (*steresis*) . . . Real relations are infinitely organic, always infallibly reflected back and integrated.[55]

The principle of contradiction, as Blondel uses it, is inseparable from human experience of the moral order and of freedom. Blondel's logic of the moral life thus illumines, from within action itself, the consequences of freedom. Rooted in human psychological and social life, the logic of action is a logic of morality. Its principles reveal that the final justice of our lot is contained within our very actions.[56]

In *Action* Blondel had expressed his answer to the question of human destiny in Augustinian terms, as the unavoidable alternative: "to love oneself to the contempt of God, to love God to the contempt of self."[57] The *Letter* with its philosophical apologetics suggested that the moral logic of action is the logic of faith and concrete love called for by the Gospels. "Elementary Principle" provides a non-apologetic approach to the Blondelian notion of the truth of human being: "the agreement of thought and life with themselves, no longer in the purely ideological sense, but in the concrete sense, and according to the demands or credits of the interior life: to attain, to enter into possession of oneself, to equal oneself explicitly, such as one is in the

[54] *PE*, pp. 132–133. Cf. John J. McNeill, S.J., "The Necessary Structures of Freedom," *Proceedings of the Jesuit Philosophical Convention* (1968), pp. 41–42.
[55] *PE*, p. 139 (emphasis added). Cf. Somerville, *Total Commitment*, p. 345.
[56] See *PE*, pp. 141–145.   [57] *Action*, pp. 327, 355.

implicit concrete."[58] In terms of a living logic, Blondel demonstrates that, "at the bottom of all possible solutions there remains one and the same subject of inherence"[59] with regard to whom various possible solutions are not equal. Among the various objects proposed to our activity, an absolute is at stake. Our actual choices with all their relativity determine us absolutely.

Although Blondel never fully developed an ethics, the technical precision of "Elementary Principle of a Logic of the Moral Life" marked a new phase in Blondel's dialogue with modern philosophy in the academy. A discussion arose between Léon Brunschvicg and Blondel, which drew to the young philosopher the affirmation of Henri Bergson and strengthened the sympathies of the president of the International Congress of Philosophy, Xavier Léon, and his former mentor, Emile Boutroux, toward him. As a result of this encounter, Blondel's philosophy of action was officially recognized as a philosophy of knowledge, even if reservations continued about what was perceived as its "mysticism."[60]

From 1902 onward, through the journal of the *Société française de philosophie*, Blondel worked with his peers and under the leadership of André Lalande to develop a philosophical vocabulary.[61] His written contributions to the dictionary discussions were well received and often included as further explanations or variant interpretations. I emphasize this aspect of Blondel's early career to situate Blondel where he placed himself, as a professional philosopher committed to dialogue with those outside ecclesiastical circles. At the same time, Blondel's deep religious convictions and his love of the church kept him intensely involved in intra-Catholic disputes. If anything, these twin circles highlight the challenge Blondel took upon himself to live with creative integrity in both contexts.

Although Blondel worked on the vocabulary project until 1923, with the condemnation of the *Annales*, the period of his early works comes to a close. One reaction from within the Catholic community

[58] *PE*, p. 144.   [59] *PE*, p. 146.
[60] Jacques Servais, S.J. "Le Principe élémentaire d'une logique de la vie morale," Mémoire présenté pour l'obtention du grade de licencié en Philosophie (Université Catholique de Louvain, Faculté de Philosophie et Lettres, June 1980), p. 16.
[61] This project which regularly appeared in the *Bulletin de la Société française de philosophie* was published by Lalande in 1923 as the *Vocabulaire technique et critique de la philosophie*. The publication of the second volume of the *Œuvres complètes de Maurice Blondel* (Paris: Presses Universitaires de France, 1997) enables scholars to read the collection of Blondel's contributions to the *Vocabulaire*. Thus gathered they stand as a philosophical work on their own.

just prior to the forced demise of the journal suffices to indicate that during this most troublesome time there were those who already recognized the importance of Blondel's philosophy for the future. Joseph Maréchal, who had never met Blondel, came across a reference to *Action* in an article on religious psychology. He penned the following to the philosopher of Aix:

Dr. J. Maréchal, S.J., is happy that a little philosophical work of vulgarization offers him the opportunity of presenting his respects to M. Blondel, as a token of admiration which, though obscure, is considered and very sincere. With several of his colleagues, all of them eager to understand before judging, he read and re-read *Action*: they were won over by the vigor and fullness of a thought which has known how to get back to the great metaphysical tradition without ignoring any of the exigencies of the critique of knowledge . . . Convinced Thomists, and devoted sons of the Church, they beg him to believe in their profound and respectful sympathy not only for the man but for the philosopher.[62]

Blondel's response is not noted, but no doubt the philosopher welcomed the recognition of what had always been his fundamental intent, to serve the modern world and the church through the practice of philosophy.

RE-PRESENTING BLONDEL AT THE CROSSROADS

As suggested at the beginning of this essay, Blondel knew that limitations of perception come largely from *a priori* filters. I conclude, therefore, by narrowing the focus of this representation of Blondel's thought to the personal and religious context of his life. In his diaries Blondel's loves, fears, deeply held spiritual convictions, and philosophical aspirations emerge with new clarity. A careful re-reading of the recollection he sent to M. Bieil, the director of the Seminary of St. Sulpice,[63] for example, reveals how pervasive was Blondel's sense of religious vocation. He describes himself as a youth "filled . . . by pious influences, raised by a deeply Christian mother and aunt, surrounded with affection by the good Sisters of the Convent where

---

[62] *BV* II, p. 266. Cited by Dru, "Introduction," in Blondel, *Letter*, p. 62.

[63] *CI* I, pp. 545–558; see above, note 11, for published English translation. While the *Carnets* identify the recollection as directed to M. R., prêtre de Saint-Sulpice, Blondel's correspondence more specifically identifies the recipient. See *BV* I, p. 22 note 5,2, for further comments on Blondel's relationship with M. Bieil. In addition to Abbé Bieil, Blondel also consulted Abbé Huvelin, the spiritual director of Charles de Foucauld. Cf. Henrici, "Blondel and Loisy," p. 363 note 38.

[he] would go to spend a part of recreation, every day of vacation, having for walking companion and playmate a young priest full of zeal for vocations."[64] Although he gradually transformed this yearning for an apostolic life, as he discerned that God was calling him to be a layman and a philosopher in the academy, the account reveals that letting go of the idea of priestly ministry was a great sacrifice.

Hidden influences

As he reflects on his attachment to his family, Blondel notes the fear lurking behind his decision to study philosophy: "Extremely pusilla-nimous in the face of every unknown, I never would have conceived of this project, if I had not been *sustained by the idea which secretly urged me on.*" A question crucial to understanding Blondel is what this "secret idea" is that gave him the courage to be "one of the soldiers of the small group of resolutely Catholic students at the Ecole Normale." First and foremost, as Blondel articulates, is a deep desire to bring the truth to unbelievers, to dispel their errors by speaking their own language, "to prove that Catholic thought is not sterile" and to give it a place in the conflicting teachings of modernity from which it seemed to be excluded.[65]

Poulat reminds us that the date of this *mémoire*, between Blondel's thesis defense and his marriage to Rose Royer, is also not signif-icant. One line of research that may shed new light on Blondel's religious motivation, but is only beginning to be pursued, concerns the influence of his wife. The diaries indicate that Blondel saw the gift of their love as part of his call "to draw from his most intimate joys" as well as his struggles, "the great law of human move-ments."[66] Right after their marriage Blondel and his spouse kept a joint diary; however, only Blondel's entries have been published. Rose's subsequent illness was a source of profound suffering for Blondel, as was her death in 1919. A study of this relationship may prove helpful in assessing the influence of Blondel's personal piety on his philosophical career.

In fact, another hidden dimension of Blondel's religious back-ground has been suggested by Poulat. Rose's mother was Edith

---

[64] *CI* I, p. 545. Blondel's mother died 1 October 1900. See *BV* I, p. 33 note 13, for his account of this painful loss.
[65] *CI* I, pp. 546–547 (emphasis added).   [66] *CI* I, pp. 538–539.

Royer (1841–1924), a visionary and "confidante of the Sacred Heart," whose revelations have become public knowledge only since the thirties. Mme Royer saw herself as divinely commissioned to initiate the Archconfraternity of Prayer and Penance of Montmartre. She maintained that, by God's design, the devotion to Sacred Heart she had been chosen to proclaim was to inaugurate a new stage in the Christian vocation of France. The addition of penance to the national vow of adoration of the Sacred Heart was to "extend to all Christianity and even to unbelievers the benefits of this repentance called for by the Sacred Heart."[67]

Blondel is mentioned in her biography, although not by name. Mme Royer had a premonition about a "young secondary school teacher," the best man at her daughter Jeanne's wedding and friend of Jeanne's husband. Although Mme Royer soon forgot the feeling, when Blondel came to ask her for Rose's hand in marriage, the presentiment returned. She confided to the suitor, "I don't know if she is made for you: she is not very intellectual. But she will be someone who will respond effectively to your vocation, your aspiration."[68] Mme Royer wrote about the encounter to Mme Henri Boissard, Jeanne's mother-in-law:

He spoke to me as to a spiritual mother: he recounted with touching simplicity the stages he had gone through for his vocation; on the advice of his spiritual directors, he had decided to marry, to look for a very pious woman, not at all worldly, whose feelings were lofty enough to understand the apostolate that he had desired to carry out in his university career . . . I told him that Rose had a very devout heart of gold, and a soul and a mind that were fresh and guileless . . . although she already had a lot of judgment and understanding from her practical side as a spiritual woman.[69]

In light of Blondel's overwhelming sense of apostolic vocation and his wife's love, Rose's intense religious background merits reflection. As Poulat infers, uncovering these family relations (which must be done carefully and with respect for all persons concerned) may alter our perspectives on Blondel, his inner life, his ideas, and his position in the church and the world of his era. Are there not lines that might be drawn between the social reign of the Sacred Heart as preached

[67] Charles Boissard, *La Vie et le message de Madame Royer (1841–1924)* (Paris: Lethielleux, 1966), p. 5. See also Poulat, "La Pensée Blondélienne," pp. 26–27, and references there.

[68] Poulat, "La Pensée Blondélienne," p. 27.

[69] Boissard, *La Vie et le message de Mme Royer,* p. 177. Henri Boissard's son and Jeanne's husband, Adéodat Boissard, and Henri Lorin founded the *Semaines sociales* to which Blondel was a regular contributor.

by Mme Royer through her confraternity and Blondel's pan-christism?[70] Poulat further notes that after a diocesan inquiry attested to the spiritual authenticity of Mme Royer, Leo XIII in 1894 raised her Archconfraternity from a national level to a universal one, and Cardinal Sarto, patriarch of Venice and the future Pius X, became one of the first members. Virgoulay points out that it is through Mme Royer that Blondel knew so quickly that P. Jean-Baptiste Lémius was the author of *Pascendi*.[71]

Was Mme Royer, along with Wehrlé, Laberthonnière, and Valensin, among those to whom Blondel confided his sufferings and struggles of conscience during the Modernist crisis? Might not Blondel's family milieu have influenced his understanding of miracle, his own mystical bent, and even his political views expressed in the *"Semaine sociale* de Bordeaux"? At this point there can only be speculation, but the evidence supports Poulat's suggestion that contemporary Blondel studies need an intellectual biography that takes into account the influence on his work of socio-cultural and familial dynamics.[72]

Concluding reflections and judgments of perceptions

While we eagerly await that study, the angle of vision made possible by situating Blondel's thought in the multiple contexts of his life suggests the following reflective perceptions about Blondel's position in the Modernist landscape. If one defines Modernism as the great "heresy" condemned by Pius X in 1907, then Vidler is correct in saying that Blondel should not be classified as a Modernist.[73] Others have written of the difficult relations with thinkers such as Loisy, von Hügel, and Laberthonnière, of his opposition to some of their positions, and of the care Blondel took *not* to be considered one of them.[74]

In the years between *Action* and World War I, Blondel actively engaged the questions of modernity: concepts of subjectivity, auton-omy, scientific and social progress. He clearly saw himself as a

---

[70] Poulat, "La Pensée Blondélienne," p. 27. For background on other possible connections, see Komonchak, "Modernity."

[71] Virgoulay, *Blondel*, pp. 196, 237.   [72] Poulat, "La Pensée Blondélienne," p. 25.

[73] Vidler, *Variety*, p. 79.

[74] See René Marlé, *Au cœur de la crise moderniste: le dossier inédit d'une controverse* (1960); Maurice Blondel and Auguste Valensin, *Correspondance*, 3 vols. (Paris: Aubier, 1957–65); Poulat, *Histoire*; and Virgoulay, *Blondel*.

modern philosopher who embraced the modern preoccupation with freedom and the human drive to know. His perception of his philosophical career as a religious vocation drew him squarely into the religious question, but he raised that question outside the confines of nineteenth-century scholasticism and expanded the Catholic intellectual tradition of his day.

Blondel stood consistently at the critical crossroads. From the perspective of intentions and conviction, his "secret idea" never wavered: "it remained in [him] like an unchanging driving force: that pushed [him] towards the study of questions most useful to [his] plan, and defended [him] against the dangers to which [he] was exposed."[75] The *Letter* and "Elementary Principle" strengthened the fundamental position taken in *Action*. Blondel stood against immanentism[76] and argued that only a philosophy of action could reconcile modern conceptions of human autonomy and traditional Christian understandings of the transcendence of human destiny.

With the distance of a century, one observes the remarkable coherence of theory and practice in Blondel's stance. By that I mean the coherence between the principles of his philosophy of action and the positions he took during the religious crisis of Catholic Modernism. This essay has focused on the *Letter* and the "Elementary Principle of the Logic of the Moral Life"; however, the other texts of this period bear out Blondel's consistent conviction. He held that to discover the intrinsic relationship between human life and Christian revelation (nature and the supernatural, history and dogma) was to engage in a complex process of dialectical reflection.

Always for Blondel, there was a double authority to be reckoned with: rigorous critical methodology (whether historical, psychological, sociological, or philosophical) and ecclesiastical magisterium.[77] Blondel's method of immanence showed the meeting point of philosophy and theology in the condition and activity of the concrete human person. His efforts to define a philosophical position on the problem of the supernatural led him to articulate a correlation between ascertaining the supernatural and the problem of know-

[75] *CI* I, p. 547.
[76] "Immanentism" refers here to the position ascribed to the Modernists and condemned by the 1907 encyclical *Pascendi dominici gregis* that Christian doctrine is derived from religious experiences in response to human psychological needs rather than from an externally given, supra-human revelation. Included is any rejection of the "supernatural" as defined in neo-scholastic theology.
[77] Virgoulay, *Blondel*, pp. 503ff, esp. p. 519.

ledge. That knowledge arises in the unfolding logic of action, where the idea of the transcendent appears as a necessary presupposition of our very consciousness and where the willing will provides the absolute norm immanently present in human life.[78]

Nonetheless, one observes subtle shifts in Blondel's thought. He began by facing the questions of the rationalist philosophers at the Ecole normale. From the time of the *Letter* on, Blondel's piety and his fastidious personality, however, made him increasingly sensitive to questions of religious orthodoxy. After *Pascendi*, Blondel moved away from the language of immanence. By 1910, he spoke in terms of a doctrine of "double afférence" to combat the one-way tendencies of neo-scholastic extrinsicists and the immanentism of which the Modernists had been accused.[79]

Under the pen name of Testis, Blondel also defended a group of democratically oriented social Catholics against attacks by the *Action française* and anti-Modernist ecclesiastics. He supported the "integral realism" of the social Catholics who saw the interconnectedness of economic factors, social and ethical relations, and their religious convictions. Their position, analyzed philosophically, did not isolate thought, did not substitute knowledge for action, but clarified, corrected, and developed the one by the other.[80] If the full metaphysical picture of action developed later in the Trilogy is less dynamic and engaged than the one sketched during this early period, it is nonetheless true to say that from the beginning Blondel intended his philosophy of action as more than a phenomenology.

From the vantage point of the trajectory we have followed, both the *Letter* and "Elementary Principle" highlight Blondel as a modern thinker intent on finding an immanent principle of judgment, a principle that respected human freedom. While remaining within its boundaries, he extended the domain of philosophy to its limits. Yet Blondel also always had an eye on something other than modernity. He wanted to demonstrate to both his audiences that the "reality of the supernatural surpasses and unites at one and the same time the lived supernatural and the known supernatural."[81]

[78] Ibid., pp. 313–366; also James Le Grys, "The Christianization of Modern Philosophy according to Maurice Blondel," *Theological Studies* 54 (1993), 476.

[79] "*Semaine Sociale* de Bordeaux," *Annales de philosophie chrétienne* 159 (1909), 271. *Double afférence* is Blondel's term to express the nuanced dialectic of the interior reality of faith and the exterior order as it actually is, neither of which can be separated from grace, because neither is merely natural.

[80] Virgoulay, *Blondel*, p. 295.   [81] Ibid, p. 523.

Speculating on the point of encounter of divine action and human action in the final chapter of his thesis, Blondel introduced a christological hypothesis: the transcendent God, source and end of being, is immanent to human action through the Divine Mediator. In the *Letter*, he stated his preference for the Scotist view that the original plan of creation embraces the incarnation, the mystery of the Human-God.[82] I suggest that Blondel's logic of action and his epistemology are more successful responses to modernity than this theological hypothesis. The dialectic of life engages human beings fully. We constitute ourselves and shape reality by our actions, but we never fully effect all that we will. At the beginning of this century Blondel reminded his world that we can neither disregard human action nor confine ourselves to its limits. In its radical insufficiency action remains all that we have. If we do reject or disregard what is found to be implied by human action, this rejection is not simply the privation of some higher gratuitous state. It is a positive failure. "The human order is not only sufficiently solid and subsistent to be the foundation for all divine projects, but also remains indestructibly itself even beneath the weight of eternal responsibilities."[83]

Blondel's stress on the logic implicit in moral choices opened the possibility of dialogue with others. He did so in a way which did not compromise the autonomy of the temporal or the political.[84] Yet to the degree that the fixed point of Blondel's position rested on Catholic dogmatic assumptions about the created order and God incarnate in Jesus Christ, it failed to speak to non-believers on their own terms. Blondel's pious scruples and christological assumptions were troublesome to modern thinkers (even those who shared his faith), but his insistence that the solution to the problem of human destiny is not speculative, but practical, has borne fruit. Blondel's use of Aristotle and his phenomenological method contributed more to the renewal of twentieth-century Catholic theology than it did to modern philosophy. The aspect of his position that speaks most strongly to a world still caught in the clash of contradictory, irreconcilable forces is his enduring conviction that humanity's ontological vocation is also an ethical one.[85] The tensive relation of Blondel's personal piety, his religious world and his cultural one, needs further probing. The interaction of these multiple contexts

---

[82] *Letter*, pp. 202–203 (89–90).   [83] *Letter*, p. 200 (87).   [84] Virgoulay, *Blondel*, p. 524.
[85] See Gregory Baum, "Modernity: A Sociological Perspective," in Geffré and Jossua (eds.), *The Debate on Modernity*, pp. 4–9.

may explain more fully why someone of such intellectual caliber has been a paradoxical figure to philosophers, theologians, historians, and sociologists in Catholic circles and a figure largely ignored in the wider modern world he felt so deeply called to serve.

CHAPTER 5

Blondel's Action *and the problem of the University*

George H. Tavard

While introducing his readers to his doctoral thesis, *Action: Essay on a Critique of Life and a Science of Practice* (1893), Maurice Blondel asks: "Is There a Problem of Action?"[1] He immediately delineates the parameters of the question in a formula that at first sight seems very different: "How one claims that the moral problem does not exist." Thus, at the beginning of his investigation Blondel identifies the problem of action with the moral problem. When we act, do we act morally? Is the Good always implied in whatever we do? Shortly thereafter the problem appears to have two faces, speculative and practical. The speculative problem relates to thought. It is, so to say, located in the mind, concerned with the nature of knowledge and the process of cognition as presuppositions of action. However, what Blondel calls the "dilettantism of art and science,"[2] denies the existence of the speculative problem, which has then been all but eliminated from the field of vision of philosophers. The practical problem, for its part, resides in "sensation and action," the "dilettantism" of which also denies that there is a problem. In the eyes of "many contemporary minds,"[3] knowing and acting, the conjunction of which is constitutive of life, are equally void of real substance and of philosophical meaning.

Blondel thus opens a perspective which offers no fundamental choice, as in Kierkegaard's *Either/Or*, between the esthetic and the ethical. The religious will not be reached by transcending the esthetic and the ethical. Blondel's "dilettante" is not Kierkegaard's esthete, but the person who, whether promoting beauty in art or exactness in science, refuses to reach below the surface of lines and numbers. This surface covers the void of thought, if whatever lies underneath is not considered worthy of attention. The choice lies

---

[1] Blondel, *Action*, p. 16.   [2] Ibid., p. 20.   [3] Ibid., p. 25.

between all and nothing, fullness and void, life and death. Life, made of meaningful thought and action, is intrinsically religious, while the renunciation of meaningful thought and action in the dilettantism of solipsistic and egotistic existence, of thoughtless survival without a commitment to real life, is no other than death.

My hypothesis at the start of this paper is that in France in the nineteenth century there was a twofold context or background for the question of the place of religion in relation to philosophy. This context was on the one hand philosophical and religious, related to basic human options regarding the nature and purpose of life, on the other hand academic and institutional, related to the problem of the University, at a time when the University of France was acquiring a new structure, and philosophy still had to find its place in the University. The interaction of these themes made it urgent in the 1890s to ask the question raised by Blondel about the nature of action and gave his answer a practical and theoretical importance that has not been fully recognized.

FELICITE DE LAMENNAIS

Blondel's concern at the end of the nineteenth century had an important antecedent in a philosophical investigation that had, in a sense, opened the century. When, beginning in 1817, Félicité de Lamennais (1782–1854) published the three volumes of his *Essai sur l'indifférence en matière de religion*, he articulated a point of view about action that shows similarities with that of Blondel, although it was conceived and formulated at another level, focused as it was on the political dimension of religious faith. Lamennais asked how the Christian faith can be lived in the actions of the public domain, or, equivalently, how it can be lived as political action.

After the turmoil of the Revolution and the fall of Napoleon, who had brought a definite though questionable order out of the revolutionary chaos, the restored monarchy was vainly trying, through a series of political adjustments, to draw again the main lines of the pre-revolutionary situation. However, Lamennais did not believe that society could return to the past. A sign of this impossibility lay at hand. The Revolution had given respectability to indifference to God, religion, and ultimately truth. Revolutionary action had denied and attempted to destroy the fundamental truths, not only of belief in God and of the Christian faith, but also of human nature. In spite of the relative religious freedom of the Napoleonic order, that the restored monarchy of Louis XVIII adorned with official religiosity, the restoration does not seem to have triggered a new surge of faith.

Lamennais put the issue of human nature in terms of truth and of life: "Truth is life."[4] The promoters of the Revolution "attacked all truths at the same time."[5] These truths are relative to the two powers that are at war in human nature, "in each man and, by a necessary tie, in each people, the senses and reason . . . flesh and spirit; and, as the one or the other prevails, it is truth or error, virtue or crime, which dominates in society and in the individual."[6] Those who read the signs of the times could learn from the Revolution that "the corruption of mores begets the corruption of the mind; disorder in actions entails disorder in thoughts, or error; and depravation of moral being entails a similar depravation of intelligent being."[7] Whether thought follows action or action thought, the two are inseparable, and all the more so as thinking is itself an act.

Against this backdrop Lamennais investigated the religious consequences of the recent chaos. A growing indifference to the question of God had reached not only esoteric philosophical circles, but European society as a whole. It fostered a tendency toward "absolute skepticism."[8] The problem of indifference in matters of religion is analyzed in volume I of the *Essai*. Volume II posits a philosophical foundation for an eventual reversal of the trend of society toward its own destruction. Volume III purports to show, on the basis that has thus been established, that Catholic Christianity is the only true religion.

As Lamennais's later writings indicate, the thrust of his solution was to elicit a kernel of truth that had been stifled by the Revolution itself. How this kernel of truth was identified, however, depended entirely on the philosophical basis chosen for reconstruction. The leaders of the Revolution had asserted the necessary priority of the nation over the citizens. Translated at the universal level, this meant the priority of the race over the individual. Such a priority prevails in nature in the animal species. Humanity itself experiences solitude as destructive: "Absolute isolation, the immediate result of the absolute independence to which the men of our century are inclined,

---

[4] Félicité de Lamennais, *Essai sur l'indifférence en matière de religion* (2nd edition; Paris: Tournachon-Molin et Seguin, 1818), vol. I, p. 5.
[5] Ibid., p. 6.   [6] Ibid., p. 9.   [7] Ibid., pp. 12–13.
[8] *Essai* (5th edition; Paris: Tournachon-Molin et Seguin, 1925), vol. II, p. 2.

would destroy the human race by destroying faith, truth, love, and the relationships that are constitutive of the family and the State."[9] In regard to knowledge and its certitude the Creator has endowed, not individual minds, but the universal consensus of humanity, with infallibility. Universal consensus, *le sens commun*, is therefore the key to knowledge, morality, and civilization. The way to truth is obedience, immediately to the authority of nature and of the human race and remotely, but no less directly, to the Creator's authority. Hence the statement, "The principle of certainty and the principle of life are one and the same thing."[10]

A basic tenet of the school of thought that will be called traditionalism flows from this: "Man could not exist as an intelligent being, could not speak, without knowing God, and he could know God only through language. It is therefore impossible that language be a human invention."[11] Thought and language were given jointly by the Creator to the first humans, along with a core of essential knowledge of God and of self: "Thus, thought and speech were revealed together."[12] At this point Lamennais explicitly endorses the thesis of Louis de Bonald[13] (1754–1840) and Joseph de Maistre (1753–1821) regarding the divine origin of language. The source of all knowledge is direct revelation by God at the beginning of the human race. Renewed by the incarnation of the divine Word, this direct revelation is not offered again privately to anyone. Today, therefore, neither "feeling or immediate revelation" nor reasoning is the way to truth. This way can only be authority and obedience: the authority of the primitive revelation, supported by the teachings of Christ transmitted by the church, and the obedience of faith.

As he looked toward the future, however, Lamennais parted with Bonald and Maistre. Beginning as a political revolt against tyranny, the Revolution had tried to give power to the people. It had failed, for it had left the people without the needed guidance. Yet the basic insight was right. "The people" has the responsibility to govern itself. Lamennais therefore endorsed the republican form of government that came from the Revolution. However, he added, in the current state of society the pope alone is able to direct the people and to protect it from the tyranny of king, emperor, or whatever clique would reserve power to itself. Conversely, the church cannot

---

[9] Ibid., p. 25.   [10] Ibid., p. 368.   [11] Ibid., p. 223.   [12] Ibid., p. 225.
[13] *Recherches philosophiques sur le premier objet des connaissances morales* (4th edition; Bruxelles, 1845), ch. 2: *De l'origine du langage*, pp. 72–139.

count on kings, emperors, or any form of government to ensure the triumph of the Catholic religion over other forms of the universal belief in God. Only "the people," properly led, is in the long run reliable, because only "the people" is identical with universal humanity and the repository of *le sens commun*.

As detailed in the newspaper that Lamennais started in 1830, *L'Avenir*, this endorsement of the democratic implications of the Revolution ran afoul of the reactionary policy of Gregory XVI (1831–1846). The pope condemned Lamennais's doctrine and movement (*Mirari vos*, 1832); and, after the publication of *Paroles d'un croyant* (1834), he excommunicated Lamennais (*Singulari nos*, 1834).[14] All subsequent popes of the nineteenth century, including Leo XIII (1878–1903), rejected the philosophical and political principles of the Revolution, which they saw at work not only in Freemasonry and in other secret societies marked by the philosophy of the Enlightenment, but also in all forms of communism, socialism, liberalism, and Protestantism. That there could be an acceptable core in the Revolution did not enter their minds: seeking to overthrow the divine authority of kings over their nation and of the church over the whole world, Satan was working on two fronts.

Lamennais advocated nothing less than a reconciliation of the church with the Revolution, a reconciliation that would have determined the legitimate scope of political authority, against revolutionary tyranny on one side and the denial of the revolutionary truth on the other. This denial, however, was basic to the Restoration and was shared by Gregory XVI and his successors: they saw a Christian monarchy as the only God-given means that would bring back the church's authority over the people. Both Lamennais and the pope found the key to the future in authority and obedience, but Lamennais had in mind the obedience of all to the universal consensus of humanity, and the pope meant the obedience of the people to a God-given king and a God-given church and clergy.

If the problem is put in terms of action, Lamennais's solution affirmed the intrinsic value of collective action. The collective movement of the Revolution was not without a positive meaning, which

14 Lamennais had made an effort to be understood by the pope. In 1831 he travelled to Rome with Jean-Baptiste Lacordaire (1892–1861) and comte Charles de Montalembert (1810–1870). Their audience with Gregory XVI led nowhere. After his condemnation Lamennais gave up his trust in the papacy but maintained his hope of Christianizing democracy: his disciples went in diverse ways.

Lamennais identified as the capacity of the people at large to express   ⸗ ᴮ͢ᵘᶜ
in collective action the fundamental human nisus for liberty and
responsibility. This so colored his view of the church's role that he
wanted the pope to make himself the interpreter and guide of the
people's implicit desires and demands against the tyranny of mon-
archic governments. However, if the popes of the times were not
averse to manipulating politics for religious purposes, they could not
admit that the church be used for any other aim than advancing the
kingdom of God, and they were blind to the shortcomings of the
legitimacy theory based on the divine right of kings. Only with Leo
XIII were cracks introduced in the ties between the throne and the
altar, at least in regard to the acceptance of a republican system of
government in America, and to the advisability for French Catholics
to accept and support the Third Republic.

The condemnation of Lamennais was in any case entirely sterile
in regard to the fundamental issue that Lamennais had raised: How
can the truth of faith and the action necessary to life in society be
reconciled? Gregory XVI, by vocation the defender of truth, opted
against the sort of action which, by groping for the truth in social
relations, can allow the future to be better than the past.

MAINE DE BIRAN

Before he was condemned, Lamennais had time to inspire a whole
generation of the Catholic youth. Yet the theoretical basis of his
system came under heavy fire. The divine origin of language and
thought was sharply criticized, on strictly philosophical grounds, by
the most impressive philosopher of the period, Maine de Biran
(1766–1824). When Maine de Biran died, he had gathered material
for a major study, *Les Fondements de la morale et de la religion*, that would
have touched on Lamennais's fundamental question. Biran, who had
analyzed the phenomenon of thought in *Mémoire sur la décomposition de
la pensée*[15] (1805), used a philosophical method centered on analysis.
The analysis of psychological consciousness occupied most of his life
and led him to a number of inferences regarding the nature of mind.
From an analysis of the moral conscience he inferred the nature and

---

[15] Pierre Tisserand (ed.), *Œuvres de Maine de Biran* (Bibliothèque de philosophie contemporaine)
(Paris: Félix Alcan, 1924), vols. III–IV.

rules of morality: these, he found, rest essentially on sympathy for others and on an intimate awareness of God in the soul.

The basic contention of traditionalism was therefore clearly erroneous. Neither the actual transmission of human knowledge nor universal consensus about the existence of God proves anything in regard to the nature of truth, for "error is transmitted as well as, or better than, truth."[16] The traditionalist theory of the origin of language is without merit. If language were indeed revealed, it would be most peculiar that the biblical revelation says nothing of it.[17] Biran's argumentation, however, was mainly logical and philosophical: "M. de Bonald gives us gratuitously as an article of faith an arbitrary and antiphilosophical hypothesis."[18] In a word, the divine origin of language is a mere hypothesis, saddled with too many contradictions to be valid. It rests on the contention that modern languages are too complicated to have been invented by human intelligence, a point that is itself based on its conclusion, namely on the notion that human intelligence is such that it could not have developed along with and through a progressive experience of speaking. The opposite hypothesis is not disproved: "Such a system [as that of modern languages] was formed little by little, starting from a first layer of signs given by nature itself, repeated and imitated intentionally. This first language, natural or even native, is the necessary means to arrive at the perfected languages."[19]

Before turning to the shortcomings of traditionalism, Maine de Biran had analyzed what he identified as three lives, or, one could say, three levels of human life. On 11 June 1820 he wrote in his journal:

I thought yesterday . . . that there are three kinds of very diverse dispositions of the mind or the soul. The first, which is that of nearly all men, consists in living exclusively in the world of phenomena that are taken for realities; along this way there is inconstancy, disgust, perpetual mobility, etc. The second is that of the most reflective minds, who have long sought for the truth in themselves or in nature, separating appearances from realities, and who, finding no stable basis for the latter, fall by desperation into skepticism. Finally the third is that of the souls enlightened by the

[16] *Notes sur le deuxième volume de l'indifférence en matière de religion*, vol. XII of *Œuvres de Maine de Biran*, ed. Pierre Tisserand (Paris: Fondation Debrousse et Gas, 1939), p. 250.
[17] *Origine du langage*, in *Défense de la philosophie*, vol. VII of *Œuvres de Maine de Biran*, ed. Pierre Tisserand (Paris: Fondation Debrousse et Gas, 1930), p. 170.
[18] Ibid., p. 171.   [19] Ibid., p. 181.

lights of religion, the only true and immutable lights: These alone have found a stable point; they are made strong by what they believe.[20]

In the "third life" nothing happens "in sense or imagination that is not inspired by the supreme power to which the I [*le moi*] comes in order to be absorbed in it."[21] This, Biran added, "may have been the primitive state from which the soul fell and to which she aspires to return. Christianity alone explains this mystery; alone it reveals to man a third life, superior to that of sense and to that of human reason or will." Although the first and the third life are the reverse of each other, there is a sort of continuity between them: the meaning of the first lies in the second, and the meaning of the second in the third. The third life is the specific domain of religion. Two centuries before Paul Tillich, Maine de Biran could then affirm: "Religion alone solves the problems that philosophy raises."[22] As is explained in *Nouveaux Essais d'anthropologie* (1823–1824), the third life is the ultimate goal of the second.

Maine de Biran shared Lamennais's conviction that humanity had reached a low ebb. Yet there were major differences between them. Lamennais's attention was pastoral, turned to society and to the deleterious effects of the general indifference to religion in the life of individuals. He was accordingly concerned about action: what should be done to reconcile the church and the Revolution? Biran's way was more interior and meditative, and ultimately more detached than that of Lamennais. He totally disapproved of the philosophical methodology of the traditionalists and notably of "the common error of MM. de Bonald and de Lamennais," which is "to derive every human science from universal reason, from the revealed language, from the authority of testimony . . ."[23] He generally missed the importance of the social dimension, which was the strength of traditionalism, and he disagreed with Lamennais's politics. Like Bonald, he remained a monarchist and a legitimist. Whether he was a professing Catholic or even an orthodox Christian is debatable, but he affirmed his belief in God.

Yet Biran and Lamennais pointed towards a common point: there

---

[20] Henri Gouhier (ed.), *Maine de Biran. Journal* (Neuchâtel: Editions de la Baconnière, 1955), vol. II, p. 276.

[21] *Anthropologie*, vol. XIV of *Œuvres de Maine de Biran*, ed. Pierre Tisserand (Paris: Fondation Debrousse et Gas, 1949), p. 372.

[22] A. de Lavalette-Monbru (ed.), *Journal intime de Maine de Biran* (Paris: Plon, 1927), vol. II, p. 104.

[23] Tisserand (ed.), *Notes*, p. 235.

is a mystery in each human person. One is "unceasingly brought back to the great mystery of one's own existence by the very astonishment it causes in every thinking being."[24] The key to this mystery, Biran admitted, "unceasingly escapes me, as it shows itself with a new face when I think I hold it under another face." Unlike Descartes, Biran did not locate the awareness of self in thought, but in the feeling of effort and in the will to make the effort that is needed for action. The self does not rest until it has discovered the concrete unity of the three lives of sense, thought, and faith. It is not "I think therefore I am," but the effort that is made when "I will" and "I do," that identifies the self and is the key to self-awareness. When Lamennais sought to reconcile the sovereignty of the people and the hierarchic structure of the church, he perceived that the fundamental human mystery is not a matter of the self, but is essentially social or collective. In their different queries, however, both thinkers were focusing on diverse forms of the basic question: what is the true locus of the human relation to God? This, incidentally, will also be Blondel's problem. However, Blondel will not seek for it, with Lamennais, in the progressive structures of human society, or, with Biran, in the psychology of willing and acting, but where it hides in the structure of human action.

The conflict between Lamennais and Gregory XVI did not put an end to Lamennais's influence. Many young clergy had felt the impact of his thought. Emmanuel d'Alzon had written to a friend in 1827, "I am enthused for M. de Bonald's system. . . his philosophy is totally divine, his way of proceeding is perfection itself."[25] D'Alzon, then eighteen years old, met Lamennais for the first time, in Paris, on 11 April 1828. In January 1830, he asked the master for "a plan of studies that would give me a total system, as I have already outlined for myself a plan of life."[26] The two corresponded until the condemnation of Lamennais dealt a hard blow to his admirer, who was then preparing for ordination in Rome. It was the influence of Bonald, Maistre, and Lamennais that made the later d'Alzon a determined opponent of the Gallican party at the First Vatican Council. Indeed, in March 1871 d'Alzon, who was then vicar general of the diocese of Nîmes and director of a secondary school,[27]

---

[24] Gouhier (ed.), *Journal*, vol. II, p. 378 (July 1823).
[25] Siméon Vailhé (ed.), *Lettres du P. Emmanuel d'Alzon* (Paris: Bonne Presse, 1923), vol. I, p. 8.
[26] Ibid., p. 33.
[27] In 1843 d'Alzon and another priest, abbé Goubiot, had bought a small private school,

informed the students, all of them sons of the bourgeoisie, that since they showed no interest in serving the church as priests he would henceforth seek for vocations among the poor.[28] This announcement was a distant but faithful echo of Lamennais's populism.

Even apart from a direct influence on specific members of the clergy and the educated laity, Lamennais's impact was felt in another way. He had been an opener of minds, an inspirer of ideas, and the mentor of a whole generation of devout Catholics. Others took over this function, though without his brilliance and thrust. At this point, however, we should look at a recurrent problem of French society after the Revolution, the problem of the University.

L'UNIVERSITE DE FRANCE

The university system, which included twenty-two independent universities in 1789, was, like all institutions of the *ancien régime*, destroyed by the Revolution. When Napoleon reorganized national education, the new system was quite different from the old. The Concordat of 1801 did not foresee the involvement of the church in education. The law of 10 May 1806 created a state monopoly under the name of the Université impériale, which later became the Université de France. The word "University" was taken in its original sense as *universitas studiorum*, the universality of studies. The University therefore included three levels of instruction or education: primary, secondary, and superior (which alone corresponds to the contemporary meaning of "university" in the English language). The institutions of the three levels were grouped geographically in "academies," seventeen all told, each closely supervised by a rector. The superior level consisted of unrelated faculties or schools of higher learning, among them several faculties of theology, notably at the Sorbonne. No longer, however, was theology treated as "queen

Pensionnat de l'Assomption, that, like others, was functioning illegally. On 21 August 1845, Narcisse de Salvandy (1795–1856), Minister of Public Instruction, granted full authorization to this school for the elementary level (*classes de grammaire*). After the school was renamed Collège de l'Assomption, d'Alzon became its sole owner in November 1848, and on 20 December 1848, the first Minister of Public Instruction of the Second Republic, Alexandre Freslon (1808–1867), granted it a charter as an institution of secondary education with the same rights and responsibilities as a state school. A similar status was given at the same time to three other Catholic schools. See Paul Gerbod, *La Condition universitaire en France au XIXe siècle* (Paris: Presses Universitaires de France, 1965), p. 227.

[28] Polyeucte Guissard, *Histoire des Alumnats: le sacerdoce des pauvres* (Paris: Bonne Presse, 1954), p. 13.

of the sciences" (Thomas Aquinas) or were "the arts reduced to theology" (Bonaventure). The entire system functioned under the absolute direction of a *Grand Maître*, who later became, more prosaically, the Minister of Public Instruction. Ideally, the professors formed a distinct order in the nation, sharing a common life and table in each institution, and they were invited to practice celibacy.

The decree of 17 March 1808 stated: "All schools of the University will take the precepts of the Catholic religion as the basis of their teaching . . ." The schools had chaplains, and several priests were appointed to teaching or administrative posts. Yet bishops exercised no supervision over the schools.[29] In 1811 Napoleon reopened the Ecole normale supérieure, which had been created in 1793 by the Convention as the first school for the formation of teachers and had been abolished by the Directory a few months later. Other Ecoles supérieures were created later in several fields of science. Their vocation was to serve the country by forming its professors and engineers.[30] Philosophy was frowned upon as potentially subversive. The Ecole normale supérieure eventually became the gate to professorial rank at the highest levels. Napoleon himself wanted it to be the seedbed of higher education in the post-revolutionary spirit, in which arts and sciences were to be pursued for themselves, each according to its proper method, yet for the sake of an academic career in the University system of the nation.

After the restoration of the monarchy, neither the revision of the Concordat in 1817 nor the Ordinances on education of 16 June 1828 departed from the basic principles of Napoleon's work. By the same token, however, philosophy was not at home in the monopoly of education. The most influential of the traditionalists, Louis de Bonald and Joseph de Maistre, functioned outside any academic setting. They were philosophers in a broad sort of way, Bonald chiefly while in exile and Maistre, who was not of French but of Savoyard citizenship, while working in a badly paid diplomatic post representing the reactionary monarchy of Sardinia. Maine de Biran did not teach; and his public career, after he was named to the

---

[29] The decree of 17 March 1808 foresaw ten faculties of Catholic theology and five of Protestant theology. Faculties of Catholic theology were established at the Sorbonne and at Aix-en-Provence, Bordeaux, Lyon, Rouen; faculties of Protestant theology in Paris and Montauban. See below, note 38.

[30] The model for these Ecoles nationales supérieures may have been the old military schools, Bonaparte having been a student at the school for artillery in Brienne.

Conseil des Cinq-cents in 1797, was chiefly in politics. Yet he was more of a philosopher in the academic sense, even though his most important works were hardly known while he lived.

The policies of the University were necessarily affected by the dominant orientations of the successive régimes and governments of the nineteenth century: the First Empire, the restored Bourbon monarchy (1814–1830), the "monarchy of July" (1830–1848), the Second Republic (1848–1852), the Second Empire (1852–1870), and finally the Third Republic (beginning in 1871). As a point of fact, higher education deteriorated steadily after Napoleon I. By 1850 only nineteen cities had faculties of some sort.

CHURCH AND UNIVERSITY

The domination of the University by the Minister of Public Instruction became a major source of conflict with the Catholics, clerical or lay, who affirmed the church's exclusive mission and right in regard to education, in what they still identified as a Catholic country.[31] Philosophy, banned from the University by Napoleon, was restored under Louis XVIII. Victor Cousin (1792–1867) became the quasi-official philosopher of the University. In 1840 he was made director of Ecole normale supérieure, Minister of Public Instruction, and a member of the Royal Council. His philosophical system, "eclecticism," amalgamated four schools of thought: idealism, materialism, scepticism, and mysticism. Cousin made philosophy politically correct, but until he retired in 1851 he ruled the official philosophical scene with absolute authority. His system then rapidly disappeared from the scene, where it was easily replaced by the "positive philosophy" of Auguste Comte[32] (1798–1857). While he kept generally good relations with the bishops, Cousin did not believe the Christian dogmas, and he fought the mild revival of scholasticism, tainted with traditionalism, that was known as "the philosophy of Lyon."[33]

---

[31] On this conflict see Gerbod, *La Condition*; Evelyn Martha Acomb, *The First Laic Laws (1879–1889): The First Anti-Clerical Campaign of the Third French Republic* (New York: Octagon Books, 1967).

[32] Comte's *Cours de philosophie positive* was published from 1830 to 1857 and his *Système de politique positive* from 1851 to 1854.

[33] Jean-Marie Doney (1796–1871), *Philosophie de Lyon, ou Institutionum philosophicarum cursus ad usum studiosae juventutis praesertimque seminariorum accommodatus*, 3 vols. (3rd edition, 1850). Doney became bishop of Montauban in 1844; he was an active ultramontane.

To the traditionalists, however, openness to modern trends meant endorsing the inane philosophical disquisitions of the Enlightenment that were largely responsible for the Revolution and listening to the voices of untruth that could be heard from liberals, Gallicans, Protestants, Freemasons, socialists, and other people of the same ilk. The critics of the University equated Cousin's eclecticism with pantheism, indifferentism, free thought, Gallicanism, liberalism, and Protestantism. They saw the University as a tool of Satan undermining the truths of the Catholic Church. While the bishops throughout the nineteenth century were divided about relations with the University, the clergy by and large thought of it as an instrument in the dechristianization of society.

FIGHTING THE MONOPOLY OF EDUCATION

The bishops who led the Catholic attack on the University belonged indifferently to the Gallican or the ultramontane persuasion. Among the ultramontane bishops, Pierre Parisis (1795–1866), bishop of Langres in 1844, of Arras in 1851, a former disciple of Lamennais, and a convinced republican, and Louis Regnault (1800–1896), bishop of Chartres since 1852, were the most outspoken opponents of the monopoly of education. However, the bishop of Orléans, Félix Dupanloup[34] (1802–1878), who would vehemently oppose the definition of papal infallibility at the First Vatican Council, was also highly critical of the monopoly. Hundreds of pamphlets were written on all sides, and the debate was all the more confused as all governments in the nineteenth century favored Gallicanism. The ultramontane writers frequently accused the Gallicans of playing into the hands of the liberals who dominated the University and wanted to perpetuate the state monopoly of education, lest bishops would dictate beliefs and morality in the schools.

The Bourbon monarchy kept the pattern adopted by Napoleon, precisely because it ensured the dominance of the state in public instruction. The Orléans monarchy, more open to liberal ideas, let philosophy, in the form of the ambiguous eclecticism of Cousin, flourish again. Yet minor victories were registered by the bishops. The short-lived Second Republic and the Second Empire allowed

[34] Dupanloup wrote several pamphlets on the matter of education, notably, *De la liberté d'enseignement. Véritable état de la question du point de vue constitutionnel*, 1848. Parisis wrote against the law of 1850.

the opening of private schools at the primary and secondary levels, the state monopoly ending with the *loi Falloux* of 15 March 1850. The same law created a *Conseil supérieur de l'instruction publique*, that was to supervise public instruction. Emmanuel d'Alzon was among those who were appointed to the first *Conseil supérieur de l'instruction publique*.[35]

The conflict between public instruction and the Catholic schools was worsening. In 1871, after the fall of Napoleon III and before the votes that established the Third Republic[36] were even taken, religious instruction was removed from the program of the baccalauréat examinations by Jules Simon (1814–1896), the Minister of Public Instruction in the Government of National Defense. Yet the law of 12 July 1875 further broke the monopoly of the University, as it authorized the creation of "free," that is, private, faculties of higher education to prepare students for the state examinations, the examining juries being at first selected from both public and private institutions. The bishops opened such institutes of higher education in Paris, Lille, Angers, and Lyon.[37] On 16 March 1880, however, the mixed juries were abolished, examination for the degrees being reserved to professors of the University of France; and private faculties of higher learning could no longer legally call themselves universities. A law that was adopted on 15 December 1884 by the Chamber of Deputies abolished the faculties of Catholic theology in the Université de France.[38] Finally, a series of laws adopted in

---

[35] D'Alzon represented the private schools (decree of 31 July 1850). D'Alzon's appointment must have been prompted by his success in making his school the best in southern France. But, far from being commited to the *Instruction publique*, d'Alzon did his utmost to undermine the generally respected and larger Collège royal of Nîmes. With its mixture of Protestant and Catholic students and its two chaplains of rival confessions, this was, d'Alzon claimed in a newspaper article of 1875, "the most powerful machine to destroy the faith" in the city. Louis Secondy, *Aux origines de la maison de l'Assomption à Nîmes*, in *Emmanuel d'Alzon dans la société et l'église du XIXe siècle. Colloque d'histoire (décembre 1980)*, ed. René Rémond and Emile Poulat (Paris: Editions du Centurion, 1982), p. 238.

[36] The Republic was proclaimed on 4 September 1870; the armistice was signed on 28 January 1871; the Third Republic received its constitution on 15 and 16 February and 16 July 1875.

[37] In addition, the Institut catholique de Toulouse was opened in 1877 and its faculty of theology in 1879. The faculty of Catholic theology of the University of Strasbourg was created on 5 December 1902, after the German annexation of Alsace, by virtue of an agreement between the Holy See and the Prussian government.

[38] These faculties of theology had never been favored by the bishops or in Rome because, created by the state, they were seen as Gallican institutions. They offered lectures rather than courses and never had many students. Yet their suppression was an openly anti-Catholic gesture, since the two faculties of Protestant theology were not suppressed. The

1896–1897 reorganized the official system, the diverse faculties of a city being then grouped into a university, while the *Ecoles supérieures* kept their separate administration. A new setting was thus created for higher education. Yet this did not quiet down the basic opposition of a number of Catholics. Two aspects of the struggle may be briefly considered.

THE GAUMIST PHASE

In late 1851 abbé Jean-Joseph Gaume (1802–1879), vicar-general of Nevers, published a small book, *Le Ver rongeur des sociétés modernes, ou, Le Paganisme dans l'éducation.*[39] His thesis was that the deterioration of Christian society was entirely due to the study of pagan authors from antiquity – the classics – rather than the great writers among the fathers of the church. Gaume claimed, incorrectly, that the pagan classics had never been studied in Christian society before the Renaissance, that the Reformers in the sixteenth century were steeped in pagan literature, that the French Revolution could be attributed to the same cause, and therefore that contemporary Catholics should wage a relentless war against the use of pagan authors in the schools. Gaume accused the University of systematically trying to paganize its students. He found a modest amount of support in the episcopate and the clergy, though the bishop of Orléans rejected the thesis and denied the value of the argument, and most bishops would not enter the controversy. Emmanuel d'Alzon, who was inclined to accept the principle, wanted it applied with discernment. His Collège de l'Assomption eliminated pagan authors from the first cycle of studies (*classes de grammaire*) while maintaining some of them in the more advanced cycle (*classes d'humanité*).[40] D'Alzon, however, mistrusted those who, like Dupanloup, rejected Gaume's ideas out of hand. He attributed such a rejection to the fundamental blindness of Catholic liberals, who did not recognize the modern forms of evil; in this they undermined the very task of the church.

Law of Separation between the churches and the state (7 July 1904) did away with the Protestant faculties, which then became private and strictly confessional.

39 It was immediately translated into English: *Paganism in Education* (London: Charles Dolman, 1852).

40 The Collège de l'Assomption published several Christian classics for use in the study of Latin.

The active controversy lasted a few years. In 1857 and 1858, the Italian exile Gioacchino Ventura[41] (1792–1861), by far the most able theologian of the traditionalist school, attempted vainly to revive it during Lenten sermons given in the presence of Napoleon III in the chapel of the Tuileries palace. The pagan authors of antiquity remained in the curriculum, but the very discussion was symptomatic of the distrust of public instruction that was rampant among large sections of the clergy.

DELENDA CARTHAGO

"The most terrible enemy of pagan Rome was Carthage; and the Senate did not rest until this long invincible rival was reduced to ashes. Here, the greatest enemy of Christian Rome, of the Church, is the University, and this is why we have shouted, *Delenda Carthago* . . ." These words were written by d'Alzon in 1871.[42] The fall of the Second Empire seemed a favorable time to attack the state system of education. D'Alzon's aim was to destroy what remained of the monopoly of instruction and to sever the ties between the government and the University. His strategy was, by improving the quality of its professors, to bring the Collège de l'Assomption to the point where it would offer advanced courses at the faculty level. The next step would be to open an unofficial Catholic University in Nîmes, and then to push for an official charter. This strategy, which had been used to obtain recognition of the Collège de l'Assomption in 1848, did not succeed in the 1870s. It even failed to move the French bishops to favor Nîmes, when the law of 12 July 1875 authorized the creation of private faculties.

The Catholic campaign against the monopoly of the University was, in reality, counterproductive. All governments since the Revolution had been suspicious of religious orders as being less pliant under political pressure than bishops. The more strident opponents of the University belonged to religious communities, which were also responsible for the greater number of private schools once it became

---

[41] Ventura was *persona non grata* in the Papal States after the attempted revolution of 1848, when he supported Mazzini's proclamation of the Roman Republic on Piazza Navona.

[42] *Revue de l'enseignement chrétien*, 2nd series, 1871, cited in *Ecrits spirituels du Serviteur de Dieu Emmanuel d'Alzon* (Rome: Maison généralice, 1956), p. 1420. Founded by d'Alzon in 1851 to counter the official *Revue de l'Instruction publique*, this periodical was discontinued in 1855 and revived in 1871.

legal to open these. Hence, there followed the decree of 29 March 1880, under the Freycinet government, by which the Society of Jesus (which ran the greatest number of "free" schools) was "dissolved," and other "unauthorized" communities were given an ultimatum to apply for authorization within three months or else to face extinction.[43] As the communities refused to abide by an unjust law, the government of Jules Ferry, in October of the same year, forcibly closed 261 religious houses and expelled 5,643 religious from the country. This extreme measure was intended to close most of the Catholic schools.[44]

Yet not all devout Catholics, in the middle years of the nineteenth century, wanted to "destroy Carthage." Most Ministers of Public Instruction tried to keep correct relations with the clergy; and the struggle against the University was never openly supported by the episcopate. Some prominent figures in the clergy and the Catholic laity did not share the misgivings of d'Alzon and others about the University. I will draw attention to two intermediate figures, the Oratorian priest Alphonse Gratry (1805–1872) and the philosopher Léon Ollé-Laprune (1839–1898), who will lead us directly to Maurice Blondel.

A continuity between them emerges from their own declarations. Blondel acknowledged Ollé-Laprune as his mentor when he dedicated *Action* to him "as a token of gratitude, devotion, and respect." In a diary entry for 7 June 1862 Ollé-Laprune recorded his resolution to follow the plan of studies outlined in Gratry's book, *Les Sources*.[45] Gratry in turn, after reading Maine de Biran's posthumous *Journal*, praised his predecessor as "the most independent, the most sincere, the most persevering in his research, among those who in our century have born the name of philosopher."[46] Gratry placed

---

[43] All political regimes of the nineteenth century followed the principle of the Revolution, that citizens have no right to form associations of more than twenty members without an official authorization. Since few religious communities applied for authorization, most were illegal, though their existence was in fact tolerated until the Third Republic adopted its anticlerical laws and decrees.

[44] Ways were found to turn the law. The easiest way was to designate a qualified layperson as official director of a school, while the religious continued to teach without wearing their habit. Between the two World Wars, when the anticlerical laws were still in the books, my father, Henri Tavard (1878–1940) was the unpaid official director of such an elementary school in the city of Nancy.

[45] See Stephen Brown's introduction to his English translation: *The Well-Springs* (London: Burns, Oates and Washbourne, 1931), p. xix.

[46] *Les Sources*, 2 vols. in one (Paris: C. Douniol; J. Lecoffre, 1864), p. xxx.

Biran's "third life" at the center of his thought: "everything hinges on this question: Is there a supernatural order?"[47] That Blondel was aware of this filiation of his thought and of its distant roots in the work of Maine de Biran, seems clear: Biran is one of the few philosophers whom he names and quotes with approval in *Action*.[48]

ALPHONSE GRATRY

A graduate of Ecole polytechnique, to which he had been admitted in 1825, Alphonse Gratry underwent a conversion in 1831. He gave up the scientific career he had dreamed of and studied philosophy under Louis Bautain at the Seminary of Strasbourg, where he was ordained in 1832.[49] In 1851 he joined the Oratory that was being restored in France after having vanished, like all religious communities, during the Revolution.

Although he is largely forgotten today, Gratry had considerable influence, at least until his opposition to the definition of infallibility cast a shadow on his last years. In 1869, in a series of letters to the archbishop of Malines, the future Cardinal Victor Dechamps (1810–1883), Gratry led a forceful campaign, not against the opportunity of the definition but against the truth of the doctrine that was based, as he believed, on forged documents.[50] What entitles him to

---

[47] "As Maine de Biran noted, if we knew how we moved the members of our body, we would know everything" (Blondel *Action*, p. 152). Biran is also named and quoted on p. 157: "I think I am in a position to prove that there is no intellectual idea, no distinct perception, nor any knowledge properly speaking, that is not originally tied to an action of the will."

[48] That as a rule philosophers are not named in *Action* (exceptions are Aristotle, Leibnitz, Kant . . .) may derive from Blondel's reaction to the status of philosophy in the Université de France. When, at the Restoration, lectures in philosophy were introduced they came under the quasi-dictatorship of a selected few. This philosophical monopoly was broken by the explosion of the end of the century, when new disciplines were born from it (sociology, psychology . . .). The acceptance of Blondel's doctoral topic was itself a sign that *les pontes* no longer reigned supreme.

[49] On 18 November 1835 Bautain subscribed to five theses on faith and reason at the request of the Bishop of Strasbourg, Lepappe de Trévern. Gratry and others of Bautain's students also subscribed to them. Bautain's acceptance of the theses was renewed on 8 September 1850 (see H. Denziger and A. Schönmetzer, *Enchiridion* [Barcinone: Herder, 1967], [DS] 2751–2756).

[50] Gratry was a close friend of the bishop of Orléans. In *La Philosophie du credo* (Paris: C. Douniol; J. Lecoffre, 1861) he attributed to the bishop of Rome "a primacy of honor and jurisdiction over the whole Church" (p. 198). But in his letters to Dechamps, Gratry blamed Satan for pushing toward the definition of papal infallibility on the basis of the False Decretals (that had been carelessly cited by Dechamps against Dupanloup's position). Yet he does not seem to have discussed the heart of the question, namely whether, in spite of the False Decretals, the unique magisterial function that he himself recognized in the bishop of Rome was correctly expressed by the doctrine of infallibility.

be considered in this paper, however, is his philosophy of the Christian life under the circumstances of the nineteenth century, when, as he thought, a scientific approach to reality was finally coming into its own. Writing on logic and on the knowledge of God and of the soul, he was himself chiefly a philosopher. However, his lasting impact on the intellectual life of the time derived from his experience as chaplain at the Ecole normale supérieure, a post he occupied from 1846 to 1851. From this chaplaincy he learned to speak to potential intellectuals among the youth of the well-to-do bourgeoisie, and he became convinced of the importance of writing and publishing to spread progressive ideas.

In 1861 Gratry published *La Philosophie du credo* and, in 1862, *Les Sources*, two volumes that present his understanding of life in a brief form. *Les Sources* describes the sources of the intellectual life. "Do you know why it is that some minds, well prepared in other respects, often remain unproductive and do not write? . . . They are ignorant of the undeniable truth that in order to write one must take up one's pen and that so long as one does not take it up, one never writes."[51] This underlining of the obvious may be taken to mean that action adds something to thought. The act of taking up a pen is the beginning of writing and already holds in itself all the potentiality of what can be written.

Gratry was aware of living in a crucial moment of world history. Looking at the past he saw "a century of faith, the seventeenth, a century of unbelief, the eighteenth, and a century of strife between faith and unbelief, our own."[52] The seventeenth century was,

from an intellectual standpoint . . . on the whole the brightest epoch in history . . . the father of sciences, the creator of that Science of modern times of which . . . we are so proud . . . This century was, moreover, the most exact and complete of all centuries as regards theology, the greatest beyond comparison in philosophy, and the greatest in literature.

On the contrary, "the object of the eighteenth century was to banish theology from the human mind. This was, it is true, done in the name of philosophy . . . But I know of no century in which there was less philosophy . . ." Nonetheless, "its one plea in the sight of God . . . is that at times it spoke sincerely of justice and of the love of mankind . . ."[53] The task of the nineteenth century should be to reunite what was separated in the eighteenth by reason of the

[51] Brown, *Well-Springs*, p. 14.   [52] Ibid., p. 42.   [53] Ibid., p. 43.

"centuries-old prejudice that philosophy and reason are opposed to faith."[54] Such a project needs thinkers and writers, but what should they write about? There is "in reality but one subject" for all writers in all languages: "God, man, and nature in their relations to one another, a relation wherein good and evil, truth and beauty, life and death, history and futurity meet in one."[55] Now if God, man, nature, and their mutual relations constitute the only topic for writing, they must also be the only topic for thought. Nothing, and by the same token no action, is without an essential relationship to God. Yet this self-evident truth has not always been perceived.[56]

Gratry then proposes a "plan of studies" for modern times that will cover all sciences from mathematics to ethics, and then pass on to theology. In theology one will read Augustine, Thomas Aquinas, Bossuet for the classics, then Thomassin (1619–1695) and, among the contemporaries, the *Praelectiones theologicae* of the Roman professor Giovanni Perrone (1794–1876). The aim of this course of study should be strictly moral. One will acquire from it "the science of duty,"[57] a science that "will bring into full relief . . . and will develop, the rich beauty of the primitive inspirations of men's consciences, and the divine fruitfulness of the precepts and counsels of Christ our Lord and of the Church." Here, Gratry's thought is not far from the traditionalist notion of the primitive revelation. This science of duty has two basic principles: "assistance [is] due by every being to every being," and "the fulfillment of Duty in the full sense of the word is the effort of the whole man to lead all creation towards its goal."[58] Each human creature is responsible for the universe. And each has the capacity to serve the universe effectively in whatever place or situation.

The philosophical perspective is centered on effort and work, more precisely, on *le travail sous la loi*, "labor under law." As such it implicitly raises the question of action. In *La Morale et la loi de l'histoire*

---

[54] Ibid., p. 44.   [55] Ibid., p. 118.

[56] Blindness to the transcendent implications of science is called "the metallic state of the mind." *La Morale et la loi de l'histoire*, 2 vols. (Paris: C. Douniol, 1871), vol. I, p. 305. Gratry had progressive social concerns. He blamed his century for encouraging systematic "spoliation" through a capitalist system that is based on the selfish acquisition of wealth (pp. 310–313), and for endorsing the potential "homicide" that is implied in the maintenance of "permanent armies" (p. 314). These two "great visible forms of injustice" (p. 310) are associated to its "general and latent form, *vice*, which is at work in the heart of everyman" (p. 312). Gratry nonetheless believed the progress of humanity toward justice to be a divine law, the effectiveness of which was guided by divine providence.

[57] Brown, *Well-Springs*, p. 132.   [58] Ibid., pp. 133, 134.

Gratry prophesied that science was about to demonstrate in regard to physics what was already established "for history and the life of societies,"[59] namely, that two forces are at work in every fact, "the one coming from the first cause, the other from the secondary cause." It follows that every fact or act conceals a core that cannot be adequately explained by the forces of the material world or by those of intelligent and free creatures. Full explanation requires recourse to the first cause.

This philosophical reflection is completed by a more theological perspective that Gratry sums up in *La Philosophie du credo*: "God is . . . in all your thoughts, in all your feelings and motions, in the physical light that illumines us, in the sun, in all creatures, in the air we breathe, in the savors and substances that nourish us . . ."[60] The universe enfolds an infinity of "natural sacraments." Moreover, God also

comes and knocks at the heart of man a thousand times a day, awakening for him this awareness of life that wants to say, "God and I," and the soul, instead of each time responding, "God, God!" the blind, senseless soul does not cease repeating its sterile and monotonous refrain, "I, I!" . . . until the moment when by constantly resisting it hardens itself . . . or else until the happy moment when, by the determination of its free will, under grace, it says, "Yes, Lord!" . . . It is this moment, "this pure moment," that allows God to pour the Holy Spirit into us. Then the Word, conceived in us of the Holy Spirit at this pure point of our life, makes us children of God. This is regeneration.[61]

Léon Ollé-Laprune

It was Maurice Blondel who, on 8 January 1899, pronounced the eulogy of his late professor Ollé-Laprune at the annual meeting of the alumni of Ecole normale supérieure, where Ollé-Laprune had lectured from 1875 to his death. The eulogy was printed in February 1922 in the magazine, *La Nouvelle Journée*. In 1923 Blondel added considerably to his text and had it published as a book.[62]

Ollé-Laprune's "dominant thesis" is formulated by Blondel in these terms:

[59] *Morale*, vol. 1, p. 307.   [60] *La Philosophie du credo*, p. 140.
[61] Ibid., pp. 140–141. On 25 November 1872, two months before he died, Gratry wrote to the archbishop of Paris: "like my brothers in the priesthood I accept the decrees of the council of the Vatican. All that on this topic, before the decision, I can have written against the decrees, I delete." Quoted in a reprint of *L'Ecole du mensonge au sein du catholicisme, ou Seconde lettre de l'abbé Gratry au Cardinal Dechamps, Archevêque de Maline* (no place indicated, 1964), p. 5.
[62] *Léon Ollé-Laprune. L'Achèvement et l'avenir de son oeuvre* (Paris: Bloud & Gay, 1923).

Philosophical knowledge, rational certainty, is not a task of pure understanding and pure reason. Belief is an integral element of science, as
science is an integral element of belief itself; that is to say, the mind's view is
always solidary with the being's life; that is to say, philosophy is indissolubly
a question of reason and a question of soul; that is to say, finally, neither is
thought sufficient to life, nor can life find in itself alone its sole light, power,
and total law.[63]

As Blondel noted, this fundamental conception called both for a
renewal of the theory of knowledge and for the rejection of a
rationalist conception of "separate philosophy." The point was so
radical at the time that it was not understood, and the implications
could not emerge immediately. Faith has to be part of life and of
thought:

to believe is not to make an affirmation simply on the strength of extrinsic
reasons, or to attribute to the will the arbitrary power to go beyond
understanding; it is to vivify intrinsic, demonstrable, and demonstrative
reasons with the adhesion of one's whole being . . . ; to treat Truth as
Living or even as a Person . . . ; to understand that this Living Truth is not
only an object of inquiring science or belief, but that it demands trust and
the mutual gift of self . . .[64]

In light of this view of faith Ollé-Laprune affirmed that philosophers should lead a normal and full human life. For "to think
normally is to think with one's body, that is, in action."[65] Ollé-
Laprune was thus the first in the French philosophical tradition to
conceive "an integral philosophy, which makes man commune with
the total order, with the other humans, and, if one may say so, with
himself and with God."[66] He did no less than "enmesh effective
action, its unforeseeable teachings, its irreplaceable reality, in the
living woof of thought . . ." He made it possible, in Blondel's
words,

at last to pose rationally the problems that Catholicism alone will solve, but
concerning which it is of essential importance to show that, born of the
concrete state of humanity, they are at the same time – unavoidable, – real,
– insoluble, even for the most developed philosophy: so that in the oneness
of life and destiny that we constitute, there are a truly unconfusable
heterogeneity and a psychologically and intimately cooperating solidarity
between man's natural activity, the contribution of the universe, and the
supernatural stimuli of grace.[67]

---

[63] Ibid., p. 69.   [64] Ibid.   [65] Ibid., p. 74, note.   [66] Ibid., p. 239, note.
[67] Ibid., pp. 173–174, 175–176.

It was precisely this line of thought that led Blondel to recognize the filiation of his own philosophy: "One clearly sees here how a 'philosophy of action' normally prolongs a 'philosophy of belief,' which normally completes a 'philosophy of the idea.'"[68]

THE MEANING OF *ACTION*

Our survey of the problem of the University in nineteenth-century France throws light on the project and the achievement of Maurice Blondel in his doctoral thesis of 1893. As I stated earlier, Blondel wrote in a variegated context that was philosophical and religious, academic and institutional. The religious and the institutional aspects of this context were closely related in the century-long protest against the monopoly of the University, that is, against the elimination of theology and religion from public instruction. Among its most adamant partisans, the protest movement aimed at destroying public instruction as a state monopoly.

In actual fact, the opposition was not absolutely exclusive. The law had itself inserted several wedges into the concept of the state as *un Etat laic*. There were chaplains in secondary schools, and the *loi Falloux* authorized *l'école libre* (private schools), though not financed by the nation. Private institutes of higher learning were eventually authorized. Yet this was never enough for those who were leading the Catholic opposition to the state. The slogan, *Delenda Carthago*, expressed in negative terms an absolute ideal, the ultimate and utopian purpose of eliminating the state from the educational structures of the nation, which would then become, as in the remote past of some idealized Middle Ages, the exclusive domain of the church.

In this context it is not surprising that the young Maurice Blondel had difficulties obtaining the approval of his topic for a doctoral thesis. The very nature of the University made his project dubious. The University was the creature of a state that, whatever its provisional name as a monarchy, an empire, or a republic, and whatever the kind of tradition to which it appealed for legitimacy, considered itself to be the sole voice of the nation, with exclusive responsibility in the education of its future citizens. Largely for this reason, philosophy still needed to prove that it was not an alien body

[68] Ibid., p. 74, note.

in the University. The only major philosophical attempt to explore the supernatural dimension of human life in the context of the University had ended with Auguste Comte's absurd project of establishing a religion of Humanity with a scientific basis. Though his project was welcome in principle by the most influential branch of French Freemasonry, the Grand Orient de France, Comte had no following. Blondel, who was known at Ecole normale supérieure, as a "tala,"[69] would not pursue his topic in the direction of Comte. However, if his analysis of action discovered within human existence itself a desire for the Absolute, would it not undermine the basis of the University, and even that of the Third Republic, in the autonomy of human reason?

As analyzed by Blondel, action as such, regardless of conscious intentions and obvious circumstances, is always virtually religious. Admittedly, "there are dead acts, without spirit and without soul . . ." Yet when an act arises from the depths of the human will, it is virtually richer than even its point of origin: "In a word, there is an infinite present in all our voluntary actions . . ."[70] The itinerary through which Blondel guides his readers in *Action* ends up precisely at the point where it parts both with the secularist (*laiques*) presuppositions of the University and with what, in the wake of the First Vatican Council, neo-scholasticism considered to be a valid and effective use of reason for Christian apologetics.

If action is a language that says more than is recognized by "reasoning reason" (*la raison raisonnante*) within the parameters in which it has been confined by academia, then the whole Université de France has been set on a false basis. Yet the church officials of the late nineteenth century and their theological supporters had no cause for triumph. For if "reasoning reason" has often failed to recognize the supernatural implications of action, it is not by "reasoned reason" (*la raison raisonnée*) that, despite the affirmation of the rationality of faith by the First Vatican Council (constitution *Dei Filius*), one can properly gauge the value of religion. It is rather by the acts of the men and women who profess the faith. And one cannot deny that there are actions by unbelievers, agnostics, atheists, and by believers in other religions that have more supernatural weight than the actions by which some of the Christian faithful are

---

[69] This nickname was given to those who attended mass on Sunday. (Possible etymology: "il va-*t-à la* messe"!).

[70] *Action*, pp. 383, 384.

identified. True religion is manifest in action, not in thought, even though, in the proper order, action and thought should be in harmony. By further affirming that "heterogeneous with regard to us, practice and dogma are in themselves identical,"[71] Blondel introduced a critical standard regarding the practice of ecclesial authority. If praxis and dogma are in themselves identical, then dogma belongs in praxis and vice versa, with the logical result that claims to ecclesial authority have to be commensurate with the evidence of behavior. And the behavior in question does not reside in the external issuing of commands and prohibitions, but in the internal attitudes that transform life through self-transcending action. In simpler terms, the exercise of authority is effective by the power of inspiring examples. In this case, jurisdiction is not a primary but a secondary concept, not a matter of principle but of organization. The primary concept is prophecy. The principle is the sense of the divine presence. The tradition that is at the heart of the spiritual community is not a habit of thought but a pattern of behavior.

As Blondel admitted in the last chapter of *Action*, such a point of view "appears to disconcert our habits of mind."[72] Disconcerted as they were by the supernatural that Blondel's philosophical analysis posited as a postulatum of action, neo-scholastic theologians denounced it as not being the supernatural that has been graciously revealed and gratuitously given in Jesus Christ. For the church, however, the critique was dysfunctional. As it rejected the necessary ties that Blondel unveiled between action and faith, the critique blocked the way of a new apologetics without being able to restore the credibility and the "credendity" of faith on the basis of universal consent (as in traditionalism) or of reason (as in neo-scholasticism).

From within the University system Blondel showed both the inadequacy of the official policy of public instruction regarding philosophy, and the possibility, even the necessity, of opening philosophy, on the basis of scientific or objective reason, to the concept and eventually the history of revelation. At the same time, however, from within the church, Blondel implicitly showed that the fight of prominent Catholics against the University was aimed at the wrong target. Far from being the school of anarchy in society and immorality in personal life that it was accused of being, the University offered a platform from which human reason could

---

[71] Ibid., p. 385.   [72] Ibid., p. 391.

register the highest demands of human life. It could not only postulate its own grounding in an Absolute that is both immanent and utterly transcendent, but also allow for the identification of this Absolute with the personal God of the Judeo-Christian tradition. What should be destroyed was not the University but the refusal to recognize it as a proper milieu for the formation of a Christian elite.

The program of Lamennais for reclaiming post-revolutionary society for religion through education had sown seeds that matured, once the extreme traditionalist theses had been abandoned, and in spite of the opposition of Pope Gregory and his successors, as they were nurtured by such men of thought and of action as Ollé-Laprune and Alphonse Gratry. Beginning outside, the program had found a path into the University through the Ecole normale supérieure. And it was within the University that it flourished in the form of Blondel's doctoral thesis of 1893. It would come to fruition a little later in the *Lettre sur les exigences de la pensée contemporaine en matière d'apologétique* (1896).

By this time, however, traditionalism was dead; the wind was blowing, in ecclesiastical quarters, for a few years, in the sails of neo-scholasticism; and the reaction against the modernity issued from the French Revolution, which had motivated many of the actions of the papacy during the nineteenth century, was about to lead the next pope, Pius X, into the repression of Modernism, as it had already led Leo XIII to condemn Americanism.

The chief lesson of the story that has been told in these pages relates precisely to the context of Modernism and to the conflicts it provoked. Whether or not Maurice Blondel is seen as a Modernist he shared the social, political, and cultural context of the Third Republic with Alfred Loisy, Edouard Le Roy, Lucien Laberthonnière, and the other French intellectuals who were affected by the movement and by the magisterial reaction to it in the Catholic Church. The tradition that carried the Third Republic went back at least to the Revolution.

The value of a school of thought does not lie only in what it says and in the method it uses to reach its conclusions, it is also to be found in the way it owns or disowns the past and anticipates the future. These two outlooks were, one may recall, among the marks of a true development of doctrine, as John Henry Newman had analyzed them in his *Essay on the Development of Christian Doctrine* (1845). I have tried to show what the past, in the form of the problem of the University in the wake of the French Revolution, brought to Blondel, and by the same token to all the Catholic scholars who worked in connection with the University scene. The French bishops of ultramontane orientation and the Roman authorities, simply rejected the revolutionary tradition, along with what they took to be its Protestant roots. They may well have suspected the depth of the problem that faced the Christian community, but they did not seek for a solution in what Newman called "conservative action upon the past," which could have required an acknowledgment of indebtedness to actions that they were not prepared to approve, but rather in condemnation of the recent past in the name of a more ancient one.

As to "anticipation of the future," few of course were the intellectuals in 1893 who could have foreseen that fifty years later Pope Pius XII, through the secretariat of state of the Vatican, would recognize the merits of Maurice Blondel as a Christian and as a philosopher. This recognition came in a letter dated 2 December 1944 and signed by Cardinal Montini, the future Paul VI.[73] Twenty years later, echoes of Blondel's ideas would resound in the constitutions and decrees of the Second Vatican Council. Fewer still were the theological critics of Blondel who could have expected a future encyclical on faith and reason to place the promotion of philosophy among the central tasks of the Church and its bishops. This, however, is said by John Paul II in *Fides et ratio*, a text which contains more than one echo of the "philosophy of action." If someone in 1893 did anticipate the future, it was precisely Maurice Blondel.

[73] Text in *La Documentation catholique* 42 (1945), 498–499.

CHAPTER 6

The politics of Loisy's Modernist theology

Harvey Hill

An introverted scholar with few outside interests, Alfred Loisy (1857–1940) wrestled with questions of the Catholic faith based on his reading of the Bible and other biblical critics. However, Loisy was not just an intellectual working out religious ideas in a vacuum; rather, he was a Roman Catholic priest with a personal commitment to the church and a high regard for it as an important institution in French life. His own experience of a crisis of faith and the more general alienation from the church in France therefore shaped his work in profound ways. As a biblical critic and historian of Christian origins, Loisy emphasized the intellectual roots of this alienation, and subsequent students of his thought have tended to follow his lead. I will argue, however, that Loisy also considered politics as a contributing factor to the religious crisis and that politics therefore played an important role in his theology.

This essay consists of two sections. In the first, I will discuss the place of politics in Loisy's view of the theological task. At a time when the church espoused an anachronistic political theory, theologians, he believed, had to translate Christian truth into modern terms. This translation necessarily included relinquishing the church's political pretensions, which, in Loisy's view, were clearly exposed as unwarranted by contemporary events. The second section of the essay will review particular political questions and their relationship to Loisy's theology. Loisy formulated his theology in the context of political discussions about moral education in the newly secularized primary school system. The *Ralliement*, Pope Leo XIII's effort to encourage French Catholics to accommodate to the government of the Third Republic of France, gave Loisy further opportunity to reflect on the role of the church in French life, as well as hope that the church would eventually recognize the necessity of the reforms he proposed. Unfortunately for Loisy, events leading to the separation of church and state intervened, effectively eliminating any possibility of the reforms that he sought in the near future and setting the stage for his excommunication in 1908. At every point, political events exercised a significant influence on the direction of his Catholic career and the shape of his "Modernist" theology.

RESPONDING TO THE RELIGIOUS CRISIS

The religious crisis

Events surrounding the establishment of the Third Republic set the terms for much of the subsequent intellectual work in France. Military defeat at the hands of Prussia in 1871 inspired dreams of revenge and an increased concern for the glory of the Fatherland, particularly relative to the German aggressor. At the same time, the fall of the Second Empire (1870) and the excesses of the Paris Commune once again raised the question of the best political regime for ensuring social stability in France. As republicans gained and consolidated political power in the wake of these events, political leaders turned to the educational system to provide both national glory and social stability.[1] Increased devotion to science at the upper levels would contribute, they hoped, to French prestige and power, while reforms in primary education would instill in an enlightened citizenry the virtues necessary for social stability and economic growth. The reformed French Université became the ideological backbone of the Third Republic, with the enthusiastic (or at least politically expedient) support of many of the most prominent French historians.[2]

C. J. T. Talar discusses these developments and their role in creating an institutional culture heavily influential in the intellectual formation of scholars interested in critical history.[3] As Talar notes, however, Catholic historians found themselves in an awkward position. The institutional culture of the Université was frequently defined in explicit opposition to Catholicism. Catholics who wanted to participate in the new intellectual movements had to stand in two worlds separated by a gap that many colleagues on both sides considered impassable. This gap between republican policies and

---

[1] See Weisz, *Emergence*, pp. 3, 8–10, 90–133.
[2] Keylor, *Academy*, pp. 41–53, 90–96.
[3] C. J. T. Talar, "Innovation and biblical interpretation," pp. 194, 206–207.

the scholarship of the Université on one hand and the political and doctrinal teachings of the church on the other precipitated a crisis of faith for many Catholic intellectuals.

Loisy first experienced this crisis as an intellectual problem. His doubts about Catholic doctrine and his efforts to remedy them through the academic study of religion are well known. Already in the late 1870s, when he first encountered scholastic theology at seminary, he despaired of "theorems" of the faith based on abstract speculations unconnected to "reality."[4] Addressing the church, his notes from 1883 proclaimed that "Your God has become an immense abstraction, or rather the synthesis of all the abstractions of the human mind."[5] By the 1890s, he no longer accepted the literal truth of a single article of the creed except Jesus' crucifixion under Pontius Pilate, and he spent his time "in the endeavor to adapt Catholic doctrine to the exigencies of contemporary thought."[6] These intellectual questions always remained central to Loisy's work as a scholar.

Intellectual questions were not the whole story, however. Loisy's notes from 1883 identified three elements in the teaching of the church: religious (by which he meant doctrinal), moral, and political. Intellectual and political developments outside the church had made the church's doctrines and political theory hopelessly anachronistic, leaving only the moral teaching of the church with any modern relevance at all.[7] In his notes, a subsequent dialogue concluded with the assertion of the relative character of all doctrinal formulas.[8] Although now outdated, Loisy insisted, Catholic doctrine had once been an adequate expression of religious truth and could change in order to be so again. This idea provided the foundation of his "Modernist" efforts to reform Catholic theology, but it did not resolve his religious crisis. Three years later, still in the grip of prolonged doubts about Catholicism, Loisy's notes show him rededicating himself to the service of the church "to which pertains the

---

[4] Loisy, *Duel*, p. 71, where "théorèmes" is translated "doctrines."
[5] Loisy, Notes, 1883, in Papiers Loisy (Department of Manuscripts, Bibliothèque nationale de France), vol. x, p. 10/33, quoted in Loisy, *Mémoires*, vol. I, p. 123. Here and elsewhere when I cite the Loisy collection in the Bibliothèque nationale, I will include the volume number of the Loisy collection, Loisy's own pagination, and then the pagination of the Bibliothèque nationale.
[6] Loisy, *Duel*, p. 168; *Mémoires*, vol. I, pp. 362–363. This was Loisy's later interpretation of his Catholic career, but it seems an accurate summary of his earlier theological agenda.
[7] Loisy, Notes, 1883, vol. x, p. 2/29, quoted in *Mémoires*, vol. I, p. 119.
[8] Loisy, Notes, 1883, vol. x, p. 15/36, quoted in *Mémoires*, vol. I, p. 125.

education of the human race ... She has also gathered up the principles of order, of devotion, of virtue, which guarantee the happiness of the family and the peace of society. To attempt today a reorganization of the moral life apart from Christ and his Church would be utopian." Thus, even though "the material sense of the theological formulas becomes less sustainable day by day," the church remained an important, if often controversial, institution in French life.[9] Despite the church's anachronistic theology and politics, the continuing social and moral relevance of Catholicism held Loisy in the church.

Loisy used his own religious struggles to diagnose the crisis facing the French Church as a whole. He addressed this larger crisis most fully in an unpublished manuscript from the late 1890s entitled "Essais d'histoire et de philosophie religieuses" (originally the title began with "La Crise de la foi dans le temps présent" ["The Crisis of Faith in the Present Time"]). The preface of the "Essais" explained Loisy's view of the crisis: it stemmed from the fear that Catholicism held people "in a state of perpetual childhood." Protestants and rationalists claimed that Catholicism "undermined the autonomy (l'autonomie) of the individual ... the autonomy of science and reason ... [and] the autonomy of familial society and political society by the interference of a professedly spiritual power claiming jurisdiction over every manifestation of life and human activity."[10] Offended by the apparent opposition of the church to individual, intellectual, familial, and political autonomy, many modern people renounced their religion, thus creating a widespread religious crisis in France. As in his personal crisis, so in the larger one, modern scientific advances represented the sharpest challenge to traditional Catholicism, but political developments posed a parallel challenge which undermined the religious faith of those people committed to modern political freedoms.

Modern(ist) theology

Loisy's understanding of the theological task made his diagnosis of the religious crisis relevant for modern theology. The initiative for reforming the church to meet the modern crisis had to come, he

---

[9] Loisy, Notes, 1886, vol. x, p. 2/45, quoted in *Mémoires*, vol. i, pp. 150–151 and *Duel*, p. 101.

[10] Loisy, "L'avant propos," in "Essais d'histoire et de philosophie religieuses," in Papiers Loisy, vol. iii, p. 17/18, quoted in *Mémoires*, vol. i, p. 447.

explained in 1892, from theologians whose task it was to adapt "revealed doctrine to the different states of culture" throughout history. The historical study of the Bible, he continued,

shows us how, in primitive epochs, revealed truth was molded into the contours of an almost infantile thought, and how it was successively emancipated; it gives us the historical sense of the development of religious truth in humanity; it teaches us *to conceive and to present [religious] truth under the form which best suits the contemporary spirit.*[11]

Like the biblical authors, contemporary theologians had to present religious truth in a form appropriate to their own day. Loisy repeated this view of theology in his "Modernist" works. In *The Gospel and the Church*, he said that "no one will contest the [theologian's] right" "to supply an interpretation [of the biblical idea of the kingdom of God] for the needs of the present time" ("l'interpréter, pour l'adapter aux conditions du temps présent").[12] A theologian, when speaking in the name of the church, Loisy added in *Autour d'un petit livre*, "draws from the gospel the teaching which suits the needs of modern times without regard for the limitations of its primitive sense."[13]

With this claim Loisy proposed a new direction for theology. No longer was it limited to the intellectual theorems of the faith that he found so distasteful at seminary; rather it consisted of the effort to reconcile the Christian tradition with the modern spirit in all its manifestations. In addition to incorporating, or at least making room for, the latest discoveries of historical science, theologians had to acknowledge the political shifts taking place in western Europe, as people increasingly gained liberty from oppressive *anciens régimes* and their ecclesiastical backers. The challenge of the Third Republic, with its ideal of political liberty, was as relevant for modern Catholic theology as was the challenge of historical scholarship, with its ideal of intellectual freedom. Both called into question the viability of Catholic teaching in its inherited form. Both were therefore important to Loisy's ideal theologian.

Despite his occasional protestations to the contrary, Loisy himself did theology in this sense. At least as early as 1883 his notes show

---

[11] Loisy, *Etudes bibliques* (3rd edition; Paris: Alphonse Picard et Fils, 1903), pp. 120–121, emphasis added.

[12] Loisy, *Gospel*, p. 73. He added that no one would contest this right only so long as theologians did not confuse their interpretations with "the primitive meaning of the gospel texts."

[13] Loisy, *Autour*, p. 143.

him worrying about the anachronistic teaching of the Catholic
Church, political as well as religious. In his first publication, he
claimed "to conciliate the tradition and a sane criticism, to join the
prudence of a theologian to the sincerity of a [historical] scholar,
without sacrificing one to the other."[14] His subsequent publications
had the same goal, if stated less explicitly. Loisy might have preferred
to leave the actual work of theological reform to others (although I
think not), but, because almost no one else in the Catholic world
seemed to him to be capable of it, he would try. "In order to preserve
his faith" with integrity, wrote Loisy, the Catholic historian "had to
become a theologian . . . He has to do for himself the work that
theologians have to do for everyone."[15]

Still, Loisy published little on politics. How, then, can I propose
that political events played an important and formative role in his
theology? First, Loisy linked his critical scholarship to liberal politics.
Loisy concluded *The Gospel and the Church* with the assertion that "as a
result of the evolution, political, intellectual, economic, of the
modern world, as a result of all that may be called the modern spirit,
a great religious crisis . . . has arisen to a greater or less extent
everywhere . . . [T]he adaptation of the gospel to the changing
conditions of humanity is as pressing a need today as it ever was and
ever will be."[16] Along with scientific progress, political developments
contributed to the religious crisis that theologians had to address. In
Autour d'un petit livre, a book designed to "clarify" some of the
ambiguities in *The Gospel and the Church*, Loisy added that

Catholicism must not be a party of reaction in either the political or the
social order . . . [But] Catholicism will necessarily be . . . a reactionary
party destined to an incurable enfeeblement and to total ruin as long as
ecclesiastical teaching tries to impose a conception of the world and of
human history which does not agree with the scientific work of the last
centuries.[17]

The church's teachings reinforced its reactionary politics, which, in
turn, exacerbated the religious crisis. Therefore, when Loisy addressed the religious crisis by battling the church's outdated historical and theological teaching, his work had political implications.
Loisy published little on specific political issues, but his critical work
was itself political.

[14] Loisy, *Histoire*, p. 2.
[15] Loisy, "Le Régime intellectuel de l'Eglise catholique," in "Essais," vol. v, p. 741/48.
[16] Loisy, *Gospel*, p. 276.   [17] Loisy, *Autour*, p. xxxiv.

The structure of the "Essais d'histoire et de philosophie religieuses" reinforced the subtle connection that Loisy made in his published works between his historical scholarship and liberal politics. Loisy drew his major Modernist publications, the "Firmin" articles, *The Gospel and the Church*, and *Autour d'un petit livre*, largely from the first seven chapters of the "Essais."[18] In the "Essais," however, these chapters did not stand alone, but rather set the stage for the more concrete reform proposals of the concluding section, where the larger theological agenda in Loisy's notoriously ambiguous publications was developed at great length. *The Gospel and the Church* itself ended by looking beyond the historical and theological argument of the book to these reform proposals. It raised the question of how truly modern people could conceive "the agreement of dogma and science, reason and faith, the Church and society."[19] *The Gospel and the Church* did not offer a solution to these problems, but they were the topics, and almost the titles, of the last chapters of the "Essais." After chapters on the proper relation of "Dogma and Science" and "Reason and Faith," Loisy explained in a chapter on "Religion and Life" that "The solution of this intellectual difficulty [the subject of the two preceding chapters] prepares and favors the solution of the difficulties in the real world."[20] "Religion and Life" then used the ideas that Loisy developed in his discussions of "Dogma and Science" and "Reason and Faith" to analyze several of the burning political issues of the day, before concluding that the Church could surmount the religious crisis by renouncing its excessive political pretensions.[21] The conclusion of the "Essais," a chapter on "The Past and the Future," ended with the optimistic hope that the church would successfully combat the religious crisis. "That which is now certain," Loisy insisted, is

that the unfortunate and almost universal antagonism which is established between the Church and modern society will diminish and then disappear because the Catholic Church, with faith, theology, ecclesiastical authority on its side, and modern society, with science, civilization, the ideal of social justice (!) on the other, will understand better and better the proper object

---

[18] See Normand Provencher, "Un inédit d'Alfred Loisy," *Eglise et théologie* 4 (1973), 394–395.
[19] Loisy, *Gospel*, pp. 276–277.
[20] Loisy, "La Religion et la vie," in "Essais," vol. v, p. 985/292.
[21] See, for example, Loisy, "La Religion et la vie," in "Essais," vol. v, p. 1010/317.

of their respective missions, their mutual independence and, at the same time, the essential need that they have for each other.[22]

Loisy's work embodied his own effort to resolve the religious crisis by facilitating this reconciliation between the church and modern society in all areas, including politics.

BETWEEN CHURCH AND STATE

I have argued that the primary theological task, according to Loisy, was reformulating Catholic teaching in modern terms. This reformulation included reflection on the meaning of political developments for Catholic faith. I have also suggested that Loisy himself did theology in this sense. Let us now turn to specific cases. We will focus on three fights about the proper relationship of church and state and on Loisy's reaction to each of them. Beginning in the late 1870s, republican politicians attacked Catholic education and the Catholic presence in state schools. With the *Ralliement*, Pope Leo XIII tried to strengthen political ties between the church and the state in order to weaken the anticlericalism that made such attacks threatening. Events in the first years of the new century upset Leo's careful political balance and precipitated the separation of church and state. Loisy's comments about all three events illustrate the theological significance that he accorded to political questions.

Catholicism and moral education?

From the early 1870s until 1886 (and even, with a few breaks, into the next century), politicians debated the proper role of the church in training French children to be good citizens. Anticlerical politicians attacked Catholic education as an instrument of division that taught young people at every educational level to distrust the republican government and to think in ways no longer appropriate for an enlightened country. Political and academic leaders raised the specter of two groups of French youth divided by patterns of thought and fundamental loyalties, with nothing promoting national unity. To counter the divisive effects of Catholic education, these politicians proposed two measures: the strict regulation of Catholic

[22] Loisy, "Le Passé et l'avenir" in "Essais," vol. v, p. 1131/438, quoted in Provencher, "Un inédit d'Alfred Loisy," p. 411.

schools and the secularization of state schools. Both measures proved controversial, but passed the Parliament by 1886.

Jules Ferry, the Minister of Education for much of this period and the sponsor of these bills, defended the regulation of Catholic schools as necessary to protect the state from the church's perfidious influence. He called the battle over education a struggle between the secular and the theocratic spirits, between the Revolution and the Syllabus.[23] Rhetorically he asked if Catholic education conformed to French laws, if it formed citizens loyal to France and its liberal institutions, if it was truly national.[24] At least in the case of Jesuit schools, he added, the answer was clearly no, and he quoted extensively from their textbooks to prove his point. "Our fathers," he proclaimed, "fought for a long time to obtain these great things which constitute a secularized society: a free State, master of itself; liberty of conscience, the greatest value in the world . . ." These principles, the "essence" of the Revolution itself, were under attack by lessons promoting ultramontane and absolutist doctrines of papal authority.[25] Ferry concluded that the state should inspect Catholic schools and close those which undermined the political independence of the secular government.

Secular education, and specifically secular moral education, was the anticlerical alternative to Catholic schools. For example, Paul Bert, Ferry's lieutenant in the debates on primary education, declared the independence of morality from religion and defended secular moral instruction.[26] He advocated "the separation of the school and the churches," with morality going to the schools.[27] Secular moral education, according to Bert, Ferry, and others, emphasized eternal principles that could be illustrated from French history rather than religious dogmas based on "revelation."[28] Historians, including Loisy's teacher, Ernest Renan, eagerly assumed the burden of teaching secular morality. They allied themselves with the government of the Third Republic and leapt into the debates on national educational policy.[29] In William Keylor's words, these

[23] Jules Ferry, *Discours et opinions de Jules Ferry*, ed. Paul Robiquet, 3 vols. (Paris: Armand Colin et Cie, 1895), vol. III, p. 353.
[24] Ibid., pp. 298–301.   [25] Ibid., pp. 96–116, especially p. 99.
[26] Paul Bert, *Discours parlementaires* (Paris: G. Charpentier, 1882), pp. 371–377.
[27] Ibid., p. 330.   [28] Ferry, *Discours*, vol. III, pp. 271–272; Bert, *Discours*, pp. 371–377.
[29] Renan, "Qu'est-ce qu'une nation?" in *Œuvres complètes de Ernest Renan*, ed. Henriette Psichari (Paris: Calmann Lévy, 1948), vol. I, p. 903, and *La Réforme intellectuelle et morale*, in *Œuvres complètes*, vol. I, pp. 333–367. See also Pierre Giolitto, *Histoire de l'enseignement primaire au XIXe*

historians set out "to deduce general maxims of right conduct from the great book of the past just as the curé before [them] discovered such prescriptions in the gospels and the writings of the church fathers."[30]

Not surprisingly, the Catholic Church took a dim view of these attempts to establish a secular moral education. In a joint letter in 1892, the French Cardinals summarized the official Catholic attitude to the republican policies: for the previous twelve years, the government had adopted "a doctrine and program in absolute opposition to the Catholic faith . . . Practical atheism had become the rule of action for everyone in France who had an official title, and the law for everything done in the name of the State."[31] Pope Leo XIII concurred. He protested that the church, "who, by the order and commission of Jesus Christ, has the duty of teaching all nations, finds herself forbidden to take part in the instruction of the people." "A State from which religion is banished," he continued, "can never be well regulated; already perhaps more than is desirable is known of the nature and tendency of the so-called civil philosophy of life and morals. The Church of Christ is the true and sole teacher of virtue and the guardian of morals."[32] Ferry passed his laws, but only over vigorous and continued Catholic opposition that kept the issues very much alive, at least in Catholic circles.

The debates over the church's role in education were raging in the early 1880s, the period of Loisy's crisis of faith, and they figured prominently in his unpublished writings of a few years later. In the mid-1890s, Loisy composed his "Dialogue des morts sur la question religieuse dans le temps présent," a dialogue in seven parts. Jules Ferry appeared in two (more than any other figure except Ernest Renan), one on "The Church in France" and one specifically on "The Secular Laws." Loisy's Ferry said that the church could again contribute to French life if it would stay out of politics, but he anticipated continued hostility between the church and the government of the Republic because of differences on "the question of national education, the rights of reason, and the autonomy of the

siècle: l'organisation pédagogique (Paris: Nathan Université, 1983), pp. 10–11; Keylor, Academy, pp. 90–96.
30 Keylor, Academy, p. 93.
31 Florian Desprez et al., "Exposé de la situation faite à l'Eglise en France et déclaration des Em. Cardinaux," Le Correspondant, n.s. 130 (1892), 416.
32 Leo XIII, "Immortale Dei," in Great Encyclical Letters of Pope Leo XIII, ed. John J. Wynne (New York, Cincinnati, Chicago: Benziger Brothers, 1903), pp. 121, 124.

civil power."[33] Loisy returned to these debates and their implications for the church at much greater length in the penultimate chapter of the "Essais" on "Religion and Life." Here Loisy tried to show that a reformed Catholic moral education could still play a valuable role even in a secular society.[34] In both works Loisy reflected theologically on the implications for the Catholic Church of the political battles over education.

In the "Dialogue des morts," and even more clearly in the "Essais," Loisy expressed his ambivalence on the question of Catholic education. On one hand, Loisy supported the general outlines of Ferry's program to secularize the schools as part of an unwavering opposition to any theological control over academic instruction.[35] Modern intellectuals no longer looked to the church for insights or approval on strictly scientific questions. The failure of the electorate effectively to support religious education bore witness to the inroads that secularization had made even among nominal Catholics.[36] With the laws of secularization, the republican government simply gave institutional form to this intellectual reality.

Furthermore, Catholic schools often fell prey to the same problems that alienated so many people from the church as a whole.[37] Loisy stressed two problems in Catholic education. First, the church taught palpably untrue stories from the Bible as scientific fact, thus sowing the seeds for future apostasy. As in the country more generally, so in the primary schools, false intellectual claims undermined the potentially valuable moral lessons of the church. To make matters worse, even properly moral teaching failed to reach students, because it did not foster in them a healthy moral autonomy. Students were taught little about the process of independent moral decision-making, and, as a result, they had to form their moral consciences on their own. Little wonder, then, that they drifted from the church in subsequent years.

On the other hand, Loisy shared the general Catholic view on the necessary place of religion in all *moral* education. Despite the anti-

---

[33] Loisy, "Dialogue des morts sur la question religieuse dans le temps présent," in Papiers Loisy, vol. IX, pp. 7–8/13–14.

[34] Loisy, "La Religion et la vie," in "Essais," vol. V, pp. 986–987/293–294, 994–996/ 301–303, summarized in *Mémoires*, vol. I, pp. 474–475, and *Duel*, pp. 187–188.

[35] Loisy, "La Religion et la vie," in "Essais," vol. V, p. 1043/350.

[36] Ibid., pp. 1031–1032/338–339, quoted in *Duel*, p. 189, and *Mémoires*, vol. I, p. 475.

[37] For this and what follows, see Loisy, "La Religion et la vie," in "Essais," vol. V, pp. 1031–1032/338–339, partially quoted in *Duel*, pp. 189–190, and *Mémoires*, vol. I, p. 475.

clerical attacks of politicians like Jules Ferry or the anti-Modern fulminations of church leaders like Pius IX, the church still had an essential role to play in modern moral education. "The domain of religious teaching," wrote Loisy, "no more pertained to the masters of science than the domain of science pertained to the church."[38] The church could complement the academic instruction offered at secular schools by promoting the moral formation of the students, "the great goal of life and the primary social necessity."[39] After all, people could only become intellectually and morally autonomous when a religious society like the church awakened, guided, and sustained their religious consciences.[40] On this ground, the church could meet even obstinate anticlericals, who had to admit that the church alone considered "the religious and moral education of all people" to be its "raison d'être." The church "created this function . . . and . . . performed it during the long centuries . . . To take from the church the moral formation of individuals is to renounce . . . the fraternity of peoples and the union of humanity."[41] In the "Dialogue des morts," Jules Ferry admitted as much. At least in theory, Loisy's fictionalized Ferry conceded, the church could benefit France by developing the religious and moral instincts of humanity.[42]

Loisy concluded that schools should, therefore, leave room for some religious instruction, so long as it was confined within proper limits.[43] Loisy advocated the suppression of religious teaching as part of the regular curriculum, with allowances made for special instruction by ministers of the different religions if desired by the children's parents.[44] As models Loisy suggested the collège Stanislas, which had ecclesiastical directors and lay teachers, or Bossuet,

---

[38] Loisy, "La Religion et la vie," in "Essais," vol. v, p. 1041/348. See also ibid., pp. 988/295 and 994–1006/301–313, partially quoted in Mémoires, vol. i, p. 474; and Loisy, "Le Dogme et la science," in "Essais," vol. v, pp. 870–874/177–181, partially quoted in Duel, pp. 183–184.

[39] Loisy, "La Religion et la vie," in "Essais," vol. v, pp. 988/295, 992–1005/299–312, 1032–1038/339–345, and 1044–1048/351–355, partially quoted in Mémoires, vol. i, p. 475. See also Loisy, "Dialogue des morts," vol. ix, pp. 9–10/15–16.

[40] Loisy, "La Religion et la vie," in "Essais," vol. v, pp. 1022–1024/329–331, partially quoted in Mémoires, vol. i, p. 475 and Duel, pp. 188–189.

[41] Loisy, "La Religion et la vie," in "Essais," vol. v, pp. 994–996/301–303.

[42] Loisy, "Dialogue des morts," vol. ix, pp. 7–8/13–14.

[43] Loisy, "La Religion et la vie," in "Essais," vol. v, pp. 994–996/301–303, partially quoted in Mémoires, vol. i, p. 474, and summarized in Duel, p. 190.

[44] Loisy, "La Religion et la vie," in "Essais," vol. v, pp. 1048–1049/355–356, partially quoted in Mémoires, vol. i, p. 475.

Fénelon, and Gerson, Catholic schools that allowed their pupils to take courses at nearby public institutions.

Loisy had no effect whatsoever on the course of the political struggles surrounding the state schools, but what did his reflections mean for his own theology? As we saw above (pp. 171–172), his view of the role of the church in moral education was central to the "resolution" of his crisis of faith. It was similarly important in the religious reforms that he sought as the best theological response to the wider religious crisis, of which the debates on education were one manifestation. Growing out of his discussion of Catholic moral education, Loisy proposed a new vision of church authority to replace the more traditional, authoritarian model. The modern, reformed Catholic Church, he suggested, is (or would be) "an educator, rather than a dominating mistress: she instructs rather than directs, and he who obeys her only does so according to his own conscience, and in order to obey God." As such, Loisy continued, the church could contribute to the goal of all true moral education, the formation of autonomous individuals, "religious personalities, souls masters of themselves, pure and free consciences."[45] For this task the church required only a pedagogical authority, nothing more. Then, Loisy thought, the religious crisis would pass. Having renounced the authoritarianism so strongly opposed by the modern spirit, the church would no longer inspire legitimate anticlerical hostility.

Church and state? The Ralliement

During and immediately following the enactment of the laws secularizing education, some French Catholics began to seek an accommodation with the republican government that would allow them to influence national policy. At the center of the *Ralliement*, as this effort at accommodation came to be called, stood the recognition of the basic legitimacy of the Republic. Pope Leo XIII told Catholic monarchists to accept the Republic. As conservatives committed to the defense of religion but flexible on the constitutional question, he said, French Catholics could more effectively oppose anti-Catholic legislation such as Ferry's educational laws.[46] Catholics

---

[45] Loisy, *Gospel*, pp. 175–176.
[46] Leo XIII, "Au milieu des sollicitudes," in *Great Encyclical Letters*, pp. 254–256, 258–260, and "Lettre de S.S. le Pape Léon XIII aux Cardinaux français," *Le Correspondant*, n.s. 131 (1892), 604, 605, 607.

might even win the support of the French government for Vatican attempts to recover the papal lands lost under Leo's predecessor, Pius IX.[47]

Although the *Ralliement* (temporarily) helped to improve relations between the Vatican and the government of the Third Republic, Loisy opposed its political goals as contrary to the best interests of religion in France. Leo wanted to strengthen the alliance of church and state, but, Loisy argued, this alliance benefited the civil government more than the church. Under the terms of the Concordat which codified the relationship of the two, "the most secular of all governments" had the right to nominate Catholic bishops. The church received little or nothing in return. In fact, Loisy continued, a more Catholic Parliament might initiate separation as a way of restoring the church's religious authority.[48] Making the same basic point, he rejoiced at the earlier loss of the Papal State. "I see precisely there," he wrote, "a guarantee of spiritual independence." The loss of temporal power increased the moral prestige of the papacy without sacrificing any freedom of religious action, a freedom now "only limited by the artifices of [Leo's] diplomacy."[49]

Furthermore, Loisy condemned Leo's diplomatic efforts as a continuation of the illegitimate political pretensions of Leo's predecessors in the Vatican. Renouncing these pretensions was, Loisy thought, an essential step for the full entrance of the church into the modern political world. He noted that "Leo has not denied Pius IX's Syllabus; he has not even withdrawn the propositions that condemn the principles of modern society . . . He wants all the forces of humanity, science, industry, art, and politics to obey the church."[50] By contrast, Loisy advocated the separation of church and state and concluded the chapter in the "Essais" on "Religion and Life" with the claim that "The reciprocal action of the church on the state and of the state on the church will eventually be exercised in mutual respect of the autonomy which is necessary to both."[51] A few years

---

[47] See William S. Halperin, "Leo XIII and the Roman Question," in *Leo XIII and the Modern World*, ed. Edward T. Gargan (New York: Sheed & Ward, 1961), pp. 115–116; Leo XIII, "Immortale Dei," p. 114.

[48] Loisy, "La Religion et la vie," in "Essais," vol. v, pp. 1079–1082/386–389, partially quoted in *Duel*, pp. 191–192. See also ibid., p. 1084/388.

[49] Loisy to Baron von Hügel, 12 January 1900, quoted in *Mémoires*, vol. i, p. 542.

[50] Loisy, "La Religion et la vie," in "Essais," vol. v, p. 1080/387. See also ibid., p. 1087/394.

[51] Ibid., pp. 1083–1085/390–392, partially quoted in *Mémoires*, vol. i, p. 476. Loisy concluded the "Essais" as a whole the same way. See "Le Passé et l'avenir," in "Essais," vol. v, p. 1131/438, quoted above, pp. 175–176.

later Loisy added that no pope would ever again have the political authority of Leo's predecessors in the see of Peter. Loisy therefore hoped Leo would renounce his anachronistic pretensions and concentrate on developing his religious authority, which the church's political engagements only compromised.[52]

Despite these criticisms of Leo's diplomacy, Loisy appreciated Leo's impact on the church, where the *Ralliement* contributed to a new, more open spirit. At the height of the *Ralliement*, Loisy wrote that "Leo's will had separated the papacy from the politics of the *ancien régime*: only the future will reveal the consequences of this act, which is irreversible and which opens new destinies to the church in joining it, although still insufficiently, to the modern world."[53] A few years later, in the midst of his struggles with Leo's successor, Loisy again praised Leo's efforts to find "the means of reconciling Catholicism with contemporary society," and he called Leo's service to the church "glorious and good."[54] Loisy made such statements even in the face of Leo's ongoing political pretensions (and in the face of Leo's repeated assertions of ecclesiastical authority over biblical scholarship), because Leo's efforts to open the church to the currents of the modern world created an atmosphere in which Loisy could refine and express his own more radical ideas about accommodating to modernity.[55] By thus encouraging Loisy to believe in the possibility of a truly modern Catholicism, the *Ralliement* contributed directly to the development of Loisy's Modernist theology. If Leo's efforts at modernization were not fully adequate, Loisy could still pray that they would grow to encompass all areas of Catholic life, and he worked for this goal.

Church and state? Separation

Leo's efforts notwithstanding, events that climaxed with a law on separation soon ended the *Ralliement*. Already reeling from poor election results in 1898, the fate of the *Ralliement* and of the abortive Catholic effort to win political influence within the republican

[52] See Loisy, *Gospel*, pp. 163–164.
[53] Loisy, "Le Passé et l'avenir," in "Essais," vol. v, p. 1113/420, quoted in Provencher, "Un inédit d'Alfred Loisy," p. 401.
[54] Loisy, *Autour*, p. 186.
[55] Loisy said that the spirit of openness engendered by the *Ralliement* "turned the best heads in French Catholicism," including his own (*Mémoires*, vol. 1, p. 365).

framework were sealed by the Dreyfus Affair. A new wave of anticlerical legislation imposed civil authority over religious orders and instituted more academic reforms. Elections in 1902 returned a larger republican majority, allowing Emile Combes, the new premier, to engage in what he called "a campaign of secularization." Even the diplomatic Leo would have had trouble with Combes, but Leo's death in 1903 and the election of Giuseppe Sarto as Pope Pius X set the stage for a pitched fight. Events in 1904 kept political tensions high and led to the severing of diplomatic relations between France and the Vatican. The following year the French Parliament passed a law ending state support for religion (Catholicism, Protestantism, and Judaism), subjecting church property to the French legal system, and requiring parishes to seek civil authorization.

In this battle between the Vatican and the government of the Third Republic, the nomination and election of bishops was a contentious issue in which Loisy figured directly. Already in 1901, Cardinal Richard, the archbishop of Paris, lamented that "the question of episcopal candidatures is one of the great sorrows and one of the great dangers of the present hour."[56] The next year Loisy exacerbated the danger. First, Loisy learned that Prince Albert of Monaco wanted to present Loisy's name, along with two others, to the Pope as candidates for the one bishopric of Monaco. A professed unbeliever, Albert had little desire to cooperate with Rome and often worked against the political interests of the church. For example, he leaked sensitive information to the socialist press in France in 1904 and broke off diplomatic relations with the Vatican following the separation crisis. His nomination of Loisy and the two other candidates in 1902 fell into the same pattern. All were compromised in the eyes of Rome, and all were rejected. On receiving Loisy's approval, the Prince responded by resubmitting the same names in an effort to force the Vatican to accept one of them.[57] At the same time Loisy learned that the French Minister of Religious Affairs had added Loisy's name to a list of prospective nominees for a bishopric in France. The Minister told Loisy that Combes planned to present the nominations without the customary prior negotiations as part of

---

[56] Richard to M. Valansio, 21 January 1901, in Clément, *Vie du Cardinal Richard, archevêque de Paris* (Paris: De Gigord, 1924), pp. 426–427.
[57] Loisy, *Mémoires*, vol. II, pp. 92–93, 96, and *Duel*, p. 218. For more details, see Marvin O'Connell, "The Bishopric of Monaco, 1902: A Revision," *The Catholic Historical Review* 71 (1985), 26–51.

his campaign of secularization. The Minister added that he expected opposition from Rome, but explained that "Rome always ends in yielding to those who are strong."[58] To this proposal, too, Loisy consented. Consistent with his support for separation and his opposition to the political pretensions of the pope, Loisy knowingly allowed himself to be used as a weapon against the Vatican in the developing struggle between Paris and Rome.

In his later writings Loisy downplayed his efforts to become a bishop, but he did campaign for the position, and his campaign intersected in interesting ways with the beginnings of the Modernist "crisis." While waiting for the final word on his two candidacies, Loisy published *The Gospel and the Church* and promptly sent his new book to an influential contact in an effort to garner his support for Loisy's episcopal ambitions.[59] Contrary to Loisy's hopes, however, *The Gospel and the Church* won him ecclesiastical censures, not advancement. On the recommendation of a theological commission called to draft a condemnation of Loisy's work, Cardinal Richard, "reprobate[d] this book and for[bade] the clergy and faithful of [his] diocese to read it." Cardinal Perraud and several bishops followed Richard's lead and banned the book in their dioceses as well.[60] Loisy attributed these judgments against his book to a desire to forestall his nomination to a French bishopric, indicating the connection that he drew between the book and his episcopal candidacy, and he responded by advising one of his allies in Rome to spread the word that further condemnations would have adverse political consequences in Paris.[61] At the same time Cardinal Richard and others increased their efforts to secure Loisy's condemnation in Rome. They were successful, and, on 16 December 1903, the Holy Office inscribed five of Loisy's publications on the Index of Forbidden Books.[62]

---

[58] Loisy, *Mémoires*, vol. II, pp. 125, 143–144; Francesco Turvasi, *The Condemnation of Alfred Loisy and the Historical Method* (Rome: Edizioni di Storia e Letteratura, 1979), p. 70.

[59] Loisy to Cardinal Mathieu, 27 October 1902, quoted in *Mémoires*, vol. II, pp. 145–148, and *Duel*, pp. 219–221.

[60] Loisy, *Duel*, pp. 230–231, 341, and *Mémoires*, vol. II, pp. 193–194, 199, 200; Clément, *Vie du Cardinal Richard*, pp. 398–399. See also Poulat, *Histoire*, pp. 136–142, 244; Roger Aubert, "Aux origines de la réaction antimoderniste: deux documents inédits," *Ephemerides Theologicae Lovanienses* 37 (1961), 567–572.

[61] Loisy, *Duel*, pp. 230–231, and *Mémoires*, vol. II, p. 148; Loisy to Genocchi, 30 October 1903, quoted in Turvasi, *The Condemnation of Alfred Loisy*, p. 94.

[62] Clément, *Vie du Cardinal Richard*, pp. 399–402; Loisy, *Duel*, p. 247, and *Mémoires*, vol. II, p. 283. See also Poulat, *Histoire*, pp. 245–248.

If the political situation initially contributed to the Vatican's reaction to Loisy's episcopal candidacies and to his works, it quickly shifted ecclesiastical attention away from Loisy and onto parliamentary proceedings. As Parliament debated the terms of separation, and particularly after the Law of Separation was promulgated in 1905, the Vatican fought the French government rather than Loisy. In a series of encyclicals on the Law of Separation Pius railed against the injustices done to God, to the church despite its almost excessive willingness to compromise, to religion in France, and to civil society itself.[63] Pius condemned the law, refused to allow French bishops to establish the "Religious Associations" that it required, and ended with the (unavailing) prayer that Catholic opposition could overturn it.[64]

Enraged by Pius' condemnation of the Law of Separation, Loisy wrote three anonymous articles attacking the reaction of the Catholic hierarchy and supporting the law.[65] In his articles, Loisy attributed Catholic hostility to the French law to the church's loss of political influence and power, not to properly religious concerns. "Nothing," Loisy wrote, "was really threatened in the new order of things except the political prestige of the Roman pontificate, and perhaps also, in the long run, the dogmatism of its authority, which a concordat with the civil power protected more effectively against schisms. But this interest . . . is not at all religious."[66] In order to protect its political prestige, Loisy insisted, the Vatican sought to dominate the civil government of France, even against the will of the majority of French people. As evidence, Loisy pointed to Pius' effort to annul a French law, an effort that Loisy described as a "violent anachronism."[67] Contrary to Pius' understanding, "the constitution

[63] See, for example, Pius X, "Vehementer nos," in *Actes de S.S. Pie X*, 4 vols. (Paris: Bonne Presse, n.d.), vol. ii, pp. 124–129. This edition of Pius' acts includes the Latin originals and facing French translations.

[64] Pius X, "Vehementer nos," vol. ii, pp. 140, 141, and "Gravissimo officii munere," in *Actes de S.S. Pie X*, vol. ii, pp. 220, 221, 224, 225.

[65] The three articles were: "Réflexions d'un historien sur la lettre précédente," *Libres Entretiens* (June 1905), 438–452; "Sur l'encyclique de Pie X," *Union pour la Vérité* (June–September 1906), 162–175; and "Lettre aux évêques français à propos de leur dernière assemblée," in Papiers Loisy, vol. x, pp. 1–18. The first two duly appeared, but Loisy's publisher withheld the third, the bitterest of the three, for fear that Loisy would be recognized (Loisy, *Duel*, p. 292).

[66] Loisy, "Lettre aux évêques français," vol. x, p. 9.

[67] Loisy to Sir R. B., 10 December 1906, in Loisy, *Quelques lettres sur des questions actuelles et sur des événements récents* (chez l'auteur, 1908), p. 55. See also Loisy, "Sur l'encyclique de Pie X," quoted in *Duel*, p. 289.

of modern States leaves no room for the intervention of his authority in political affairs."[68] "The Church," Loisy concluded, abdicated "none of those pretensions which contemporary society cannot admit without self-destruction."[69] "It is not the state, it is not the bishops, except by their obedience to the Pope, who will have produced this sad result. It is Roman absolutism which, in order to protect its pretensions, will have lost what remained of the church in which shone Saint Bernard, Saint Louis, and Fénelon."[70] Loisy later added that "the pretensions of Pius X to interfere [réglementer] in political matters seemed to me as illegitimate and as disturbing as his pretensions to dominate [réglementer] in the realm of scholarship. Only, here the practical consequences appeared immediately, and it was a vital interest of France that was involved."[71]

The battle over separation exposed the gulf between Loisy and the Vatican and prepared the way for the official condemnation of "Modernism." Roman intransigence killed Loisy's commitment to the church, thus ensuring that he would not submit to further demands. At the same time, political events fueled the hostility of many Catholics to anything smacking of "liberalism." After the immediate urgency of the separation crisis began to wane, Vatican theologians returned to the theological questions raised by Loisy and others and saw there political implications that appeared to defend the recent French outrages against the church.

The Vatican made its dissatisfaction with Loisy's position clear in the summer of 1907, shortly after the French government began enforcing the Law of Separation. On 3 July, Pius released *Lamentabili sane exitu*, a syllabus of sixty-five condemned propositions. Two months later, Pius followed *Lamentabili* with a long encyclical entitled *Pascendi dominici gregis* that described the "Modernist system."[72] Modernists, *Pascendi* claimed, disingenuously presented their views in

---

[68] Loisy, "Sur l'encyclique de Pie X," quoted in *Duel*, p. 289.
[69] Ibid., quoted in *Duel*, p. 289. See also Loisy, "Réflexions d'un historien," p. 444, and "Lettre aux évêques français," vol. x, p. 9.
[70] Loisy to Sir R. B., 20 December 1906, in *Quelques lettres*, p. 58.
[71] Loisy, *Duel*, p. 291. See also Loisy, *Mémoires*, vol. ii, pp. 441–442.
[72] Scholars have amply discussed both *Lamentabili* and *Pascendi*. See, for example, Albert Houtin, *Histoire du modernisme catholique* (chez l'auteur, 1913), pp. 165–184; Jean Rivière, *Le modernisme dans l'Eglise: étude d'histoire religieuse contemporaine* (Paris: Letouzey et Ane, 1929), pp. 333–372; Poulat, *Histoire*, pp. 103–112; Daly, *Transcendence*, pp. 165–217, 231–234. I will not repeat their arguments here but will focus only on the connections the two papal documents drew between the theological ideas they condemned and the political issues raised by the separation crisis.

unsystematic form in order to deceive people as to their full intentions, while simultaneously trying to replace scholasticism with scientific history, democratize ecclesiastical government, and change the social and political policies of the church.[73]

The encyclical did not emphasize Modernist efforts to change the church's social and political policies, but it clearly associated the well-known Modernist commitment to critical scholarship with support for the separation of church and state. As *Pascendi* put it,

the rules to be applied in this matter [church–state relations] are those which have been laid down for science and faith . . . In the same way, then, as faith and science are strangers to each other by reason of the diversity of their objects, Church and State are strangers by reason of the diversity of their ends, that of the Church being spiritual while that of the State is temporal.

Again drawing the parallel with the Modernist treatment of faith and science, the encyclical accused Modernists of going still further.

It is not enough for the Modernist school that the State should be separated from the Church. For as faith is to be subordinated to science, as far as phenomenal elements are concerned, so too in temporal matters the Church must be subject to the State. They do not say this openly yet – but they will say it when they wish to be logical on this matter.[74]

Thus, according to *Pascendi*, Modernists not only supported the separation of church and state, but they actually advocated, at least in principle, the subordination of the church to the state. The anticlerical offenses against the church in the Law of Separation were the practical application of Modernist theology and philosophy, even if Modernists themselves did not yet openly support it.

Loisy generally rejected the picture that *Pascendi* drew of the Modernists, but he accepted parts of its description of Modernist politics. Like *Pascendi*, Loisy interpreted the Modernist crisis in terms of first principles that had political as well as academic implications. The controversy involved "the very notion of authority in the church" and the appropriate limitations of this authority in a modern society.[75] Modernists, Loisy proclaimed, "have recognized the independence of temporal society with regard to the church, and . . . they approve, in the political order, the separation of the church

[73] Pius X, *Pascendi dominici gregis*, §8 in *Actes de S.S. Pie X*, vol. III, pp. 144–147.
[74] *Pascendi*, §25, pp. 120–121. I have altered the last word of the English translation from "head" to "matter."
[75] Loisy to A.M. l'abbé X., 17 June 1907, in *Quelques lettres*, p. 157.

and the state." By contrast, the encyclical presupposed a model of "autocratic" and "tyrannical" authority "incompatible with the normal development of civilized nations."[76] Modernists fought this authoritarianism in the name of "the autonomy of the religious conscience . . . the autonomy of science with regard to theology, [and] that of civil society with regard to the church."[77]

CONCLUSION

That the challenge of Modernism was not simply doctrinal, but rather involved the most basic principles of church authority and the relation of church and state helps to explain the ferocity of the Vatican reaction in the disciplinary section of *Pascendi* and the decisions of the next few years. David Schultenover has shown how some conservative Catholics interpreted Modernism within the context of an ongoing battle against liberalism, and he suggests that Pius hoped *Pascendi* might be the final blow.[78] Seen in this way, the crisis over separation did not interrupt an isolated attack on Loisy's ideas in 1903 so much as force the Vatican to address political questions that had always stood in the background of Loisy's thought. When the immediate pressures of separation waned, the church could continue the same struggle on the intellectual front with the bitterness to be expected against traitors who aided and abetted an intractable foe.

In this assessment of Loisy's theology, the Vatican was partly right. Already by the middle 1880s, Loisy opposed the political pretensions of the Catholic hierarchy as an important factor in the religious crisis, and he accepted, as part of the work of modern theology, the necessity of moderating them. Loisy therefore watched the fluctu-ating relationship between the Vatican and the government of the Third Republic from 1880 to 1907 with a critical eye and commented on the battles over secular education, the *Ralliement*, and the Law of Separation. Throughout his Catholic career, then, politics played a part in his theology, and political events in France influenced the development, course, and outcome of his Modernism.

What can a better awareness of this political component of Loisy's theology teach us about his Modernism more generally? Scholars

---

[76] Loisy, *Simples réflexions sur le décret du Saint-Office "Lamentabili sane exitu" et sur l'encyclique "Pascendi dominici gregis"* (2nd edition; chez l'auteur, 1908), pp. 198–199.

[77] Ibid., p. 150.   [78] Schultenover, *View*, pp. 23–33.

have sometimes claimed that Loisy was an exegete who addressed theological questions only when he encountered resistance to his biblical critical conclusions.[79] As a result, they have stressed his opposition to late nineteenth- and early twentieth-century expressions of Catholic doctrine, with less attention to his more "constructive" theological proposals and their relationship to a larger program of ecclesiastical reform. At least in his aspirations, however, Loisy was more than a biblical critic; he wanted to be a doctor of the church who taught the church to be truly modern.[80] Loisy's interest in politics and the link that he drew between politics and his Modernist works illustrate one aspect of this broader ambition, and thus demonstrate that students of his thought must pay greater attention than is usually the case to his theological agenda as a whole and its relation to his historical context.

[79] See, for example, Normand Provencher, "The Origin and Development of Alfred Loisy's Modernism," *Science et Esprit* 32 (1980), 324.
[80] Loisy, Notes, 1884, quoted in Houtin, *La Vie d'Alfred Loisy,* in *Alfred Loisy: sa vie – son œuvre,* ed. Emile Poulat (Paris: Centre national de la recherche scientifique, 1960), pp. 40–41. See also my "La Science catholique: Alfred Loisy's Program of Historical Theology," *Zeitschrift für neuere Theologiegeschichte/Journal for the History of Modern Theology* 3 (1996), 39–59.

7

Innovation and biblical interpretation

C. J. T. Talar

This book showed that M. Loisy stood in the forefront of the biblical controversy, that several of the ideas for which he had been persecuted have become part of what is taught, that those who had opposed him had been able to counter only with a puerile apologetic, tainted by bogus methods: brazen denials, shameless affirmations, cynical retractions . . . Several excused the author for recognizing the importance of Loisy's role, but they did not pardon him for exposing the weakness of the official apologetics of M. Vigouroux.

Albert Houtin, on his *La Question biblique chez les catholiques de France au XIXe siècle* (1902)

LOISY: INTELLECTUAL AND INSTITUTIONAL CONTEXTS

In any account of the Modernist movement Alfred Firmin Loisy (1857–1940) would claim a central role, given the prominence of his own person and that of biblical criticism in shaping the crisis. The sheer quantity of his published output contributed to Loisy's preeminence. That, however, is merely the backdrop. More salient would be the notoriety gained by a few of those publications, most notably *L'Evangile et l'Eglise* (*The Gospel and the Church*) (1902), the book that could be said to have precipitated the Modernist crisis. Part of Loisy's prominence could also be attributed to the background from which he stood out: the state of biblical studies in latter nineteenth-century Catholicism. Even to those untrained in exegesis the rather low level of Catholic scholarship in this area was glaringly apparent. In 1906, while at Issy, J.-K. Huysmans remarked on "an enormous library of exegetical studies" that he had "dipped into" there, concluding that "the ineptitude of Catholic exegetes is frightful! Ah – they are even lower than I thought."[1] Even if these remarks are

---

[1] Joris-Karl Huysmans to Vicomte d'Hennezel, 26 August 1906 in *The Road from Decadence*.

discounted, given the novelist's rarely restrained tendency to rail against the mediocre state of contemporary Catholicism, they are reinforced by others who went through the seminary system and thus had exposure to the full course of training allotted to the church's professional servants. The testimony of Ernest Dimnet covers the years of his theological studies at Cambrai (1890–1893), which coincide with the final portion of Loisy's career at the Institut catholique.[2] While describing his seminary biblical studies from 1894 to 1897, Prosper Alfaric echoes Dimnet's experiences.[3] Their observations reinforce Loisy's more familiar representations of the received scholarship he encountered in the 1870s and 1880s.[4] By the 1890s, however, things had progressed to the degree that there was growing awareness of Catholic alternatives to the then dominant exegetical and apologetical approach. Dimnet exemplified this awareness as well as the anxieties these alternatives were evoking:

I also kept up a brisk correspondence with my friend Joseph Bricout, who had become the secretary of the illustrious Monsignor d'Hulst and was, in Paris, the pupil of Duchesne and Loisy. Three or four times a year he paid me a visit and I got illuminating glimpses of the speedy transformation of Catholic scholarship. Sometimes the gulf between what I heard and what I had been taught appeared frightening, but I was told that the new scholarship had also developed a new apologetics and there was no cause for alarm.[5]

While Loisy stood apart from the dominant trend in Catholic exegesis, he did not stand alone. In Francophone biblical studies he shared the spotlight (or searchlight) with others, most notably the Dominican Marie-Joseph Lagrange (1855–1938). Not only the critical character of Loisy's work but its quality contributed to its enduring prominence. In her comparison of the two exegetes, Nadia

---

From Brothel to Cloister: Selected Letters of J. K. Huysmans, trs. and ed. Barbara Beaumont (London: The Athlone Press, 1989), p. 230.

[2] See Ernest Dimnet, My Old World (London: Jonathan Cape, 1935), pp. 203–242.

[3] Prosper Alfaric, De la foi à la raison (Paris: Publications de l'Union rationaliste, 1959), pp. 53–84. On Alfaric see Vidler, Variety, pp. 75–78.

[4] Loisy's characterization of the tenor of Vigouroux's teaching at the Institut catholique was incorporated into his autobiographical Choses passées (Paris: Nourry, 1913), pp. 58–60. See Loisy, Duel, pp. 88–89. For Vigouroux's influence on French biblical studies, see Christoph Théobald, "L'Exégèse catholique au moment de la crise moderniste" in Le Monde contemporain et la bible, ed. Claude Savart and Jean-Noël Aletti (Paris: Beauchesne, 1985), pp. 405–409.

[5] Dimnet, My Old World. p. 223. Some of the factors that contributed to the anxieties of church authorities are noted by Normand Provencher, O.M.I., "Loisy's Understanding of Theology and History," Science et Esprit 36 (1984), 117.

Lahutsky has remarked that, "By today's standards Loisy's critical work sounds eerily contemporary and Lagrange's quaint and traditional."[6] In their own time their published work was debated in a setting deeply divided on matters of criticism. In 1902 the American Sulpician James Driscoll wrote to Houtin to offer his congratulations on *La Question biblique chez les catholiques de France au XIXe siècle*. In his letter he remarked that "controversy between Catholics on questions of Biblical criticism appears more bitter in France than anywhere else."[7] Loisy himself noted that he was targeted in France for saying things that passed without polemic in Britain.[8] However, he undoubtedly contributed to the climate in French Catholicism by choosing as his opponents, on those occasions on which he deigned to reply to critics, conservative rather than more moderate Catholics. Lastly, Loisy's person and his work achieve a prominence in their connection to the condemnation of Modernism, a condemnation that led to his excommunication in 1908, putting an end to his ecclesiastical career and placing him at the threshold of another in the Collège de France.

Given his prominence, Loisy has been approached on any number of fronts. Both adversaries and advocates then and since have debated the sincerity of his beliefs.[9] Numerous inquiries have investigated the sources of his thought and the degree of his dependence on them.[10] His relationship to the papal condemnations of Modernism set forth in *Lamentabili* and *Pascendi* is an area of inquiry opened up by Loisy himself.[11] His relationship to other principal figures of the movement has also attracted interest.[12] Our

---

[6] Nadia M. Lahutsky, "Paris and Jerusalem: Alfred Loisy and Père Lagrange on the Gospel of Mark," *Catholic Biblical Quarterly* 52 (1990), 445.

[7] Albert Houtin, *Une vie de prêtre* (1926). English trs. *The Life of a Priest*, by Winifred S. Whale (London: Watts & Co., 1927), p. 142.

[8] *Mémoires*, vol. I, p. 391.

[9] Ronald Burke has incorporated the work of a number of scholars in his treatment of this issue in "Loisy's Faith: Landshift in Catholic Thought," *Journal of Religion* 60 (1980), 138–164.

[10] A favorite tactic used by his contemporaries was to cast him in the same mold as Renan, i.e., as a mere popularizer of the work of German biblical scholarship. On the subject of his connection with John Henry Newman's work on development there have been a number of studies, among them Nicholas Lash, "Newman and 'A. Firmin'" in Jenkins (ed.), *Newman*, pp. 56–73; Francesco Turvasi, "The Development of Doctrine in John Cardinal Newman and Alfred Loisy" in *John Henry Newman: Theology and Reform*, ed. Michael E. Allsopp and Ronald R. Burke (New York: Garland, 1992), pp. 145–187.

[11] Alfred Loisy, *Simples Réflexions sur le décret du Saint-Office "Lamentabili sane exitu" et sur l'encyclique "Pascendi dominici gregis"* (Ceffonds: chez l'auteur, 1908).

[12] This is exemplified both in writings of fellow Modernists, e.g., Albert Houtin, and of

concerns here will be in part intellectual, situating Loisy with respect
to developments occurring in historical disciplines during the period,
and in part institutional, situating him in relation to Catholicism and
the secular university.

In France *fin-de-siècle* biblical exegesis was affected by a complex
of ideational and institutional changes. History was undergoing a
transformation from a strongly literary enterprise to a critical
discipline. It received competition from the emerging "science of
society" advanced notably by the Durkheimians, and both of these
disciplines informed the aims and methods of the history of
religions. These developments can be seen as part of a larger
transition from "intellectual genres" to more strictly organized
disciplines that was occurring in the latter portion of the nineteenth
century. Moreover, this shift from "rather flexible intellectual
genres to more organized disciplines was directly linked to the
institutional shift from academies and learned societies to reformed universities and professional schools."[13] These emerging
disciplines, along with exegesis, were to a degree influenced by
German currents of thought, as were their institutional settings:
from the 1860s until World War I the French university underwent
structural reform. Greater prominence was given to research and
the creation or upgrading of institutions in which to conduct it. In
this respect as well, Germany provided models, but always with a
certain tension: if the German victory of 1870 was popularly
credited to the Prussian schoolmaster – thereby enhancing the
prestige of German academic achievements – it was nonetheless a
German victory. Ambivalence toward German scholarship increased, fueled by factors such as the Dreyfus Affair and the series
of political crises leading up to 1914.

The secular university became increasingly allied with the Third
Republic. Historians were especially prominent as evangelists of the
republican ideal – with predictable results where the majority of
active Catholics were concerned. The Catholic camp, meanwhile,
had not been devoid of innovation. The Instituts catholiques were
established, critical methods in historical research were not entirely

subsequent scholars. Loome in *Liberal* has situated Loisy in relation to von Hügel in a way
that does little justice to either.
[13] See Johan Heilbron, *The Rise of Social Theory*, trs. Sheila Gogol (Minneapolis: University of
Minnesota Press, 1995), p. 269.

absent (e.g., Louis Duchesne), journals such as the *Revue biblique* were founded, and the French clergy contributed to the membership of the Pontifical Biblical Commission.

From the 1880s, when Loisy was establishing himself at the Paris Institut catholique, until his excommunication in 1908, his exegetical work spanned two worlds, that of Catholicism and that of the secular academy. From his studies at the Ecole Pratique des Hautes Etudes (EPHE) and the Collège de France in the course of his years at the Institut catholique, to his acceptance of a lectureship at the EPHE (1901–1904), he forged institutional links to the university and the scholarly ideas and ideals it represented. His scholarship was open to the more advanced trends in German exegesis – in contrast to the prevailing Catholic biblical scholarship, which exhibited a marked preference for the more conservative British and German exegetes.

This survey situates, in outline, Loisy's exegetical practice in the context of the institutional as well as the intellectual ferment of the Modernist period. Without taking account of his multiple and varied contacts with the university, it is not possible to understand Loisy's emergence as a critical scholar or the course of his critical career. To appreciate the alternative horizons opened via contact with the secular academy, some account must be taken of the thought world of the Catholicism in which Loisy was initially formed. This analysis emphasizes the *practical* assimilation of critical exegesis by Loisy and the secular academy as the decisive context for its acquisition and continued refinement. The progress of critical biblical study in the university is linked to a broader movement, marked by the secularization of disciplines over the period, and reflective of a larger shift in consciousness that occurred in the course of the nineteenth century. The next section will trace the exegete's development from seminary through the publication of *The Gospel and the Church*, highlighting the theology dominant in Catholicism, alternative perspectives to which he was exposed, and some of his strategies for importing those into the church.

FROM MANUAL MEMORIZATION TO EXEGETICAL PRACTICE

From the 1880s Loisy had the impression of witnessing what Emile Poulat has called "the end of the mental universe consecrated by the

Council of Trent."[14] This mental universe reflected and, reciprocally, legitimated a set of institutional structures shaped by that
council. Avery Dulles has identified and analyzed this version of
church in his institutional model, "the view that defines the church
primarily in terms of its visible structures, especially the rights and
powers of its officers."[15] More concretely, in his study of the theology
of the magisterium of the Roman School which was influential
throughout much of the nineteenth century and well into the
twentieth, T. Howland Sanks has stressed the divine-human character of this conception of ecclesiastical authority. As a continuation
of the Incarnation, the church united the divine and human on
earth. This view lent a more than human character to its teaching
authority and reinforced its hierarchical nature.[16] The attempts to
extend the church's authority into the political order, the socio-
economic order, and the cultural order have been discussed earlier
in Paul Misner's "Catholic anti-Modernism: the ecclesial setting."
Moreover, Ralph Keifer has argued that this institutional, hierarchical, and juridical understanding of church was not simply promulgated by theologians, but the very experience of worship
communicated it more pervasively to the faithful.[17]

An institutional emphasis on hierarchical authority found its
analog in the understanding of theology and its relation to other
disciplines. By the latter nineteenth century neo-Thomism had
largely succeeded in eliminating potential rivals and establishing
theological hegemony.[18] As a supernatural science of faith
("science" being understood in an Aristotelian, deductive sense)
theology derived its first principles from revelation: "In an Aristotelian 'science of faith' the Catholic theologian can proceed from
his revealed first principles through his naturally known minor
premises to his theologically certain conclusions."[19] Its status as a
genuine science was secured with the aid of philosophy. The latter
provided the structure through which the various parts of theology
were organized into a single, interrelated body of knowledge. Since
philosophy derived its first principles from the natural light of

---

[14] Quoted in Raymond de Boyer de Sainte Suzanne, *Alfred Loisy, entre la foi et l'incroyance* (Paris: Editions du Centurion, 1968), p. 36.

[15] Avery Dulles, S.J., *Models of the Church* (Garden City, New York: Image Books, 1978), p. 39.

[16] T. Howland Sanks, *Authority in the Church: A Study in Changing Paradigms* (Missoula, Montana: Scholars Press, 1974).

[17] See Ralph A. Keifer, *Blessed and Broken* (Wilmington, Delaware: Michael Glazier, 1982).

[18] See McCool, *Catholic.*   [19] Ibid., p. 225.

human reason (hence its character as a natural science), it remains subordinate to theology.

On this conception the higher certitude of theology's first principles, being revealed, served to distinguish theology from every other science. As a corollary it established the subordination of philosophy and history to theology. Hence the tendency to want "to set up history as judge, to consider it the primary element in the formation of judgments and the foundation of opinions, outside of and anterior to all doctrinal authority" is censured as "unfortunate and false" by one scholastic writer. He counterposes theology as "the science of the principles whose application and facts are studied by history; but, these principles are infallible insofar as they are revealed; and if history takes them as the norm of its judgments, it has every guarantee against error."[20]

If history is tied to theology, ecclesiastical history is all the more so, specifically to doctrine. Indeed, this form of historical study becomes less the study of facts than of doctrines. This same doctrinal emphasis reappears in this theology's conception of the proper role of exegesis.[21] The proof-texting role assigned to exegesis recapitulates the ahistorical, "essentialist" character of neo-scholasticism generally and neo-Thomism more particularly. The comparatively marginal status assigned to biblical studies in the seminary curriculum for much of the nineteenth century reflects its marginality in neo-scholasticism.[22]

Homologous with this understanding of theology is a conception of the role of the theologian. Under the rubric of theological responsibility John Thiel has examined the theological vocation as it relates to the issue of authority. An emphasis on God as the author of the truth of salvation in scripture and tradition, coupled with the conviction of the perennial and unchanging nature of that truth, yielded what he terms the "classical paradigm" of theological responsibility. It viewed the theologian's task as "the mimetic *representation* of an objective revelation," which "took the form of speculative commentary on scripture or commentary-based speculation."[23] The

---

[20] J.-B. Aubry, *Essai sur la méthode des études ecclésiastiques en France*, vol. II (Lille: Desclée, De Brouwer, n.d.), pp. 457, 452.

[21] Ibid., p. 382.

[22] See, for example, Christian Dumoulin, *Un séminaire français au 19ème siècle: le recrutement, la formation, la vie des clercs à Bourges* (Paris: Téqui, 1978).

[23] John E. Thiel, *Imagination & Authority* (Minneapolis: Fortress Press, 1991), pp. 21, 19.

stress on faithful representation of a perennial tradition devalues the theologian's creativity and originality – traits that, by contrast, will figure more heavily in theologies that bear the imprint of the Enlightenment.

This sketch has identified the intellectual and institutional matrix which initially formed Loisy and which he sought to reform through his teaching and publications. A look at his early reactions is now in order.

Since Vigouroux's *Manuel biblique*, which came to enjoy a considerable authority, was not published until 1879, Loisy had to wait until his entrance into the Institut catholique to encounter the Sulpician's exegesis and apologetic.[24] His autobiographical writings do not name the manual in use during his years at the Châlons seminary, but a brief remark does reveal the caliber of the teaching. The professor of scripture and church history is characterized as "a pious individual, as innocent as possible of critical method, who had us recite from the most pitiful manuals, and who was capable of pointing out to us how St. John the apostle had predicted in his *Apocalypse* – in rather obscure but nonetheless intelligible terms – the Vatican Council."[25]

Despite the very real shortcomings of the instruction in scripture that Loisy received at the Institut catholique, it served to enlarge his critical horizons, if only backhandedly. In the course of refuting rationalist positions, Vigouroux did have the merit of representing them rather faithfully. He thereby acquainted Loisy with conclusions reached by critical exegesis along with the insufficiency of Catholic responses. Thus "the weakness of the official apologetics of M. Vigouroux," which Houtin set before readers of *La Question biblique chez les catholiques de France au XIXe siècle* in 1902, had already been apparent to Loisy more than two decades earlier. Still, exposure to critical conclusions is one thing, acquiring critical methods another. Here the Institut faculty was helpful – to a point – in the person of the church historian, Louis Duchesne. The latter had already achieved a certain notoriety for the corrosive effects his critical approach had worked on Christian legends. However, he resolutely avoided using those methods on scriptural terrain. Thus in March of 1882, in reflecting privately on the difficulty of finding the proper

---

[24] It was not actually until the academic year of 1881–1882 that Loisy followed Vigouroux's lectures.

[25] *Duel*, p. 62 (my translation).

balance between faith and science, and on the danger of according too little or refusing too much to rationalism, Loisy wrote that he found himself without a guide into that middle way.[26] Much of his progress to that point had been the fruit of independent study, initially in Châlons and continuing at the Paris Institut. To learn critical *practice* he would have to go beyond the institutional confines of Catholic instruction. He found it at the Collège de France in the lectures of Ernest Renan.

In his autobiographical writings Loisy has left a description of Renan's approach to teaching, making clear that it emphasized procedure over conclusions.[27] In a short piece devoted to Renan's instruction at the Collège de France, Loisy left a more detailed recollection, showing that he not only gained exposure to the most recent German scholarship but also learned how to use the French critical works that he had previously tried to work with on his own.[28]

Thus, throughout the 1880s Loisy came increasingly to live in two intellectual worlds, a condition he had to reckon with when he began to publish in the 1890s. On the one hand, while Catholic exegesis was not immune to the effects of rationalist criticism, for the most part it continued to function along traditional lines. In 1897 a member of the Paris Institut faculty wrote that "our professors of sacred scripture, very well-informed about the results of criticism, safeguard with a pious respect all the rights of tradition." Those rights included the Mosaic authorship of Genesis, defended against the theories of rationalist critics by Vigouroux, and the authenticity of the book of Daniel, upheld by Fillion.[29] On the other hand, by this time there was a discernible "scientific" approach to exegesis, captured in W. Ward Gasque's description of New Testament scholarship:

New Testament criticism became a "science" in its own right, entirely independent of the work of the ordinary literary critic or historian of antiquity; and there developed a body of "assured results of criticism", based on the principles of "scientific" exegesis, which was accepted as

[26] Ibid., p. 90. Loisy, *Mémoires*, vol. I, pp. 102, 103.
[27] *Duel*, pp. 92–93. *Mémoires*, vol. I, pp. 117–118.
[28] Alfred Loisy, "Le Cours de Renan au Collège de France," *Journal de psychologie normale et pathologique* 20 (1923), 325–330.
[29] Alfred Baudrillart, "La Faculté de théologie catholique de Paris à la mort de Mgr d'Hulst" in *L'Enseignement catholique dans la France contemporaine* (Paris: Bloud & Cie, 1910), pp. 463–465. Non-coincidently, Renan had dealt with the areas addressed by Vigouroux and Fillion in his lectures at the Collège de France.

200 C. J. T. TALAR

authoritative. *Neutestamentler* began to understand their task as that of adding to the work of previous scholars, rather than starting on the basis of inductive exegesis. New Testament research came to be regarded as *new* discovery, each successive scholar re-working the material of his predecessor, accepting the bulk of his conclusions (*if* he happened to be in the right critical tradition!) and adding a new point or two – thus advancing the cause of scientific exegesis.[30]

Cast in a Kuhnian framework, this sounds much like an emerging paradigm beginning to develop its tradition of "normal science." Even without the Kuhnian conceptualization it indicates an emerging alternative to the traditional orthodoxy. *Mutatis mutandis,* something similar could be said regarding Old Testament scholarship.[31]

The traditional–critical divisions in French biblical studies represented thus far were further complicated by confessional differences. Any attempt to understand the exegesis of the period must include not only Catholics of whatever critical persuasion and "independent" critics who stood outside any confessional allegiance, but Protestants as well. In his study of French exegesis that encompasses the period of interest here, Alan Jones used these cutting points to divide the field, distinguishing Catholic, Protestant, and Independent sectors. Renan may be taken as a point of reference in situating all three.

The Independent sector constitutes a tradition of French-speaking scholarship, initiated with Renan's work on the origins of Christianity, which treated it as "a religious phenomenon to be investigated with all the resources of history, unaided by theology."[32] Jones takes care to note that this position was far from static. It was "a stance continually to be redefined according to religious and academic circumstances"[33] whose boundaries were fluid with respect to the other two confessional sectors. Renan also had a hand in shaping the Catholic sector, generating antipathy toward critical methods and German scholarship, while reinforcing the defensive position

[30] W. Ward Gasque, *A History of the Interpretation of the Acts of the Apostles* (Peabody, Massachusetts: Hendrickson, 1989), p. 106. Cf. John Riches' assessment in *A Century of New Testament Study* (Valley Forge, Pennsylvania: Trinity Press International, 1993), pp. 1–2.
[31] See, for example, John Rogerson, *Old Testament Criticism in the Nineteenth Century: England and Germany* (Philadelphia: Fortress Press, 1985), especially part three; Henri Cazelles, "L'Exégèse scientifique au XXe siècle: l'Ancien Testament" in Savart and Aletti, *Le Monde,* pp. 441–471. Thomas Kuhn's analysis of scientific development can be found in his *The Structure of Scientific Revolutions* (Chicago: University of Chicago Press, 1970).
[32] Alan H. Jones, *Independence and Exegesis* (Tübingen: J. C. B. Mohr, 1983), p. v.
[33] Ibid., p. vi.

that had come to characterize Catholicism more generally.[34] It is worth recalling that Loisy attended Renan's lectures in the early 1880s with the ambition of someday refuting him with his own critical weapons.[35] By a sizable majority Catholic biblical scholars largely rejected outright critical methods and their conclusions. However, a handful of Catholic scholars cautiously accepted the methods and searched for more palatable results from their application. Renan may additionally serve as a touchstone for situating the Protestant sector. The Liberal Protestant presence in this area was very prominent, and Protestants exercised an influence disproportionate to their relatively small numbers. Liberal Protestant exegesis served as a conduit for German critical scholarship. It also borrowed methods from psychology, ethnography, the history of religions, and philology. Unlike the Catholic sector, an influential portion of the Protestant sector openly embraced historical criticism and could share some of the same positions on the biblical documents as Renan. Nonetheless, as both sides perceived, the animating spirit in each case was different. If from Renan's point of view the orthodox theologian could be compared to a caged bird, the liberal theologian resembled a bird with clipped wings. The theologian of whatever stamp retains a dogmatic interest; only the historian is disinterested and enjoys full freedom of movement.[36]

Having delineated something of the topography of biblical studies, Jones goes on to suggest some of its movement:

Any serious "scientific" work could only be found in the thinly-inhabited and difficult terrain in between the contending forces. In practice, this meant the work of Catholic "progressives", of Liberal Protestants and of those "independents" who avoided the extremes of dogmatic rationalism. Each of these categories was able to draw upon established traditions: not only was there the dominant presence of Renan behind them, but Catholics had a master in Duchesne, Protestants had a close affiliation with the world of German scholarship and in the independent sector, the school of Durkheim was building a tradition of the scientific study of religion as a social force, as well as the less radical but solid work undertaken in the history of religions at EPHE.[37]

---

[34] A survey of Catholic response to Renan's *Vie de Jésus* (1863) can be found in Vytas V. Gaigalas, *Ernest Renan and His French Catholic Critics* (North Quincy, Massachusetts: Christopher Publishing House, 1972).

[35] *Duel*, p. 94.

[36] Renan's comparison is quoted in Jean Pommier, *Renan et Strasbourg* (Paris: Félix Alcan, 1926), pp. 54–55.

[37] Jones, *Independence*, pp. 52–53.

The task of Loisy and other critical exegetes within Catholicism, then, was to *make* a space for critical methods and positions "tainted" by French Liberal Protestantism or German rationalism, marry those to the approaches opened up by the emergent disciplines of the history of religions and sociology, but without compromising the essentials of the tradition. The task was one of negotiating a field of forces to migrate Catholic opinion from its defensive posture.

Loisy formulated a strategy for this ideological migration during his tenure at the Institut catholique. He saw the formation of ecclesiastical students as crucial to a receptive climate for critical work and a future source of support in its favor. While forming a cadre of clerics who would greet criticism with understanding instead of scandal, he would concentrate on works of detail, leaving their larger implications implicit, and confine himself to less controversial areas of biblical studies.[38] Accordingly his early publications were detailed histories of the canons of both testaments[39] or analyses of less controverted areas of the Old Testament.[40]

Despite his caution, Loisy's work encountered opposition. In a climate in which Vigouroux's *Manuel biblique* could prove unsettling for some ecclesiastics, such opposition would have occasioned little surprise.[41] When, such gradualist strategies notwithstanding, Loisy did run afoul of church authorities, however, the catalyst came from an unexpected quarter: from a well-meaning advocate rather than an adversary. It took the form of Mgr Maurice d'Hulst's 1893 article, "La Question biblique," which set in motion a series of events that led to Loisy's dismissal from his position at the Institut.[42] The exegete used the controversy generated by d'Hulst's article as an occasion to set out rather clearly his own position on biblical inspiration and the related larger question of the connection between exegesis and theology. It reads like a mirror image of Aubry's position, noted earlier.[43] Loisy advocated the independence

[38] *Mémoires*, vol. 1, p. 136.
[39] Loisy, *Histoire*, and *Histoire du canon du Nouveau Testament* (Paris: J. Maisonneuve, 1891).
[40] "Les Proverbes de Salomon," *Revue des religions* 2 (1890), 28–44, 97–115, 217–240, published in book form that same year, and *Le livre de Job* (Amiens: Rousseau-Leroy, 1892).
[41] See *Mémoires*, vol. 1, pp. 80, 139–142, 215–221, for instances of anxiety provoked by Vigouroux and opposition aroused by Loisy's teaching and publications.
[42] Loisy describes these events in *Duel*, pp. 137–154, and in *Mémoires*, vol. 1, ch. 8–9. More sympathetic to d'Hulst is Alfred Baudrillart, *Vie de Mgr d'Hulst* (Paris: J. de Gigord, 1928), vol. 1, pp. 480–492, and vol. 11, ch. 21.
[43] See note 20.

of criticism from the outdated traditional notion of inspiration and from theological control more generally. As he later summed up his article, "basically, it sanctioned the emancipation of scientific exegesis from dogma and theology, while at the same time it announced the formidable loss suffered by the traditionally received opinions as a result of critical work."[44]

Loisy's forced exit from the Institut catholique marked the end of his teaching career in Catholic higher education. It would have the unforeseen result of facilitating an alternative career in the secular university and an unforeseen impact on the nature of his published work. In the position given him as chaplain of a convent school in a Paris suburb, Loisy was largely deprived of the bibliographic resources necessary to do serious exegetical work. At the same time, obliged to give religious instruction, he was motivated to reflect on the presentation of Christian doctrine. This reflection engaged him with apologetic issues and was reinforced by his contact with the work of John Henry Newman. Part of these labors found published expression in the series of "Firmin" articles, interrupted by Cardinal Richard's censure in 1900. Another portion formed the core of *The Gospel and the Church*, in which critical exegesis of the Gospels was brought to bear on issues of contemporary concern for the church. The portrait that emerged from Loisy's reconstruction was markedly different from the traditional one. In lieu of the church founded by Jesus Christ with its essential hierarchical structures in place, its sevenfold sacramental system operative, and its "deposit" of faith handed over in order to be faithfully handed on, Loisy accentuated the apocalyptic element in the gospel tradition. Jesus preached the kingdom, a future event very near at hand. Under the influence of this eschatological perspective Jesus could not consciously and intentionally have founded a church replete with hierarchy, worship, and doctrine. This element of discontinuity was resolved by recourse to a developmental perspective, couched in organic metaphors. The church in its various aspects developed after the death of Jesus in response to the varied environments in which his followers found themselves. His teaching was brought to new expression in Greek philosophy, the church was structurally influenced by the political conditions in which it existed.

---

[44] *Mémoires*, vol. 1, p. 261. The complete text of "La Question biblique et l'inspiration des écritures" is accessible in Alfred Loisy, *Etudes bibliques* (Paris: Alphonse Picard et Fils, 1901), pp. 38–60.

For this mode of apologetics, then, continuity is not secured by the faithful repetition of content, or the replication of structure, but by the ongoing, vital activity of Catholicism itself. Put another way, continuity is not dependent fundamentally on content or on structure, but on process: "the best apology for all that lives lies in the life itself."[45]

This approach has important implications for the vocation of the theologian in the present and for the directions the church may take in the future. John Thiel's typology of theological responsibility counterposed a "romantic" paradigm to the "classical" conception exemplified earlier in neo-Thomism. A developmental understanding of tradition, a development primarily accessible via experience, privileges the theologian's creativity in "the imaginative *construction* of the historical experience of salvation." The romantic paradigm values theological originality and recognizes that "the theological innovation of today could very well be the time-honored belief of the future."[46] Both stand in marked contrast to the classical paradigm's devaluation of the theologian's creativity and its readiness to equate theological novelty with error.

The theological innovation of today might also be the time-honored structure of the future – which returns us to the discussion of church in *The Gospel and the Church*. As a living organism, the "Church became, at important moments, what it had to become in order not to decline and perish, dragging the gospel down with it."[47] Since with Loisy the developmental process is left rather open-ended, there is the distinct possibility that in a political climate that has moved from monarchy to republic, the church may continue to adapt and modify in fundamental respects.

We may even go further, and conjecture that the Church, when dealing with those who recognize her authority, will find a procedure more conformable with the fundamental equality and personal dignity of all Christians. In the universal levelling of ranks which is in prospect, the members of the ecclesiastical hierarchy may be less great personages in the eyes of the world, without in any way losing the rights of their ministry, which will assume again, more visibly, their essential form of duties.[48]

On substantive issues (e.g., its reconstruction of Christian origins,

---

[45] Alfred Loisy, *L'Evangile et l'Eglise* (Paris: Alphonse Picard, 1902), p. 170. *Gospel*, p. 220.
[46] Thiel, *Imagination*, pp. 21, 23.   [47] *Gospel*, pp. 149–150.   [48] Ibid., p. 175.

its ecclesiology); on methodological approaches (e.g., its exegesis, its apologetics); on its conception of theology and the theological vocation, Loisy's work stood at variance with the dominant theology. Furthermore, in *The Gospel and the Church* he presented the product of his thought in popular form rather than in the technical accents of scientific scholarship. Condemnation of this book and several of its companions was but the prelude to a more detailed, encompassing, and violent condemnation of the movement of thought it was perceived to represent.

To sum up, Loisy was exposed in seminary and later at the Institut catholique to the ready-made models of dogmatic exegesis, which utilized Scripture in a subordinate, proof-texting role. He developed a critical alternative to that inductively, first comparing the Hebrew and Greek versions of the Old Testament on his own. Without access to any critical commentaries he "could make no troubling discovery."[49] His private study of Tischendorf's classical edition of the New Testament, while he was at the Institut catholique, provided him with an acute sense of the contradictions among the Gospels. Vigouroux's lectures afforded abundant evidence that in non-Catholic scholarship there were (unacceptable) alternative ways of resolving them, but the acquisition of a method for dealing with such anomalies came through Renan. What Renan transmitted to Loisy was not so much theories or conceptual models, but certain skills. Newman's work appears to have played a role in furnishing a conceptual framework and, equally importantly, a legitimation for lines of thought Loisy was already working through on his own. That developmental approach undergirds both the "Firmin" articles and *The Gospel and the Church*, incorporating the results of Loisy's exegetical practice into Catholicism in the form of an innovative apologetic.

FROM CATHOLIC SECTOR TO INDEPENDENT SECTOR

Thus far the exposition has highlighted intellectual tensions in Loisy's work vis-à-vis Catholicism and the Catholic institutional context, while leaving the role played by the French university largely in shadow. Since the latter constituted the institutional context for the independent sector of exegesis, some attention must

[49] *Duel*, p. 79 (my translation).

be devoted to its structure and its relationship to the politics of Republican France.

Although the French educational system had been the target of intermittent attempts at reform prior to the Franco-Prussian war, in the aftermath of defeat a general consensus favoring significant change developed within the academy, and higher education became an important political issue. A viable university system was perceived to be vital to the survival of the Third Republic. By the mid-1880s various constituencies favoring reform had coalesced and over the next two decades succeeded in reconstituting the system of higher education. In these various initiatives historians played a prominent role. Already under the Second Empire the practice of historical study underwent increasing professionalization as it moved from a more literary orientation to one that emphasized an objectivity immune to the influences of ideology. This period also saw the founding of journals that enforced professional standards of scholarship. Of considerable importance for the development of the profession and for the course of university reform were the historians who were strategically placed to extend the pedagogical innovations of the EPHE to the entire French university system. The "scientific" research orientation of the latter, with its emphasis on the small, specialized seminar oriented to the practical formation of future professionals, signaled a decisive shift away from the large lecture format with general topics aimed at heterogeneous audiences.[50] Within the university they found allies in the practitioners of sociology and the history of religions, especially at the time of the Dreyfus Affair. Outside the university their decision to defend the political institutions of the Third Republic forged a *mariage de convenance* with republican statesmen. This arrangement proved to be a mixed blessing. As George Weisz points out, "The controversy over the liberty of higher studies was essentially a struggle for political control over educational institutions. The Université and the Church, which had once been at the center of the debate, were now little more than pawns in the strategies of rival political

---

[50] Sandra Horvath-Peterson, *Victor Duruy & French Education* (Baton Rouge: Louisiana State University Press, 1984); George Weisz, *The Emergence of Modern Universities in France, 1863–1914* (Princeton, New Jersey: Princeton University Press, 1983); William R. Keylor, *Academy and Community* (Cambridge, Massachusetts: Harvard University Press, 1975); and Charles-Olivier Carbonell, *Histoire et historiens* (Toulouse: Privat, 1976) provide background to these developments.

groups."[51] Despite opposition of the type described by George Tavard earlier in this volume, reformers succeeded in establishing scientific methods of research in French scholarship, expanding the institutional positions from which such research could be conducted, and gaining political support for their endeavors.

The secular university was not only the site of critical historical scholarship in nineteenth-century France. On Paul Desjardin's testimony it also provided a conduit for these methods to influence Catholics. "The initiation into critical methods, unexpected and unwanted by the clergy, came to it from without. The secular laboratories, particularly the Ecole des Hautes Etudes, little by little opened new horizons in three or four gifted clerical minds."[52] Two of those "gifted clerical minds" that Desjardins undoubtedly had in mind were Louis Duchesne and Alfred Loisy. Duchesne had been formed at the EPHE after attending the course at the Roman College. He brought the ethos of the former to his teaching at the Institut catholique, both in the Faculty of Letters and in the Faculty of Theology.[53] In 1882, the same year Loisy began to attend Renan's lectures at the Collège de France, he took up Assyriology and Egyptology at EPHE. Though he dropped the latter after one year as less important to his biblical work, he remained with the former for four consecutive years. In 1883 he added a course in Ethiopian, where he met Père Méchineau, S.J.[54] The tenor of this Jesuit's later work[55] argues against any simple evaluation of the EPHE as an academic equivalent to the magical role ascribed to the Gare de Montparnasse in transforming the faith of French rural Catholics who passed through it into unbelief. Surely, however, it is non-coincidental that the two faculty members at the Institut outstanding for their commitments to a scientific approach to history with modern methods had exposure to a model very different from the one prevalent in Catholicism.[56]

While still at the Institut catholique Loisy aspired to a position at

[51] Weisz, *Emergence*, p. 107.
[52] Paul Desjardins, *Catholicisme et critique* (Paris: Cahiers de la quinzaine, 1905), p. 21.
[53] Claude Bressolette, "De l'école de théologie à l'unité d'enseignement et de recherche de théologie et de sciences religieuses" in *Les Cent Ans de la faculté de théologie*, ed. Joseph Doré (Paris: Beauchesne, 1992), pp. 22–23.
[54] *Mémoires*, vol. I, p. 117.
[55] See, for example, Lucien Méchineau, S.J., *L'Idée du livre inspiré* (Rome: Imprimerie Pontificale de l'Institut Pie IX, 1908).
[56] See Bernard Sesboüé, "Avant le modernisme: Louis Duchesne et Alfred Loisy à la faculté de théologie de l'Institut catholique de Paris" in Doré (ed.), *Les Cent Ans*, pp. 99–139.

the EPHE, but his hopes were not then realized.[57] Toward the end of 1900 he was more successful: though no chair was available, he received an appointment as a free lecturer with a temporary grant in the section of the science of religion. His teaching served as the basis for future publications. More importantly, a post in the secular academy provided an institutional support for the exegetical auton- omy he claimed in principle. As he later observed, "to censure teaching given at the Sorbonne appeared too daring a measure, and it was not dreamed of, at least under Leo XIII."[58] Loisy continued at the EPHE until 1904, when he gave up his lectureship in the midst of the protracted negotiations surrounding his submission to the condemnation of five of his books by the Holy Office at the end of 1903.

The excommunication he expected in 1904 did not arrive until 1908. Shortly thereafter the death of Jean Réville created vacancies at both the EPHE and the Collège de France. Loisy opted to offer himself as a candidate for the latter position in the history of religions. He was ultimately successful and delivered his inaugural lecture in April of 1909.[59] In assuming the chair he was obliged to enlarge his scholarly horizons beyond the Judeo-Christian tradition and to expand his intellectual horizons to engage disciplines such as sociology.[60] These changes soon made their impact on his published work. In *A propos d'histoire des religions* (1911) he gathered a number of articles previously published over the two preceding years in various periodicals. In the course of this work he acknowledged that "the science of religions is still in its infancy"[61] but argued that it had a significant role to play in national education following the Law of Separation. As a science, the history of religions is committed to a rigorous neutrality: it is neither an advocate of any confessional position nor an adversary of religious belief. In treating the "facts" alone it is well suited to an educational system which claims

---

[57] *Duel*, pp. 117–118.   [58] Ibid., p. 213 (my translation).

[59] Loisy details the events surrounding his candidacy in his *Mémoires*, vol. III, chs. 42 and 43.

[60] Loisy acknowledged the importance of the sociology of religion in his *Leçon d'ouverture du cours d'histoire des religions au Collège de France* (Paris: Nourry, 1909), pp. 33–37. For continuities and divergences with the Durkheimian school, see W. S. F. Pickering, *Durkheim's Sociology of Religion* (London: Routledge & Kegan Paul, 1984).

[61] Alfred Loisy, *A propos d'histoire des religions* (Paris: Nourry, 1911), p. 9. Some years earlier Durkheim had advocated that lessons on the history of religions should replace those on the history of philosophy in the French educational system. Steven Lukes, *Emile Durkheim* (Stanford, California: Stanford University Press, 1985), p. 360 note.

autonomy vis-à-vis religious confessions. He makes it clear that Catholic Modernism has well and truly been left behind.[62]

Loisy's intellectual evolution from the Catholic sector to the Independent sector can be seen against the backdrop of a larger series of shifts that occurred over the course of the nineteenth century. Roman Catholic Modernist attempts to revolutionize Catholic theology form but a small episode in the larger drama of political and industrial revolutions. In France the former had a greater impact on perceptions of a breakdown of intellectual and social structures than the latter. In various ways political thinkers, novelists, theologians, historians, and social scientists responded to what Bruce Mazlish has termed "the 'connections problem.'"[63] Behind the diversity of forms which responses – whether celebrations or laments – assumed, he sees a shift in primary metaphor: "the snapping of belief in the Great Chain of Being, and the substitution for it of a Newtonian . . . and then, additionally, an evolutionary universe." The metaphor for the latter was a "web of interconnections," and this became "the image which summed up the way human beings thought of themselves in relation to God, Nature, and their fellow Men."[64] While the hierarchical thinking that characterizes the "chain" metaphor can be traced back at least to Plato, it assumed special prominence in the eighteenth century and then in the following century underwent an intensity and quality of challenge that differed from anything preceding – precisely what made the challenge "modern."

Mazlish not only surfaces these metaphors but also suggests something of their implications:

A chain . . . involves the notion of a linear linking, a hierarchical ordering, a unilateral causal relation, which either has to be rigidly maintained or painfully broken. It speaks either of secure restraint or oppressive servitude, depending on one's attitude and place in the chain. Web, on the other

---

[62] See "De la vulgarisation et de l'enseignement de l'histoire des religions," *A propos d'histoire des religions*, pp. 100–165.

[63] Bruce Mazlish, *A New Science: The Breakdown of Connections and the Birth of Sociology* (University Park, Pennsylvania: The Pennsylvania State University Press, 1989), pp. ix–x.

[64] Ibid., pp. 32, 24. The reception of evolutionary perspectives in France via Lamarck, Spencer, and Darwin is treated in Linda L. Clark, *Social Darwinism in France* (Tuscaloosa, Alabama: University of Alabama Press, 1984).

hand, is many-stranded, and represents an awareness of constant pulls and tugs, emanating from many directions, of many possible lines that hold one to others. It is an organic metaphor (whereas chain is largely mechanical), and it speaks of living adjustments and of growth.[65]

The neo-Thomist conception of theology and its relation to other disciplines reflects the chain metaphor. As a former partisan of neo-Thomism, the modernist George Tyrrell was well situated to criticize this theological attitude. In the course of doing so he communicates a sense of the security that could be derived from theology's qualitatively superior status:

If God's word vouches for any one science that science must be the rule and criterion of all the rest. To be under its control is not slavery but liberty – liberty from error. Nay, it must be a cause of rapid and fruitful progression. While an unaided astronomy or geology or history is delayed and weakened by uncertainties; that which derives were it only three or four fixed and infallible truths, from Scripture or Tradition, has a solid foundation to build upon, and builds itself up rapidly and securely.[66]

As Mazlish points out, one person's security is another's constraint. Loisy's call for autonomy for historical-critical exegesis vis-à-vis theology and dogma was seconded by other biblicists such as Mgr Mignot and echoed by practitioners of other disciplines. Maurice Blondel, for instance, rejected a conception of philosophical apologetics that would entail that "philosophy lends its services and, so to speak, commits itself in advance, or that its conclusions can be homogeneous or continuous with those of theology or subordinate to them, or if it is expected to take account of claims which exceed its competence or to sacrifice, even on a single point, its method and its scientific autonomy."[67]

The "web" metaphor privileges process over position, an emphasis that is particularly apparent in Loisy's apologetic, and most notably in *The Gospel and the Church*. The prominence in that book of an organic metaphorical network has received attention elsewhere.[68] Autonomy in the intellectual realm finds its analog in the political

---

[65] Mazlish, *A New Science*, p. 245. Heilbron's depiction of a transition from intellectual genres to disciplines fits with Mazlish's "web" metaphor. In the area of sociology the metaphor resonates well with Warren Schmaus's characterization of the Durkheimian research program in terms of "intellectual niches." See Warren Schmaus, *Durkheim's Philosophy of Science and the Sociology of Knowledge* (Chicago: University of Chicago Press, 1994).

[66] Tyrrell, *Medievalism*, p. 123.   [67] Blondel, *Letter*, p. 165.

[68] C. J. T. Talar, *Metaphor and Modernist: Alfred Loisy and His Neo-Thomist Critics* (Lanham, Maryland: University Press of America, 1987).

realm in the call for autonomy from ecclesiastical control.[69] It is worth recalling here the interdisciplinary character of exegesis in the Protestant sector, with its methodological interconnections. And it is hardly coincidental that, when Loisy received his lectureship at the EPHE in 1900, Cardinal Richard felt obliged to warn him of the dangers of exposure to the Protestant presence there and the nature of their ideas.[70] After Loisy's break with the church a weblike interconnectedness is present in his interdisciplinary characterization of the history of religions and the role he conceives for the latter in an ideologically diverse educational system. "Anthropology, ethnography, sociology come to the aid of history and help it to understand better the religious phenomenon in all its diversity."[71]

Poulat has noted that Modernism was a consequence of the secularization of religious sciences.[72] Access to the secular university enabled a number of Roman Catholic scholars to gain contact with these disciplines and their ethos. This contact either occurred directly, as in Loisy's case at the EPHE and Collège de France, or less directly, via exposure to the teaching and publications of scholars such as Duchesne and Loisy. Given the manual tradition of theological formation in Catholicism and the way in which it was taught in seminaries, the emergence of an initial generation of critical scholars within the church is impossible to understand without taking account of the development of the secular academy over this period. Mazlish's work can suggestively illuminate this secularization of disciplines as part of a larger shift in consciousness that occurred in the course of the nineteenth century, for the most part lamented by Catholic theologians and hierarchy, but welcomed by some. In this latter current, Modernism can be situated.

---

[69] See *Gospel*, pp. 172–175.   [70] *Duel*, pp. 209–210.
[71] *A propos d'histoire des religions*, p. 102.
[72] De Boyer de Sainte Suzanne, *Alfred Loisy*, p. 38.

PART III

*Friedrich von Hügel and Maude Petre
in England*

CHAPTER 8

The Modernist as mystic

Lawrence Barmann

The questions a historian puts to his evidence determine the quality of the history he writes. Of equal importance to this quality is the level of analytic consciousness attained by the historian concerning the assumptions underlying his questions. To ask what the Roman Catholic Modernist crisis was and why it occurred when it did presupposes a number of assumptions about the ecclesial culture within which the crisis took place and about the individuals caught in the conflict. This last point about the individuals caught in the conflict is of special importance because the papal encyclical *Pascendi dominici gregis* not only created *Modernism*; it also created *Modernists* – as though dozens of individuals of varying ages and experiences and of a multitude of nationalities, with different degrees of religious development and levels of intellectual culture, thought with one mind and pursued one goal.[1] The reality was rather different. No two so-called Modernists, in fact, shared more than a superficial identity; and one of them, at least, was simply unique, not only, of course, in who he was, but also in what he thought and did and why. The operative questions, then, in the task undertaken in these pages, will be: what can we know of Baron Friedrich von Hügel's personal religious development?; what was the ecclesial cultural context of this development?; and what was von Hügel's perception of and reaction to this context? To delineate responses to these questions in their inter-relationships would go a long way to help one understand why von Hügel was a Modernist, to determine what kind of Modernist he was, and to correct some of the misapprehensions

---

[1] Obviously this is not to deny that, in an era when theological pluralism in both methodology and concept was unthinkable to church authorities, many individuals in every western European nation and elsewhere were rethinking the great questions of Christianity. What it does deny is that this was an organized movement of rebellion as *Pascendi* would have it, and that the individuals involved were destructive-minded persons out to ruin the church as, again, *Pascendi* argues.

about him which have become accepted in the historiography of both von Hügel and Modernism.[2]

On 5 May 1870 Friedrich von Hügel turned eighteen years old, and within the next several months two events took place which would radically shape the remainder of his life. One of the events was existential, and the other institutional. The first was a personal religious crisis and subsequent religious commitment. The second was the Vatican Council's proclamation that the pope was infallible. The unfolding results of both events as they affected von Hügel's life in its development within the Roman Catholic Church over the next half century would make his ecclesial conflicts, if not inevitable, at least not unlikely.

As a boy and adolescent von Hügel's religious involvement seems to have been curious and detached at best, and traditional and perfunctory at worst. He even acknowledged in later life that between the ages of thirteen and eighteen he would have hesitated to claim himself a Catholic.[3] Nevertheless at the age of fifteen he made his first Holy Communion,[4] and a little over two years after this he

[2] The historiographical tradition concerning von Hügel and Modernism is more easily deconstructed at the end of the twentieth century than at any earlier period because of the increasing availability of letters and documents from various participants in the Modernist crisis. Some of von Hügel's contemporaries who were involved began the interpretation of him after his death which suggests that the Baron was either duplicitous or naive or, somehow, both. Alfred Fawkes (1925), Maude Petre (1927 and 1937), Alfred Loisy (1933), and Maisie Ward (1937), all writing within the first dozen years following von Hügel's death, laid the foundations and set the structure within which subsequent writers would mostly frame their interpretations of him. Loisy had been formally repudiated by Catholicism, and Fawkes had himself formally repudiated the Roman Church; but von Hügel had remained faithful to the end. Both men subtly scapegoated the Baron in self-justification. Maude Petre had been in love with Tyrrell and would accept no criticism of her hero or of his memory; and von Hügel had criticized Tyrrell. During a period of aggressive thought control within Catholic orthodoxy, Maisie Ward was concerned to protect the reputation of her father, Wilfrid Ward, whom she idolized. So the father was measured against the Baron, and the latter alone of the two, in the daughter's estimation at least, had tried to stretch the Catholic framework too far. Of those writing about von Hügel in the 1930s only Maurice Nédoncelle (1935) tried dispassionately to get at the real meaning of von Hügel's life, without using him for idiosyncratic purposes, and, as a Catholic cleric, he was dogged by censors for his efforts. After World War II, these first interpretations, except for Nédoncelle's, were again picked up and redeveloped, first by Michael de la Bedoyère (1951), then, but more critically, by John J. Heaney (1965 and 1968), and finally, and most bizarrely, by Thomas M. Loome (1973 and 1979). The history of von Hügel's fate at the hands of ideologically driven interpreters is outlined in Lawrence Barmann's "Friedrich von Hügel As Modernist and As More Than Modernist," *The Catholic Historical Review* 75, no. 2 (1989), 211–232.
[3] Von Hügel to Edmund Bishop, 23 May 1906, in Nigel Abercrombie, "Friedrich von Hügel's Letters to Edmund Bishop," *The Dublin Review* 227 (1953), 289.
[4] "My 1st H. Communion, 55 years ago!," von Hügel to Maude Petre, 29 June 1922, British Library (hereafter, BL), Add. MS 45362.142.

read John Henry Newman's *Loss and Gain* which, he later remarked, was the first book to make him "realize the intellectual might and grandeur of the Catholic position."[5] So he was at least beginning to take Catholicism seriously before the crisis which turned his life around took place in June 1870. In an effort to fulfill his dying father's wish to see Austria and Vienna once more, Friedrich, together with his mother and younger brother Anatole, began at the end of May the trip from Torquay in England to Vienna. They had barely reached Brussels when Baron Carl von Hügel died there on 2 June. The family went on from Brussels with his body for burial in Vienna.[6] On this trip Friedrich contracted typhoid fever, which would leave him nerve impaired and increasingly deaf for the rest of his life. This illness and the personal turmoil of this father's death under such circumstances seem to have put the young man into a state of serious religious crisis by the time he reached Vienna. There he met a Dutch Dominican priest, Father Raymond Hocking, who took him in hand, read his situation correctly, and helped him to reorient his life in a new and, as time would prove, definitive direction.

It was Hocking, the Baron always maintained, who first set his face toward the religious commitment and growth which became his life's primary work. "At eighteen," von Hügel told his niece Gwendolen Greene, "I made up my mind to go into moral and religious training," as a result of this encounter with Hocking.[7] And what the priest helped von Hügel to structure into his young life was primarily a Christian asceticism, patient and plodding, based always on the realities of his here and now situation, and motivated by a desire for God. Thirty years after meeting Hocking, von Hügel commented to George Tyrrell on this issue of the essentialness of the ascetical dimension for any authentic and vibrant Christian life, and how it was Hocking, as a vowed and celibate religious, who had first exemplified this asceticism for him and had helped him to grasp and to begin to live it in his own life. "Certainly," he told Tyrrell,

all this is no paper-theory with me. It has been the vivid memory of a dearly loved and admired black-and-white clad figure of a noble-hearted,

---

[5] Von Hügel to H. I. D. Ryder, 18 August 1890, Birmingham Oratory Archives, VC 20.
[6] This information is found in Anatole von Hügel (ed.), *Charles von Hügel, April 25, 1795–June 2, 1870*, (Cambridge: privately printed, 1905), pp. 48 and 59.
[7] Von Hügel to Gwendolen Greene, 23 January 1919, in *Letters From Baron Friedrich von Hügel to a Niece*, ed. Gwendolen Greene (London: Dent, 1965), p. 16.

218 LAWRENCE BARMANN

gladly self-immolating Dominican Friar, whom God sent me, to seek and
save me when I was eighteen; it is the tonic of that closely watched and
nobly costing, richly fruitful self-renunciation and its ever vivid memory
which has braced me throughout these thirty years, which, if without any
external badge of self-renouncement, have, thank God, escaped the
unspeakable vulgarity of a hunting after pleasure, or of any consistent
attempt to keep the cross out of any part of my life . . . yet, – there it is –
the Cross of Christ is our one salvation, even in the purely intellectual
order, the one force, which, properly understood, will still redeem the
Church from all this miserable Philistinism . . .[8]

Precisely when it was that dealing with the authoritarian aspect of
the Catholic church began to be a dimension of von Hügel's ascetical
practice is unclear. What is clear is that it was early and it was
nuanced. Three years after returning to England from his father's
burial, he married Lady Mary Catherine Herbert, eldest child of
Lord and Lady Herbert of Lea and sister to the 13th and 14th Earls
of Pembroke. She was twenty-four at the time of the wedding, and a
convert to Roman Catholicism; he was twenty-one. And although
they shared a loving and fruitful married life, Lady Mary seems
never really to have understood nor fully shared the struggles
stemming from her husband's religious commitment within the
Catholic Church.[9] Just a year after his marriage, while in the south
of France with his wife, von Hügel wrote his first letter to John
Henry Newman, and it concerned the Vatican decree on papal
infallibility.

To declare the pope infallible is one thing; to understand what the
declaration means and does not mean is another. Both before and
after the Vatican Council, Catholic theologians and ecclesiastical
authorities disagreed with one another on the declaration's interpretation; so, likewise, did non-Catholics, secular politicians, and
rulers of nations who had recently lived through the conflicts and
antagonisms occasioned by papal claims to temporal power. One of
the earliest post-counciliar efforts to pin down the meaning of the
Council's declaration was made by Austrian Bishop Joseph Fessler of
St. Pölten, whom Pope Pius IX himself had appointed Secretary
General of the Council. Fessler's small book was entitled *The True and*

[8] Von Hügel to George Tyrrell, 26 December 1900, BL, Add. MS 44927.151.
[9] Telling Tyrrell why he hesitated to sign a letter defending Loisy which was to be published in
the London *Times*, von Hügel wrote: "I have not myself only to think of, but a dear wife,
only by affection with me in this attitude, and 3 good girls to marry." Von Hügel to Tyrrell, 5
February 1904, BL, Add. MS 44928.155.

the False Infallibility of the Popes: A Controversial Reply to Dr. Schulte. Schulte, chief leader of the Old Catholic movement and Professor of Canon and German Law in the University of Prague, had published an interpretation of the Vatican decree which was so broad as to make the papal claim a threat to practically everyone. Fessler's response was a moderate and very limited interpretation with which almost anyone could live; and it was, interestingly, both read and publicly approved with praise by Pius IX in April 1871.[10] Friedrich von Hügel, at the age of nineteen, read Fessler's book and found, as he told Newman, that it "has helped me very much."[11] In fact, it had helped him so much that the young Baron wrote to the Viennese publisher to ask "if he would cede me the right of translation into English, on my pledging myself to getting it done by really competent hands." While awaiting an answer to his query, von Hügel discovered that Newman's great friend and fellow Oratorian, Ambrose St. John, was already at work on an English translation but, apparently, without the Austrian publisher's awareness. So von Hügel sent Newman the publisher's eventual response to himself, telling Newman that he was delighted that St. John "should be bringing so first-rate a pamphlet before the notice of Englishmen." He concluded his letter by remarking on Gladstone's foray into the infallibility controversy, saying that

we have read much of the newspaper criticisms on, and answers to, Mr. Gladstone. I suppose his pamphlet is a good thing, inasmuch as it is the occasion of the question being thoroughly discussed and sifted. But I for one, and all who will read you with me, must, I am sure be grateful to him, for making you take up your pen. I need not say how eagerly, almost feverishly, I am looking forward to the publication of your reply. I have no doubt, that it, like your other books, will be to me a fresh starting point, intellectually, and an additional link in the chain of the many helps and enlightenments that binds me to you.

Newman, of course, had been distraught by the haste and the pressure with which the schema on infallibility had been pressed on the Council fathers by the extreme infallibilists among them,[12] and

[10] Joseph Fessler, *The True and the False Infallibility of the Popes: A Controversial Reply to Dr. Schulte* (New York: The Catholic Publication Society, 1875), pp. 1–2.
[11] Von Hügel to John Henry Newman, 13 December 1874, BOA, VC, 100a. All quotations in this paragraph are taken from this letter.
[12] See Lawrence Barmann, "Theological Inquiry in an Authoritarian Church: Newman and Modernism," in *Discourse and Context, An Interdisciplinary Study of John Henry Newman*, ed. Gerard Magill (Carbondale, Illinois: Southern Illinois University Press, 1993), pp. 191–193.

his *Letter to His Grace the Duke of Norfolk* in response to Gladstone was the very model of a limited and moderate interpretation of the Vatican decree, not unlike Fessler's. So in Fessler's and Newman's temperate and limiting explanation of papal infallibility, von Hügel found his intellectual and moral breathing space.

Such breathing space was especially important to von Hügel at this early period in his life primarily because of another influence he was experiencing just then. When the Baron had married in 1873, he and his wife moved to 4 Holford Road in Hampstead, where they found they had as neighbor the most colorful and controversial of the Catholic converts from the Oxford Movement of the previous generation, William George Ward. Although forty years separated von Hügel and Ward in age, they soon became frequent walking and discussion partners across Hampstead Heath. Two more unlikely companions could hardly be imagined than the young inquiring Baron and the old seminary professor of theology whose ideas on infallibility, articulated in his treatise *De infallibilitatis extensione*, had been so sweepingly extreme and absolute as to cause their repudiation by the Council fathers themselves.[13] What drew the two men together was their shared intellectual acuity and their love of religion and the church. When Ward's son Wilfrid came to write his father's life nearly a decade after the latter's death, he asked von Hügel to write a memoir of the elder Ward for publication in the volume. This von Hügel did in the form of a letter to Wilfrid, noting at the outset that "warm as is my admiration for him, and my gratitude for the very much I owe him of kindness, example, and stimulation, yet there are several circumstances which make it difficult for me to write upon the subject at all."[14] Among these circumstances was the fact that the infallibility issue had been for Ward "the main controversy of his life"; whereas von Hügel had to admit that "on this one set of questions, I was from the first in relations of friendly and respectful, but most frank and open conflict with him." In trying to explain why this was so the Baron wrote an extraordinarily insightful psychological profile of Ward in relation to which his own psychology and intellectual positions were expressed. If Ward could claim to be an ultramontane, so could von Hügel. But the Baron

[13] Wilfrid Ward, *William George Ward and the Catholic Revival* (London: Macmillan and Co., 1893), pp. 255–263.

[14] Ibid., p. 365. All following quotations from von Hügel's letters are taken from Ward's book, pp. 365–374.

always qualified his own ultramontanism as "in the old and definite sense of the word," by which he meant the original seventeenth-century meaning of the word as "anti-Gallicanism." "Catholics were not," he wrote,

either then or now, divided simply between the two extreme wings, the *Ultras* and the *Extras*, as they have been wittily called. The large majority no doubt belong to the centre, and to that centre I belong myself. St. François de Sales and Fénelon in the past, Bishop Fessler, M. Foisset and Father Hilarius, Cardinal Newman and Father Ryder in our time, would in various degrees and ways, represent this position.

In trying to explain why he and Ward should have been such different types of ultramontanes, von Hügel delved into the psychology of belief, and concluded that Ward insisted that "the Church is infallible as to the limits of her own infallibility" because only such power and authority could restrain "men argumentatively constituted like himself." Ward was impatient and even contemptuous of all painstaking and careful historical research bearing on ecclesiastical and theological subjects. Von Hügel observed that Ward at times spoke of those engaged in such scholarship as though they "were people who undertook this kind of thing at their own risk and peril, and who could be tolerated only if they reported themselves periodically to the ecclesiastical police." In light of all this the Baron concluded that "of this I am very sure so great a difference in degree as there was between your father's Ultramontanism and my own, results, practically, in a difference in kind, and reacts most powerfully upon one's whole temper of mind, and one's method of attacking problems and looking at things without and within."

If the authoritarian structure of Roman Catholicism in the nineteenth century was one of the dimensions of von Hügel's lived Christianity with which he constantly struggled, it was neither the only one nor necessarily always the most significant. During the thirty years he resided in Hampstead, his reading and his contacts indicate that all three of the dimensions of religion which, in his mature years, he considered essential to a full and vibrant personality, that is, the institutional dimension, the intellectual, and the mystical: all of these grew proportionately and with constant interaction among themselves in his life throughout his twenties and thirties and thereafter.[15] But it was, in fact, the mystical dimension

---

[15] In von Hügel's theory of personal religion the ideal would be composed of three interacting

which most attracted him and within which his life primarily flourished.[16]

Christianity was, after all, a life – not a theory, nor an idea, nor a club; and it was a life to be lived and nurtured within the structure of the church. To understand both the life and the structure in such a way as to make living Christianly more fully practicable became von Hügel's life's passion. He had told Hocking that he wanted to serve God and learn to love Christ, and Hocking had shown him that he had "to become free from *self*, from my poor, shabby, bad, all-spoiling *self*."[17] And this self-renunciation was necessary, he came to understand, solely for the purpose of allowing his true God-communing self to flourish.[18] How one accomplished this in the church of Pope Pius IX was not an easy thing for a man of von Hügel's temperament and intelligence. The devotional practices of the time common among Catholics tended often to sentimentality or superstition, and what passed for speculative theology among Roman Catholic theologians was mostly apologetics and the lifeless logic of a very decadent scholasticism. Neither were helpful to von Hügel's effort to grow in Christian life. He tried, nevertheless, at first to use what was available; he consulted, read, and discussed every aspect of his Catholicism with the best clerical minds in England and eventually elsewhere. He read Döllinger and Renan, as well as Newman, Cardinal Franzelin, and St. John of the Cross.[19] He consulted about and discussed religion with his parish priest, as well as with Father William Addis, Bishop John Cuthbert Hedley, and Cardinal

---

and complementary elements, namely, the institutional, the intellectual, and the mystical. – "And, everything else being equal, my faith will be at its richest and deepest and strongest, in so far as all these three motives are most fully and characteristically operative within me, at one and the same time, and towards one and the same ultimate result and end." Von Hügel, *Mystical*, vol. I, p. 54.

[16] Von Hügel, *Mystical*, vol. II, pp. 283–284.

[17] Von Hügel to a Girl on Her Confirmation, 11 April 1922, in *Letters*, p. 352.

[18] "The primary function of religion is not the consoling of the natural man as it finds him, but the purification of this man, by effecting an ever-growing cleavage and contrast between his bad false self, and the false, blind self-love that clings to that self, and his good true self, and the true, enlightened self-love that clings to the true self; and the deepest, generally confused and dumb, aspirations of every human heart, correspond exactly to, and come from precisely the same source, as the external helps and examples of miracle, Church or Saint." Von Hügel to Tyrrell, 26 September 1898, *Letters*, p. 72.

[19] *Diaries*, 13 February, 24 and 26 April, 4 August, 30 December 1878; 17 August, 5 October 1879; 31 January, 5 March 1884; 25 March, 5 September 1889; and elsewhere. Von Hügel's manuscript diaries are in the von Hügel manuscript collection at the University of St. Andrews in Scotland, and will be referred to in these pages solely by entry dates.

Manning.[20] He made annual retreats with the Jesuits at Manresa, coming to know well Father Joseph Rickaby;[21] and he welcomed for walks and visits to his home the Jesuit rector of the Farm Street residence, Father George Porter.[22] Von Hügel's mind and spirit were not restless, but they were intensely and indefatigably involved in his pursuit of God – the all-consuming passion of his life. As an old man he once reflected in print on "the far-reaching importance of our initial self-directions amidst the realities and impressions within us and without us."[23] He was, of course, speaking from hard experience.

In his pursuit of the fulness of Christian life, von Hügel met in his early thirties several men who would become, as Hocking had been for him at eighteen, his exemplars and teachers in this pursuit. In 1884 he met both Monseigneur Louis Duchesne and the Abbé Henri Huvelin.[24] Duchesne would introduce him to the use of critical historical methodology in his efforts to deal with the historical data of Christianity, including the Bible; and Huvelin would help him grow in the prayerful peace, openness, and conviction necessary for a full flourishing of the mystical element of his religious life.[25]

More than twenty years passed from the time when von Hügel

---

[20] *Diaries*, 3 October 1877; 24 January, 5 and 7 February, 27–29 May 1878; 2 June, 25 July 1879; 3 August 1884.

[21] *Diaries*, 25–30 August 1879.

[22] *Diaries*, 26 August 1879; 11 and 28 January, 3 and 8 February, 6 March 1884.

[23] Friedrich von Hügel, "Eudoxe Irenée Mignot," *The Contemporary Review* 113 (1918), 520.

[24] *Diaries*, 10 May 1884. A study of von Hügel's diaries makes incontrovertible the date of his first meeting with these two men, in spite of his own remarks in Friedrich von Hügel, "Louis Duchesne," *The Times Literary Supplement* 1062 (25 May 1922), 342, which place the date in March 1885.

[25] The mystical element in personal religion meant for von Hügel one's sense or experience, no matter how partial and inadequate and misunderstood, of God not only as immanent but also as transcendent. This experience was always in and through the material and temporal, and for its consistency depended on one's growth in openness to such experience through the continuous purification of one's false and selfish egoisms in order to allow one's true self to go forward to its intended object (God) in love. This mystical dimension had nothing to do with abnormal experiences, with visions, trances, voices, and such irrelevant trappings which is what some have thought of as mystical experience. In a review of R. J. Campbell's *The New Theology*, von Hügel criticized the author's idea that it is "an obvious truism that we have nothing real and fruitful to do with God as Transcendent; as though God's Transcendence were entirely outside of man's emotional and operative life." The Baron argued that God's transcendence does indeed have real meaning "in actual religious experience and all deeper theological thought." F. von Hügel, "The Relation Between God and Man in 'The New Theology' of the Rev. R. J. Campbell," *The Albany Review* 1 (September 1907), 659. Von Hügel wrote his *magnum opus* to try to understand how a life in which the mystical element of religion was most fully developed could also have full developments of the institutional and intellectual elements. *Mystical*, vol. 1, pp. vi–vii.

first met Duchesne and Huvelin to when Pope Pius X, in 1907, condemned most of the work of critical scholars within the church; and it was within these years that the Baron brought to a ripe maturity both his own understanding and use of critical historical methodology and his living grasp of the mystical element of Christian life within the institutional church. These two dimensions of his life were, of course, developing together in the late nineteenth century, interacting, and profoundly influencing one another. Yet they are rarely studied together by scholars, even though the evidences for both dimensions of his life are abundant. Von Hügel's growth as a serious student of the Bible and as a not insignificant critic of biblical critics is easily documentable. From his encounters with Duchesne he came to know of and learn from Gustav Bickell of Innsbruck and Alfred Loisy of the Institut Catholique in Paris.[26] His growing sense of the seriousness for Catholicism of the "biblical question" led him to master not only biblical Greek, but also classical Hebrew. He became a friend of and correspondent with Alfred Loisy, of course, but also with Heinrich Julius Holtzmann in Germany,[27] with Giovanni Semeria in Italy,[28] and with the best of the biblical scholars in England as well.[29] By 1894 he had published a scholarly and dense three-part article in response to Pope Leo XIII's encyclical on biblical studies, *Providentissimus Deus*;[30] in 1897 he

[26] Cf. *Diaries*, 22, 24, 26, 29, 30 August, 2, 4, 7, 9, 11, 14, 16, 18, 20, 23, 25, 27, 30 September, 2, 4, 8, 9 October, 4 November 1890; and 28 October 1892.

[27] Von Hügel's diaries and letters manifest a strong and consistent respect and even affection for Holtzmann and his biblical scholarship. As early as 1891 he was using Holtzmann's books for his own Bible-based religion lessons for his daughters (*Diaries*, 23 and 26 March 1891); and finally in the late summer of 1907, after the famous Modernist meeting at Molveno, von Hügel stopped in Baden-Baden to meet Holtzmann for the first and only time (*Diaries*, 13 September 1907). When the Baron first met Adolf von Harnack five years later, a year after Holtzmann's death, he commented: 'I saw *Harnack*, for the first time, last Sunday week, at Bp. Talbot's in Kensington. We had a quarter of an hour's tête-à-tête. Certainly an astonishingly active-cultivated mind; but one does not get the impression, that H. Holtzmann used to give, of utter simplicity of aim and spirit," Von Hügel to Petre, 16 February 1911, BL, Add. MS 45362.30.

[28] Von Hügel met Semeria for the first time in the autumn of 1894, and their friendship continued till von Hügel's death thirty years later (*Diaries*, 14 November 1894). The Baron's letters to Semeria have been published by Guiseppe Zorzi, *Auf der Suche nach der verlorenen Katholizität. Die Briefe Friedrich von Hügels an Giovanni Semeria* (Mainz: Matthias-Grünewald-Verlag, 1991), vol. II.

[29] These include Thomas Kelly Cheyne, Samuel Rolles Driver, Percy Gardner, William Sanday, and especially William Robertson Smith. Von Hügel began reading Smith's *Religion of the Semites* in October 1890, and met and talked with him later that same month (*Diaries*, 16, 21, 27 October 1890).

[30] Friedrich von Hügel, "The Church and the Bible: The Two Stages of Their Inter-Relation," *The Dublin Review* 115–117 (1894–1895), 313–341, 306–337, 275–304.

presented *in absentia* a paper entitled "The Historical Method and Its Application to the Study of the Documents of the Hexateuch" at the fourth International Congress for Catholics held that year in Fribourg, Switzerland;[31] with the condemnation of Loisy's *L'Evangile et l'Eglise* (*The Gospel and the Church*) at the end of 1903 he entered into intelligent debate in the public forum in defense of Loisy's rights as a scholar;[32] and in 1906 he co-authored with the Protestant biblical scholar Charles Augustus Briggs *The Papal Commission and the Pentateuch*[33] So it is hardly surprising that those who have studied Modernism and von Hügel during this period have concentrated on his involvement with biblical criticism and biblical critics, and on the growing antagonisms which this brought about with church authorities.

But to study von Hügel only in this aspect of his life is to miss the real meaning of the man. His involvement with critical biblical studies was one aspect of his over-all pursuit of God. And because this latter dimension of his life is less well studied, or studied only in isolation from his more objective intellectual pursuits, it is thus less well understood generally.[34] Yet it is von Hügel's unflagging pursuit of the mystical element of religion which both informed and guided his critical intellectual pursuits, and which ultimately explain his attitude and conduct after the condemnation of the latter by the church authorities. Henri Huvelin was the man who, more than any other person, confirmed the Baron in the pursuit of this mystical dimension of his Christian life. Although they first met briefly in 1884,[35] it was in the spring of 1886 that the French priest's influence really began to take hold in specific ways. Von Hügel had arranged to spend a week at the end of May in Paris, without his family, precisely and solely so that he could consult Huvelin in five lengthy

---

[31] Friedrich von Hügel, "The Historical Method and the Documents of the Hexateuch," *The Catholic University Bulletin* 4 (1898), 198–226, with seven separately numbered pages of appendices.

[32] Perhaps the most important of the Baron's writings in this debate is "The Case of M. Loisy," *The Pilot* 9 (23 January 1904), 94.

[33] The Rev. Charles A. Briggs and Baron Friedrich von Hügel, *The Papal Commission and the Pentateuch* (London: Longmans, Green and Co., 1906).

[34] See, for instance, the remark by Joseph P. Whelan, S.J., *The Spirituality of Friedrich von Hügel* (London: Collins, 1971), p. 21, that "much of the excitement of his spirituality arises precisely from the circumstance that the more than 800, wholly *non*-modernist pages of *The Mystical Element of Religion* are written during 1898 to 1909, the very years of the crisis and of von Hügel's major participation in its questions and affairs." The thesis of these pages is the antithesis of that statement!

[35] *Diaries*, 16 June 1884.

interviews.[36] On this occasion and again in 1893, he wrote down much of Huvelin's advice to himself. These pages remain today, and they not only show the areas of concern which von Hügel discussed with Huvelin, but they also help one to understand the absoluteness of the various statements the Baron made throughout his life about the significance of Huvelin for him.

Huvelin's remarks to von Hügel show that the priest had a keen insight into his client's temperament and personality, and that he knew how to direct this man into profound Christian growth, not in spite of the church structure but precisely through it. In their very first conversation Huvelin told von Hügel that he should not expect other people to understand him often, and, when they did, they would invariably be solitary, self-possessed individuals who had suffered.[37] Huvelin emphasized prayer for the Baron, more as a state of being than of specific acts. He thought truth for von Hügel would resemble a point of light whose edges gradually fade into the surrounding darkness. And the only safeguard against becoming self-willed in the pursuit of critical intellectual work, Huvelin warned, is prayer.

The thrust of Huvelin's counsels centered on the basic problem of von Hügel's life at the time of this consultation: how to combine a constantly growing and vibrantly open spiritual life with an ever developing critical intellect. Catholic orthodoxy of von Hügel's day was exclusively expressed in scholastic language and by scholastic methodology, and the fact that Pope Leo XIII had made St. Thomas Aquinas the paradigm of this system had not helped von Hügel to find it any more palatable intellectually. Huvelin was helpful on both scholasticism and orthodoxy. Scholastic writers, he said, have their own jargon and sense of self-importance. Von Hügel was advised not to take them too seriously, since they are dealing with formulae, not reality; they fail to grasp that all life is ultimately unanalyzable. Even the great St. Thomas did not explain everything, Huvelin said, because living truth escapes comprehensive definition.

---

[36] *Diaries*, 25, 26, 27, 28, 29, 31 May 1886.

[37] The remarks of Huvelin to the Baron were recorded in French by the latter at the time of the meetings, and were referred to by von Hügel throughout his life. For several intimates whom he believed might profit from these sayings he made copies. The copy made for his niece Gwendolen Greene was published complete by James J. Kelly, "The Abbé Huvelin's Counsel to Baron von Hügel," *Bijdragen Tijdschrift voor Filosofie en Theologie* 39 (1978), 59–69, and is the text used in this paper. This and the following four paragraphs are the author's synthesis of Huvelin's observations to von Hügel.

Contemporary scholastics think that they can put the moon into a bottle; they clarify things by impoverishing them. It is as though they construct a great road system through a pristine forest. This, of course, allows them to see the forest, but at the expense of the beautiful trees. Scholastics simply lose the living truth in the course of their argumentation.

Because scholastic thought had been a stumbling block to von Hügel, Huvelin urged him to cease to wrestle with it. But if the Baron was not destined to find religious truth through the church's scholastic orthodoxy, how was he to find it? Huvelin recommended that von Hügel's way should be to combine great freedom of spirit with great purity of heart in assessing everything which would come under his purview. To try to limit or cage the large and expansive spirit which God had given the Baron would spell spiritual death for him, Huvelin thought. One can be supremely orthodox in men's eyes, the priest said, and utterly wrong in God's. For von Hügel, orthodoxy was never to be a thing aimed at in itself; rather, conscientiousness was the thing to aim for, since conscience, not orthodoxy, always has the position of primacy.[38] Huvelin told von Hügel that he had a horror of temporizing thinkers and those who say only what others want to hear, because he was pursuing truth, not what is acceptable to men. Orthodoxy must square itself with truth. That is its responsibility. However, von Hügel was warned never to offend against charity. For von Hügel, Huvelin told him, faith and charity were the same thing. They either diminish or expand together. He should not worry if others caused him suffering; just make certain that he did not make others suffer. His own suffering would not come from what he gave of himself for others, but only from what he held back selfishly. It was the pure essence of Christianity which held him and kept him in the church, and this was a good sign.

[38] Kelly, "The Abbé Huvelin's Counsel," p. 64. That von Hügel interiorized this particular piece of advice is evidenced in his writings and correspondence. As von Hügel worked on his mysticism book, he had Tyrrell's promise to read the whole in proof. Telling Tyrrell in 1901 about the book's progress, he wrote: "When you *do* come to see it all, I shall, of course, be grateful for any help. But the 2 points on which I wd. desiderate your special kind attention, are my English, and my orthodoxy." Von Hügel to Tyrrell, 6 August 1901, BL, Add. MS 44927.169. And a few months later he told Tyrrell: "I love so much to leave to the dear Christ-Master, to Love Infinite, all dividing off of the goats from the sheep. And all, even indirect, exclusion on the score of orthodoxy, – how painful it is always, and how little Christian the temper, where this predominates!" Von Hügel to Tyrrell, 18–20 December 1901, BL, Add. MS 44927.177.

Huvelin seemed bent upon showing von Hügel how his God-given personality and temperament were a blessing, despite the conflicts and suffering which they brought him within conventionally structured Catholicism. Huvelin told von Hügel that the latter's special grace was to grasp spiritual truth with the core of his whole being and with an overwhelming profundity which made analysis and rationalistic justification for his faith impossible. Consequently, all structures and limitations would become sources of suffering. The church, Huvelin said, must have space not only for the conventional majority, but also for those of great independence of spirit who are both unable and ought not to try to force themselves to follow the conventional path. One is not free to distort or disfigure the individuality which God has given him. On the other hand, von Hügel was to remember that the conventional majority also have rights: the right to his silence, to his consideration, and to his respect. He should not try either to change them or to make them understand himself, because he would succeed in neither. Because von Hügel's temperament was naturally vigorous and impetuous,[39] Huvelin warned him against letting it lead him astray, recommending calmness, a prayerful state, and growing humility as counterbalances. Huvelin pointed out that it was in matters of religion that von Hügel was especially prone to become over intense and agitated; so he must develop composure, because divine reality would elude him to the extent that he pursued it feverishly, and it would come to him to the extent that he did not.

Throughout Huvelin's conversations with von Hügel the priest warned him never to belittle his intellectual pursuits and their costingness, stressing how interwoven suffering was to any serious pursuit of spiritual life; and he even suggested that holiness and suffering were interchangeable. Jesus saved the world not by beautiful talk, he pointed out, but by suffering. And von Hügel would do good for others, Huvelin suggested, to the extent that he suffered. This suffering would not be something extrinsic to and superimposed upon his real life; rather, it would come from his chronic poor health and a mind and temperament which ill-suited him for life within the Roman Catholic Church at the end of the nineteenth century. Huvelin thought that St. Francis of Assisi had had a temperament

[39] Cf., for example, Von Hügel to Wilfrid Ward, 30 January 1899, St. Andrews University Library (hereafter, SAUL), vH MS vii, 143 (103).

like von Hügel's, one that was full of life, vigor, insight, and intensity. And he encouraged the Baron's attraction to such large-souled Christians.

In 1922, on the occasion of Duchesne's death, von Hügel wrote a memoir of his friend for publication in which he commented on

how I was helped to keep my faith and my reason through those terrible years of 1906–1914. Two forces were by now fully organized within myself; and neither force proceeded from Duchesne or from the Modernists. I had already in 1886 come under the grandly tonic influence of the Abbé Huvelin, that truly masculine saint who won and trained so many a soul. There sanctity stood before me in the flesh, and this as the genuine deepest effect and reason of the Catholic Church; I could now utilize the sufferings of these hurricane years towards growing a little less unlike this mediator of Church and Christ and God. And then, somewhat later, the philosophical needs of my mind became more clamorous than ever before. The philosophy, the theory of knowledge, I needed and have achieved is strongly realist in character; . . . belief in our real knowledge of real objects, distinct from ourselves and from our knowledge of them. And this mentality (so full of the differences, the reality, the *knownness* and the interaction of things) left large regions of my soul unfed, unsatisfied by Duchesne, or by Loisy, even where they were otherwise entirely acceptable.[40]

Duchesne, then, as well as von Hügel's other mentors and fellow workers in the area of critical historical studies, had helped him to develop part of the intellectual dimension of his religious life; Huvelin, on the other hand, had helped him to develop the mystical dimension which, ultimately, was the most important and integrative dimension of all.

Huvelin's suggestion to von Hügel that he look to the great-souled heroes of Christian history for inspiration and support was unnecessary. Long before he came under Huvelin's influence the Baron was studying the lives of various mystics and, where possible, reading their own writings as well.[41] In the preface to his own two-volume study of Saint Catherine of Genoa and mysticism he explained what the attraction for him was, and how it had worked in his life. "Born as I was in Italy," he wrote,

certain early impressions have never left me; a vivid consciousness has been with me, almost from the first, of the massively virile personalities, the spacious, trustful times of the early, as yet truly Christian, Renaissance there, from Dante to the Florentine Platonists. And when, on growing up, I

---

[40] Friedrich von Hügel, "Louis Duchesne," p. 342.   [41] *Diaries*, 22 January 1878.

acquired strong and definite religious convictions, it was that ampler pre-Protestant, as yet neither Protestant nor anti-Protestant, but deeply positive and Catholic, world, with its already characteristically modern outlook and its hopeful and spontaneous application of religion to the pressing problems of life and thought, which helped to strengthen and sustain me, when depressed and hemmed in by the types of devotion prevalent since then in Western Christendom. For those early modern times presented me with men of the same general instincts and outlook as my own, but environed by the priceless boon and starting-point of a still undivided Western Christendom; Protestantism, as such, continued to be felt as ever more or less unjust and sectarian; and the specifically post-Tridentine type of Catholicism, with its regimental Seminarism, its predominantly controversial spirit, its suspiciousness and timidity, persisted, however inevitable some of it may be, in its failure to win my love. Hence I had to continue the seeking and the finding elsewhere, yet ever well within the great Roman Church, things more intrinsically lovable. The wish some day to portray one of those large-souled pre-Protestant, post-Mediaeval Catholics, was thus early and has been long at work within me.[42]

The opportunity to write such a life came in 1898, when the Protestant publisher of *The Hampstead Annual* invited von Hügel to write an article on some Catholic mystic for that year's issue.[43] He chose St. Catherine of Genoa, and though the article was limited to sixteen printed pages, he managed to touch on nearly all of the major questions provoked by the topic of Christian mysticism at the end of the nineteenth century. Sydney Mayle, the publisher, was sufficiently impressed by his effort to propose to him "to publish at his own risk and expense, a little book on St. Catherine of Genoa, and the questions suggested by her life – something six times the length of the article as finally accepted."[44] This, then, is the humble origin of what became the greatest literary undertaking of his life, which he himself called his *magnum opus, The Mystical Element of Religion As Studied in Saint Catherine of Genoa and Her Friends*, published finally not by Mayle but by J. M. Dent and Company in London in 1908 in two volumes. The ten years spanning the publication of his original article and the publication of the two-volume book are usually considered to be the peak of his Modernist activity. While they are this, indeed, they are also the peak of his historical and theological work on mysticism and its integration into his own life.

[42] Von Hügel, *Mystical*, vol. 1, pp. v–vi.
[43] Von Hügel to Tyrrell, 3 October 1898, in M. D. Petre, *Von Hugel and Tyrrell: The Story of a Friendship* (London: J. M. Dent and Sons Ltd., 1937), p. 42.
[44] Von Hügel to Tyrrell, 21 November 1898, *Letters*, p. 74.

In fact, his Modernist activity, in terms of supporting Loisy and Tyrrell, and to a lesser extent others in France, Italy, and England, was always subordinate to, if not in effort and energy expended, at least in ultimate evaluation, his work on mysticism.[45]

This ten-year period, with one year added both to the beginning and the end of that span, is the entire duration of Friedrich von Hügel's relationship with George Tyrrell. And while this relationship, too, is commonly considered to be at the center of whatever one might mean by Roman Catholic Modernism, the pursuit of the mystical element of religion by von Hügel was both the origin of the relationship and, from the Baron's perspective at least, its consistent *leit-motif*. Von Hügel's introductory letter to Tyrrell is dated 20 September 1897, and it makes the point that he wants to meet Tyrrell because of "all the furtherance and encouragement that I have so abundantly found, in your *Nova et Vetera*, of ideas and tendencies that have now for long been part and parcel of my life, its aims and combats."[46] Tyrrell was invited to Hampstead for a walk and talk, and the rest, as they say, is history!

What cannot be over-emphasized here, however, is that for von Hügel, at least, the relationship was based on what he perceived to be their mutual attraction to the mystical element of religion. Their early letters center mostly on Tyrrell's help to von Hügel's oldest child, Gertrude, in regaining her religious convictions after passing through a period of nerve-agitated skepticism; and on the Baron's own pursuit of mystical theory and practice. As von Hügel prepared his article on St. Catherine in 1898, he consulted Tyrrell at length on various aspects of his thinking; and when Mayle proposed that the Baron write a book, the latter asked Tyrrell to write an introduction for it. By the time the book was actually ready for the printer Tyrrell was in no position to attach his name to anything which one wanted to escape ecclesiastical condemnation; but he did correct proofs for the volumes, making suggestions on both style and content.[47]

[45] Von Hügel to Tyrrell, 18–20 December 1901, *Letters*, pp. 102–103.
[46] Von Hügel to Tyrrell, 20 September 1897, in Petre, *Von Hugel and Tyrrell*, p. 10.
[47] "And lastly, my Book. You know how sincere was (indeed *is*) my conviction, that I could nowhere secure for myself a more competent, valuable critic of it, than *him* . . . What does distinctly distress me is, that I will not only be sending my 2 vols for judgment to a more than ever indiscreet person, who now puts even upon P.C.s things most of us would have only in registered letters, – and whose share in the book will doubtless be well known, even before its publication, to all this now organized company of delators: I willingly accept this cost: but that the subject-matter and the intricacies of the book *of course* demand quiet,

The years at the end of the nineteenth century and beginning of the twentieth were also a time when von Hügel spent about half of every year on the continent and especially in Rome. Because of his ready *entrée* into high clerical and aristocratic circles there, he was in a position to give Tyrrell his perceptions of the temper and trends among Roman authorities. And as Tyrrell's own problems with ecclesiastical superiors increased, from the censorship of his writings to his dismissal from the Society of Jesus, his deprivation of the sacraments, and the final refusal to allow his burial in a Catholic cemetery, von Hügel's interaction with him was always supportive and encouraging, but increasingly alarmed, restraining, and, finally, disappointed. Early in their relationship von Hügel had told Tyrrell that he was

the Catholic, with whom of all English-speaking ones, I feel myself the most completely at one. I have, of course, other gratefully cared for friends amongst them, but they are either not intellectually alive, or active largely on other subjects or in other directions, – at least more so than you are. The mystical *attrait* is a point that really speaks volumes, all round.[48]

But as Tyrrell's troubles escalated, his mystical sensitivity became swamped by his sense of injustice suffered and by his anger. This, more than anything else in their relationship, seriously upset von Hügel; and it caused both men, for the first time, to withdraw a bit from the almost total openness which had previously characterized their interaction. At first the Baron simply urged Tyrrell to regain his composure and to strive to live in his depths rather than on the surface of his life, buffeted by the polemical agitation in which he reacted to each new authoritarian assault on his integrity and intelligence. But in the autumn of 1907, with Tyrrell's equivalent

peace, etc., for the critic to be competent (he is that overflowingly), and for the critic *to be himself* (is he that?)." Von Hügel to Petre, 3 July 1906, BL, Add. MS 45361.39.

[48] Von Hügel to Tyrrell, 17 November 1899, BL. Add. MS 44927.88. And again: "no one knows and loves your mind . . . but must feel that not since Newman have we English-speaking Catholics had anything like as sweet and deep an 'organ-voice', as adequate an expression of the truest, most constitutive forces within ourselves, as is that which God has now given us in you." Von Hügel to Tyrrell, 28 May 1901, BL, Add. MS 44927.162. And more than two years after the Roman condemnation of Modernism and nearly five months after Tyrrell's death, von Hügel told Maude Petre: "There is such a beautiful German article abt Fr. T. that I cannot now lay hands on, saying that unless his deep, positive religiousness can permeate the Latin Modernists, the movement of the latter is lost, as a beneficient force. Indeed Rome will easily win in that case, and deserve to do so, in a very real way. It is just so that I too feel. I do not fear the anti-Romanism of a Troeltsch or a Eucken; I fear the anti-Romanism of a Houtin or a Minocchi." Von Hügel to Petre, 7 December 1909, BL. Add. MS 45361.106.

excommunication, and the seeming triumph of his antagonists in the press, von Hügel insisted that Tyrrell cease temporarily from this war of words. In frustration the muzzled priest wrote to A. L. Lilley: "I have never been so nearly hating the Baron as during these days when Gasquet have [*sic*] been having it all their own way; & the other side so freely represented; & then two letters a day from Dell urging me on."[49] Early in 1908 Tyrrell actually flirted with the idea of joining the Old Catholics and was in contact with their leaders. He kept this from von Hügel at first, and only after Tyrrell's death did von Hügel realize the full extent of Tyrrell's attraction to and dealings with this group. How foreign even the possibility of such a move would have been to von Hügel, and how contrary to his most basic *raison d'être*, is indicated in a letter which he wrote Tyrrell in the weeks between Tyrrell's excommunication and his contact with the Old Catholics. Von Hügel had just been to the dinner meeting which opened the 1907–1908 session for the London Society for the Study of Religion, and he told Tyrrell that

although at our Dinner Meetings we are not supposed to have any but merely little business speeches, they asked me, after these were over, to speak to them about you and us all, – our position, aims, hopes etc. – tho' tired, and hence inclined to be over emphatic, I hope that what I said was to the point; in any case, they were very kind and sympathetic. I specially tried to draw out two facts: that your position was in no sense an excentric [*sic*] or isolated one – the three groups of protesters in Italy, taking up practically the same attitude; and that we, in no wise, aimed, even as a second and possible policy, either at forming or at joining any other religious body, – our very strength and *raison d'être* consisting in the deep Catholicism of our non-Ultramontanism, our anti-absolutism. Chevalier told me that Newsom and Lilley specially endorsed and drove home this second point of mine, and the former criticised the formation of the separate Old Cath. Church in 1870 as a profound mistake, and spoke strongly against Anglicans hoping or wishing to have any of us. Caldecott, as usual, showed himself much less wide, and Wicksteed seemed to think us Agnostics at heart, – like himself, in fact.[50]

After Tyrrell's death various continental Modernists who found themselves outside the Roman Church tried to claim Tyrrell's legacy as their own, and they cited his letters to and about the Old

---

[49] Tyrrell to A. L. Lilley, 12 November 1907, SAUL, MS. 30840.
[50] Von Hügel to Tyrrell, 6 November 1907, BL, Add. MS 44930.84. Newsom and Lilley were both Anglican clerics.

Catholics in proof of their claims.[51] Both von Hügel and Maude Petre were anxious to save Tyrrell's reputation in and for the church, though they disagreed on how this might best be done. For Miss Petre, Tyrrell was quite simply a hero who had fallen in the battle to save Roman Catholicism from its own worst tendencies. And in her opinion nothing about Tyrrell needed explanation or apology. Von Hügel, on the other hand, saw Tyrrell as a flawed man, whose flaws should be acknowledged but not allowed to obscure his real greatness and meaning. A few months after Tyrrell's death von Hügel gave an address to the London Society for the Study of Religion on his evaluation of Tyrrell's life, and these remarks were re-organized and published two months later in the *Hibbert Journal*. This article dealt with both the flaws and the greatness, and it also attempted to explain the essence of von Hügel's relationship with Tyrrell.

Father Tyrrell was ever a mystic; and I myself have found full religious peace only since deeply spiritual Catholic clerics helped me to understand and to assimilate the simpler elements of the great Catholic mystics. So we had a central requirement and help in common; and it was in this interior life that I ever longed to see his sorely harassed soul continuously find its fundamental peace.[52]

In the article von Hügel dealt with the conflicts in Tyrrell's life with honesty and balance, but noting that "if I speak at all, I cannot avoid speaking with some fulness of utterance and fearless accuracy about certain sides of current Catholic Church life with which he came into collision, and which broke his life."[53] But despite Tyrrell's struggles within Catholicism and the bitterness and isolation of his final years, von Hügel stressed Tyrrell's genuine Catholicism. "Is it not, then," he asked, "a clear duty for me (a Catholic born and, I pray, a Catholic to live and to die) to speak out clearly concerning that which I know about my friend's Catholicism?"[54] And what followed was a summary attempt to demonstrate Tyrrell's deep Catholic spirit throughout the most conflicted period of his life. In conclusion, von Hügel said that it was Tyrrell's "rare combination of gifts" which made it possible for him to render to religion the great services which he did. "As to the combination," von Hügel wrote,

there was on the other hand, his deep religiousness and delicate spirituality.

[51] Von Hügel to Petre, 18 February 1910, BL, Add. MS 45361.120–121.
[52] Baron F. von Hügel, "Father Tyrrell: Some Memorials of the Last Twelve Years of His Life," *The Hibbert Journal* 8 (January 1910), 235.
[53] Ibid., p. 234.   [54] Ibid., p. 235.

I have known hundreds of clerics and of laymen of various countries, but I have only found three or four individuals who, in this respect, equalled, and no one who, in this, surpassed him. It is this rare spiritual instinct that speaks so powerfully out of all his books, from the first to the last. The aesthetic sense, the scientific interest, the political bent, the moral law, he understood them all; yet in religion alone, as specifically distinct from all else, did he ever find full peace and his real self. Yet, unlike most religionists, he was keenly awake to the obligations of religion to respect, sympathise with, even learn from, and gently to purify those other worlds and their specific immanental rights and duties. In his intentions and instincts a Christian and a priest to his finger-tips, he had thus, of necessity, much to strain and to distract him. It is only if we take him thus, at his deepest and widest, that we can understand the deeply experimental character of his best work, and can be just to his labours, faults, and limitations.[55]

Before publishing the article von Hügel sent it to Maude Petre, giving her the right to correct or change anything in it, and explaining why he had written it in the way that he had. She returned it, noting that she did not see "the necessity to raise any points of detail," but also telling him quite frankly that

I won't venture to say that I find the article as a whole quite sympathetic. I suppose it expresses what I have felt in my intercourse with you since his death – viz: that you seemed more conscious of things to be excused than of things to be admired. To me the full meaning and explanation of his life has come even more fully – indeed with a fulness that has made me rather proud and humble – since his death than it did before – To you it has perhaps been otherwise; and some things have come to you as a surprise which were familiar to me. I should not be honest if I omitted to say this – while liking so much a great deal that you have said. And I daresay you will think that I am not the best judge in the matter.[56]

While their different approaches to interpreting Tyrrell remained, indeed hardened, the difference did not lessen von Hügel's support and concern for Miss Petre. She kept him abreast of her work on Tyrrell's biography and of her harassment by Bishop Amigo and others; and he shared with her his best lights on how to meet and deal with the various situations as they arose. When Amigo tried to make her subscribe to *Lamentabili* and *Pascendi*, von Hügel told her that he would pray very seriously for her "because, besides my long-standing most respectful affection and sympathy for and with you, I

[55] Ibid., pp. 249–250.
[56] Petre to von Hügel, 17 November 1909, BL, Add. MS 45361.97.

have a growing sad feeling that my own turn too will not be long in coming. May God bless and keep you in spite of all these troubles, full of Catholic faith and piety and give you the deepest strength and peace."[57]

While Maude Petre was preparing her biography of Tyrrell, von Hügel had accepted the invitation of Dr. James Hastings to write the article on "Eternal Life" for the latter's *Encyclopedia of Religion and Ethics*. Hastings told von Hügel that he could "make the paper as long as the subject-matter might seem to deserve or require." Von Hügel, however, became so engrossed in the subject that he simply let his material lead him where it would. When his article was sent in, it was found to be much too long for the *Encyclopedia*, so Hastings arranged with his Edinburgh publisher to issue von Hügel's work as a separate book.[58] Both Maude Petre's and the Baron's books were to be published in 1912, but the latter wrote to the publisher to insist that his book must be published first and told Miss Petre that

I explained to them that I hoped this my book might help somewhat to deflect and to break such blows as may be leveled at your publication, but that, for such a purpose, my book should come first. And they have hurried at the last, very commendably, and have promised to have the book out 'in any case, before the 30th.' You will see, if and when you read it that especially the chapter on 'Institutional Religion' contains emphatic, clear-cut sentences which the present authorities will not like, and which, I hope, may have the more of an effect, as they certainly were written outside of all excitement or nervous irritation and come, as the Preface explains, as an inevitable part of the book's central argument and point.[59]

The anticipated blows leveled against Maude Petre's *Life of George Tyrrell* were not slow in coming, one of the first appearing in *The Tablet*, unsigned, but thought by von Hügel to be by James Moyes, the official theologian of the Catholic archdiocese of Westminster. When Miss Petre consulted von Hügel about how to handle *The Tablet*'s attack, he advised her to do nothing, but said that he felt "distinctly inclined to write a signed letter to the Editor myself." He told her he was certain that "if my speaking is to do any good, it must be well-weighed, very dignified, significant, emphatic, calm, with anger, yes, but with perfect, self-possession. Am below par to-

[57] Von Hügel to Petre, 8 October 1910, BL, Add. MS 45362.1.
[58] Von Hügel, *Eternal*, pp. v–vi.
[59] Von Hügel to Petre, 15 October 1912, BL, Add. MS 45362.55.

day, but may be fit for that combination to-morrow."[60] He was, and the letter was duly sent and printed.[61]

The chapter in von Hügel's *Eternal Life* which he believed the contemporary church authorities would not like demonstrates his understanding of the Roman Catholic ecclesial culture of his day and also makes clear how he, as a Modernist and a mystic, dealt with it. The chapter deals with institutional religions "in so far as these are the homes and training-grounds of the experiences and convictions concerning Eternal Life, and in so far as they bring helps, or occasion obstacles, to these convictions, or contrariwise, are themselves checked and purified by these convictions."[62] Von Hügel's first principle here was that religious institutions are "the normal requirements, expressions, and instruments of the religious sense," and that religion and institutions not only need one another but must also be sensitive to all the other levels of human life and their own corresponding organizations. Yet in spite of this, he noted, in contemporary society there is widespread alienation from all institutional religion. If, then, religion is life's most profound truth and deepest joy, and if people everywhere possess some glimpses of truth and experience some goodness, and long for more of such God-given graces; why is there this alienation? To answer this question von Hügel discussed both the positive and negative aspects of the institutional dimensions of religion, and used as his representative institution "the Roman Catholic Church, as by far the oldest, most widespread, and most consistent of all such bodies; and as alone, so it happens, known and well-known from within to the present writer." He also believed that his diagnosis can apply, *mutatis mutandis*, to all institutional religion worldwide. What becomes clear from a reading of this book is that von Hügel's idea of intimations of eternal life, which can be experienced in this present life by the religiously alive person, are, from another perspective, what he means elsewhere by the mystical element of religion. And both the mystical element of religion and intimations of eternal life *should* find support and confirmation from religion's institutional element, when in fact, very often, they find frustration or even opposition instead.

In typical Hügelian fashion this was not merely a negative

[60] Von Hügel to Petre, 25 November 1912, BL, Add. MS 45362.60.
[61] Friedrich von Hügel, "Father Tyrrell," *The Tablet* 120 (30 November 1912), 866–867.
[62] Von Hügel, *Eternal*, pp. 323–324. This quotation and all those in the following seven paragraphs are taken from pages 323 to 378 of *Eternal*.

critique; it was, in fact, negative only in the sense of showing how certain human defects within the institution were hindering the institution's positive purposes and meaning from attaining their fulfillment. So he began his remarks by saying that he had "long and profoundly benefited by Institutional Religion," but that he also watched "wistfully its present-day operation and men's alienation from it." Both the intrinsic strength and attraction of institutional religion and its actual weakness and repulsiveness "are closely intertwined." He thought that this can be demonstrated "in five pairs of nearly related power and defect. The first two pairs are primarily concerned with intellectual matters; the last three pairs, with moral affairs." And he treated them "approximately in the order of their increasing influence with the majority of men."

The first pair of strength and defect had to do with the Catholic Church's "tradition of a large and continuous utilization, discussion, acceptance or rejection of Philosophical Systems and Scientific Hypotheses on the part of Religion." From the very beginning of Christianity the church had made use of philosophical ideas and systems, both because religion has an absolute need for philosophy in general and because the church has a practical need for some workable philosophy at any given period in its history. The problem developed when the institution embraced one philosophy, neo-scholasticism, as coextensive with the authoritative voice of the institution to explain and interpret the whole Christian experience and tradition. This does violence to philosophy, von Hügel insisted, because philosophy is essentially free, following "its own specific requirements and self-criticisms, or it is nothing." Church authority has the fullest right and duty to criticise or condemn any philosophical doctrine or system as incompatible with Christian faith. But philosophy's integrity is destroyed when church authority is used to enforce this or that philosophical proposition or system as true. Yet this was what was happening, and it was causing bitter and excessive reactions in some, causing them to turn against all philosophical ontology and religious institutionalism. On the other hand, said von Hügel, while contemporary church authorities have gone after many new philosophical ideas, it is "highly instructive to note how entirely silent concerning" physical and natural science "the recent most strenuous papal campaign against all and every 'Modernism' has remained throughout."

Von Hügel's second pair of strength and weakness within

institutional religion, and specifically Roman Catholicism, concerned history. This pair, together with his third pair which followed, he
believed to be simply, "*the* crux of every Institutional Religion, and
especially of one so deeply Historical as the Roman Catholic
Church." Religion in general and Rome in particular are right, he
said, in their insistence on the historicity of certain facts, "since only
in and through History, only by means of concrete happenings in
time and space, does man awaken to, does he apprehend, Eternal
Life and God, and do they penetrate and win him." He rejected
outright any "systematic or radical distinction between Historical
Happenings and Dogmatic 'Facts' or Doctrines." All genuine religion, he argued, "absolutely requires, at every stage, *Ontology*, a really
extant God, and really *happened* Historical Facts and Persons." And
this is especially true of Christianity because its "greatness resides
especially in its all-pervasive and persistent Incarnational trend;
since God, the Eternal Spirit, here reveals Himself to us, and
touches us, in Duration and through Matter." In fact, he said,
Christianity itself has helped us gradually to distinguish between
historical facts and merely ideal symbols in religion; so Rome, "the
chief representative of Christianity, which is itself so nobly Ontological and Factual, cannot but be and remain profoundly wedded to
Reality and Facts." The problem, then, has arisen with the modern
refinement of the historical sense. Religion begins with some actual
historical event. The religion's followers continue in their conviction
that the event really happened, but they also continue to probe it for
spiritual substance and meaning, and they grow in their "sense of
the Eternal's Self-manifestation in these temporal events." Here is
the problem. Those with faith in the historical happening symbolize
their interpretation of that happening "by means of fact-like historical pictures which (once a keen discrimination between factual and
non-factual becomes irresistible) cannot be taken as directly, simply
factual in the manner and degree in which those Happenings can be
taken." Certain scenes in the Fourth Gospel, said von Hügel, are
such an example. So what is Rome to do? She cannot let go of the
historical happenings, nor can she forbid historians to critique those
happenings' historical dimensions.

Yet, on the other hand, Rome cannot make the historical evidence other
than what it is; nor appeal to it, and yet insist upon keeping it above all
discussion; nor change the simple, broad facts that men in the past were
but little alive to the difference between Factual Event and Symbolic

Narrative, and that men in the present are keenly sensitive to this difference. And yet even to insist upon the strict Factualness of all the factual-seeming narratives, but to abandon the insistence upon the demonstrative force of the documents concerned, would already, no doubt, be a serious modification of the very ancient, predominant attitude of traditional theologians.

Here von Hügel dealt boldly with the essence of Rome's conflict with Loisy. Loisy was demonstrating the less-than-factualness of many passages in the New Testament, whereas a certain amount of traditional and authoritatively enforced Roman theology was premised on that factualness. So the authorities who held power in the institutional church, that is, determined who was and who was not orthodox, expelled Loisy from the institution. Von Hügel's solution, on the other hand, would have been that Roman theologians "both as Catholics and as reasonable men, will have not to insist upon historians finding more, or different, historical Happenings in documents put forward as historical proofs, than those documents will yield to careful and candid critical analysis."

Von Hügel's third set of power and weakness in the institutional side of religion derived from the Catholic Church's emphasis on the importance of truth and unity in religion. Just as religious indifference is a destructive thing in the potentially religious individual; so, in another direction, is the use of coercive force in the name of religion an ultimately destructive thing for a religious institution. The Baron briefly sketched both the Catholic history of coercion and its opposite history of "shrinking from the application of physical force in spiritual things." He addressed the issue of excommunications, calling them "admittedly fallible" and pointing out that such exclusions and even consequent schisms are not necessarily merely the fault of those excommunicated. And even if the fault is clearly and predominantly on the part of the one excluded, various degrees of truth and grace are soon evident in those who follow him. Roman Catholicism must never forget her historical many-sidedness, von Hügel urged, a many-sidedness expressed in multiple spiritualities, schools of theology, and religious orders. If Catholicism is to become "fully lovable and entirely trusted," it must recapture that larger and gentler approach, "fervent without fanaticism and universally just and encouraging without indifference." This, too, surely, was a lesson derived from Loisy's experience.

The fourth pair of strength and weakness in institutional religion which von Hügel considered was, on his own admission, "hardly distinguishable from the preceding one." This pair concerned canon law and the question of what religion has to do with law. Religion is neither a mental abstraction nor something which exists in a vacuum. Von Hügel said that "the spirituality and liberty of the Gospel have ever to develop, and to show, their full force in contact with, and through the transformation of, matter and law." So there should be no problem with the idea of law as a legitimate factor of institutional religion; the problem comes with "the spirit, character, position, and effects of such law." His approach to the problem was again historical, and he showed that the strongly theocratic Middle Ages have left too strong an imprint on current canon law. And he argued that now, in his own day, the papal curia was pursuing the application of this law with medieval fervor. Ever since the French Revolution one could witness the unrelenting "absorption or elimination of all non-Papal, non-Curialist powers and activities by Rome throughout this time, until the Vatican Council, in 1870, placed all the Church's doctrinal and disciplinary powers in the hands of the Monarch Pope." Since the accession of Pope Pius X in 1903, von Hügel argued, things have become much worse. "Indeed, Rome's action in the matter of the Separation of Church and State in France, and in the numberless condemnation of books, doctrines, and men during these eight years, also illustrates this pure autocracy." Yet he attempted to find some comfort in several facts. The first was that support for this stringent policy by papal Rome had come, throughout the nineteenth century, primarily from laymen and non-Italians, men like de Maistre, Chateaubriand, Veuillot, and William George Ward. Von Hügel was also consoled to think that "the Curialist presentation of the situation, as a simple alternative between anarchy or autocracy, revolt or self-stultification, will not forever terrify into nonentity or goad into scepticism the freely docile children of Jesus Christ and of His Vicar, the Servant of the servants of God." And, finally, he was consoled to find that, even in the midst of these distressing autocratic acts and consequent revolts against them, there yet remained "much sincere and dignified Catholic loyalty and submission, and genuine, because humble and creaturely, freedom, operating amongst numberless souls, cleric and lay, persistently devoted lovers of the great Roman Church." A more appropriate description of the Baron himself could not have been written!

Von Hügel's final pair of complications for institutional religion
had to do with politics. Politics and institutional religion cannot
mutually exclude one another, and yet as soon as religious leaders
have gained political power they have historically abused it in the
name of transcendent values. He observed that "all the world knows
how apparently incapable of dying is the Roman Curia's thirst for
the old Temporal Power over the Roman States, and its hunger for
external, political recognition and influence amongst the governments of the world." He further argued that "similarly, the political
system of Papal Nuncios, and even, recently, of semi-secret political
agents of small capacity and denunciatory procedure, has more and
more crippled the authority of the Bishops in times and countries
most in need of such an undisputed, public, essentially spiritual,
authority representative of these Churches' special needs and
wishes." That comment, read now at the end of the twentieth
century rather than at its beginning when it was written, sounds
sadly prophetic. So, too, does von Hügel's recommendation that in
the face of such politicization of the institution, "we can only do our
best, and trust God and the interconnection (ever so real even when
most obscure) of all men and classes and forces in this our wondrous
existence."

This whole lengthy chapter of von Hügel's *Eternal Life* concluded
by using the experiences of several saints and holy people whose
lives demonstrated variously how "to avoid, bear, mitigate, abolish,
or utilize the evils we have found to be closely intertwined with the
benefits of institutionalism." He listed several spiritual characteristics
and insights found in these people, some more and some less, and, as
usual, he was eclectic in his choices. He began with Charles Booth,
mentioned his good friend Claude Montefiore, specified the John
Henry Newman of the *Parochial and Plain Sermons*, the Belgian Father
Damien of the Lepers, Jean Baptiste Vianney the *Curé d'Ars*, Eugénie
Smet who became Mère Marie de la Providence, and finally,

there is before my mind, with all the vividness resulting from direct
personal intercourse and deep spiritual obligations, the figure of the Abbé
Huvelin, who died only in 1910. A gentleman by birth and breeding, a
distinguished Hellenist, a man of exquisitely piercing, humorous mind, he
could readily have become a great editor or interpreter of Greek
philosophical or patristic texts, or a remarkable Church historian. But this
deep and heroic personality deliberately preferred 'to write in souls,' whilst
occupying, during thirty-five years, a supernumerary, unpaid post in a large

Parisian parish. There, suffering from gout in the eyes and brain, and usually lying prone in a darkened room, he served souls with the supreme authority of self-oblivious love, and brought light and purity and peace to countless troubled, sorrowing, or sinful souls.

Friedrich von Hügel spent all of his adult years working and struggling to achieve the fullest expression of mystical Christianity possible in his own life, and to share that life with the institutional church in a mutually re-enforcing symbiotic relationship. He had a mind and a character which could have been of immense value to the whole visible church had the church leadership been capable of appreciating his worth and of incorporating what he himself achiev-ed into its own life and expression.[63] But it did not; and part of von Hügel's greatness is his ability to use consistently the friction and pain of this rejection by the institution he valued most for the ongoing purification of his own motives and efforts. He looked for support in his mystical pursuit wherever he could find it, and he took keen delight in individuals whose long-term performance did not disappoint him in this ultimate value.[64] After the death of his friend Archbishop Eudoxe Irenée Mignot of Albi, von Hügel tried to explain what it was about the prelate which had so attracted him. And one of the characteristics in Mignot which he mentioned, and which he himself especially shared with Mignot, goes very far in

[63] This difference between the mind-set of turn-of-the-century clerical Rome and von Hügel, the Baron once demonstrated in a letter written from Rome to Tyrrell: "M. Brunetierè has been here, lecturing on . . . Bossuet; and this spiritually utterly cold and empty rhetorician, this panegyrist of an ecclesiastical police, had some 8 cardinals and practically all the official clerical world at his Conference. There is no doubt that he represents *exactly* the type best understood here; and again, the type we *don't* want. They enormously over-estimate the power of the press for one thing; then they understand rhetoric, and don't understand specialism, or severe method, critical or any other; and lastly they understand religion as an external institution, a social force, a polity and policy. And B., of course, represented and gave them encouragement along all these their lines." Von Hügel to Tyrrell, 4 March 1900, BL, Add. MS 44927.105.

[64] One of these, not a Catholic, and of great intellectual and spiritual importance to von Hügel, was Ernst Troeltsch, whom he first met in 1902. "He is another man from whom I have learned and am learning indefinitely much . . . He has the most sensitive consciousness of the complexity and relativity of all history and its evidences; and extraordinary speculative, metaphysical competence and revealing power; and finally a truly touching and personally devotional sense and experience, which runs through all, and hallows, steadies and deepens it. And his knowledge of the history, of the literature, of the present requirements of all these three things is astonishing; and his honesty, and straight cleanness and clearness of vision is, of itself, a true moral tonic, which stems from a robust, truly manly faith, and leads straight on to its strengthening in others." Von Hügel to Tyrrell, 4 June 1902, BL, Add. MS 44928.16–17.

helping one understand both von Hügel's intellectual and moral stances throughout his life. Of Mignot he wrote:

There was a quite spontaneous, quite simple, activity of all the natural faculties – of these as the prerequisites, the substrates, occasions and materials of grace. When at eighteen I made my full and deliberate submission to the Catholic Church, to her as my teacher and trainer throughout my life, it never entered my head during that now well-nigh fifty years of my Catholic practice – to ask for permission to think – also to think my religion – any more than it occurred to me to get leave to be hungry and thirsty and to eat and to drink, or to feel the impulsions of sex-life, or to love my family or country. Every one of these things was and is continuously felt to require a continuous purification, correction, supplementation by grace and training within and through the Church; yet not one of these things but is felt, in its essence, to possess a certain spontaneity, autonomy, right, duty, method and range of its own. And such a relation between Nature and Grace is felt to be inherent in God's own planning and formation of us, so that intrinsically some such autonomies of Nature are necessary for the full penetrations and mouldings of Grace. Now in M. Mignot I always perceived this same unquestioned, quite unquestioning presupposition – this activity of his mind, as frank and spontaneous as was the activity of his senses or of his affections.[65]

But thinking one's religion, spontaneously and naturally, whether by an archbishop or a baron, was unacceptable to the Rome of Pius X. And when Mignot sent Christmas greetings to von Hügel in 1912, he told him that he as archbishop had "been denounced in Rome as half or three quarters a heretic, and that he has now wrapped himself in an *obstinate* silence, whilst such raging wolves are abroad with impunity."[66]

Any reform movement necessarily attracts supporters with a wide spectrum of motives, both conscious and unconscious, which justify to themselves their support. Friedrich von Hügel was a major contributor to the Roman Catholic Modernist movement because he sincerely believed that many of its suggested reforms could have made the institutional church a more effective vehicle for fostering sanctity. He also believed that the pursuit of intellectual "truth" was radically important for this mystical dimension of religion, and that policy was no substitute for truth. But the church as nurturer of saints was the prime object of his ecclesial affection. Unlike many of his fellow Modernists, he really believed that the institutional church

[65] Friedrich von Hügel, "Eudoxe Irenée Mignot," p. 520.
[66] Von Hügel to Petre, 7 January 1913, BL, Add. MS 45362.71.

was, despite all its faults and even downright corruption, an undeniable *given* of Christianity, and the God-given instrument within which Christians were meant to realize their spiritual potential. Years before the anti-Modernist crusade of Pius X, von Hügel had expressed this conviction of his in a letter to Wilfrid Ward, in which he delineated how he and Ward differed in their attitudes toward the Catholic saints and church reform. He told Ward that

I feel that we ought not to specially seek out in saints, and put forward as the classical ideal, an admission, however full and painful, of abuses, desirable reform etc., all to lead up simply to a making the best of the de facto situation, and a philosophy of preference for unreformed Rome over any and every heresy or schism. But that the far more complex and difficult, but alone fully adequate ideal should be sought (and it can certainly be found) amongst them, of every kind and degree of reformatory claim, action, ideal and (partial) achievement, within the limits of a refusal to break with the Church. The Church as it is, would thus never be a thing to just simply put up with; and our energies would never be spent in elaborating theories either to show that things as they are, really will *do*; or that, not to so accept them thus, involves the alternative of leaving the Church. But the soul of the Church alone would be, not thus simply put up with, but heartwholly endorsed and willed, for its own sake; and the body of the Church, just because it was loved too, but loved only on account of its being a means and expression of that soul, would be both worked *at* and worked *for*, and would in every act of acceptance, be accepted also to be improved.[67]

This "complex and difficult, but alone fully adequate ideal" was von Hügel's own throughout the Modernist crisis; and because it was complex and difficult, involving strong faith and deep asceticism, and thus was not a simple black-and-white affair, it was not understood by most of his fellow Modernists and has been misunderstood by most of those since who think they can explain him.[68] One

---

[67] Von Hügel to Ward, 10 October 1900, SAUL, VII, 143 (119).
[68] At the end of 1909, after Tyrrell's death, he told Maude Petre that she was "about the only English Catholic, with whom I have felt, with whom I do feel, profoundly at one, in these most complex and straining transition-problems." Von Hügel to Petre, 12 November 1909, BL, Add. MS 45361.94. In 1910 he made it clear how little he had in common with Ernesto Bonajuti and Salvatore Minocchi (Von Hügel to Petre, 18 February 1910, BL, Add. MS 45361.120–121); and upon receiving Albert Houtin's *Histoire du Modernisme catholique* from the author, he remarked that it was "surely a most painful performance, at least as much so because of the writer's all-pervading corrosive embitterment as for the saddening facts he has to tell. What a dangerous man, poor thing. No, no: the way out is not through and into this kind of thing." Von Hügel to Petre, 15 October 1912, BL, Add. MS 45362.55–56. And finally, any reader of Loisy's *Mémoires* quickly comes to realize how little he ever really understood von Hügel or had been at one with him. Perhaps nowhere is this better

cannot understand von Hügel on the level of ideas alone. From his late adolescence to this death, sanctity, the fruition of the mystical element of religion in his own life, an element which involved full human experience and more than the rational faculties alone, was his conscious goal.

More than twenty years after articulating his ideal to Ward, he was asked by Professor Norman Kemp Smith of the University of Edinburgh if he still believed that the Roman Catholic Church was capable of assimilating the best in the modern world. That question, he told Kemp Smith, "is one that certainly, after suffering under Pius X, I ought fully to understand."[69] His answer was threefold. First, he knew individual Catholics, clerics and laypersons, who had achieved this assimilation. And, though individuals are one thing and whole institutions another, yet, "in this poor world of trouble and inevitable, difficult choosings, it is not nothing to find such an assimilation a *fact*, and no mere hope." He cited Huvelin as having been such an individual. Secondly, he said that he could not "do more, with regard to the Church authorities, than to include such assimilative action of theirs, amongst the objects of my faith." And he told Kemp Smith that in all the many winters he had spent in Rome before Pius X, he had found individual authorities who were not opposed to such assimilation; and that since Pius X there have again been like-minded individual authorities. Von Hügel's third point in his answer to Kemp Smith was the one he considered the most important, and the one which his own experience especially demonstrated. He reminded Kemp Smith that "the essential, the most indispensable of the dimensions of religion is, *not breadth, but depth*, and above all, *the insight into sanctity and the power to produce saints*." And with the conviction born of a lifetime's struggles, he concluded: "Rome continues – of this I am very sure – to possess this supernatural depth – possesses it in far greater degree than Protestantism, and still more than the quite unattached moderns."

expressed than in the letter which Loisy sent to Semeria in April 1906 and which Loisy himself quotes: "Notre cher baron von Hügel pense que la raison conduit au monisme, mais que la coeur suffit à trouver Dieu" (Our dear Baron von Hügel thinks that reason leads to monism, but that the heart suffices for finding God). He goes on to say that von Hügel's God is very like Harnack's, and that von Hügel's mystical element of religion is an illusion! Loisy, *Mémoires*, vol. ii, p. 469.

69 Von Hügel to Norman Kemp Smith, 31 December 1921–3 January 1922, in *The Letters of Baron Friedrich von Hügel and Professor Norman Kemp Smith*, ed. Lawrence Barmann (New York: Fordham University Press, 1981), p. 161. The other quotations in this paragraph are from the same letter.

After von Hügel's death in January 1925, his longtime friend Abbot Cuthbert Butler of Downside Abbey wrote an obituary appreciation of him for *The Tablet* of London. In his piece Butler emphasized von Hügel's intellectual contributions to religious and theistic thought, pointing out "the intellectual qualities that gave von Hügel his special power as an apostle of theism and of religion to a generation whereof the intellectuals largely know not God, the personal God of Christianity."[70] And though Butler's treatment of von Hügel stressed the latter's intellectual qualities and contributions, it concluded by saying that "beyond all compare greater than the intellectual appeal was the moral appeal of von Hügel's personal religion." Not only those who read him, but most especially everyone who came into close personal contact with him, "could not but feel that religion was the great all-absorbing interest of his life, the one thing he supremely cared about. And not merely religion, but Catholic religion." Butler said that von Hügel's writings "proclaim Catholicism to be of all religions the highest, fullest, richest, most helpful, most powerful, true; again and again he says he could not think of himself as anything else than a Catholic." Von Hügel's widow wrote to thank Butler for the article, telling him that it "said so many things about him which I longed should be said & which the other articles had not said; excellent as several of them were."[71]

Von Hügel's appeal to those outside the Roman Catholic Church who took religion seriously had been very great. And though he not only did not minimize his Catholicism, but in fact proclaimed it boldly, he was treated by the Catholic institution as a leper. Butler's article had given a nod to this fact by noting that the Baron's "works probably would not be given an *Imprimatur.*" He believed that this was much less important than what von Hügel had achieved in his life. It was the combination of von Hügel's intellectual and mystical dimensions of religion, within the institutional church, which made him "if not an 'apologist,' certainly himself an arresting 'apology' for those religious truths, for that Catholicism, that were the very life of his life."

[70] Abbot Butler, "Friedrich von Hügel," *The Tablet* 45 (14 February 1925), 202.
[71] Mary Catherine von Hügel to Cuthbert Butler, 16 February 1925, Downside Abbey Archives, vH papers. The articles referred to by Lady Mary were by Professor Norman Kemp Smith in *The Scotsman*; by Bishop (soon to be Archbishop of York, and eventually of Canterbury) William Temple and Evelyn Underhill (Mrs. Stuart Moore) in *The Guardian*; and a sermon by W. R. Matthews, the Dean of St. Paul's.

CHAPTER 9

English Catholicism and Modernism

Ellen M. Leonard, C.S.J.

Friedrich von Hügel (1852–1925) and Maude Petre (1863–1942) were deeply committed Roman Catholic lay persons who saw the need for reform in the Catholic Church and worked toward that end. They did so while maintaining a remarkable openness to members of other Christian churches and other religions. Each spent considerable time in France and Italy, but for both England was home. Petre belonged to an old English Catholic family, while von Hügel, who had been born in Florence and remained an Austrian citizen until 1914, lived most of his life in England. The church was the primary focus of their lives and their writing. Both were major actors in the development of what became known as Roman Catholic Modernism and particularly in the drama surrounding George Tyrrell's brief and brilliant career and untimely death.

This paper focuses on English Catholicism between 1890 and 1910, crucial years in the history of the Catholic Church in England and in the lives of both von Hügel and Petre. During these transitional years, that church was coming to a new sense of itself. It ceased to be a "missionary outpost" and became "more Roman." Against this changing background von Hügel and Petre resolutely maintained their Catholic identity. While some have considered them to be only marginally Catholic, they considered their lives to be shaped decisively by their Catholicism. Although both were uncomfortable with the form English Catholicism was taking between 1890 and 1910, their understanding of Catholicism was broad enough and deep enough to sustain their Catholic identity – an identity that was at once both critical and faithful.

The first section of the paper explores some of the factors which shaped English Catholicism. Section two situates Friedrich von Hügel and Maude Petre within that tradition, indicating how they appropriated it without becoming submerged within it. Section three considers a number of significant ecclesial events between 1890 and 1910 which reinforced a particular approach to Catholicism and indicates how von Hügel and Petre responded to these events. The final section suggests that von Hügel and Petre were not only influenced by the religious context in which they lived and wrote but made their own unique contribution to English Catholicism. That contribution was not appreciated by their fellow Catholics during their lifetime, although their work was recognized by Christians outside the Roman Catholic Church. This they were able to do by combining a deep love for Catholicism with a critical spirit.

FORMATIVE FACTORS THAT SHAPED ENGLISH CATHOLICISM

The year 1890 marked the death of the great Cardinal Newman, whose conversion to Catholicism in 1845 had so profoundly influenced the Catholic Church in England. In July 1852, at the first Provincial Synod of Westminster, he had preached his famous sermon on "The Second Spring," in which he described in negative terms the position of Catholics at the end of the eighteenth century:

No longer the Catholic Church in the country; nay, no longer, I may say, a Catholic community, but a few adherents of the old religion, moving silently and sorrowfully about, as memorials of what had been. "The Roman Catholics" – not a sect, not even an interest, as men conceive it, not a body, however small, representative of the great communion abroad, but a mere handful of individuals, who might be counted like the pebbles and detritus of the great deluge, and who, forsooth, merely happened to retain a creed which in its day indeed was the profession of a Church.[1]

Although Newman's description was somewhat exaggerated, it provides a vivid contrast to the situation a hundred years later in 1890.

From the Reformation until 1850, the Catholic Church in England had been a mission from Rome under the care of vicars apostolic. During this wintry season in which Catholics were banished from public life, the faith had been kept alive by a faithful remnant of families, such as the Petre family, who had remained loyal to Rome since the Reformation. John Bossy, in his description of the Catholic gentry of East Anglia, refers to the Petres as "the one family of cast-iron landed magnates to remain invincibly Catholic

---

[1] J. H. Newman, "The Second Spring," *Sermons Preached on Various Occasions* (London: Longmans, Green and Co., 1892), pp. 163–182.

from the sixteenth century onwards and one in a very advantageous position for making its wealth felt."[2] These recusant Catholics had a sense of themselves as part of a universal body with a loyalty to Rome, but also as loyal English citizens. While their Protestant neighbors might question their dual loyalties to pope and crown and look upon them as politically subversive, the recusants were able, in spite of restrictions, personal hardship, and persecution over the centuries, to work out and to maintain their delicate position. Because of the restrictions placed upon Catholics, ecclesiastical property and appointment of priests were under lay control, a practice which Rome accepted as a necessary exception to general rules. The faith of the recusant Catholics was marked by fidelity in spite of opposition, by loyalty, and by lay leadership.

The Catholic population of Britain had probably fallen by about forty percent between 1720 and 1780, rising thereafter chiefly through Irish immigration to a total of 129,000 in 1800. By 1850 the number of Catholics had reached 846,000. This growth continued during the second half of the century reaching 1,691,000 by 1890 and 2,016,000 by 1900.[3] The Catholic Church had to reorganize in order to meet the pastoral needs of a more diverse and expanding population. In 1850 Pius IX restored the diocesan hierarchy by appointing Catholic bishops to twelve dioceses. Wiseman, vicar apostolic of London since 1849, became the first cardinal archbishop of the newly established metropolitan see of Westminster. The restoration of the Catholic hierarchy, under the leadership of Cardinal Wiseman, was greeted with joy by most Catholics. Wiseman proudly proclaimed: "Catholic England has been restored to its orbit in the ecclesiastical firmament, from which its light has long vanished, and begins now anew its course of regular adjusted action round the centre of unity, the source of jurisdiction, of light, and of vigour."[4] For many members of the Church of England, however, this change was seen as an act of "papal aggression." Angry mobs burned effigies of the pope and cardinal. In a more ecumenical age it is difficult to imagine how upsetting the restoration

[2] John Bossy, *The English Catholic Community 1570–1850* (New York: Oxford University Press, 1976), p. 101.
[3] Robert Currie, Alan Gilbert and Lee Horsley, *Churches and Churchgoers: Patterns of Church Growth in the British Isles since 1700* (Oxford: Clarendon Press, 1977), pp. 23–29.
[4] From Wiseman's pastoral, *Out of the Flaminian Gate*, quoted by J. Derek Holmes, *More Roman than Rome: English Catholicism in the Nineteenth Century* (London: Burns & Oates, 1978), p. 75.

of the Catholic hierarchy was, not only to many of the general population, but also to the bishops of the Church of England, who protested to the Queen against "this attempt to subject our people to a spiritual tyranny from which they were freed at the Reformation."[5] Wiseman wrote his "Appeal to the Reason and Good Feeling of the English People," published in five London papers, explaining that as Archbishop of Westminster he would be responsible not for the Abbey but for the destitute people needing spiritual as well as material sustenance. The anti-papist demonstrations died down, although anti-Catholic sentiments remained.

In colorful language of a "second spring," Newman described his vision of the Catholic Church in England at the beginning of the second half of the nineteenth century – but it was a particular kind of spring: "Have we any right to take it strange, if, in this English land, the spring-time of the Church should turn out to be an English spring, an uncertain, anxious time of hope and fear, joy and suffering, – of bright promise and budding hopes, yet withal, of keen blasts, and cold showers, and sudden storms?"[6] This accurate description conveys the sense of excitement experienced by Catholics who for centuries had been largely "invisible" in English society. Now their numbers were increasing, both by the conversions of influential people, such as Newman himself, and by large numbers of Irish immigrants swelling the Catholic population of the cities. The number of Catholics was still small (about three and a half percent of the population in England and Wales in 1850), but there was a sense of expansion.[7] The restoration of the hierarchy introduced England to a more rigid form of Tridentine Catholicism. Norman describes the effect:

To the exultant converts, anxious to luxuriate in everything which differentiated themselves from the English religion they had abandoned, this was splendid; to the Old Catholics, however, it was a lamentable and insensitive renunciation of a religious tone which echoed centuries of sacrifice and common-sense adjustment to Protestant sensibilities.[8]

The influence of the clergy over the laity was extended, and the old

---

[5] Quoted by Holmes, ibid., p. 76.   [6] "The Second Spring," pp. 179–180.
[7] Edward Norman, *The English Catholic Church in the Nineteenth Century* (Oxford: Clarendon Press, 1984), p. 3; see also Currie, Gilbert and Horsley, *Churches and Churchgoers*, pp. 23–29.
[8] Edward Norman, *Roman Catholicism in England from the Elizabethan Settlement to the Second Vatican Council* (Oxford: Oxford University Press, 1985), p. 84.

Catholics no longer enjoyed the hegemony that had been theirs under the vicars apostolic.

The growing Catholic population was by no means homogeneous and represented different classes. As a result of the French Revolution many priests, religious, and lay people had fled to England, some of them staying and helping to transform the Catholic Church in that country. The old Catholic families were a small but influential group with their own quiet English spirituality. Increasing numbers of converts to Catholicism, some like Newman connected with the Oxford Movement, formed a third group. These conversions continued throughout the nineteenth century. In the 1890s converts probably numbered ten thousand a year.[9] Finally, the influx of Irish immigrants greatly increased the Catholic population, particularly in cities such as London, Birmingham, and Liverpool. Catholics in each of these groups had their own needs and priorities.

Von Hügel, Petre, and Tyrrell reflect three of these different backgrounds. Von Hügel represented the European Catholics who brought their own international flavor and breadth to English Catholicism. Maude Petre was an articulate representative of the old Catholics, that strong, independent group of laity who had kept Catholicism alive in England during and after the Reformation and whose courage she praised in her work on *The Ninth Lord Petre*.[10] George Tyrrell, himself a convert, joined the Society of Jesus with the expressed desire to work with others who, like himself, had to struggle to come to faith. Much of his ministry of writing and spiritual direction was directed to those who were interested in becoming Catholics or who had recently joined the church.

Most numerous within English Catholicism were the Irish immigrants. Gerard Connelly describes how the influx of Irish affected the Catholic clergy, who struggled to minister to their flock amidst dreadful poverty and lack of adequate places for worship. Concern about "leakage" among the immigrants motivated the extensive building of churches and the struggle to provide Catholic education. Gradually the Catholic clergy were able to reclaim leadership of English Catholicism from aristocratic laity such as Petre's father, who considered the clergy to be their employees. In Connelly's

---

9 Walter L. Anstein, *Protestant Versus Catholic in Mid-Victorian England: Mr. Newdegate and the Nuns* (Columbia, Missouri, and London: University of Missouri Press, 1982), p. 216.

10 Maude Petre, *The Ninth Lord Petre: Pioneers of Roman Catholic Emancipation* (London: SPCK, 1928).

words, the result of this clericalization was "the appearance in nineteenth-century England of an aggressive and exclusive Roman Catholic Church with an appetite for contentious dogma, authoritarian rubric, clerical omnicompetence and an often tasteless obsequiousness toward the papacy."[11]

The bond which united the disparate groups of English Catholics under their leaders was a strong allegiance to Rome, and to the person of the pope. This loyalty caused them to be viewed with hostility or at least suspicion by their Protestant neighbors. After great struggle and amid fear of "popery," Catholic emancipation had been achieved during the early nineteenth century, but anti-Catholicism was still widespread. Foreigners, especially southern Europeans, were suspect. Holmes describes the view held by many: "Catholics were unenlightened, intolerant bigots whose religion was opposed to sound economic progress and liberal political development."[12] In Marvin O'Connell's words: "Catholicism for most Englishmen remained beneath contempt, representing for them as it did mummery and priestcraft indulged in by inferior Latins and Celts."[13]

A history of popular antipathy had its impact on English Catholics. They were somewhat defensive and often viewed as outsiders. In his own way von Hügel was an "outsider." He chose England for his home, but his German name and accent set him apart within his adopted country. Gradually he found a place within the larger religious milieu of his day, and through his writings and lectures he challenged the perception of Catholics as removed from the mainstream of religious life and thought. As a recusant Catholic, Maude Petre, although thoroughly English, grew up in a church which she described as embracing her, but it also set her apart from the dominant culture.[14] Like von Hügel she tried to present Catholicism in a favorable light to a public which looked upon Catholics with suspicion.

The English Catholic community in the nineteenth century generally remained socially and politically isolated. According to

---

[11] Gerard Connelly, "The Transubstantiation of Myth: Towards a New Popular Nineteenth Century Catholicism in England," *Journal of Ecclesiastical History* 35 (January 1984), 78–104; quote from p. 94.
[12] Holmes, *More Roman than Rome*, p. 44.
[13] O'Connell, *Critics*, p. 95.
[14] Petre, *My Way of Faith* (London: Dent, 1937), p. 61.

Owen Chadwick it put out "prickles against its environment." "For it mostly consisted of working men who felt half-foreigners and knew that they were disliked; and where it did not consist of Irish, it consisted either of old-fashioned recusant aristocrats with a long tradition of quiet separateness, or of a small number of converts from other churches who knew themselves disapproved as converts by the main body of society."[15]

This attitude of isolation was encouraged by the clergy. The hierarchy discouraged Catholics from attending the older universities, which were seen as dangerous to faith and morals. Manning, who succeeded Wiseman in 1865 as second archbishop of Westminster, attempted unsuccessfully to provide a Catholic university in Kensington, but lacking both personnel and money, as well as support from the laity, it only lasted from 1875 to 1882.

The appointment of Henry Edward Manning, a convert, as archbishop of Westminster was a triumph of ultramontanism and romanization. Under his leadership English Catholics were encouraged to be "more Roman than Rome, and more ultramontane than the Pope himself."[16] In their devotional life and even in their dress, the English clergy were to be romanized. Manning endeavored to raise the prestige of the secular clergy by introducing the use of the title "father," which had previously been used only for priests in religious orders. He was one of the most enthusiastic supporters of papal infallibility, both before and after its proclamation at the First Vatican Council in 1870. Newman, who believed in papal infallibility, was opposed to its definition, as were some others, but the majority of English Catholics, following the leadership of Manning, favored it.

Improved communications, combined with a strong ultramontane spirit and a distrust of liberal ideas, enabled the Vatican to exert rigid control over the Catholic Church in different countries. The men who were chosen as bishops were strongly committed to carrying out Vatican policy. This practice seems to have been particularly true in England. Wiseman (1850–65) and his successors, Manning (1865–1892) and Vaughan (1892–1903), had all been educated in Rome and were deeply committed to ultramontane

[15] Owen Chadwick, *The Victorian Church*, Part II (London: A. & C. Black, 1970), pp. 402–403.
[16] H. E. Manning, "The Work and the Wants of the Catholic Church in England," *Dublin Review*, n.s. 1 (1863), 139–166; quote p. 162; reprinted in *Miscellanies*, vol. 1 (London: 1877), pp. 27–71.

attitudes and policies.[17] Unlike the traditional old Catholics who were more independent and insular and espoused their own form of Gallicanism known as Cisalpinism, many of the recent converts as well as the priests and members of religious orders from other countries who now settled in England gave English Catholicism a strong Roman stamp. Devotion to the person of the pope became a characteristic mark of the true Catholic.

Did English Catholicism enjoy that second spring predicted by Newman? Certainly the second half of the nineteenth century was a time of tremendous growth, as numerous churches and schools were built to meet the needs of the rapidly increasing Catholic population. Religious houses were established. The Jesuits, Benedictines, and Dominicans flourished once again. Other orders such as the Redemptorists, Passionists, Oratorians, and the Premonstratensians made foundations in England. Numerous orders and congregations of women opened monasteries and convents. These included the Carmelites, the order which von Hügel's youngest daughter Thekla entered in 1907, and the Filles de Marie, the society in which Maude Petre was a member from 1890 to 1908. Some orders brought with them new devotions which seemed strange to English sensibilities. The numerous religious orders with their schools contributed to the transformation of English Catholicism, while their service to the poor and sick was recognized and appreciated by the general public.

With the exception of Cardinal Manning, who was a strong supporter of labor, the English Catholic bishops were less involved in the politics of social reform during the closing decades of the nineteenth century than the Anglican leaders. The Catholic bishops focused more on the pastoral than the political, as they struggled to meet the needs of their diverse population. Even after the publication of Leo XIII's *Rerum Novarum* in 1891, social Catholicism developed slowly among English Catholics.

The Catholic press was growing, and both Petre and von Hügel published in it as well as in the secular press. A number of periodicals which still publish in England date back to the nineteenth century: *Dublin Review* (1836), *The Tablet* (1840), and the Jesuit periodical *The Month* (1864). Other periodicals such as *The Rambler* (1848), which became *The Home and Foreign Review* (1862), were

[17] J. Derek Holmes, "English Catholicism from Wiseman to Bourne," *Clergy Review* 61 (1976), 57–69, 107–116. While acknowledging the influence of these three churchmen, it is important to remember that London is not England and the church is not just its leaders.

discontinued because of conflict with ecclesiastical authorities. Vaughan bought *The Tablet* in 1868 and the *Dublin Review* in 1878 and used these journals to promote loyalty to Rome and ecclesiastical authority. Catholic periodicals that survived did so because they were able to meet the requirements of censorship.

Gradually the diverse elements which made up English Catholicism were assimilated into a more homogeneous reality, as may be exemplified in the men who were appointed archbishops of Westminster. Herbert Vaughan, the third archbishop of Westminster, was the oldest son of an old Catholic family. His mother was a convert from Anglicanism. Francis Bourne, who succeeded Vaughan as archbishop of Westminster in 1903 and continued in that post until 1935, was the son of a convert English father and an Irish Catholic mother. Although the elements were fusing, it is possible to identify a number of strands which made up English Catholicism. From the old Catholics the tradition of lay leadership continued among an elite. The sense of being an oppressed minority within the dominant culture also endured, as well as a strong loyalty to the papacy and to Rome as their spiritual center. As the church moved toward the end of the nineteenth century, however, the belated effects of the Council of Trent and the more recent influence of the First Vatican Council were felt under the strong leadership of Manning and Vaughan. English Catholicism had become more romanized and clerical.

Rather than seeing itself as a component of English Christianity, the Catholic Church in England saw itself as a "(beleaguered) outwork of 'The Church', a divine institution founded by Christ in person and entrusted to Peter and his successors in Rome."[18] No opportunities were lost in making the Roman claims. When Vaughan was appointed archbishop of Westminster in 1892, he chose to receive the *pallium* in London rather than in Rome, remarking that it was "too good a trump-card against the Anglican to throw away."[19]

Isolation was giving way to cautious involvement, as Catholics began to participate in the social and political life of the country while still forming their own clubs and unions and supporting their own schools. In February 1893 Friedrich's brother, Anatole von

---

[18] Connelly, "Transubstantiation," p. 96.
[19] Holmes, *More Roman than Rome*, p. 200. Quote from Vaughan's letter to Lady Herbert, 15 May 1892. Shane Leslie (ed.), *Letters of Herbert Cardinal Vaughan to Lady Herbert of Lea 1867–1903* (London: Burns & Oates, 1942), p. 405.

Hügel, robed in his Cambridge gown and hood, attended a papal audience and presented an address to the pope from Catholic undergraduates of Cambridge University who, "according to ecclesiastical authorities, were not supposed to exist."[20] In January 1895 the bishops, with some reluctance, decided to ask the Roman authorities to allow Catholics to attend the old universities, and Leo XIII gave his approval. The "Church of outsiders" was taking root in English soil. It was becoming more confident, distinctive, assertive, and ultramontane.

In spite of the rapid growth during the second half of the nineteenth century, English Catholicism was still under the jurisdiction of the Propaganda in Rome and therefore considered a mission church. England itself was seen as a mission field awaiting conversion. However, Vaughan called upon English Catholics as members of the British Empire to support a college to train foreign missioners. Under his persistent leadership the St. Joseph Missionary Society at Mill Hill was founded and flourished. It opened in 1866 with one student and one professor. Even after Vaughan became bishop of Salford and later archbishop of Westminster, he continued as superior general of the Mission Society.

In founding the English Foreign Mission Society Vaughan was supported by Lady Herbert, Friedrich von Hügel's mother-in-law, whom he met in 1866, a year after she had become a Catholic. Following her reception into the Catholic Church, as part of a determined effort to ensure the Protestant succession of the Herberts, her children were taken as wards in Chancery and brought up in the Church of England. With the exception of her daughter Mary, who became a Catholic before marrying Friedrich von Hügel, Lady Herbert was unable to share her faith with her children, a situation which grieved her. The missionary students at Mill Hill became the focus of her life. When buried along with Vaughan at Mill Hill, her tomb bore the simple epitaph, "The Mother of the Mill."[21]

The church that the English missionaries transported to foreign lands was both distinctively English and Roman, although it seemed to Maude Petre and others that it was becoming less English and more Roman. She and von Hügel, though loyal members of the Roman Catholic Church, envisioned a more open church than that of the late nineteenth century. For Petre her Catholic ancestors

---

[20] Holmes, *More Roman than Rome*, pp. 233–234.   [21] Leslie, *Letters*, introduction.

provided a model, while von Hügel looked to the saints and mystics, particularly to those before the division of Western Christendom. Both had a strong sense of their responsibility as lay Catholics to participate in the mission of the church. Both were financially able to devote their time and energy to what they understood to be their vocations within the church. They appropriated the tradition of English Catholicism, but they did so in a critical way. In the following section I will consider briefly how each expressed his or her Catholicism in terms of lay responsiblity, participation in the church's mission, and relationship with Rome.

VON HÜGEL'S CATHOLICISM

The characteristics of von Hügel's Catholicism have been carefully developed in Barmann's essay, "The Modernist as mystic."[22] As Barmann emphasizes, the mystical dimension was central to von Hügel's Catholicism throughout his life. His earliest religious memories went back to the "mysterious divine Presence in the churches of Florence."[23] Three other aspects of von Hügel's Catholicism are particularly significant: his understanding of his vocation as a lay scholar, his appreciation of the richness of the Catholic tradition, and his conviction concerning the place of loyal critique within the church.

Von Hügel carefully explained in the preface of *The Mystical Element*, dated Easter 1908, just a few months after the condemnation of Modernism, how he understood his contribution to the life of the church. Describing himself as "a proudly devoted and grateful son of the Roman Church," he recognized the many different kinds and degrees of light both within and without the Christian and Catholic Church.[24] He then situated his work as a lay person, acknowledging that the official church has "the exclusive right and duty to formulate successively, for the Church's successive periods . . . normative forms and expressions of the Church's deepest consciousness and mind." However, this articulation does not take place in a

---

[22] See Lawrence Barmann, "The Modernist as mystic," pp. 215–247 above. See also Leonard, *Creative Tension: The Spiritual Legacy of Friedrich von Hügel* (Scranton, Pennsylvania: University of Scranton Press, 1997).

[23] Von Hügel, *The Reality of God and Religion and Agnosticism*, ed. Edmund G. Gardner (London: Dent, 1931), p. 80.

[24] Von Hügel, *Mystical*, vol. I, p. ix.

vacuum. The role of what he called "the Church's unofficial members" is to do the "tentative, and preliminary work" that is necessary if the church is to express its deepest consciousness.[25]

Von Hügel's status as a layman gave him a freedom of expression that his clerical friends, bound by rules of censorship, did not enjoy. "I am a layman, who, just because he speaks with no kind of official authority, can the more easily say simply what he knows."[26] This freedom must have seemed especially precious, when he saw many of his friends who were priests deprived of their professorships, among them Tyrrell, Loisy, Semeria, and Genocchi. Von Hügel believed, however, that the independence and freedom which he enjoyed as a lay person also carried responsibilities. In discharging his scholarly work, he strove for "a layman's special virtues and function: complete candour, courage, sensitiveness to the present and future."[27]

While von Hügel recognized the importance of ecclesiastical "officials" and was a personal friend of many bishops, both English and Roman, he resolutely refused to limit the church to its "officials." When Tyrrell was experiencing difficulties with Cardinal Ferrata, the Prefect of the Sacred Congregation for Religious, von Hügel reminded him:

> The Church is more and other than just these Churchmen; and religion is more, and largely other, than even the best theology: and we, i.e. he, L (Loisy), you, M.D.P. (Petre), I – our housemaids too, are true, integral portions of the Church, which in none of its members is simply teaching, in none of its members is simply learning.[28]

Von Hügel's view of Catholicism had an openness that was unusual for the period. No doubt his childhood experiences helped to shape his ecumenical approach to religion. Son of an Austrian Catholic father and Scottish Presbyterian mother who converted to Catholicism, Friedrich's education had an ecumenical dimension under private tuition by a Protestant woman, a Lutheran pastor, a German Catholic historian, and a Quaker geologist. The fact that

---

[25] Ibid., p. xi.
[26] "Father Tyrrell: Some Memorials of the Last Twelve Years of His Life," *Hibbert Journal* 8 (January 1910), 234.
[27] Von Hügel, *Mystical*, vol. 1, p. xi.
[28] Von Hügel to Tyrrell, 18 December 1906, British Library (hereafter BL), Add. MS 44929; published in von Hügel, *Letters*, pp. 136–137; quote p. 136.

he belonged to no particular school or academic discipline gave von Hügel a freedom to pursue whatever interested him.

The wider, richer Catholicism that von Hügel envisioned and hoped to see embodied in English Catholicism was more concerned with truth than with orthodoxy, an attitude he had learned from his spiritual director, Abbé Huvelin.[29] Huvelin helped him to appreciate the rich Catholic tradition as it found expression before the defensive reactions of the Tridentine and Vatican Councils. In the great pre-Reformation Catholic tradition he discovered wisdom which relativized the difficulties that he experienced within the church of his day. And yet he knew that it is only in the present that the church in each generation must respond to its own challenges. Through his writing and his personal contact with ecclesiastical superiors he tried to help the church in England embrace the larger Catholicism which he loved.

Von Hügel's loyalty to the Catholic Church included critique. He considered himself an ultramontane, but not in the narrow political sense of the late nineteenth century. In 1892 he wrote to Wilfrid Ward: "Personally, I have never been anything but an Ultramontane, in the old and definite sense of the word, ever since I have been a convinced Catholic at all."[30] He acknowledged the centralizing process that had placed all "doctrinal and disciplinary powers in the hands of the Monarch Pope." His hope was that just as laymen, including W. G. Ward, had pressed this policy on Rome, "zealous believers, perhaps again mostly laymen and non-Italians, may arise who will successfully aid the return to a wider and richer, a truly Catholic, action."[31] Writing in 1912, von Hügel expressed his hope that the church would eventually work out a fruitful relationship between authority and freedom. He was convinced that: "The curialist presentation of the situation, as a simple alternative between anarchy or autocracy, revolt or self-stultification, will not for ever terrify into nonentity or goad into scepticism the freely docile children of Jesus Christ and of his Vicar, the Servant of the servants of God."[32]

As a lay scholar von Hügel used his influence to further the study of religion within the Catholic Church, both by his own contributions to scholarship and by his support of other scholars. He

---

[29] For Huvelin's influence on von Hügel see Barmann, pp. 225–229 above.
[30] Wilfrid Ward, *William George Ward and the Catholic Revival* (London: Macmillan and Co., 1893), p. 371.
[31] Von Hügel, *Eternal*, p. 359.   [32] Ibid., p. 360.

freely drew upon the work of German Protestant critics and attempted to disseminate this information to an English readership. For Catholics to engage in critical scholarship there had to be freedom for enquiry, or what von Hügel called "elbow room." Throughout the 1890s and the early years of the twentieth century von Hügel worked for a more open Catholicism, one which could stand up to the challenge of historical criticism. He encouraged reform within the Roman Catholic Church while at the same time attempting to bring that church into dialogue with the larger religious world.[33] This expansive vision was particularly needed among English Catholics whose Catholicism was often insular and defensive.

MAUDE PETRE'S CATHOLICISM

Maude Petre's mother was a convert to Catholicism, and her father was the son of an old Catholic family. In her memoirs, *My Way of Faith*, she described how she had been influenced both by the "religious ardour and imagination, fervour and devotion" of the convert and the "religious firmness, tenacity, and independence" of the old Catholic.[34] Her early faith development had been nourished by her mother's faith, but as she matured she grew in her appreciation for her father's faith. In him she discovered one of the last representatives of Cisalpinism, the English form of Gallicanism which upheld the independence of the state in civil matters and the independence of the church in religious matters. She doubted that her father ever fully accepted the definition of papal infallibility. According to Maude Petre, the Cisalpines believed in the unity of the church and considered the papacy as "the most potent factor of that unity," but they also recognized the limits of ecclesiastical authority. They stood for "a faith and loyalty blended with criticism and discrimination."[35] It was this strong faith, developed over centuries of persecution and accommodation to the Protestant majority, that characterized Maude Petre's Catholicism.

Petre's education, like von Hügel's, took the form of private tuition, but, unlike von Hügel's, hers was exclusively Catholic. In her memoirs she described how the feasts of the liturgical year shaped

---

[33] Von Hügel's participation in the London Society for the Study of Religion is one example of the kind of dialogue in which he wanted Catholics to participate.
[34] *My Way of Faith*, p. 14.   [35] Petre, *The Ninth Lord Petre*, pp. 323–324.

their lives as children and they pitied those who were not Catholic.[36] When she was twenty-two, Petre spent a year studying theology in Rome under the direction of a professor from the College of Propaganda. She appreciated this exposure to Aquinas, although the experience did not provide the answers to her persistent questions, as her confessor had hoped when he suggested that she study scholasticism in Rome to remedy her doubts concerning faith.

In 1890 Petre joined the Filles de Marie, a religious congregation founded during the French Revolution, a time when traditional religious orders suffered persecution. The Filles de Marie began as a secret society and resembled what later would be called "secular institutes." The members did not wear religious habits, retained their own names, and maintained their place in society. Pope Leo XIII gave final approbation to this new form of religious life in 1890, the year that Petre joined. Seventeen years as a member of this international apostolic religious society shaped Petre's Catholicism. She served both as a local superior and as English provincial. Her work included giving retreats and conferences to the sisters as well as work with the poor. Although she was particularly moved by the poor, she gradually came to see writing as her most important task. In order not to involve the Filles de Marie in the ecclesiastical difficulties which arose over the publication of her book, *Catholicism and Independence*, Petre left the society on 2 February 1908 when her vows expired.[37] She continued her vocation as a dedicated single laywoman, writing and speaking to various groups on a wide range of topics.

Like von Hügel, Petre believed in a less rigid, more open Catholicism than that of either the leadership of the church or the mass of Catholics. A number of ecclesial events during the period 1890–1910 illustrate the growing gap between those Catholics such as Petre and von Hügel who had an appreciation of the tradition in its richness and diversity and others who equated Catholicism with a certain Roman style which emphasized submission to the pope, devotion to Mary and the saints, and the use of relics and ceremonies.

[36] Petre described her Catholic childhood in *My Way of Faith*, pp. 61–70; see especially pp. 61–62.
[37] *Catholicism and Independence: Being Studies in Spiritual Liberty* (London: Longmans, Green and Co., 1907).

KEY ECCLESIAL EVENTS BETWEEN 1890 AND 1910

Papal condemnation of Anglican orders (1896)

The discussion on the validity of Anglican orders, which occurred between 1894 and 1896, had a profound effect on English Catholicism. Encouraged by reports of conversions occurring in England, Leo XIII hoped for a corporate reunion of the Church of England with the Catholic Church. According to recent scholarship, Leo saw reunion as a powerful weapon against the upheavals taking place in society, but the reunion which he sought was the conversion of all "separated Christians" to the ultramontane form of Roman Catholicism. George Tavard suggests that Leo made John Henry Newman a cardinal as one of the first acts of his papacy because he wanted to honor one who had found the right way to unity and encourage other Anglicans to follow Newman's path.[38]

The historian Abbé Louis Duchesne argued for the validity of Anglican orders, and there was some interest among a group of Anglo-Catholics in union with Rome. However, any recognition of Anglican orders was strongly opposed by Cardinal Vaughan, whose position was supported by the other English bishops, the Irish and Scottish bishops, and the influential English member of the Vatican, Raphael Merry del Val, secretary of the Commission on Anglican Orders, later to become secretary of state for Pius X.[39] These men feared that the recognition of Anglican orders would discourage individual conversions. For Vaughan, corporate reunion meant corporate submission, something which he realized would be impossible for the Church of England. It did not have the teaching authority to order such a collective submission.

During the 1890s von Hügel was involved in the discussion on the validity of Anglican orders. He was uncertain about the issue but was opposed to an absolute negative ruling. In a brief letter to the editor of *The Tablet*, he pointed out that the more significant issue was the question of jurisdiction and of unity.[40] He added that the

---

[38] George Tavard, "*Apostolicae Curae* and the Snares of Tradition," *Anglican Theological Review* 78 (1996), 30–47.

[39] Because of his English background Raphael Merry del Val (1865–1930) took great interest in and exercised a powerful influence on ecclesiastical life in England.

[40] "L'Abbé Duchesne and Anglican Orders," *The Tablet* 83 (2 June 1894), 857–858.

consensus over the past twenty years was that Anglican orders were "not certainly invalid, yet not certainly valid."

The hope for reunion on the part of some Catholics and Anglo-Catholics was squelched when Leo issued his papal bull, *Ad Anglos* (1895), calling for the conversion of England. Another papal bull followed in 1896, *Apostolicae Curae*, declaring Anglican orders to be null and void, defective in form and intent. The condemnation of Anglican orders strengthened the self-understanding of English Catholics that they belonged to the one true church and that all other Christians were either heretics or schismatics.

Von Hügel and Petre were ecumenical Christians before the Roman Catholic Church entered the ecumenical movement. They continued to maintain close relationships with many Anglican friends, including Lord Halifax, one of the promoters of church reunion. Both saw the importance of working closely for the cause of religion with Christians of other traditions, something they were able to do as Catholic lay persons. They longed for visible unity and believed that it would come through Rome but as von Hügel noted "in a temper and with applications more elastic than those of the later Middle Ages and especially than those of post-Reformation times."[41] It would not be simply a "return to Rome" but would take into account Protestant instincts and objections. Von Hügel's hope was that one great international church would lead Christians beyond "our noblest, national aspirations."[42] Petre and von Hügel saw their work with Anglicans and Protestants as a remote preparation for such a church.

Joint Pastoral (1900)

"The Church and Liberal Catholicism: A Joint Pastoral Letter by the Cardinal Archbishop and the Bishops of the Province of Westminster" began with the words: "It has become a dominant principle in England that all power and authority in civic, political, and religious matters are ultimately vested in the people." In such a climate some Catholics had been "infected by the critical spirit of private judgment." The Pastoral sought to correct those "liberal Catholics" who freely expressed their own opinions on church

---

[41] *Essays and Addresses on the Philosophy of Religion* (London: Dent, 1921), p. 276.
[42] Ibid., pp. 276–277.

doctrine.[43] Although the Joint Pastoral was signed by the English bishops, Merry del Val was its principal fabricator. Editorial assistance came from Luis Martin, General of the Society of Jesus, who shared Merry del Val's concern about liberalism among England Catholics.[44]

The Pastoral emphasized that the teaching authority of the church resided in the hierarchy. It separated the *ecclesia docens* (teaching church) and the *ecclesia discens* (learning church) and insisted on the "assent of religious obedience" to the ordinary teaching of the church. Included among these teachings were pastoral letters of bishops and all decisions of the Roman congregations. The Pastoral illustrates the strong influence of Rome and particularly of Merry del Val on English Catholicism. It also reveals their distrust of "liberal" Catholics and the emphasis placed on obedience by the hierarchy. The tone throughout the document was negative. Those who experienced difficulty were urged to develop "a more docile spirit."

Maude Petre's immediate reaction was evident in her diary entry for 2 January 1901: "The bishops of England have put forth a letter on 'Liberal Catholicism.' black! black! It will disturb many in the Church and keep many out." She prayed for "light for the rigid, conservative and narrow – humility for the more enlightened" adding: "How different all will be in a hundred years! What changes in the Church!"[45]

The issues of authority and of religious obedience became important topics for Petre. She devoted a chapter to the significance of the Joint Pastoral in her *Life of George Tyrrell from 1884 to 1909*.[46] A number of her essays reflect on obedience and authority and suggest a form of "limited obedience."[47]

Von Hügel and Tyrrell had long talks on the questions raised by the Pastoral. In January 1904 von Hügel presented a paper to a group of Anglican clerics on the topic "Official Authority and Living Religion." The paper, which was subsequently edited with suggestions from Tyrrell, was not published until after von Hügel's death,

---

[43] The text was published in *The Tablet* 97 (5 January 1901), 8–12, and was endorsed by Leo XIII.

[44] Schultenover, *View*, p. 151.

[45] Petre Papers, BL, Add. MS 52372.

[46] Petre, *Life*, vol. II, pp. 146–161.

[47] "Obedience Spiritual and Not Military," *Catholicism and Independence*, pp. 33–54; "The Advantages and Disadvantages of Authority in Religion," *Hibbert Journal* 12 (1914), 295–305; "Religious Authority," *Modern Churchman* 13 (1923), 176–185.

and even then his literary executor, Edmund Gardner, had some reservations about including it in a collection of essays and addresses.[48] Gardner expressed his reservations in a letter to Hildegard von Hügel, 24 April 1926, adding: "Being the earliest of them, it will stand first in the volume, and therefore will not be taken as your Father's final and matured utterance on the subject."[49] This nervousness about discussing the question of authority within the church illustrates the devastating effect that the 1900 condemnation of "liberal" Catholics and the subsequent condemnation of Modernism had on English Catholicism.

Condemnation of Modernism (1907)

If the Joint Pastoral had the effect of raising suspicion against "liberal" Catholics, the papal documents *Lamentabili* and *Pascendi*, which condemned the errors of Modernism and indicated the remedies to be applied by the bishops, were even more disturbing for those who had hoped for reform within the church. Whatever "elbow room" there had been for the critical study of religion was virtually eliminated. Tyrrell reacted strongly in the secular papers, an act interpreted as disloyalty to the pope and punished by excommunication. Von Hügel was disturbed by the course of events, although he expressed some sympathy for Pius X and urged Tyrrell to be patient.[50]

Bishops were required by *Pascendi* to set up Vigilance Committees in order to stamp out any Modernist tendencies within their jurisdiction. The little village of Storrington in Southwark diocese was of special concern to the Southwark Vigilance Committee, because it was the home of Maude Petre. There the notorious Modernist George Tyrrell and his friend Friedrich von Hügel met with other like-minded persons.[51]

The timing of *Pascendi* was bad for both Petre and von Hügel, who had books ready for publication. Petre's book on *Catholicism and Independence*, published in December 1907, just three months after the

---

[48] *Essays and Addresses on the Philosophy of Religion*, second series (London: Dent, 1926), pp. 3–23.
[49] Letter to Hildegard von Hügel, von Hügel Papers, Downside Abbey Archives, MS 1272 (uncatalogued).
[50] Von Hügel to Tyrrell, 1 October 1907, 21 October 1907, BL, Add. MS 44930.
[51] Archives of Diocese of Southwark, Vigilance Committee file, includes minutes of meetings and letters.

condemnation of Modernism, pointed out to the reader "the right, the necessity, the duty of every mind to work out its own salvation by the courageous facing of its own difficulties, the following of its own lights."[52] This critical approach to faith was certainly not the spirit of *Pascendi*. The previous February Petre had tried unsuccessfully to obtain an *Imprimatur* because, as she wrote to Archbishop Bourne, "The chief desire of my heart is to help our own through these difficult times."[53] When the book came out, she sent a copy to the archbishop, who immediately instructed her to withdraw it. She explained that this was not possible because the book had been handed over to the publisher.[54] Toward the end of May 1908 Bourne asked her to come for an interview, during which he requested that she not allow a second edition. Petre responded that she had no control over a second edition, that she could not make a formal retraction, but that she would reconsider the matter if the question of a second edition arose. The question did not arise and Bourne allowed the matter to rest.

Von Hügel too was concerned about his book, a two-volume critical study of religion, *The Mystical Element of Religion as Studied in Saint Catherine of Genoa and her Friends*. It was the fruit of over ten years of research and was his first book. Even before *Pascendi* he had feared that it might be placed on the Index of Forbidden Books and had asked Tyrrell, who had served as a resource at every stage of the work, if he would be willing to waive a formal acknowledgment in the preface.[55] When published in November 1908 it was generally well received, although the anti-Modernist campaign caused a certain cautiousness among Catholics.

The premature death of George Tyrrell in July 1909, the refusal of the ecclesiastical authorities to allow Catholic burial, and the activities of Petre and von Hügel both before and after Tyrrell's death were reported by Bishop Amigo to Cardinal Merry del Val.[56] The latter replied in a confidential letter deploring the behavior of

---

[52] *Catholicism and Independence*, p. ix.
[53] Petre to Archbishop Bourne, 3 February 1907, Francis Bourne Papers, Archives of the Archbishops of Westminster, Bo.1/32. For an account of Petre's efforts to obtain the *Imprimatur*, the response of the censor, and subsequent correspondence with the Archbishop, see Leonard, *Unresting Transformation: The Theology and Spirituality of Maude Petre* (Lanham, Maryland: University Press of America, 1991), pp. 46–47, 49–53.
[54] Petre to Archbishop Bourne, 13 December 1907, Bo.1/32. A draft of the archbishop's reply is on the reverse of Petre's letter.
[55] Von Hügel to Tyrrell, 30 December 1905, BL, Add. MS 44929.
[56] Amigo to Merry del Val, 24 July 1909, Vigilance Committee file, MS 60.

Petre, von Hügel and the others involved in the funeral, and raising the question whether in view of the public scandal they ought to be refused the sacraments in their respective dioceses. He instructed Amigo to discuss the matter with the archbishop and other bishops.[57] Archbishop Bourne, who had been away at the time of Tyrrell's funeral, knowing the English ethos, suggested that action should not be taken, reminding Merry del Val that "it is always dangerous to arouse in England the morbid unreasonable sympathy which people so readily give to every wrong-doer whatever the nature of his crime." Bourne had no desire to create "martyrs for a cause."[58]

Following Tyrrell's death Maude Petre devoted her energies to continuing what she understood to be Tyrrell's life work. Von Hügel urged her to exercise caution. Various motivations have been suggested for the difference in approach adopted by Petre and von Hügel, but the key seems, at least in part, to have been personality. Petre was like the early Christian martyrs who said "Take me too!" whereas von Hügel was more like Thomas More who avoided condemnation as long as it could be done with integrity. Von Hügel chose this more cautious approach, not only because of his work, which would be adversely affected by a condemnation, but because of his concern for his family, especially his wife, Lady Mary, and their three daughters. Petre was motivated by her loyalty to Tyrrell.

The personalities of Archbishop Bourne and Bishop Amigo also played a part. Bourne maintained a wise and charitable attitude during these difficult years, refusing to engage in heresy hunting. He took under his protection Catholic scholars suspected by the zealots, in particular Wilfrid Ward, the editor of the *Dublin Review* from 1906 to 1916, and von Hügel.[59] Bishop Amigo, under pressure from the Prior of Storrington, Xavier de la Fourvière, who had refused communion to Petre, took a hard line and forbade her to receive communion in his diocese. In the exchanges between Petre and Amigo, a determined man met an equally determined woman.[60]

In 1910 Pius X issued a Motu Proprio, *Sacrorum Antistitum*, demanding that all priests take the anti-Modernist oath or give up

[57] Merry del Val to Amigo, 30 July 1909, Vigilance Committee file, MS 71.
[58] Bourne to Merry del Val, 15 August 1909, Bo.124/5.
[59] E. I. Watkin, *Roman Catholicism in England from the Reformation to 1950* (London: Oxford University Press, 1957), p. 218.
[60] See *Unresting Transformation*, pp. 55–56, 62–63, 66–67, 72–74.

their ministry. As lay persons, neither von Hügel nor Petre were required to take the oath, although Bishop Amigo requested that Petre take it in order to show her acceptance of the teachings of *Pascendi*. She resolutely refused, asking Amigo for an assurance that "every condemnation or proposition of these documents without a single exception, is *de fide* [of the faith] now, and will always be in the same sense *de fide*," an assurance which no one was willing to give.[61] Dr. Scannell, one of Amigo's advisors, reminded him that "she is a lay person, and therefore not liable to the ordinary penalties. She is also a woman and therefore not a fit subject for persecution at the hands of men."[62] For Maude Petre the ancient creeds recited by her ancestors were a sufficient expression of faith, a faith for which she, like the English martyrs of the sixteenth century, would have been willing to die. But Petre was not willing to remain silent.

In "An Open Letter to My Fellow Catholics," published in the *London Times* on 2 November 1910, Petre called upon Catholics to resist tyranny within their church. She expressed her sympathy with priests who in conscience could not take the anti-Modernist oath and urged them to band together, something explicitly forbidden by *Pascendi*. Von Hügel considered her letter "most dignified, courageous, touching." Although he agreed with her that "God would make up to her fully," he expressed his fear that it might mean her exclusion from the sacraments for the rest of her life."[63] He himself did not want to risk such a loss. Because of Bourne's tolerant attitude Petre was able to continue to receive the sacraments in Westminster archdiocese, although she was barred from doing so in Southwark diocese, and no action was taken against von Hügel.

Coming of age

In the epilogue of *Catholicism and Independence* Petre urged the church, like good parents, to recognize that her children have come of age and not continue to treat them as children.[64] Such a view was unaccepted in the Roman Catholic Church, particularly in England where Catholics were a minority and where maintaining a strong identity and a united front were considered necessary. Through

---

[61] Petre to Amigo, 14 October 1910, Vigilance Committee file, MS 112.
[62] Scannell to Amigo, 17 October 1910, Vigilance Committee file, MS 120.
[63] Von Hügel to Petre, 3 November 1910, BL, Add. MS 45362.
[64] *Catholicism and Independence*, pp. 171–174.

separate schools and Catholic guilds and societies, the church permeated the daily lives of Catholics. The papal revision of marriage law, expressed in the decree *Ne Temere* (1908), ruled that Catholics could only validly marry before a priest and two witnesses, a restriction which meant that marriages of Catholics in Protestant or Anglican churches were no longer considered valid. The church's control over the lives of Catholics extended from birth to death. Most individual Catholics seem to have unquestioningly accepted their place as loyal children of Mother Church. Their task as loyal children was to pay and obey.

Three events toward the end of the period, 1890–1910, suggest that English Catholicism itself was coming of age. In 1908 the Apostolic Constitution *sapienti consilio* declared England and Wales no longer missionary districts subject to the jurisdiction of Propaganda. That same year the Eucharistic Congress was held in London, and for the first time in three centuries a papal legate, Cardinal Vanutelli, visited England. Finally in 1910 Westminster Cathedral was consecrated.

The Eucharistic Congress of 1908 was an international celebration of the church triumphant firmly established once again on English soil. In addition to the papal delegate, seven cardinals and over a hundred archbishops, bishops and abbots graced the occasion. Plans were made for an outdoor procession of the Blessed Sacrament through the streets on the last Sunday of the Congress. A few days before the scheduled procession an indirect message from the Home Secretary, followed by an official order for its cancellation, was sent to Archbishop Bourne. The procession was considered "provocative to Protestant sentiment."[65] There was disappointment at being confined to the area of the Cathedral, but Benediction was given from the balcony over its portal.

The Congress, occurring just a year after the condemnation of Modernism, raised problems for von Hügel and Petre. Their diaries reveal their conflicting emotions. On Wednesday, 9 September, von Hügel wrote to Tyrrell, asking him and Petre to telegraph their opinion as to whether he should attend the legate's reception on Friday. Thursday night he had one of his "white nights," unable to sleep as he tried to decide whether to go up to London. On Friday

---

[65] E. E. Reynolds, *The Roman Catholic Church in England and Wales: A Short History* (Wheathampstead: Anthony Clarke Books, 1973), pp. 356–357.

he noted in his diary: "Cab came but was taken by mistake (I not seeing it by another man) [*sic*]. I gave up going up to London today, for Legate's reception." On Sunday afternoon he and his family watched the procession in front of the Cathedral from the flat roof of a house on Victoria Street where they had a fine view of the legate "in his robes with train."[66]

Petre expressed her views on the Congress in her journal entries. On 12 September, noting that the Congress was in full force, she wrote: "Card. Vanutelli said that the two fundamental truths of our religion were 'the eucharist and the Papacy.' The Duke of Norfolk made a foolish speech in the same sense. How blind they all are!" On 14 September she commented: "The speeches of the Congress were painful in their adulation of the Papal Power."[67] Such an attitude was not part of her heritage as an old English Catholic.

A symbol of English Catholicism coming of age more permanent than the Eucharistic Congress was the consecration of Westminster Cathedral in 1910. The foundation stone had been laid in 1895. Cardinal Vaughan's funeral mass on 25 June 1903 had been the occasion for its official opening.[68] With its high tower, it is a worthy monument to the persistent faith and generosity of English Roman Catholics. Maude Petre herself donated one thousand pounds to the building fund in 1900.[69] Leo XIII also donated one thousand.[70] The Cathedral, which was constructed in the manner of a Roman basilica in the Byzantine style, symbolized the ultramontane spirit. This imposing building a few blocks from Victoria Station stands as a monument to the triumphant "Roman spirit" of English Catholicism which emerged during the late nineteenth century. By 1910 the "church of outsiders" had its own cathedral and was becoming a force to be reckoned with in English society.

[66] Diary, 9 to 13 September 1908, St. Andrew University Library, von Hügel Papers, MS 36362.
[67] Diary, 12 to 14 September 1908, Petre Papers, BL, Add. MS 52374.
[68] O'Connell, *Critics*, p. 273.
[69] Letter from Vaughan, 20 March 1898, thanking Petre for her donation of 1,000 pounds, Petre Papers, BL, Add. MS 45744.
[70] Gordon Wheeler, "The Archdiocese of Westminster," in *The English Catholics 1850–1950: Essays to Commemorate the Centenary of the Restoration of the Hierarchy of England and Wales*, ed. George Andrew Beck (London: Burns & Oates, 1950), p. 169.

CONCLUSION

As we have seen, both Petre and von Hügel were influenced by European Catholicism and scholarship, but English Catholicism, as it developed during the critical years 1890 to 1910, was the context in which they lived and wrote. Petre, with her recusant background, was more self-consciously English than von Hügel, whose Catholicism reflected a number of European influences, particularly seventeenth-century French spirituality and nineteenth-century German scholarship. The triumphant Catholicism symbolized by the new cathedral was distasteful to both von Hügel and Petre. The events of the years between 1890 and 1910 might seem to have marginalized them from the body of English Catholics, but their vision of Catholicism was wide enough for them to continue to find a home within English Catholicism. Through their writings and their lives they offered their own critical appropriation of the tradition, adding to English Catholicism an intellectual component that was in danger of being lost in the anti-Modernist period. Owen Chadwick refers to "the suppression of the modernists in 1907 and after" as the rejection of "the most promising and courageous ways by which Catholics of that generation might aim to meet the intellectual challenges of the age."[71] Although the influence of von Hügel and Petre was restricted among Catholics, neither was silenced. Both continued to speak and to write until their deaths, von Hügel in 1925 and Petre in 1942.

We have seen that Petre and von Hügel had a strong sense of their lay vocation and saw themselves actively participating in the mission of the church. In the tradition of the old English Catholics they did not ask permission to act but took the initiative themselves. Because of their class they were able to continue the tradition of lay leadership which had characterized the old Catholics. As members of a religious minority they saw themselves as "unofficial" spokespersons for their tradition, addressing various audiences through lectures and writing.

Von Hügel and Petre both recognized the importance of the pope and Rome as the center of the universal church, but they objected to the exaggerated devotion to the person of the pope and to the centralized control that Rome was exercising over national churches. During a period in which the Catholic Church was still operating

---

[71] Chadwick, *Secularization*, p. 251.

out of a siege mentality, they believed in dialogue with other faith traditions. As lay Catholics they engaged in ecumenical dialogue, anticipating by more than fifty years the official commencement of their church's dialogue with other Christian churches and other religions.

Von Hügel and Petre lived and wrote during a particularly difficult period in the history of the church, but they maintained their hope in the future. By their ability to combine criticism of their tradition with loving fidelity to it, both in their daily lives and in their writing, they made their own unique contributions to English Catholicism. The kind of openness that they exemplified had to wait for several more decades before becoming an accepted part of Catholicism in England.

PART IV

Social modernism and anti-Modernism in France

CHAPTER 10

Social modernism: the case of the Semaines sociales
Peter Bernardi, S.J.

An under-studied dimension of the Modernist crisis is social modernism. During the pontificate of Pius X (1903–1914), the Vatican grew increasingly apprehensive about the way many lay Catholics and clergy were responding to the clamor of the working classes. Approaches to the "social problem" that seemed to undermine the traditional hierarchical and paternalistic structures of authority and social organization were viewed with suspicion. Shortly after the promulgation of the anti-Modernist encyclical *Pascendi* (1907), the French Catholics of the *Semaines sociales* were accused of social modernism. This essay will review the *Semaine sociale* teachings and the accusations of their anti-Modernist critics in order to cast light on the complex conflict of mentalities that divided French Catholics under the Third Republic (1870–1940).

French Catholics were divided over what strategy to adopt to re-Christianize French society. Catholic "restorationists" sought to restore the institutional prerogatives of the Roman Catholic Church, even by way of an alliance with the agnostic, anti-Christian ideologist Charles Maurras and his neo-monarchist political movement of *Action française*. Catholic "transformationists," many of whom participated in the *Semaines sociales*, rejected a top-down, authoritarian imposition of Catholicism in favor of a democratic strategy that viewed the aspirations of the working class for justice as an implicit cry for the kingdom of God.

I will contend, on the one hand, that the dividing line between the social Catholics of the *Semaines sociales* and their anti-Modernist opponents did not precisely follow the dividing line between doctrinal Modernists and the integralists who were their opponents. Indeed, the founders of the *Semaines sociales* aspired to be Catholic "integralists," that is, those who refused to compromise their Catholic approach to the social problem with the spirit of the age. In contrast, some of their anti-Modernist critics showed greater sympathy for economic liberalism, fruit of the French Revolution, that official church teaching increasingly criticized. On the other hand, I also argue that these anti-Modernist critics were not wrong to suspect the influence on the *Semaines sociales* of one seminal thinker whose thought was targeted by *Pascendi*, namely Maurice Blondel (1861–1949). I contend that Blondel had a direct influence on the efforts of the *Semaine sociale* Catholics to forge a new vision of Christian economic life that eschewed both positivism and neo-scholasticism.[1] Detecting the stamp of Blondel's philosophy in the keynote addresses of the *Semaines sociales*, their critics sought to make a direct link between doctrinal Modernism and what they called "sociological modernism." While it exceeds the scope of this essay to elaborate on the affinity between Blondel's philosophical project and the social teaching of the *Semaines sociales*, I do call attention to a specific theological criticism made against both: the confusion of the natural and supernatural orders.

What were the *Semaines sociales*? Literally, "social weeks," the *Semaines sociales* were a sort of peripatetic university (*université sociale ambulante*) founded in 1904 by Marius Gonin, director of the *Chronique des comités du Sud-Est*, and Adéodat Boissard, Maurice Blondel's brother-in-law and professor at the School of Social and Political Sciences at the Catholic University of Lille.[2] Seeking to propagate Catholic social teaching beyond the urban centers of Paris and Lille,

---

[1] Blondel had been engaged with the social Catholic milieu in which the *Semaine sociale* movement had its origins. Blondel's brother-in-law, Adéodat Boissard, was a co-founder; his brother Georges was a *conférencier*; Charles Flory, his son-in-law, became its president in 1947. The first *Semaine sociale* Blondel attended was in 1906. For further bibliographical information, see Paul Poupard, "Blondel et les catholiques sociaux," *Nouvelles de l'Institut Catholique de Paris* (December 1974), 49–71. See also Joseph Vialatoux, "Maurice Blondel et les Semaines sociales," *Chronique sociale de France* 59 (May–June 1950), 195–209; and Paul Melizan, "M. Blondel et les catholiques sociaux," *Bulletin de la societé des amis de Maurice Blondel*, n.s. 4 (June 1992), 4–5.

[2] See Misner, *Social*, pp. 288–318, especially pp. 296–298; Philippe Lécrivain, "Les *Semaines sociales* de France," in *Le Mouvement social catholique en France au XXe siècle*, ed. Denis Maugenest (Paris: Editions du Cerf, 1990), pp. 151–165; and Robert Talmy, *Le Syndicalisme chrétien en France (1871–1930): difficultés et controverses* (hereafter, *SCF*) (Paris: Bloud & Gay, 1965), pp. 91–105. The general inspiration for this initiative was expressed by Henri Bazire, then president of *Association catholique de la jeunesse française* (*ACJF*). Bazire uttered the famous dictum: "Social because Catholic" which became a *mot d'ordre* for Catholics responsive to the "social problem" (see Talmy, *SCF*, p. 84). For a personal account of the founding and early history of the *Semaines sociales*, see Joseph Folliet, *Notre ami Marius Gonin. Un témoin du Christ dans le temporel* (Lyon: Chronique sociale de France, 1944). Gonin was the organizational genius behind the success of the *Semaines sociales*.

the *Semaines sociales* brought together for a week in a different city each summer, a varied group of professionals, workers, clergy, and students. As many as two thousand participants followed courses given by experts on the church's social doctrine and practice.[3] Specific proposals for improving the workers' lot were shared and discussed. From its inaugural assembly in Lyon, these annual gatherings generated an enormous enthusiasm and energy.[4]

Veteran social Catholic Henri Lorin served as the first president of the *Semaines sociales.*[5] He defined their aim at their 1905 assembly: "To perfect the knowledge of Christian morality in our own consciences and to prepare us to make the social importance of Christian dogmas better known to people outside: this is our objective."[6] Implied in this program are both a method and a spirit. The method was distinctive for the two sources it employed: "the fundamental moral teachings of Catholicism and the observation of facts, the science of sociology in the proper sense." The spirit was characterized by simple obedience to Christian conscience and a "disinterested attitude" reflected in their "concern to place themselves outside existing groups, whatever they may be."[7] Evidence of this disinterested attitude can be seen in the composition of its founding "patronage committee" and in the variety of its professors.[8] The *Semaines sociales* received a broad range of support among leading social Catholics, including Albert de Mun and Marc

---

[3] The *Semaines sociales* billed themselves as "Cours de doctrine et de pratique sociales"; their motto: "La Science pour l'Action." For information about topics addressed, see Lécrivain, "Les *Semaines sociales* de France," pp. 154–155.

[4] Lyon was a center of Catholic social activism. Gonin's Lyon-based *Chronique des comités du Sud-Est* became the *Semaine sociale* publishing arm in addition to housing its secrétariat. In 1909, this organ became the *Chronique sociale de France.* See Christian Ponson, *Les Catholiques lyonnais et la Chronique sociale: 1892–1914* (Lyon: P.U.L., 1979).

[5] Lorin (1857–1914), a lawyer from the *grande bourgeoisie parisienne,* was very influenced by Pope Leo XIII's Thomistic revival. He was an "assiduous reader" of the *Summa.* He was a member of the influential Fribourg Union (1883–1891) which helped prepare the founding document of modern Catholic social teaching, *Rerum Novarum* (hereafter, *RN*), promulgated by Pope Leo XIII in 1891. At the time of the *Semaine sociale* founding, he was president of the *Union d'études des catholiques sociaux.*

[6] "La *Semaine sociale*: son caractère – son objectif – sa méthode, déclaration faite par M. H. Lorin," *Chronique des comités du Sud-Est* 14 (August–September 1905), 267.

[7] From a prospectus published in advance of the 1909 Bordeaux *Semaine sociale,* Archives Chronique sociale de France, *malle* 1.

[8] The founding *comité de patronage* included bishops: Couillé, Péchenard, Dadolle, Battifol, Petit; other clergy: Blanc, Cetty, Dehon, Garnier, Gayraud, Lemire, Naudet, Quillet, Roche; and lay Catholics: Bazire, Berne, Crétinon, Estrangin, Fonsegrive, Goyau, Gonin, Harmel, Lorin, Mun, and Sangnier. See Lécrivain, "Les *Semaines sociales* de France," p. 153.

Sangnier, and among clergy, especially several prominent democratic *abbés*. For example, though Christian democrats predominated among the leadership of the *Semaines sociales*, Gonin and Boissard turned down an invitation to join Marc Sangnier's national democratic political movement *le plus grand Sillon*. Furthermore, the directors of the *Semaines sociales* invited Fr. Georges de Pascal, O.P., a sympathizer of the neo-monarchist political movement *Action française*, to give lessons in its early years. The leading social Catholic monarchist René de La Tour du Pin also lent his support. The *Semaines sociales* aspired to bridge the rancorous political divisions among French Catholics.

The *Semaines sociales* must be understood in the larger context of the history of the French Catholic response to the "social problem."[9] The Enlightenment, the French Revolution, and the Industrial Revolution had initiated a vast and ongoing process of change. Secularization and new social configurations, especially a growing proletariat class, posed a growing challenge to the church's pastoral mission.[10] In the course of the nineteenth century, tensions increased among Catholics about what strategies to adopt to accomplish the Christian renewal of society and, more fundamentally, how to conceive of this renewal.[11] Beginning in the 1830s with the school of l'abbé Félicité de Lamennais, a strain of "liberal" Catholicism developed that was characterized by its openness to the democratic values championed by the first phase of the French Revolution (1789). This strain, a minority voice in French Catholic life during the nineteenth century, came into increasing conflict with the dominant strain of intransigent Catholicism that repudiated the French Revolution "root and branch" and was dedicated to a "restorationist" project.

The awakening of conscience that was prompted by the violence of the Commune insurrection in the spring of 1871 led to the first sustained efforts to respond to the workers' plight. Under the leadership of intransigent Catholics Albert de Mun and René de La Tour du Pin, French "social Catholicism" had its modern

---

[9] My account draws largely upon Misner, Talmy, Mayeur (see n. 14), Lécrivain and several other sources that will be cited when appropriate.

[10] See Chadwick, *Secularization*.

[11] See Misner, *Social*; Adrien Dansette, *Religious History of Modern France*, trs. John Dingle, 2 vols. (New York: Herder, 1961); and Gérard Cholvy and Yves-Marie Hilaire, *Histoire religieuse de la France contemporaine: 1880–1930* (Toulouse: Bibliothèque historique privat, 1986).

beginnings.[12] Ultramontane and counter-revolutionary, de Mun and La Tour du Pin fervently adhered to Pope Pius IX's anti-liberal Syllabus of Errors (1864). They rejected "the prevailing secular ideology, economic liberalism, as well as its younger rival, socialism, in the name of Catholicism or tradition."[13] They favored a corporatist and hierarchical type of social organization that evinced a certain nostalgia for the medieval guilds. However, as the century drew to a close, this paternalistic and counter-revolutionary mentality found itself in growing tension with proponents of "Christian democracy" who were feeling their way to a less traditional, more democratic approach to the social problem.[14] When Pope Leo appealed to French Catholics to "rally" to the Third Republic, French Catholics divided along political lines.[15] The split was conspicuously exemplified in the contrasting responses of social Catholicism's two most venerable figures: La Tour du Pin, a dyed-in-the-wool monarchist, refused the Pope's appeal; on the other hand, de Mun set aside his monarchist sympathies to become a "rallié" (that is, one who supported the Third Republic).

The promulgation of *Rerum Novarum* (1891) gave the encouragement of the magisterium to the groundbreaking efforts of the "social Catholics." Opposing socialism and laissez-faire capitalism, *Rerum Novarum* affirmed both the right to private property and the right of workers to organize and to be protected, when necessary, by intervention of the state. However, *Rerum Novarum* left open many practical questions concerning the nature and function of unions as well as the limits of state intervention. The thorny questions concerning the composition and status of unions were to become

---

[12] In 1871, these army officers co-founded the *Œuvre des cercles catholiques d'ouvriers (OCCO)*. These Catholic workers' clubs became "one of the best known collective efforts in the history of social Catholicism." La Tour du Pin was the primary intellectual architect of the socio-economic theory of "corporatism" which promoted intermediate, organic associations of workers and owners. He was one of the principal theoreticians of the Fribourg Union. See Misner, *Social*, pp. 148–168.

[13] Misner, *Social*, p. 320.

[14] Jean-Marie Mayeur observes: "The heart of social Catholicism resides in the affirmation of the church's competence to address the problems of society. The specificity of social Catholicism lies in its rejection of liberal 'separatism'" (*Catholicisme social et démocratie chrétienne* [Paris: Editions du Cerf, 1986], p. 267).

[15] Leo's *Ralliement* encyclical, *Au milieu des sollicitudes*, issued in February 1892, was a long plea for French Catholics to honor the institutions which the French people had chosen for themselves. See John McManners, *Church and State in France, 1870–1914* (New York: Harper & Row, 1972).

especially divisive.[16] The divided response to the *Ralliement* and the
different readings of *Rerum Novarum* contributed to growing divisions
among Catholics.[17] These divisions, however, are complicated
because they cut across political, social, economic, and religious
planes. The political differences among Catholics were exacerbated
by the harsh anticlerical policies of the Third Republic that were to
culminate in the hostile revocation of the church–state concordat
effected by the 1905 Law of Separation. New political movements
arose that further polarized Catholics. On the one hand, *Action
française* promoted a political monarchism and a social corporatism
that appealed to the traditionalists. On the other hand, the movement known as "*le Sillon*" promoted a visionary political and social
democratism. In any event, a "dualist" interpretation that pits
"intransigents" against "liberals" is to be avoided in explaining the
evolution of social Catholicism.

In 1901, in view of the growing prominence of the Christian
democratic tendency, Pope Leo XIII exhorted Catholics to promote
"a beneficent action among the people" (*aller au peuple*), a "Christian
democratic" action in a non-political sense.[18] Seeking to practice
"integral" Catholicism, Gonin, Broissard, and their collaborators
organized the *Semaines sociales* to energize efforts on behalf of social
justice. Like the *Association catholique de la jeunesse française (ACJF)* and
Action Populaire (AP), they conceived of a new strategy for enabling
Christian values to penetrate an increasingly secular and pluralist
society.[19] These Catholic movements shared a "progressive" spirit in

---

[16] Catholics of the liberal economic school, such as Joseph Rambaud of the Catholic Institute
of Lyon, put primary stress on the individual wage contract (*liberté du travail*). They saw the
specter of socialism in the promotion of state intervention and independent unions. On the
other hand, corporatist social Catholics were committed to the paternal and hierarchical,
"mixed" unions of workers and owners that maintained proper authority and avoided
exacerbating class conflict. This latter approach was challenged by democratic-minded
social Catholics who promoted independent workers' unions in which the workers could
truly "participate" and not be simply subservient to the owners and their managers (*classes
dirigeantes*). A further question arose as to whether unions should be strictly "confessional,"
i.e. Catholic and thus under the church's aegis, or "a-confessional," i.e., open to other
Christians. See Talmy, *SCF*, pp. 79–129.

[17] See Jacques Gadille, "*Rerum Novarum* et les protagonistes du catholicisme social en France,
1891–1911," *Bulletin de la société des amis de Maurice Blondel*, n.s. 4 (June 1992), 10–23.

[18] "Graves de communi," *Acta Sanctae Sedis* 33 (18 January 1901), 385–396.

[19] Mayeur observes: "Voie réformiste fondée sur une compétence technique, refus de l'utopie,
c'est la ligne de l'*ACJF* et des *Semaines sociales* qui s'affirme là" (*Catholicisme social et démocratie
chrétienne*, p. 264). The *ACJF* was the national youth organization founded in 1886 by Albert
de Mun. Its motto was: "Piety, Study, Action." Under the inspiring presidency of Henri
Bazire, mentioned above, it took a more activist role vis-à-vis the workers, including the

that, in contrast with intransigent reactionaries, they considered society to be reformable within its republican framework. When the Law of Separation threw French Catholicism into disarray, Pope Pius X took an uncompromising stand of "religious defense." On another – but not unrelated – front, the pope declared war on "Modernism" in its many expressions.[20] These events intensified a traditionalist (*intégriste*) reaction which received encouragement from the highest levels of the Vatican.[21] Despite their ultramontane pedigree, social Catholics were not immune from attack, especially if they promoted "egalitarianism" and democratic structures.[22]

How and why did the *Semaines sociales* become a target? A month before their 1909 assembly convened at Bordeaux, Julien Fontaine, S.J., had published *Le Modernisme sociologique: décadence ou régénération?* (*Sociological Modernism: Decadence or Regeneration?*)[23] Fontaine, described in the Jesuit periodical *Etudes* as a "franc-tireur" (literally, "sniper"; figuratively, "freelancer"), was a well-known crusader against suspected Modernists and their innovations.[24] His earlier books had

support of independent workers' unions. *AP* (not to be confused with the political party *Action libérale populaire*) was founded in 1903 by Fr. Henri-Joseph Leroy, S.J., but the leadership quickly passed to Fr. Desbuquois, S.J. Its purpose was to gather and disseminate research data relating to the social question. For the definitive account, see Paul Droulers, *Politique sociale et christianisme, le Père Desbuquois et l'Action Populaire*, vol. 1: *Débuts, syndicalisme, et intégristes (1903–1918)* (Paris: Editions Ouvrières, 1969).

20 See *Pascendi dominici gregis* ("On the Doctrines of the Modernists") (8 September 1907) and *Lamentabili sane exitu* ("Syllabus Condemning the Errors of the Modernists") (3 July 1907), *Acte Sanctae Sedis* 40, 593–650.

21 Emile Poulat has done the basic research on "intégrisme." See especially *Intégrisme et catholicisme intégral. Un réseau secret international antimoderniste: la "Sapinière," (1909–1921)* (Paris, Tournai: Casterman, 1969). For a summary treatment, see "Integralism" in *History of the Church* (abridged edition), ed. H. Jedin, vol. III: *The Church in the Modern World* (New York: Crossroad, 1993), pp. 632–639.

22 Mayeur notes the irony: "One witnessed then a regrouping: social Catholics (who accepted political democracy – the Republic and universal suffrage – and social democracy-equality) were accused of liberalism and of 'social modernism' by those with whom they had often been very close . . . The very fact that 'brother enemies' were opposed explains the intensity of the conflicts" ("Catholicisme intransigeant . . . ," *Catholicisme social et démocratie chrétienne*, pp. 26–27).

23 *Le Modernisme sociologique: décadence ou régénération?* (Paris: Lethielleux, 1909) (hereafter, *LMS*). Fontaine dedicated his volume to Pope Pius X. The preface states: "This book is born of an attentive study of the encyclical *Pascendi gregis* . . . Modernism . . . has changed its forms; the dogmatician has turned himself into a sociologist. His aim is to ruin the social order by attacking the principles of natural law which support it, just as he recently attacked the principles of the faith" (p. v). Fontaine (1839–1917) was ordained a priest for the diocese of S.-Brieuc in 1863; in 1873, he entered the Paris province of the Society of Jesus, which assigned him to teach apologetics at Angers.

24 See A. d'Alès, review of *Le Modernisme sociologique* in *Etudes* 121 (20 October 1909), 271–272. The reviewer judged the volume to be "somewhat sad," because it neglected the positive

won official Vatican approbation and this latest volume also received a warm commendation from the Vatican secretary of state Merry del Val. *Le Modernisme sociologique* devoted a chapter to exposing the "excessive and dangerous tendencies" that had been taught at the 1908 *Semaine sociale* of Marseilles by Henri Lorin and Maurice Deslandres.[25] Fontaine's general accusation was that the *Semaines sociales* were propagating "social modernism."[26] In the volatile ecclesial atmosphere that followed the publication of *Pascendi*, the accusation of "social modernism" was extremely serious.[27] Though the encyclical did not employ the term "social modernism" or condemn any particular social doctrine or individual, it had warned Catholics about possible deviations on the social terrain. At the *Semaine sociale* of Bordeaux, the directors, in keeping with their practice of seeking a papal blessing, received a reminder from Cardinal Merry del Val that echoed Fontaine's criticisms. While commending their filial sentiments, the Vatican secretary of state reminded the participants to seek their inspiration "from the true Christian principles concerning work, property, [and] the family."[28] This triad touched on the controversial areas which had drawn Fontaine's censure.

What exactly was "social modernism"? In the fall of 1907, six weeks after the appearance of *Pascendi*, Father V. Loiselet had publicly accused the *Semaines sociales* of "Modernism."[29] He made the accusation at a regular meeting of the industrialists (*patrons*) of the north of France, but he did not offer a definition.[30] The chosen venue for the charge, however, reflected its underlying "liberal"

---

developments in social Catholicism. Fontaine wrote a number of anti-Modernist works including: *Les Infiltrations protestantes et le clergé français* (1901); *Les Infiltrations protestantes et l'exégèse du Nouveau Testament* (1905); and *Le Modernisme social* (1911).

25   *LMS*, pp. 427–481. Maurice Deslandres was a professor of constitutional law at Dijon and a regular *conférencier* at the *Semaines sociales*.

26   For treatments of "social modernism," see Talmy, *SCF*, pp. 79–129, and Misner, *Social*, pp. 303–312.

27   "The attacks of Fr. Fontaine provoked a great reaction among social Catholics" (Talmy, *SCF*, p. 111). Fontaine's accusations were echoed by the *intégriste* Catholic press.

28   *Cours de doctrine et de pratique sociales: VIe session – Bordeaux 1909. Compte rendu in-extenso* (hereafter, *CR*) (Lyon: Chronique sociale de France, 1910), p. ii.

29   Fr. Loiselet, S.J., was the director of the Jesuit retreat center at Mouvoux (patronized by the owners and their managers [*classes dirigeantes*]) in the industrialized northeast of France. When he subsequently softened his views on the workers' right to unionize, he was moved to Nancy.

30   See Talmy, *SCF*, p. 106, and Droulers, *Politique sociale et christianisme*, p. 239. Loiselet did not qualify his charge with the adjective "social."

economic orientation, hostile to efforts promoting a strong and independent syndicalism.

Two years later, Julien Fontaine supplied a content and a distinctive label, namely, "sociological modernism":

In the name of Christian fraternity, [sociological modernism] professes an egalitarianism incompatible with any hierarchy and any idea of authority and subordination. It extols the autonomy of the human person, the equal worth of human agents, the equation of rights . . . , equation that necessarily involves the equality in the possession and the enjoyment of the goods of this world. Private property, diverse and unequal like the sources that produce it, should henceforth disappear.[31]

Fontaine claimed that Lorin had taught these ideas in his 1908 Marseilles declaration, either explicitly or by implication. Whether the president of the *Semaines sociales* intended it or not, the end result of his teaching was to promote socialism (*collectivisme*) by undermining the foundation of society in natural law. According to Fontaine, the true source of Lorin's ideas was not Christianity, but the revolutionary ideas of Jean-Jacques Rousseau. These notions dissolved the organic, hierarchical social order by promoting pernicious "egalitarianism."[32]

Fontaine's apprehensions must be viewed in the social context of his time. In the previous decade, socialist and Marxist political parties had been launched in France. The period between 1905 and 1910 was especially tense for French society. At their 1906 Congress, the socialist workers' movement (the C.G.T.) had reaffirmed and intensified their revolutionary program. Between 1907 and 1909, massive strikes paralyzed industries in the northeast of France. All of this served to accentuate Fontaine's criticism of Lorin.

THE *SEMAINE SOCIALE* OF MARSEILLES

Before proceeding to an exposition of Fontaine's critical chapter, I will give a précis of the central points contained in Lorin's 1908 declaration.[33] Lorin's seminal insight was grounded in biblical revelation: the "equality of dignity" and "the equivalence of human

[31] *LMS*, p. v; ellipsis in original. See Misner, *Social*, pp. 308–309, whose translation I have used.
[32] *LMS*, p. 451.
[33] "Déclaration de M. Henri Lorin," *Semaine sociale de Marseille 1908* (hereafter, "1908 declaration") published as brochure no. 39 in the series *Actes sociaux* (Reims: Action populaire, 1908), pp. 8–33.

agents" that flowed from the divine paternity. The ontologically
based "dignity of the human person" that flows from God's creative
and redemptive action has consequences for the socio-economic
order. Though Catholic doctrines do not dictate a socio-economic
system, Lorin asserted that "there is a Catholic way of envisaging,
orienting, and constructing" the discipline of economics:

> to take the point of view of human beings and not of things; to have for a
> goal not the description of that which is, but the search for that which
> ought to be; to take for foundations the affirmations of Catholicism relative
> to the dignity of the human person, the fraternity of all people, the
> universal purpose of earthly goods; and to take for guides its conceptions of
> justice and of progress, and, for a rule, the principle of fraternal
> equivalence which it posits and the positive determinations which the
> church has made of this principle.

Lorin concluded that "the goal of the discipline of economics will be
the search for the organization of work the most conformed to
justice, the most apt to further progress, the most fitting to assure the
conservation and development of individual and social life."[34] Over
against the notions of "orthodox" (i.e., liberal) economics grounded
in materialist theories of human nature, Lorin elaborated the
consequences of a Christian anthropology for the socio-economic
order. He stressed the progressive pursuit of "fraternal justice"
which strives to overcome the natural and artificial inequalities
which divide and diminish people. He emphasized the social
implications of the Christian idea of work by which human beings
"prepare the future of God's reign by putting justice into practice."
For Lorin the effort to extend the rule of spirit over matter is "the
radiating of a supernatural light which, by the clarity it spreads over
the origins and role of work, shows forth its nobility and highlights
its attraction and which, by the infinite receding which it assigns to
the goals of work, opens an unlimited field before it."[35] We can
detect in this dynamic understanding of work the influence of the
philosophy of action of Maurice Blondel, Lorin's philosophical
mentor. Blondel's phenomenology of human willing that seeks
fulfillment in ever-widening circles of action is implicit in Lorin's
perspective. Concrete human nature is dynamically oriented to a
unitary, supernaturalized end.

Lorin drew out specific implications from this conception of work

---

[34] Ibid., pp. 16–17.   [35] Ibid., pp. 19–20.

and the biblical ideal of "fraternal equivalence." In contrast to liberal economic theory, he criticized the "absolute liberty" of contracts and the absolute right to private property.[36] Property has an ultimately social purpose and everyone has a right to a living wage (*salaire vital*). *Rerum Novarum* had endorsed the "means of association" (*la société professionnelle*) and the "means of legislation" as legitimate methods for securing justice. Lorin chided those who refused to cooperate with the social legislative initiatives of the Third Republic, because such measures have their true source in the Decalogue and not the principles of 1789.

After arguing for the importance of maintaining the Sunday rest in a society where unity of belief was quickly disappearing, Lorin underlined the convergence of concern between the social duties entailed by Christianity and the growing movement of workers seeking recognition of their human dignity. There is a unitary human destiny which refuses any "airtight partition" (*cloison étanche*) between the business of eternal salvation and the business of this world.

> The heavenly kingdom and the earthly domain, the religious person and the social person, are not two separately distinct realities without relation . . . they interpenetrate and, so to speak, are of the same substance and activated by the same energy: the enlightened awareness of our origin and of our end which requires us, on a single plane, to persevere in the dignity of the first by using the means assigned to it for realizing the second.

Again we find that this passage has invoked characteristic Blondelian themes which reject any artificial compartmentalizing of reality that would undermine the unitary human vocation. Thus, social Catholics are called "to participate in public affairs and to cooperate for the common good and to propagate . . . in the public mind the Christian notion of labor."[37]

JULIEN FONTAINE'S CRITIQUE

I will now sketch the "excessive and dangerous tendencies" that Fontaine found in the teaching of Lorin and, very briefly, Deslandres. Before beginning his critique, Fontaine recognized the value of the *Semaines sociales*, the quality of many of its professors, and the ecclesiastical approbations they had received. However, he

---

[36] Ibid., pp. 21–25.   [37] Ibid., p. 31.

considered it his responsibility to point out the "dangerous and excessive tendencies" which give encouragement to the "partisans of false and wicked democracy."[38] Fontaine especially took aim at the "unhealthy democratic ferment" (*malsaine fermentation démocratique*) at work among certain Catholic groups, but he added that he did not want to confuse these ruinous tendencies with the useful work of the *Semaines sociales*.

Fontaine's critical chapter comprised four sections. In the first, entitled "the address of M. Lorin; the social foundations," he asserts that Lorin's declaration, "*given its doctrinal purpose and character*, seems to us very incomplete, defective in many places, false and dangerous in others." He especially faults Lorin for saying "nothing or almost nothing concerning property and the family," while "what he tells us about work is false in part."[39] Concerning property, Fontaine scored Lorin for countenancing "collectivism" by failing to affirm "private property, family, and heredity."[40] Lorin's teachings on the universal destination of earthly goods and the social aspects of work were cloaked "in a sort of Christian mysticism which renders it infinitely more communicable and dangerous." The Jesuit accused Lorin of covering over the real consequences of his positions: "the collapse of the most essential components of the social economy itself, I mean the collapse of the most elementary principles of natural law."[41]

The next section took aim at Lorin's "egalitarianism" which, in Fontaine's opinion, implied the leveling of all social differences.[42] He asserted that Lorin's principles for grounding a just social order, "the equality of dignity of persons" and "fraternal equivalence," owed more to Jean-Jacques Rousseau than the Bible. While Fontaine allowed "the metaphysical identity" of persons, he strongly repudiated any doctrine that would indiscriminately attribute to all people the same status, regardless of their obvious moral and social differences.[43] Indeed, the major rub of Lorin's egalitarianism was precisely its socio-political implications. In Fontaine's view there were, in the end, two fundamentally opposed socio-political systems: a democratic system which enforces the tyranny of an oligarchy over the "confused mass of people," and a "corporatist" system which

---

[38] Ibid., pp. 427–428.   [39] Ibid., p. 430.
[40] Ibid., pp. 435–440. Fontaine cited *RN* to secure his argument.
[41] Ibid., pp. 439–440.   [42] Ibid., pp. 442–457.
[43] Lorin would clarify the intended meaning of the phrase "equal dignity of all human beings" in his Bordeaux declaration.

promotes healthy intermediate bodies which serve as a buffer between the populace and the government.[44] Lorin and like-minded "Christian democrats," holding that the existence of social classes is "artificial" (*factices*), would do away with all the natural hierarchies that serve to decentralize power and ground social stability.[45] By conceiving of the dignity of the person in a way that suppresses "subordination and a necessary dependence," they "canonize arrogant individualism" which undermines the natural hierarchies in society like the family structure. "It is envy which you democrats inflame when you speak to these working masses of the equality of dignity, of equivalence, of absolute autonomy, of sovereignty."[46]

In the third section, Fontaine took to task Maurice Deslandres' lesson on the question of "public assistance."[47] The disputed issue was how best to meet the needs of the vulnerable members of society, namely, the elderly, the infirm, women and children in the work force, and retired workers. Deslandres and other Christian democrats favored collaboration with the Third Republic to enact social legislation to guarantee public assistance for the needy. Though approving of the goal, Fontaine strongly disagreed with the means. Invoking *Rerum Novarum*, the Jesuit argued that social needs were better met through intermediate groups (*corporations*) that serve "as a counterweight to the omnipotence of the collectivist state." For Fontaine, state intervention was unjustified except in a few limited matters.[48]

Fontaine raised two fundamental objections to Deslandres' promotion of social assistance legislation. First, such cooperation with anticlerical politicians who were using this legislation for their own political ends was sheer "dupery." In Fontaine's opinion, Deslandres was expressing a blind optimism to assert that such legislation has a "Christian basis." These assistance laws have in fact a "Masonic base." Secondly, Deslandres and Lorin were blurring the respective

---

[44] Fontaine cited La Tour du Pin, the sociologist Le Play, and *RN* in support of corporatist organization.

[45] The passage concerning social classes cited by Fontaine differs from the official text of Lorin's 1908 declaration. This latter is more nuanced concerning the nature of social classes. There are two possibilities. Fontaine may have taken polemical liberties with the texts or, as we shall see, the official text could have been altered for publication.

[46] *LMS*, p. 453.

[47] Ibid., pp. 457–469. Fontaine did not have a copy of Deslandres' lesson. He used citations from a journal review.

[48] For example, Fontaine would allow legislation to regulate the working conditions of women and children.

roles of justice and charity by stressing the ideal of social justice to be achieved through legislation. Fontaine, echoing Pius X and Merry del Val, argued for the primacy of charity for resolving social needs.[49] Acts of charity have salvific significance because they are free. An excessive concern for justice risks supplanting the necessary role of charity in a Christian's life. Fontaine thought the Christian democrats wanted to banish charity in favor of the claims of strict justice. He saw this as leading to the destructive leveling of the natural social hierarchies, a primary goal of the collectivist state.

In the final section of his polemic against the lessons of the 1908 *Semaine sociale*, Fontaine assailed the "pseudo-democratic" spirit that had spread among Catholics during the years of the Third Republic.[50] In "the implacable and merciless war" between the Catholic Church and the Third Republic, the Christian democrats and social Catholics have undermined Catholic resistance through their collaboration with the anticlericals.[51] Further, they have even served as apologists for some of the anti-Catholic measures, including the laws dealing with education and the Law of Separation. The younger generations of Catholics have been beguiled by these Christian democrats and their publications into accepting this state of affairs as unobjectionable, even desirable.[52]

Finally, Fontaine wondered what secret complicities united the Christian democrats with "the dogmatists of Modernism" condemned by *Pascendi*:

In a matter so grave, I would not like to be unjust towards anyone and I begin by stating that a good number of democrats have always seemed to me to be strangers to the doctrinal aberrations of exegetes like Loisy and the philosophers of immanence and pragmatism. They have been quite able to ignore the speculations of Messieurs Laberthonnière and Maurice Blondel, and to devote themselves exclusively to social works. However, this was not the case with the leaders of the party to which they were attached, the writers and journalists which they had chosen as guides.[53]

As Fontaine saw it, the "dogmatists of Modernism" and the leaders of Christian democracy were conspiring parties who abetted "the

---

[49] The future Pope Pius X, Cardinal Sarto, had affirmed the primacy of charity in 1896. See Ponson, *Les Catholiques lyonnais*, pp. 279–280.

[50] *LMS*, pp. 469–481.   [51] Ibid., p. 471.

[52] Fontaine named the *Annales de philosophie chrétienne* among these publications. The *Annales de philosophie chrétienne* was secretly owned by Maurice Blondel, who had appointed Lucien Laberthonnière as its managing editor. It was condemned in May 1913.

[53] *LMS*, pp. 477–478.

Revolution" sweeping France. It was *"above all* a doctrinal revolution." Its latest phase was the "sociological" application of the doctrinal errors condemned by *Pascendi*. Among Catholics, the two types of people who are promoting this revolution are first "the dogmaticians, exegetes, philosophers, historians, critics" as named by the encyclical. Their false doctrines "are found at the heart of our social revolution, at the base of our transformed – or rather deformed and perverted – institutions, at the heart of the democracy without God, without Christ, without natural law or moral law, and, consequently, without equity nor justice . . ."[54] Among the dogmaticians of Modernism, Fontaine singled out Maurice Blondel and Lucien Laberthonnière as purveyors of the false philosophies of immanence and pragmatism. Fontaine had been a fierce critic of Blondel since 1902.[55] Two years before, Fontaine had denounced "the Kantian skepticism which is at the heart of [Blondel's] philosophy of action."[56] Now Fontaine attacked Blondel's "very carefully crafted pages on history and dogma" that have contributed to form the democratic mentality. Indeed, the "Christian democrats" make up the second type of Catholics who are abetting the revolution sweeping France. In contrast with the doctrinal Modernists, they do not really understand the fundamental ideas they are implementing. Christian democrats such as Lorin are guided more by "sentiments." The Church had the grave responsibility to intervene in this delicate matter. Though questions of a social and even political nature are not directly under the magisterium's aegis, these revolutionists were working to form a society "where the Catholic truth has no more place."[57]

In summary, let us understand Julien Fontaine's point of view from two angles. His archadversary was "collectivism" (i.e., state socialism) which he viewed, with some reason, as posing a threat to French society. The proponents of Christian democracy were heirs to the pernicious legacy of the French Revolution and its intellectual

---

[54] Ibid., pp. 478–479.
[55] Blondel held Fontaine responsible, among others, for spreading what Blondel considered to be egregious distortions of his positions. He had chosen to remain silent in the face of the Jesuit's criticisms. See Blondel and Auguste Valensin, *Correspondance, 1899–1947*, 3 vols., presentation and notes by Henri de Lubac (Paris: Aubier, 1957–1965), vol. 1, pp. 167 and 183 (hereafter, *BV*). See also Virgoulay, *Blondel*, pp. 74–75 and 125.
[56] J. Fontaine, *La Théologie du N.T. et l'évolution des dogmes* (1907), cited by de Lubac in *BV*, vol. 1, p. 130.
[57] *LMS*, pp. 478, 480.

architects such as Rousseau. Fontaine judged Lorin's social Catholic agenda with its stress on social justice, the social function of property, and an independent syndicalism as an unwittingly dangerous collaboration with the socialist agenda. He viewed Lorin's stress on "fraternal equivalence" through this optic. Lorin's teaching was undermining the natural law bases of the hierarchically constituted social order and its legitimate authorities in the name of a spurious egalitarianism *à la Jean-Jacques*.[58] Behind these social teachings, Fontaine discerned the influence of the philosophers of immanence, Blondel and Laberthonnière.

What did Fontaine favor? His attitudes and positions fit the "conservative school" that accepted the regnant theories of economic liberalism, but tempered them with the sociological theories of Le Play that stressed a social order based on organic and paternal structures such as the family and professional associations.[59] While expressing admiration for La Tour du Pin's corporatism, the Jesuit thought the state should minimally intervene in the socioeconomic order. He saw himself as faithful to *Rerum Novarum*, especially its teachings on the inviolable right to private property, the maintenance of social classes, and the importance of intermediate social bodies to curtail the power of the state. These are truths of natural law. However, Fontaine chose not to view the affirmation of independent workers' unions by the *Semaines sociales* as evidence of their promotion of intermediate bodies. He seems to have assimilated Lorin's ideas on syndicalism to the more conspicuous, antihierarchical, socialist workers' organizations. In contrast, Fontaine approved of workers' associations as mutual aid societies that served a primarily moral and religious purpose, tightly under the control of the *patrons*. In a society ordered according to natural law principles, only paternalistic, intermediate bodies qualified.[60]

THE *SEMAINE SOCIALE* OF BORDEAUX

Fontaine's attack on the Marseilles *Semaine sociale* was published in June 1909, a month before the Bordeaux meeting. At the opening

[58] Ibid., introduction, p. xxv.
[59] See Lécrivain, "La Formation sociale," *Le Mouvement social catholique*, p. 118.
[60] Could Fontaine be considered a social Catholic akin to La Tour du Pin? No. Fontaine was too accepting of economic liberalism, a doctrine that every social Catholic, whether monarchist or democrat, found unacceptable.

Mass of this gathering, Cardinal Andrieu, the hosting prelate, explicitly raised the issue of "social modernism" without naming Fontaine. Calling the dechristianization of France "a satanic work," he exhorted the freshly arrived *semainiers* to multiply their efforts to help people "continue on the road, without fear of the failings to which the thousand temptations of social modernism could drag them." Andrieu concluded: "You have entered into battle against the great enemy of the day, *sociological modernism.*"[61] If anyone was on the spot, it was Henri Lorin. A contemporary press account stated that Lorin opened the proceedings by affirming "his resolution to maintain doctrinal rectitude, protest-[ing] against sociological modernism . . ."[62] This, however, did not satisfy his anti-Modernist critics. Bernard Gaudeau, a former Jesuit and *quondam* professor of theology at the Pontifical Roman Gregorian University, joined forces with Fontaine to assail Lorin's positions.[63] In an article entitled "La *Semaine sociale* de Bordeaux," published in his journal *La Foi catholique,* Gaudeau took to task Lorin's 1909 declaration.[64]

I will begin by giving highlights of Lorin's declaration and will then summarize Gaudeau's response. Any researcher faces the initial problem of verifying the original manuscript that Lorin read at Bordeaux, the specific text that drew Gaudeau's critical fire.[65] There are certain discrepancies between the official text (*CR*) published by the *Chronique sociale de France,* the parent press of the *Semaines sociales,*

---

[61] *CR*, pp. 14–15.

[62] "La *Semaine sociale,*" *La Croix* (27 July 1909). Lorin's official text contains no mention of "sociological modernism."

[63] Gaudeau (1854–1925) had been a Jesuit until 1902, when he was secularized and incardinated in the diocese of Tours. He had held a series of teaching posts, including a brief assignment teaching dogmatic theology at the Gregorian University. After 1902 he carried on an itinerant preaching and conference ministry. In 1908 he founded the periodical *La Foi catholique,* which absorbed his energies for the rest of his life. Though he had occupied a chair at the Institute of Action française, he later became quite critical of *Action française.* In an era of self-appointed defenders of orthodoxy, Gaudeau's theological competence was generally recognized by his peers. See Roger Aubert, "L'Intégrisme du début du XXe siècle," *La Foi et le temps* 20 (1990–1), 41. Poulat terms him a "conservateur" rather than an "intégriste." See E. Poulat, "Gaudeau (Bernard)," *Dictionnaire d'histoire et de géographie ecclésiastiques,* under the direction of R. Aubert, assisted by J. P. Hendrickx and J. P. Sosson (Paris: Letouzey et Ane, 1909–1993).

[64] "La *Semaine sociale* de Bordeaux: la 'déclaration' de M. H. Lorin en 1909. – Danger d'un pseudo-mysticisme catholique en matière sociale, lequel supprime le droit naturel à base religieuse, mais rationnelle," *La Foi catholique* 2 (August 1909), 119–147. Reprinted in *Autour du catholicisme social* (Paris: Aux Bureaux de la *Foi catholique,* 1912).

[65] Lorin publicly presented only the first half of his lengthy declaration at the Bordeaux gathering. See the *CR*, p. 23.

and the text cited by Gaudeau.[66] Key phrases and words have been changed as if altered in the light of Gaudeau's critique. And that is exactly what happened! The *Nihil obstat* was given only after the text was changed in the light of the criticisms made by Fontaine and Gaudeau.[67] Indeed, Fr. Desbuquois of *Action Populaire*, who had published Lorin's 1908 declaration, declined to publish the 1909 declaration because of certain "Kantian" remarks.[68] These remarks were mostly found in the second, theoretical half of his declaration. In summarizing Lorin's lesson, I will employ Gaudeau's citations at certain points as faithful transcriptions of the original manuscript and will indicate in the notes any changes in the official *CR* version.

A second legitimate inference is that the *CR* altered Lorin's original manuscript in view of Fontaine's criticisms. Most conspicuous are several footnotes in the *CR* whose contents directly respond to some of Fontaine's criticisms.[69] These notes were presumably added to the original manuscript to secure the *Nihil obstat*. I will only briefly indicate this material, since our focus has shifted to Gaudeau's criticisms of Lorin.

Finally, I want to signal the distinctive, though implicit, stamp of Maurice Blondel's "philosophy of action" on Lorin's declaration. It is probable that Blondel influenced the composition of Lorin's 1909 declaration. We have Blondel's testimony that Lorin frequently solicited his comments and advice in preparing his declarations.[70] We also know that Lorin summoned "his father in philosophy" (*son père philosophique*) to preparatory meetings at Lorin's country estate and asked Blondel to be present at the delivery of his Bordeaux

[66] The altered passages are all in the second half, with one exception. Gaudeau had access to the entire text: "je viens de lire, d'un bout à l'autre, la déclaration de M. Lorin . . ." ("La *Semaine sociale* de Bordeaux," p. 123). I have not been able to obtain this original manuscript. Gaudeau's article appeared several months before the official *CR* was published by the *Chronique sociale de France* in January 1910.

[67] "Déjà en 1909, le *CR* de la *Semaine sociale* de Bordeaux ne reçoit le *nihil obstat* qu'après que l'on ait 'tenu compte des critiques formulées par MM. Fontaine et Gaudeau' A.A.L. [Archives de l'archevêché de Lyon], 'Com. vig.', 13 janvier 1910 et 28 décembre 1911" (cited in Ponson, *Les Catholiques lyonnais*, p. 334, n. 85). Cardinal Couillié's *Imprimatur* is dated 3 January 1910.

[68] See Droulers, *Politique sociale et christianisme*, p. 244. These "Kantian" passages will be discussed below. The description "Kantian" refers to epistemological and metaphysical positions that hold that the mind does not so much discover an object and its significance, but rather the mind construes, even constructs, reality according to the mind's own categories. Kant held that the mind is incapable of grasping the "thing in itself."

[69] Neither Fontaine or Gaudeau are named in the official text.

[70] See, for example, Lorin's letter to Blondel, 17 October 1910, *Centre d'archives Maurice Blondel* (Louvain-la-Neuve, Belgium), folder CLIV/55.

declaration. Over the objections of those *semainiers* who thought it too risky to associate the *Semaines sociales* with a determinate philosophical doctrine, Lorin dramatically appealed to Blondel from the podium at the conclusion of his conference for Blondel's "philosophical and religious witness."[71] Blondel responded by composing a series of articles under the pseudonym of "Testis" in which he defended the *Semaines sociales* from the attacks of Fontaine and Gaudeau and indicated the affinities between his own philosophy and the method of the social Catholics.[72] Respecting Lorin's declaration, Blondel's influence is most evident in the crucial second section entitled "The equivalence [*adéquation*] of Christianity to individual and social life."[73] From the title itself to the distinctive "unitary" anthropology, Blondel's influence is unmistakable. Gaudeau's criticisms will especially lock onto these passages. It is not coincidental that the anti-Modernist charge against Blondel of confusing the natural and supernatural orders was also leveled against Lorin.

The title of Lorin's 1909 declaration was "The individualist idea or the Christian idea as the foundation of law."[74] As he had in his 1908 declaration, Lorin criticized the baleful consequences of the socio-economic individualism stemming from the French Revolution. Firmly grounding the *Semaines sociales* in the tradition of the Catholic response to the "social problem" that traced its lineage back to Archbishop von Ketteler, Cardinal Manning, and *Rerum Novarum*, Lorin gave a pithy statement of their motivation:

They are everywhere a well-founded protest against the individualist conception which implies a misunderstanding of concrete solidarities, undermines the notion of human fraternity by ruining that of divine paternity, its real origin and logical foundation, [and] falsifies the idea of right by detaching it from the idea of duty, its source and *raison d'être*.[75]

"Individualism" has acted as an "enemy ideology" to dismantle the Christian framework of society that had been constructed over several centuries.

---

[71] Blondel recalled the circumstances of his involvement in his letter to Paul Archambault, 3 September 1924, cited in Maurice Blondel and Joannès Wehrlé, *Correspondance*, edited and annotated by Henri de Lubac, vol. II (Paris: Aubier Montaigne, 1969), pp. 414–415.

[72] Blondel, *LSS*.

[73] *CR*, p. 66. The term "adéquation" is both crucially significant and extremely difficult to translate. It means something stronger than "appropriateness," but not as strong as "identification." The term "adéquation" appears once in *L'Action* when Blondel refers parenthetically to "an adequation of mind and life." See *Action*, p. 283 (Fr. original, p. 303).

[74] *CR*, pp. 53–80.   [75] Ibid., p. 55.

It claimed to deliver human beings from the religious bond which united them to each other, and each of its stages of conquest was marked in our country by social disorganization: disorganization of the professional society, by the law of 1791; disorganization of the familial society by the divorce law; disorganization of the religious society by the law of separation of church and state.[76]

The social unity that had been realized by the teaching and practice of the church had been destroyed step by step. The vacuum has been filled by "human absolutism" (*l'absolutisme humain*) which, "failing to recognize not only divine authority but even the existence of the transcendent" that is the only true foundation for social unity, progresses "from the deification of reason to the apotheosis of force, from the absolutizing of the human being to his reduction to the level of matter."[77]

In the first, historical section, entitled the "Consequences of the abandonment of the social principles of Catholicism," Lorin traced the logical results of the doctrine of individualism in the political, juridical, economic, and social orders.[78] In reaction to these negative consequences, the adversely affected proletariat was clamorously demanding justice. The workers' union (*syndicat*) was the means of advancing their demands to improve working conditions.[79] These demands arise from a confused sense of human dignity and justice in a society that has lost "the transcendent norm of this justice and the primary meaning of this dignity." With great difficulty, a body of social legislation has been wrested from the propertied class, legislation that has sought to substitute itself for the individualistic law enshrined in the 1804 Code. Lorin asserted that "this new law is social, is just, only to the degree that it borrows from Christianity, consciously or not, its principles of action."[80]

Lorin's extremely important, theoretical second section, "Christianity's equivalence to individual and social life," bore the brunt of Gaudeau's critique.[81] Lorin began by articulating a framework

---

[76] Ibid., pp. 56–57.   [77] Ibid., pp. 58–59.
[78] Ibid., pp. 55–66. What is noteworthy for our purposes are his qualified support for democratic universal suffrage (it is not a necessary consequence of the Christian doctrine of fraternal equality) and his critique of the legal codification of private property as an "absolute power."
[79] The Third Republic first legalized the formation of workers' unions in 1884, as a matter of "private" law.
[80] *CR*, pp. 65–66.   [81] Ibid., pp. 66–79.

within which human beings come to realize the deepest meaning of their strivings.

There exists an order of invisible things that acts in us, manifests itself to our intelligence, determines our will, coordinates our thoughts, multiplies our desires. Our supreme good is to strive to understand, to love, to reproduce in our consciousness the image of this transcendent reality which we name God. From this reality, reason, of course, *ought to suffice* to make us know with certitude that it is. But in order to know what it is more intimately . . . it requires grace on [God's] part, and an act of faith on our part which grace inspires and supports. And although this order is transcendent, nevertheless, since everything holds together in the divine plan [and] since we are unable actually to realize a purely natural and human equilibrium, the terrestrial order itself is indecipherable and unsolvable without this divine word of the human enigma. Thus, reality, accessible to understanding, is illuminated by this act of faith which surpasses it. We are firmly established in certitudes to which scientific hypotheses do not lead; we attain the interior peace not given by the constancy of laws which our mind imposes on reality. And our faith, by the grace that makes it last and by its very action, verifies its foundations in order to all the more adhere to it.[82]

In asserting the inadequacy of the natural order and its "indecipherability" without the "divine word," Lorin was making a claim about the nature–supernature relationship. He seems to suggest that the mind, apart from supernatural revelation, is limited to a mere phenomenalism that yields no sure foundation for human life.[83] An implicit anthropology that asserts the impossibility of a "purely natural and human equilibrium" echoes Blondel's philosophy of action. This Blondelian anthropology is more pronounced in the following passage:

The life of the Christian, oriented as the Gospel commands by the constant thought of its origin and end, is essentially action . . . unceasing action because, detached from matter in its projects, it aims beyond its immediate objectives at the final end which during earthly life remains outside our attainment; indefinitely extendable action, because, alien to the beckonings of egoism, it is turned toward the service of neighbor in which the faith shows it the concrete condition of service of God here below, and which can incrementally discover points of application up to infinity.[84]

---

82 Ibid., p. 66, and Gaudeau, "La *Semaine sociale* de Bordeaux," p. 139; emphasis added.
83 The *CR* altered the second to last sentence to say: "that our mind discovers in things." Droulers corroborates this specific instance of alteration. See *Politique sociale et christianisme,* p. 244, note 36.
84 *CR*, pp. 76–77.

Thus human life has a "unitary" destiny, indicated by the dynamic orientation of action that radiates outward "up to infinity." The pivotal issue concerns the respective contributions of the human sciences and supernatural revelation to understanding this destiny:

Every discipline which treats of human acts implies, in constituting itself, a response to these questions, a response for which observable reality does not furnish the data and which, whatever its positive or negative form, constitutes a postulate of the metaphysical order. Those who refuse the divine grace and do not have the illuminations of the faith are reduced to forging this postulate according to the bent of their mind [*au gré de leur esprit*] by an entirely abstract process.[85]

Given this positivism of the human sciences which are limited to "observable reality," what are the implications for the role of Christian dogmas for human knowledge and activity?

Lorin expatiated upon the social import of Catholic doctrines that orient and motivate the progressive attempts to secure justice in society.

The visible world draws all its value from an invisible and spiritual universe. The dogmas of creation, the original Fall, the Redemption, and the institution of the Church express and enlighten for us this transcendent reality. They give the life of humans an infinite price and a dynamic meaning by making them know their origin and their end. They establish the relationships with God, in situating them in a social cosmogony. They determine the concepts upon which human beings construct the cities which they must inhabit.[86]

Thus Catholic dogmas do more than supplement the human sciences concerned with the various aspects of social life. By indicating the ultimate human origin and end, these dogmas actually determine the fundamental orientation of these sciences: "Thus the dogmas, expression of the transcendent reality, supply a metaphysics

---

[85] Cited in Gaudeau, "La *Semaine sociale* de Bordeaux," p. 134. The *CR* altered the last portion to read: "People who are closed to the insights of the faith formulate this postulate according to the light and measure of their intelligence" (p. 69).

[86] Cited in Gaudeau, "La *Semaine sociale* de Bordeaux," pp. 134–135. This passage was altered in the official version to read: "The visible world draws *a new value* from an invisible and spiritual universe, source of illuminating insights. The dogmas of Creation, of the original fall, of the Incarnation, of the Redemption, [and] of the institution of the Church determine with precision what the human being is, his origin and his end; [these dogmas] give a sure meaning and infinite price to his life; [they] situate it in a social cosmogony, define its relations with divine Being and creatures, [and] determine the concepts upon which human beings construct the cities they must inhabit" (*CR*, pp. 66–67; emphasis added).

of action and a sociology by means of which the human being situates himself in the universe, understands himself, orients himself, and interprets in a language of movement the concepts of social relations."[87] As Lorin had asserted at Marseilles, these dogmas ground and guide action on behalf of the progressive realization of the ideal of "human fraternity."[88] For example, the Christian doctrine of the divine adoption grounds the "relation of equivalence among human beings."[89] However, contrary to Fontaine's interpretation, "progress" by means of action for justice in society is not a socialistic leveling of all differences, but an effort to "diminish the gap between the human reality and the divine ideal."[90] Lorin clearly interpreted *Rerum Novarum* with individualistic capitalism uppermost in mind and not the menace of state socialism which preoccupied Fontaine and Gaudeau.

Lorin's conclusion continued in a Blondelian vein. In keeping with a "unitary" anthropology, he viewed the workers' efforts to obtain justice as taking its ultimate significance from the "Christian" notion of justice:

Let us keep from seeing in the coincidence of facts only the immanent irony of things. Rather let us take them for the effects of silent causes that shape a world in its depths, by which the necessity of earning one's daily bread imposes a sense of order, and which claims to found this order on justice . . . [J]ustice is a *Christian* notion which only makes sense as a function of the divine will, and whose constructive value and social efficacy are only

---

[87] Cited in Gaudeau, "La *Semaine sociale* de Bordeaux," p. 135. The official version read: "Thus the dogmas furnish a metaphysics and a sociology by means of which human beings are situated in the universe, are understood and oriented, and interpret the concepts of social relations in a language of movement" (*CR*, p. 68). Lorin added: "dogmas furnish human beings the clear notion of the nature of their relations with diverse elements of total reality. They constitute a metaphysic entirely oriented to action . . ." (cited in Gaudeau, p. 135).

[88] Lorin appended a note that responds to Fontaine's accusation that Lorin's egalitarianism repudiated human inequalities: "Fraternity, such as it is here defined and understood, far from putting in question the existence of human inequalities which is a natural fact, and the existence of diverse social authorities which is a necessity established by God, entails a differentiation resulting from the deployment of unequal occupations [*d'activités inégales*]" (*CR*, p. 71).

[89] Cited in Gaudeau, "La *Semaine sociale* de Bordeaux," p. 136.

[90] Touching on some of the problematic points attacked by Fontaine, Lorin reiterated his views on the divine ordination of property to the common good and the implications of the Christian doctrine of work. He fortified his unflinching critique of laissez-faire capitalism by references to the Decalogue, St. Thomas, and *RN*. The *CR* version added notes that directly respond to certain of Fontaine's criticisms. I infer that these were subsequently appended to secure the *Nihil obstat*. See *CR*, pp. 75–79, and the notes on pages 71 and 78.

fully realized in the linkage of Christian notions, within which [justice] is inserted.[91]

Hearkening back to the title of the second half of his declaration, Lorin finished his lesson by averring that the necessities of daily life inexorably lead a person of good will "to respect Christianity as an equivalence [*adéquation*] to individual and social life."

What did Lorin mean by "adéquation"? Was he suggesting that the natural order required the supernatural order to be viable? Certain ambiguous expressions in his 1909 declaration raised questions about Lorin's understanding of the natural order. Indeed, scholastic critics had posed such questions to Blondel. Picking up where Fontaine left off, Bernard Gaudeau was to put his finger on the neuralgic point: the understanding of the nature–supernature relationship

BERNARD GAUDEAU'S CRITIQUE

Gaudeau began his article "La *Semaine social* de Bordeaux" by commending Fontaine's book *Le Modernisme sociologique*. Fontaine's chapter criticizing the 1908 Marseilles *Semaine sociale* was excerpted in the same issue of *La Foi catholique*. Gaudeau cited a long excerpt from Cardinal Andrieu's Bordeaux allocution in which Andrieu excoriated the anticlerical Third Republic whose tactics of "laiciza-tion," culminating in the Law of Separation, had the ultimate aim of "dechristianizing" French society. Gaudeau indicated a striking affinity between Andrieu and Fontaine in their analysis of the causes of dechristianization and the means of social dissolution which inexorably lead to state socialism.[92] Nevertheless, Gaudeau wondered whether the awareness and the fear of the dangers of "social modernism" had really had any impact on the teachings of the *Semaine sociale* of Bordeaux.[93] In answering this question, Gaudeau first took a swipe at Lorin's style (it lacked "the happy character of a typically French style") in a way that implied that he suspected Blondel's influence. He compared the "nightmares of obscurity" of Lorin's text to certain passages in Blondel, whose obscurity is "the most cruel." Regarding the content, he concluded that Lorin had failed to do justice to the triad of "family, property, and work"; it was

[91] Ibid., p. 80, and Gaudeau, "La *Semaine sociale* de Bordeaux," p. 137; emphasis added. The *CR* version dropped the modifying adjective "Christian."
[92] Gaudeau, "La *Semaine sociale* de Bordeaux," pp. 119–122.   [93] Ibid., p. 123.

of their importance that the Vatican secretary of state, Merry del Val, had reminded the Bordeaux assembly.[94] In addition Gaudeau faulted Lorin for making no mention of the social teaching of Pius X, especially his *Motu proprio* on popular Christian action.[95] He also took Lorin to task for offering no effective refutation of state socialism and international collectivism which "already governs us," not to mention his silence vis-à-vis the notions of family and nation (*la patrie*).[96]

Up to this point, Gaudeau had not significantly added to Fontaine's critique. Now he formulated his most serious criticism. The dominant, theological error that Gaudeau discovered in Lorin's declaration was the confusion of the natural and supernatural orders: "The very subtle element of error which insinuates itself (very unconsciously under cover of the most upright, the most Christian, the most supernatural intentions, I would even say too exclusively supernatural), is precisely the confusion between the natural order and the Christian supernatural order."[97] Gaudeau's general charge was that Lorin had "supernaturalized," that is, subsumed under the province of Christian dogma, what can properly be known and established by the use of reason alone. Repeating Fontaine's accusation, Gaudeau said that Lorin seemed to deny the reality of "natural law," in its proper sense. He even conveyed the impression that there was no idea of justice and of right apart from the revealed truth of Christianity. "For M. Lorin, justice is a notion exclusively Christian . . ."[98] Such views falsify the bases of "natural religion," and thus run counter to the Vatican Council's teaching on human reason's capacity, unassisted by revelation, to conclude on God's existence with certitude.[99]

Gaudeau censured the very title of Lorin's second section, a phrase repeated in the declaration's conclusion: "Christianity's equivalence [*adéquation*] to individual and social life." He contended that the most one could say is that Christianity is "'adequate' to the

[94] Ibid., pp. 123–129.
[95] "De populari actione christiana moderanda" (18 November 1903) *Pii X Pontificis Maximi Acta*, vol. 1 (Rome: Vatican Press, 1905), pp. 117–125. Pius X affirmed that social hierarchy that subordinates lower classes to the higher was a *sine qua non* of Catholic social doctrine. Gaudeau mentions that Cardinal Andrieu had given equal emphasis to *RN* and Pius X's *Motu proprio* in his opening allocution.
[96] Gaudeau, "La *Semaine sociale* de Bordeaux," p. 131.　　[97] Ibid., pp. 131–132.
[98] Ibid., pp. 132 and 137.　　[99] Cf. the First Vatican Council's *Dei Filius*.

supernatural [*sic*; Lorin had said 'individual'; Gaudeau cites Lorin correctly below] and social life."

[F]urthermore, these words express a false notion; because if there really is [an] equivalence [*adéquation*] between Christianity and the individual and social life of man, [then] human nature demands and postulates Christianity, and this is the error of immanence, understood in the sense condemned by the church.[100]

Immanentism was, of course, the error that *Pascendi* attributed to the Modernists.[101] Gaudeau was obviously attempting to make a logical connection between Lorin's social teaching and the central philosophical position associated with Modernism.

Another example of Lorin's undermining of the proper distinction between the natural and supernatural orders was his statement that "reason . . . *ought to suffice*" for attaining a certain knowledge of God's existence.[102] Tendentiously inferring that Lorin was denying the *theoretical possibility* of such knowledge, Gaudeau asserted that Lorin should have said "really suffices" (*suffit réellement*) under pain of being anathematized by the Vatican Council.

Gaudeau decried the "formal error," apparent in Lorin's formulations, that holds that "the specifically Christian dogmas (Incarnation, Redemption, Church) determine the first principles upon which natural social law is based." Lorin had compromised the adequacy of natural reason to arrive at "conceptions of right, duty, justice, love, solidarity, the precepts of natural law, the fundamental natural laws of the family and society," independently of Christian revelation. Such an understanding was "fideism."[103]

Lorin's confusion of the respective prerogatives of revelation and natural reason was especially flagrant when he founded his notion of human fraternity upon the relationship of supernatural "adoption":

Here the ambiguity is obvious: no, it is not the relationship, purely gratuitous and supernatural, of adoption between humans and God the Father by Jesus Christ; it is not the relations, of the exclusively Christian order, which found and directly create the social bond among human beings, the rights and the duties of justice and of natural love, natural fraternity. The natural social law is founded in the first place on God,

---

100 Gaudeau, "La *Semaine sociale* de Bordeaux," p. 133.
101 See Daly, *Transcendence*, pp. 195–204.
102 Gaudeau, "La *Semaine sociale* de Bordeaux," p. 139; emphasis added.
103 Ibid., p. 135.

Creator and final End as known by reason and nature, abstracted from all Revelation: it is founded first of all on "natural religion."[104]

The cumulative impact of the incriminating passages compelled Gaudeau to make a judgment that he intoned he was loath to make lightly:

I judge that the more Modernism, condemned by the church and common sense, is a dangerous error, the more one ought to be sovereignly cautious in applying the label of "Modernist" to a person or a definite doctrine. But after all, it is not doubtful that the suppression or near ignorance of the rational bases of the faith, of the natural bases of the Christian and revealed order, the confusion of these two orders, the one necessary to the other but adequately and indispensably distinct, are the essential characteristic of the error of Modernism.[105]

Gaudeau proceeded to put Lorin in his place with masterful condescension:

The science of theology is complex and cannot be improvised; its formulas are difficult to wield; its terrain is one of those onto which one should not lightly dare to step. M. Henri Lorin, a fine talent, eminent and generous Maecenas of certain social works that intend to be Catholic, would be wise not to step out of his role and not to set foot on a terrain of doctrine which is not his own.[106]

By undermining the proper claims of the natural order for establishing the foundations of justice and the entire structure of natural law, Lorin had left Catholics bereft of an effective appeal to non-believers who do not accept Christian revelation:

there would be no common, definitive, absolute principle upon which justice and law could be based, and in the name of which unbelievers themselves could be led to the faith; there would be no possible reply to the argumentation of a-religious liberalism, of oppressive atheism. Spiritual natural law, which sociological modernism no longer wants, natural law with its rational religious base, is the only ground to which those without faith cannot object.[107]

There was no question in Gaudeau's mind that Lorin's 1909 declaration was not an improvement upon his defective 1908 presentation. If anything, the errors were more egregious.

---

[104] Ibid., p. 136.   [105] Ibid., pp. 137–138.   [106] Ibid., p. 138.
[107] Ibid., p. 143.

CONCLUSION

Having reviewed Henri Lorin's *Semaine sociale* declarations and the accusations of the anti-Modernists Julien Fontaine and Bernard Gaudeau, I want to indicate two optics that have emerged from this investigation that help to focus the conflict of mentalities involved in the Modernist crisis. First, the controversies concerning the *Semaines sociales* point to two different strategies for re-Christianizing society. The strategy of Lorin and the *Semaine sociale* organization could be termed "reformist" or "progressive." Despite a political climate unfavorable to the church and her confessional works, they saw the possibility of collaborating with non-Catholic, even anticlerical, forces to seek greater justice for the workers and the gradual transformation of society. They viewed the workers' aspirations as expressive of an unacknowledged yearning for God's kingdom. In promoting justice for the workers and their empowerment, they increasingly looked to democratic structures to secure workers' dignity. They were convinced that a strong and independent Christian workers' movement was essential if society was going to overcome the corrosive consequences of economic liberalism.

On the other hand, the strategy favored by Fontaine and Gaudeau could be termed "restorationist." This approach rejected all collaboration with those hostile or indifferent to the church as an institution. It promoted a return to hierarchical structures in which the lines of authority descended from top to bottom, that is, a benevolent paternalism. It stressed private property, the family, and "mixed" associations of workers and owners to maintain proper social order. It preferred to speak of charity in response to social misery, rather than justice. Above all, it prioritized efforts to restore the fortunes of the church because of its conviction that religion is essential to the health of a society. During the pontificate of Pius X, this strategy received papal encouragement under the label of "religious defense."

However, the contrast between these two strategies is not to be read as a conflict between "intransigent" traditionalists and "modernizing" liberals. As J. M. Mayeur has indicated, both sides were counter-revolutionary at their root:

Democrats, but not liberals, the Christian democrats and the social Catholics, even if they accept the Republic, profess in fact the vision of the world which was that of the intransigents: refusal of individualism, organicism, defense of the family, dream of an alliance of the people and the clergy against the notables, corporatism, decentralization, hostility to the established order – that of the 'right thinking' and the conservatives, the search for a third way between liberalism and socialism, anti-industrialism, [and] anti-capitalism colored by anti-Semitism.[108]

Social Catholics such as Lorin were not less upset than Fontaine and Gaudeau by the pernicious consequences of the French Revolution. For Fontaine, however, these evils consisted primarily in the socio-political "egalitarianism" propagated by Rousseau and the Revolution; for Lorin, the primary evil was not the political system, but the individualistic socio-economic system. Public enemy number one for Fontaine and Gaudeau was state socialism. Fontaine argued that the *Semaine sociale* Catholics and Christian democrats played into the hands of the socialists. As an intransigent committed to an hierarchical social order, Fontaine viewed social Catholics who promoted equal dignity and democratic procedures as subverting the bases of natural and supernatural authority. However, Fontaine was myopic about the liberal economic system that was also a fruit of the Revolution. In this he did not differ from the majority of French Catholics who were imbued with the liberal economic mindset.[109]

Besides these contrasting estimations of the political and economic legacy of the French Revolution, there were properly philosophical, epistemological differences. Fontaine and Gaudeau decried in Lorin's declarations the influence of immanentist philosophy whose ultimate provenance was Immanuel Kant. At issue was reason's capacity to attain the real, that is, to arrive at sure truths in the natural order, sufficient to establish the bases of society, without benefit of supernatural revelation. On the other hand, Lorin was opposed to the reigning, rationalistic positivism in the social sciences: economics, political science, and sociology. Positivism claimed to establish the "facts" and "laws" necessary for human prosperity, while adhering to a strict metaphysical agnosticism, if not antagonism. Lorin and Blondel faulted such scientistic positivism for artificially compartmentalizing reality and, as a result, treating the human person in isolation from his true, supernatural destiny.

A second optic was indicated by Gaudeau: the understanding of

---

[108] Mayeur, *Catholicisme social et démocratie chrétienne*, pp. 28–29.
[109] Social Catholics of any stripe were never more than a minor prophetic voice within the ranks of the *pratiquants*.

the nature–supernature relationship. Gaudeau reproved Lorin for holding a false conception of this relationship. Lorin, echoing his philosophical mentor Maurice Blondel, viewed the supernatural as investing the natural order with its authentic, spiritual finality. Consequently he was concerned to establish the Christian bases for Catholic social action. Lorin and Blondel sought to construct a third way, different from both positivism and neo-scholasticism, to understand the relationship between terrestrial realities and the invisible supernatural realm. Gaudeau objected that this approach resulted in the evaporation of the specifically natural. Different understandings of the relationship between the natural and supernatural orders were the theological pivot of the crisis over social modernism.[110]

This investigation of the controversy between the *Semaines sociales* and their critics has cast light on the complexity of the clash of mentalities vis-à-vis social modernism. While accused of social modernism, the *Semaines sociales*, especially through the presidential addresses of Henri Lorin, endeavored to articulate an integral vision of socio-economic life that was consistent with their Catholic beliefs. Julien Fontaine, on the other hand, while posing as a paladin of anti-Modernism, was actually imbued with the modernism of economic liberalism. Secondly, I have argued for the influence of Maurice Blondel on the teachings presented by Lorin. The case I have made is admittedly circumstantial, but there is both internal and external evidence in its favor. This connection is not merely a matter of historical interest. The Blondelian viewpoint continues to play a role in the spirited debate over the proper Christian understanding of the social order and the correlate understanding of the nature–supernature relationship. In *Theology and Social Theory*, John Milbank has asserted that "Blondel, more than anyone else, points us beyond secular reason."[111] But Milbank's thesis has been contested.[112] A second instance is David Schindler's argument with "neo-conservatives" George Weigel, Michael Novak, and John Richard Neuhaus. Schindler's distinctively Blondelian perspective is at odds with the

---

[110] See Peter J. Bernardi, "Theology and Politics: The Dispute between Maurice Blondel and Pedro Descoqs, S.J." (Ph.D. Dissertation: The Catholic University of America, 1997).

[111] (Oxford: Blackwell, 1990), p. 219. For Milbank's treatment of Blondel, see especially chapter 8, pp. 206–255.

[112] See, for example, Gregory Baum, "For and Against John Milbank," *Essays in Critical Theology* (Kansas City, Missouri: Sheed & Ward, 1994), pp. 52–76.

neo-conservative approach to the social order.[113] The controversy involving the teaching of the *Semaines sociales* has significant contemporary resonances.

Finally, a brief note on what happened to the *Semaines sociales*. The accusations of "social modernism" by Julien Fontaine and Bernard Gaudeau were widely echoed in the Catholic *intégriste* press. The *Semaines sociales* continued under a cloud of suspicion until almost the end of the pontificate of Pius X. At the 1913 *Semaine sociale*, Lorin rectified certain positions to which the Vatican had objected, thus staving off a rumored Vatican condemnation.[114] The *Semaines sociales* continue to meet into the 1990s.

---

[113] David L. Schindler, "The Church's 'worldly' mission: Neoconservatism and American culture," *Communio* 18 (Fall, 1991), 365–397.
[114] Talmy, *SCF,* pp. 106–129.

CHAPTER 11

Anti-Modernism and the elective affinity between politics and philosophy

Michael J. Kerlin

INTRODUCTORY COMMENTS

There are two truisms about politics and philosophy. The first is that politics bears upon the totality of philosophy. The second is that philosophy bears upon the totality of politics. However, a person can press either to the point of falsehood and foolishness. For example, one can press the first to the point of claiming that politics will explain the whole of philosophy, or one can press the second to the point of claiming that philosophy will explain the whole of politics. And the closer one comes to pressing either truism to its extreme, the closer one comes to falsehood and foolishness. The reality of the connection between politics and philosophy is, in fact, extremely complex. My objective in the present article is to show just how complex the connection can be by tracing the work of two major Catholic philosophers of the twentieth century, Reginald Garrigou-Lagrange and Jacques Maritain. I select them in particular because of their interest and my interest in the Modernist controversy within the Roman Catholic Church at the beginning of the century and because in their lives politics and philosophy affected each other throughout a long and significant personal relationship. When I say that my objective is "to show just how complex the connection can be," I have in mind showing both the extent of the variety and the degree of the complexity. The connection will, if my argument is successful, turn out to be (by a stretch of Johann Wolfgang von Goethe's metaphor) one of elective affinity. I leave the needed elaboration of this metaphor until the concluding section of the article.[1]

[1] B. Zorcolo provides a complete bibliography of the books and articles of Garrigou-Lagrange in "Bibliographia del P. Garrigou-Lagrange," *Angelicum* 42 (1965), 200–272. Donald and Idella Gallagher provide a bibliography for Maritain up to 1961 in *The Achievement of Jacques and Raïssa Maritain: A Bibliography, 1906–1961* (Garden City, New York: Doubleday, 1962).

Some clarifications are in order. The first concerns the time-frame involved. Prior to the last decade, students of the Modernist controversy focused on developments internal to the Roman Catholic Church in such areas as philosophy, theology, scripture studies, and church discipline. More recently they have given considerable attention to the impact on the Roman Catholic Church of events and tendencies within the larger society. They have usually agreed, though, in fixing the end of the controversy around the beginning of World War I. Garrigou-Lagrange and Maritain were, in contrast, figures who achieved their importance well beyond 1914. I lengthen the temporal scope because the controversy continued to have its impact for decades, indeed even until the present day, and because throughout their long lives Garrigou-Lagrange and Maritain never ceased altogether to have Modernism in mind. The second clarification is about the terms *politics* and *philosophy*. I take *politics* to be an umbrella term encompassing the struggle for and the exercise of power within any society. We may think of it as the realm studied by political philosophers and political scientists and political historians, but obviously this realm cannot be separated from those studied by the historian of ideas or by the economist and the sociologist. I take *philosophy* to be an umbrella term for the effort of people to understand their world and to justify that understanding to themselves and to others. So taken, it will include much of science and much of theology. Garrigou-Lagrange and Maritain were primarily philosophers, by my definitions, rather than politicians, although they were always interested in the political realm and did on occasions enter it. Garrigou-Lagrange would have thought himself above all a theologian in the traditional scholastic sense (one concerned with revealed truth) more than a philosopher (one concerned with the truth accessible by reason), and Maritain would have thought himself above all a philosopher. However, philosophical and theological matters intermixed in all of their thinking; and, although I understand and by and large accept the distinction between a theologian and a philosopher, it need not play a great role in these pages.

BEGINNINGS

As a twenty-year-old medical student in 1897, Garrigou-Lagrange read Ernest Hello's *L'Homme* and underwent a conversion experience that changed his whole way of life. He tried to capture the experience as he thought back on his life in 1962.

During this reading, I saw or understood that the doctrine of the Catholic Church is the absolute truth about God, his intimate life, man, his origin, his spiritual destiny. I saw as in the batting of an eye that it was not merely a relative truth for the present moment, but an absolute truth which will not pass and which will appear always more and more elevated in its splendor until the moment we shall see God immediately, *facie ad faciem*.[2]

Hello's strategy in *L'Homme* was not one of systematic analysis or argument, but of laying side by side two portraits, one repellent and the other attractive. The repellent portrait is of the modern world, rooted in error, caught up in self-contradiction, and condemned necessarily to confusion and strife. Its main embodiments are Protestantism, rationalism, and pantheism. This modern world confronts the Catholic Church, which is founded on truth, beyond all essential change, and the earthly source of unity and peace. "[T]he Catholic Church not only has not changed, but is not able to change and will not change. In proclaiming the Catholic Church immutable, the human word repeats for it the promise made to it by the word of God. This word immutable engages the future."[3] Above all, Hello, the absolute believer, wishes to take on the mediocre man, who weakens the contrast between the modern world and the Catholic Church in deference to public opinion. This mediocre man "leaves us where we are, inspires us with a dead tranquillity which is not peace."[4]

His encounter with Hello's book, as Garrigou-Lagrange would remember it, caused him to abandon his medical ambitions and enter the Dominicans, the Order of Preachers. Becoming a Dominican meant not only preparing for the priesthood, but also entering into new fields of study, mainly philosophy and theology pursued (both by the tradition of the order and by direction of the church) through the intense study of the writings of the thirteenth-century Dominican Thomas Aquinas and his commentators. Now the passion for "truth beyond all essential change" found a systematic

---

[2] From Jorge y Ramòn Maria Sans Vila and Luigi Castiglione, *Vocazione al Sacerdozio. Inchiesta. Perché divenni sacerdote* (1962) and quoted in Innocenzo Colosio, "Il Maestro Reginaldo Garrigou-Lagrange, O. P. (1877–1964). Ricordi personali di un discepolo," *Rivista di ascetica e mistica* 9 (1964), 140.

[3] Hello, *L'Homme* (Paris: Librairie Academique, 1897), p. 269. The original was published in 1872.

[4] Ibid., p. 66.

intellectual framework. His principal mentor in developing this framework was his superior and teacher at Amiens, Ambroise Gardeil, who sent him in 1903 to the Sorbonne for further studies in philosophy. Studying at the Sorbonne meant entering the maelstrom of French intellectual discussion at the turn of the century, and we are fortunate to have a collection of letters from Garrigou-Lagrange to Gardeil for this period. In them we learn of Garrigou-Lagrange's dissatisfaction with the program at the Sorbonne, a program which he found too literary and formalistic and which would eventually lead him to Vienna and Fribourg en Suisse in search of something more satisfactory.

Of special interest here are his comments on the people and the tendencies he encountered during his time at the Sorbonne. In his very first letter, he notes that Alfred Loisy is a regular visitor to his residence and that students there refer to him in hushed tones. He expresses astonishment at the severe comments by his confrere A. D. Sertillanges about the biblical scholar. Some months later he describes attending one of Loisy's lectures and discovering him to be "a priest, simple, sweet, modest . . . nearly naïve."[5] In yet another letter, he asks if Gardeil has seen Maurice Blondel's "Histoire et dogme" in *La Quinzaine*, and he notes that "these people represent a considerable part of the young clergy and that they have for us the same hatred we have for them."[6] Thus, although he does not talk directly about the Modernism to be synthesized and condemned by Pope Pius X in *Pascendi dominici gregis* (1907), he was already mentally and socially involved in the controversy surrounding people such as Loisy and Blondel. His greatest interest, though, at this time was in the lectures of his eventual philosophical nemesis, Henri Bergson, at the Collège de France. He summarizes for Gardeil one of Bergson's lectures on intuition and sciences and remarks that there is evidently something of value there. He resists those Catholics who think that "Bergson, [Edouard] Le Roy and [Raymond] Poincaré work for us." "Bergson!! I'm too much of a rationalist to get involved in that."[7] In response to Bergson and these Catholics, he begins to develop his own more rationalistic species of metaphysical objectivism and realism, one with a surprising element of the epistemological *a priori* in it. He will be a Thomist, but without the sensism

---

[5] "Lettres de Jeunesse au P. Ambroise Gardeil (1903–1909)," presented by F. van Guten, *Angelicum* 42 (1965), 141–142 and 153–154.
[6] Ibid., p. 166.   [7] Ibid., p. 179.

characterizing too many of the Thomists of his day and with more sensitivity to historical context in philosophy generally.[8]

It was in attending the lectures of Bergson that Garrigou-Lagrange met Jacques Maritain, then recognized by his peers as among the most promising and committed of Bergson's disciples. As we know, Garrigou-Lagrange and Maritain would eventually become intellectual collaborators and close friends; and in the midst of their collaboration and friendship they would look back on their first encounter as students at the Sorbonne.[9] No one has related Maritain's life story better than his wife, Raïssa Oumansoff Maritain. Her husband was born in 1882, the son of Paul Maritain, a successful lawyer, and Genevieve Favre, whose father, Jules, had been a leading figure in the Third French Republic. His parents raised Jacques within a recognizably French tradition of liberal Protestantism and humanitarianism, but, by the time he reached the Sorbonne, he had given up all formal religious doctrine or association. It was through learning and above all through philosophy that he hoped to reach his fulfillment. For him, as for Garrigou-Lagrange, but perhaps at a different level, the Sorbonne proved a disappointment. Although he liked and respected the sociologists Emile Durkheim and Lucien Lévy-Bruhl, he found the efforts of his teachers – in philosophy above all – soulless. They had much learning in the history of philosophy, but they had no answers to the great questions they studied, that is, they had no wisdom to offer the young Maritain in his quest. In the classes of these teachers he met another disillusioned philosophy student, the Russian Jewish immigrant Raïssa Oumansoff. In the meeting of their minds, they came to love each other; but, in their common despair, they made a pact to kill themselves if they did not find a path towards the answers they sought. Happily, in the lectures of Bergson across the way from the Sorbonne, they discovered a hopeful direction. Here finally was someone who offered a trail through the tangle of experience and taught with conviction; and so, for the moment, they were Bergsonians, and the cloud lifted.[10]

After an engagement of two years, Jacques and Raïssa were

---

[8] Ibid., pp. 167–171, 179, 183–189.

[9] Raïssa Maritain, *Les Grandes Amitiés* (7th edition; Paris: Desclée de Brouwer, 1949), p. 108, and M. R. Gagnebet, "L'Œuvre du P. Garrigou-Lagrange: itinéraire intellectuel et spirituel vers Dieu," *Doctor Communis* 17 (1964), 163–164.

[10] *Les Grandes Amitiés*, pp. 91–92.

married on 26 November 1904. Not long after their marriage, they were to make a discovery that transcended philosophy in their eyes. They read Léon Bloy's *The Woman who was Poor* and encountered a ring of authenticity beyond anything they had met in philosophy, even in the classes of Bergson. Perhaps it was true that "the only tragedy in life is not to be a saint."[11] When they sought out the impoverished Bloy and his family, they found that this crude man, who hated philosophy and rejected the standards of polite society, was keyed into something absent in all their studies. Bloy seemed to them to be a saint; and, despite all the prejudices of their education, they accepted the connection between his sanctity and his intense Roman Catholic Christianity. After a long and shared interior struggle, intensified by an aversion they had felt for the Catholic culture around them and by their awareness of the pain a conversion would cause their families, they received baptism along with Raïssa's sister, Vera, with the Bloys as godparents.[12] They in turn were to lead their friends, Ernest Psichari and Charles Péguy (Péguy had no admiration for Bloy), on long and troubled journeys toward Catholicism.

By necessity, I have just made two long stories, that of the young Garrigou-Lagrange and that of the young Maritains, very short. It is necessary, however, to note certain connections that are nearly invisible in the records we have about these formative years. When Jacques and Raïssa Maritain were becoming Catholics in 1906, the Roman Catholic Church was in the midst of the intellectual and ecclesial struggle known as "the Roman Catholic Modernist controversy." In *Pascendi*, Pius X would identify Modernism as the "synthesis of all heresies" and attempt to eliminate this tendency by a remarkably severe set of disciplinary measures. Although the encyclical appeared the year after the Maritains became Catholics, they could not have been oblivious to the battle going on within the church about the work of Loisy and Blondel as well as people such as the French Catholic philosopher Marcel Hébert and the Anglo-Irish theologian George Tyrrell. Yet these events seem to have had no significance for Jacques and Raïssa as they moved from despair to faith. Almost as invisible in *Les Grandes Amitiés* are the political battles around the turn of the century, first those surrounding the trial of Jewish military officer Alfred Dreyfus on treason charges and then

---

[11] Ibid., pp. 117 ff.   [12] Ibid., pp. 184 ff.

those surrounding the efforts of successive French governments to weaken, indeed destroy, the power of the Roman Catholic Church in civil society. Yet no mentally competent adult in France could have been without opinions on these matters (and we know that Bloy and Péguy gave much thought to them). Similarly, although the Gardeil correspondence reveals Garrigou-Lagrange's early thoughts about the Modernist controversy, his letters contain no references to secular politics or to the restrictive legislation that was having major consequences for religious communities such as the Order of Preachers. The absence is remarkable.

FRIENDSHIP AND CONTROVERSY

No letters remain from Garrigou-Lagrange to Gardeil for the stretch between 1904 and 1909. Not surprisingly then, we do not know his immediate reactions to *Pascendi* and to *Lamentabili sane exitu*, the syllabus of errors preceding it in 1907. In fact, though, the two papal documents were to be central to his long career as a thinker and a writer – even when he seemed to have roamed far from the issues and the battles of these early days. In his 1964 memorial, M. R. Gagnebet would summarize the achievement of his confrere as having had a consistent theme: "Garrigou-Lagrange never ceased to meditate on these acts [*Pascendi* and *Lamentabili*] of the magisterium. His entire work is their explication and defense against modernist theology."[13] Certainly, in his earliest literary achievements, *Le Sens commun, la philosophie de l'être et les formules dogmatiques* of 1909 and "Dieu," his article for the *Dictionnaire apologétique de la foi catholique* of 1911, he is not only "the unyielding champion of Thomism" remembered by Gagnebet, but also the critic of Modernism and of the Modernists. Neither *Pascendi* nor *Lamentabili* had named Modernist names. The first was a synthesis of positions and tendencies in philosophy, theology, biblical studies, apologetics, ecclesiology and politics and the second, a culling of sentences from various books and their condemnation without naming either the books or the authors. In most of his writings, especially in these first pieces, Garrigou-Lagrange stayed mainly within philosophy and theology; and he made his principal Modernists Edouard Le Roy, Maurice Blondel, and Lucien Laberthonnière. The Bergsonian Le Roy, in

---

[13] Gagnebet, "L'Œuvre," p. 168.

particular, provided the foil for the argument of *Le Sens commun*, an argument central to everything its author was to write in the next sixty years and one worth a précis here.

To understand Garrigou-Lagrange's response, we need to have some idea of Le Roy's own thinking as it appeared in "Qu'est-ce qu'un dogme?" and *Dogme et critique*, both of which made it onto the Index of Forbidden Books despite the fact that Le Roy himself lived and died within the Roman Catholic Church. "Qu'est-ce qu'un dogme?," a 1905 article for *La Quinzaine*, cited the difficulties of presenting Christian-Catholic doctrine to sophisticated non-believers and even to sophisticated believers. Thus (1) "Dogma is a statement neither proved nor provable"; (2) "any dogma whatever seems like a subservience, like a limit to the rights of thought, like a menace of intellectual tyranny. . ."; (3) "their formulas often belong to the language of a particular philosophical system" or "they contain metaphors borrowed from everyday matters"; and (4) they "form a group incommensurable with the whole of positive knowledge." The examples given are the special problems of formulas such as "God is a person," "Jesus rose from the dead," and "Jesus is present in the eucharist." None of them seem properly intelligible as "theoretical bits of knowledge." How then shall we understand them? Le Roy offers two approaches. First, they serve a negative function, excluding certain options such as God is impersonal, or Jesus is dead and gone, or the consecrated host is just a symbol. Secondly, they call for certain attitudes toward God and the world, toward Jesus and life, toward the eucharist and worship. The attitudes are comprehensible on the level of common sense and capable of persisting through many changes of theory, and the approach "permits a solution of the problem without abandoning either the rights of thought or the requirements of dogma."[14]

Le Sens commun gives short shrift to most of Le Roy's worries and solutions. Garrigou-Lagrange does object to the suggestion that dogma be made palatable to his contemporaries: "In order to know what dogma is, it is not the present needs of souls which one should study; it is dogma itself, and its study will point us to excite in souls aspirations which are profound and interesting in ways other than

[14] Le Roy, "Qu'est-ce qu'un dogme?," in Fitzer (ed.), *Romance*, pp. 349–372. For an excellent overview of the debates surrounding Le Roy's work, see Guy Mansini, *"What is a Dogma?" The Meaning and Truth of Dogma in Edouard Le Roy and His Scholastic Opponents* (Rome: Editrice Pontificia Universitas Gregoriana, 1985).

those of which one now speaks . . ."[15] However, the notion of common sense that Le Roy takes from Bergson is of more concern to him. His summary of Le Roy goes roughly as follows. Intuition grasps the deepest reality as duration and flow without any artificial separation between things or between mind and matter. Common sense, in contrast, is not a discernment of being but a pragmatic way of dealing with what cannot be conceptualized. It has no representational value, but only a value of signification orienting our attitude and conduct toward the object. Consequently, dogmatic formulas, using the terms of common sense, are significative rather than representative; and only as significative do they command the irreformable and absolute adhesion of faith. Garrigou-Lagrange strikes at Le Roy and indirectly at Bergson through a complex and sophisticated argument for a "conceptual-realist or moderate realist" view. Common sense is a way of apprehending and understanding reality on its own terms and not simply of adjusting to it. It requires conception, judgment, and reason, reaching below the flow of appearances, entailing ontological commitments and terminating in a thoroughgoing metaphysics neither reducible to nor independent of the common sense from which it springs. This metaphysics will include the principles of identity, non-contradiction, unity, causality, and finality, principles to be denied only at the risk of destroying all thought and discourse.[16] The implications for dogma should be clear. Only a realist notion of common sense and of metaphysics will allow for analogical predication; and, without analogical predication, we shall be unable to make sense of religious and dogmatic teaching, and we shall run contrary to the formal teaching of the church as promulgated by the First Vatican Council and by Pius X in *Pascendi* and *Lamentabili*.[17] Such is, in capsule, the reasoning of *Le Sens commun*. Garrigou-Lagrange sent a copy to Bergson, who, despite the rough treatment his thought had received, responded with courtesy and appreciation. The approach in "Dieu" is along the same lines, but the encyclopedia article is far shorter and appeals to papal and conciliar authority more than to philosophical argumentation. Although more detailed criticisms of Blondel and Laberthonnière are now included, Le Roy and Bergson remain the principal targets.[18]

[15] *Le Sens commun, la philosophie de l'être et les formules dogmatique* (Paris: G. Beauchesne, 1909), p. v.
[16] Ibid., pp. 31–33, 52, 50–64, 74–82.   [17] Ibid., pp. 175–177.
[18] "Dieu," *Dictionnaire apologétique de la foi catholique* (Paris: G. Beauchesne, 1911), columns 949–956.

Jacques Maritain's path into the Modernist controversy was more roundabout. When he and Raïssa fell under the influence of Bloy, they put philosophical concerns on a back burner; and after their baptism they went to the university at Heidelberg to study biological questions and particularly the work on Hans Driesch on the nature of organisms. Driesch had reinvigorated the Aristotelian notion of the entelechy as a biological principle, and the Maritains found themselves taking up an Aristotle they had so far neglected. More importantly, they had come to realize that their Bergsonianism raised problems for their new-found faith. What would happen to the teaching of the scriptures, of Jesus, of the church, if religious doctrine like all formal thought had but pragmatic value and if the underlying reality reached by intuition was always in flux?[19] Becoming a serious Catholic in 1906 meant finding a spiritual director; and it was to his spiritual director, the Parisian Dominican Humbert Clérissac, that Jacques brought his difficulties. Clérissac directed him back into philosophy, to the very same scholastic philosophy that had been the heart of Garrigou-Lagrange's own Dominican intellectual formation. For Jacques, it was a genuinely new course of studies, and he soon found in it a way to handle the difficulties created by his earlier Bergsonianism. He steeped himself in the immense literature left behind by Thomas Aquinas, all the time bringing it into dialogue and contrasting it with the thought of Bergson.[20] Articles on Bergsonian philosophy appeared in the *Revue de philosophie* and the *Revue Thomiste* in 1911 and 1912, and he lectured on "la philosophie de M. Bergson et la philosophie chrétienne" at the Catholic Institute in Paris, where he had become a professor. All of this work came together in *La Philosophie Bergsonienne: études critiques* in 1913.

The import of *La Philosophie Bergsonienne* appears clearly in the title given to the English translation of the 1929 second edition: *Bergsonian Philosophy and Thomism*. Maritain attacked his old master and recommended Thomism as an alternative to inadequate theories of knowledge and of being. The tone of the attack was biting and even haughty, and the author would regret the tone enough to modify his language for the later version. However, he did not change his basic position.[21] His principal purpose in the book was to reject the

---

[19] *Les Grandes Amitiés*, pp. 210–212, and Raïssa Maritain, *Les Aventures de la grâce* (1944), published with *Les Grandes Amitiés* in 1949, pp. 228–229.
[20] *Les Aventures de la grâce*, pp. 233–249.
[21] *La Philosophie Bergsonienne: études critiques* (second edition; Paris: Marcel Rivière et Cie, 1930),

radical distinction between intuition and intellect and to defend the
view that conceptual knowledge, the fruit of intellect, reflects the
world as it is and does so in ways that transcend the limitations of
culture and epoch. *La Philosophie Bergsonienne* was then a companion
piece to *Le Sens commun*, although it does not stress the Modernist
controversy or the work of Le Roy. As already noted, the Maritains
had come to worry about their Bergsonianism without any direct
reference to Modernism, but they could not but see that their
worries concerned matters at the heart of the storm within the
church. When Jacques came to write the 1929 preface, he noted the
link with the Modernist controversy, a link he thought his new
readers might easily miss with the struggle now something of the
past. The years of "Modernism" had been

the period in which many young priests spoke of nothing but becoming and
immanence, of the evolutive transformation of the expressions of faith, of
the prismatization of the ineffable through dogmatic formulae ever
provisional and deficient, of the evils of abstract knowledge, of the inability
of "conceptual" or "notional" reason to establish the supreme natural
truths, of the idolatrous, superstitious (and above all outmoded) character
of the principle of contradiction.

It was "a courageous generation intellectually unarmed," a generation for which "to look down upon the intellect was considered to
be the beginning of wisdom, and became axiomatic." For this
generation, Bergson seemed to have pointed up the problem and to
have provided the answer: "This was the knot which had to be cut."
And Jacques Maritain was among those who found in Thomism the
knife sharp enough to do the cutting.[22]

When Garrigou-Lagrange and Maritain had become acquain-
tances at the Sorbonne, their worlds and their loyalties had seemed
immensely different. Now, though, Maritain had become a Catholic,
and they had had a mind-match about the dangers of Bergsonianism
and the promise of Thomism. They soon found each other again
and became collaborators and friends. Not only did they share the
same mission, but they could find similarities in their spiritual
adventures. Of course, Maritain's journey had been at once more
indirect and more dramatic – a long and difficult journey from
agnosticism and despair to a faith that had never been his before, in

pp. vi–ix, and the translation by Mabelle L. Andison and J. Gordon Andison, *Bergsonian Philosophy and Thomism* (New York: Philosophical Library, 1955).
[22] *La Philosophie Bergsonienne*, pp. xvi–xviii.

contrast to the discovery of a religious and intellectual vocation on the part of one raised within the church. Yet their "paths to Rome" were not altogether dissimilar. Maritain's mentor, Léon Bloy, had himself been formed through contact with the same Ernest Hello whose *L'Homme* had so altered the life of Garrigou-Lagrange. Bloy had even taken for himself the tag "pilgrim of the absolute" in an unmistakable reference back to "the absolute believer."[23] No doubt this coincidence of influences, so distant from philosophy and theology, must have entered into their new-found relationship. The relationship took on a formal character when Garrigou-Lagrange began to preside over the annual retreats of the *Cercle d'Etudes Thomistes*, founded by the younger man at Meudon after World War I.[24] By then, the Dominican had, under papal auspices, founded and occupied the chair of spiritual theology at the Angelicum in Rome, and he began to devote considerably less energy to combating a Modernism already defeated by the strategies of Pius X and by the zeal of other church leaders and anti-Modernist intellectuals. Maritain, for his part, moved beyond the preoccupations of *La Philosophie Bergsonienne* to a broader critique of Western culture, but even books such as *Anti-Moderne* and *Trois Réformateurs* are sprinkled with asides regarding Modernism.[25]

ACTION FRANÇAISE

The mind-match of Garrigou-Lagrange and Maritain in practical politics was never as neat as in "pure" philosophy and theology. Maritain had been a republican and a socialist right through his conversion, and Garrigou-Lagrange had shared neither sympathy. By the early 1920s, however, any observer of the political scene would have located them in the same camp. How they got into that camp and what eventually happened there makes an interesting story, one at the heart of the present essay. A good part of the story concerns their relationship with *Action française*, a movement with its beginnings as the espionage case against the Jewish officer, Alfred

[23] Jacques Petit, *Léon Bloy* (Paris: Desclée de Brouwer, 1965), pp. 51–62, and Jean Steinmann, *Léon Bloy* (Paris: Editions du Cerf, 1956), pp. 107–116.
[24] Jacques Maritain, *Carnet de notes* (Paris: Desclée de Brouwer, 1965), chapter V, on "Les Cercles d'Etudes Thomistes et leurs retraits annuelles."
[25] *Anti-Moderne* (Paris: Editions de Revue des Jeunes, 1922), and *Trois Réformateurs: Luther, Descartes, Rousseau* (Paris: Plon, 1925) (translated as *Three Reformers: Luther-Descartes-Rousseau* [London: Sheed & Ward, 1950]).

Dreyfus, began to unravel after his first trial. Much of French society divided into Dreyfusards and anti-Dreyfusards with the issue soon becoming not the guilt or innocence of Dreyfus, but the integrity and the dignity of the French army. One group which arose on the anti-Dreyfusard side was *Action française*; and, although he could not claim to be its founder, Charles Maurras was from early on until his death its intellectual leader and principal spokesman, and he made it a major force in French society for at least five decades.[26] Maurras himself was a man of many sides. A poet and an essayist as well as a political figure, he had in two early works, *L'Anthinea* and *Les Chemins de paradis*, presented himself as an atheist; but, well before the Dreyfus affair had concluded, he was also a nationalist and a monarchist for whom liberalism, republicanism, and democracy had brought France to a state of moral chaos and national weakness and for whom a return to French traditions and to the monarchy was the only path to internal peace and external strength. Despite his personal disbelief, he defended the Catholic Church, very specifically the *Roman* Catholic Church, as the source of French well-being in the past and the key not only to its well-being in the future, but also to the stability and harmony of the whole international order.[27] He grounded his argument on an empiricism drawn explicitly from Auguste Comte.[28]

Most committed French Catholics sided with the army in the Dreyfus affair and were thus on the side of the anti-Dreyfusards. They soon found themselves in a state of siege as one government after another worked to weaken, in many instances destroy, church institutions in the name of the separation of church and state. The one political force effectively opposing these governments was *Action française*, and great numbers of Catholics identified formally or informally with it. Garrigou-Lagrange seems to have made his identification very early. For Maritain, the transition was more complex, and, according to Raïssa, it began with the efforts of the same Clérissac who had already turned her and her husband toward Thomism. Clérissac made no secret of his distaste for Maritain's

[26] See Maurras's own account in *L'Action française et la religion catholique* (Paris: Nouvelle Librairie Nationale, 1913), pp. 90–97, on the origins. See also Lucien Thomas, *L'Action française devant l'Eglise: de Pie X a Pie XII* (Paris: Nouvelles Editions Latines, 1965), pp. 15–37, and Eugen Weber, *Action Française: Royalism and Reaction in Twentieth Century France* (Stanford, California: Stanford University Press, 1962), pp. 1–43.

[27] *L'Action française et la religion catholique*, pp. 75–97.

[28] Ibid., pp. 6, 67, 102, Thomas, *L'Action française*, p. 167, and Weber, *Action Française*, p. 38.

republicanism and socialism, and he began to work on him in two ways, to undermine his political convictions and to point out to him the merits of *Action française*.[29] Maritain never became a formal member of *Action française* or any of its sub-groups, but the impact of the spiritual director became evident: the philosopher began to reconsider some of his positions and to publish in its journal *La Revue universelle*.

One of the most difficult elements of *Action française* for Maritain must surely have been the anti-Semitism of Maurras and many of his followers. It was an anti-Semitism never raised by Maurras to a theoretical level, but *Juif* was invariably a slur word frequently put into a string with such labels as revolutionary, Protestant, German, and Freemason.[30] How could Maritain, married to a Jew, Raïssa, to whom Bloy dedicated the second edition of *Le Salue par les Juifs*, and a friend of a Dreyfusard like Péguy, have associated himself with Maurras and *Action française*? There are some partial answers. Bloy and Péguy could combine a mystical view of Judaism and a detestation of anti-Semites with an antipathy for many everyday Jews and could worry about the influence of Jews in French society.[31] Maritain would express some of this tension in a 1921 essay, one he would come to regret for its advocacy of some institutional limitations on Jews.[32] Maurras, for his part, always insisted that people could work for the political objectives of *Action française* without sharing his personal views on every subject. Believers and unbelievers could work together for political objectives without settling their differences about truth in religion. Something similar might hold for one's ethnic biases. However, other matters also made it possible for Maritain to make the shift encouraged by Clérissac. What would have been more natural than for a convert coming into the church in 1906 to accept the linkage between social modernism and all the other modernisms of *Pascendi*? For France, social modernism was Marc Sangnier's *Sillon*, a Catholic movement flowing from the

---

[29] See *Les Grandes Amitiés*, pp. 398–413, Thomas, p. 47, and Weber, p. 220.
[30] *L'Action française et la religion catholique*, pp. 72, 91, 94.
[31] Léon Bloy, *Le Salue par les Juifs* (Paris: Mercure de France, 1949) (originally published in 1892). See also Jacques and Raïssa Maritain, *Pages de Léon Bloy* (Paris: Mercure de France, 1931), pp. 275–303, and Marjorie Villiers, *Charles Péguy: A Study in Integrity* (New York: Harper & Row, 1965), pp. 48–60.
[32] "A propos de la question juive," *La Vie spirituelle* 4 (July 1921), 305–310. Robert Royal's collection, *Jacques Maritain and the Jews* (Notre Dame, Indiana: University of Notre Dame Press, 1994), reveals the wide range of interpretations of the thought and action of Maritain, Bloy, and Péguy on Jews and Judaism.

Ralliement encouraged by Leo XIII and combining republicanism with a heady mix of democratic sympathies, even in church matters, and political independence from ecclesiastical direction. Many French bishops and lower clergy, for whom the conciliatory mentality and the tactics of Sangnier and his fellows in French politics were exactly the wrong course in meeting their civil crisis, were not at all unhappy when Pius X condemned the *Sillon* in 1910.[33] These were most often the same bishops and clergy who found hope in Maurras and *his* fellows. It is no wonder that a convert finding his way in the Catholic Church in these years would have given a sympathetic hearing to Clérissac's political advice.

Although with one important exception, to be discussed later in this section, Maritain never became a formal defender of *Action française*, there was much in *La Philosophie Bergsonienne* to please the members of the movement. For them, the Catholics of the left, first *les abbés démocrats* and then the Sillonists, were the force of subversion within the church, and they had no reservations about the connection Pius X had made in *Pascendi* between these social and political currents and the other aspects of the Modernism synthesized there.[34] It was the hard edge of Catholicism that they admired; so anyone who obscured the edges of doctrine and attenuated discipline was in league with the democrats and the Sillonists. As a result, anyone who attacked Bergsonianism, especially Bergsonianism among Catholics, seemed likely to be an opponent of the *Ralliement* and everything associated with it. Of course, a democrat or a Sillonist could well have been against Bergson in philosophy, just as V. I. Lenin and the Bolsheviks were; but the position Maritain took gave him the presumption of being on the right (in both senses of the word) side of the political as well as the theoretical divide. He had the appropriate enemies. His choice of enemies in *Trois Réformateurs* – Luther, Descartes, and Rousseau – went further to accredit him among both the religious and the political anti-Modernists. Maritain located in these three reformers the intellectual sources of modern individualism, irrationality, sentimentality, anarchism, and ultimately tyranny. All these isms had a special connection with the German spirit, so despised by Maurras and the other *Action française* intellectuals. In *Anti-Moderne*, a collection of essays and talks, Maritain

---

[33] Simone and Helene Galliot, *Marc Sangnier (1873–1950)* (Le Mans: Imprimerie Commerciale, 1960), pp. 59–66, and O'Connell, *Critics*, pp. 164–165, 364–365.
[34] Maurras, *L'Action française et la religion catholique*, pp. 39, 46, 80, 82, 107–198.

offered a way out of the morass through the ongoing renewal of Thomistic philosophy and through the liberating magisterium of the Catholic Church. All these linkages would have made sense to Pius X and the apologists of *Pascendi*, and the believing and the unbelieving members of *Action française* interpreted them as the markings of a kindred spirit. Furthermore, Thomists and Maurrasians often enough formed overlapping groups, and Maritain found his books well reviewed and his articles accepted by the periodicals of both schools.

The Catholic identification with *Action française* was, however, far from universal, and for many within the church it constituted a dangerous identification. Their concern had many dimensions, the first of which was the position of Charles Maurras himself. How could believing Catholics accept as a leader a man who was a professed atheist and a methodological positivist? The leadership of Maurras and other unbelievers seemed to mean that politics was cut off not just from any religious base, but also from any moral base. It was an objection made not just by Lucien Laberthonnière and Maurice Blondel, neither of whom carried much weight among the bishops or within the Roman curia, but also by thinkers in no way suspect and by some bishops in France and in Rome.[35] Apart from the question of leadership, the independence claimed by *Action française* vis-à-vis the hierarchy seemed to be on a plane with the independence claimed by the *Sillon*. Surely consistency required a similar censure of the two movements. And what was to be made of a slogan like "politics first" (*politique d'abord*) with its ring of Machiavellianism or of the ruthlessness with which the members of *Action française* attacked their enemies in every camp and at every level? Maurras's answers were that he honored the church and respected believers, that it was possible for believers and unbelievers to work together for a sane society, that some of the elements of sanity were open to the empirical methods of Frédéric Le Play no less than Auguste Comte, that politics was not the highest realm but the realm of prior urgency, and that the "ruthlessness" at issue was a response to the real ruthlessness of his enemies. How earnestly he and his unbelieving colleagues took the position of the Catholic Church was

[35] See Lucien Laberthonnière, *Positivisme et catholicisme: à propos de "l'Action française"* (Paris: Bloud & Cie, Editeurs, 1911), and the articles published as Blondel, *LSS*. See also Michael Sutton, *Nationalism, Positivism and Catholicism: The Politics of Charles Maurras and French Catholics (1890–1914)* (Cambridge: Cambridge University Press, 1982).

surely clear from their enthusiasm for *Pascendi* and their establishment of the "chair of the syllabus" within *Action française*.[36]

The dispute about *Action française* came to a head for the first time
in 1914, when the Prefect of the Congregation of the Index presented
Pius X with a decree placing Maurras's early writings on the Index
of Forbidden Books. Reportedly the pope received the decree with
the words "Damnable but not to be damned" ("damnabilis sed non
damnandus") and then placed the decree in his desk drawer. Some
have taken the story to mean that, because of the tensions in Europe
at the time, the pope was reserving the condemnation for a more
propitious moment. Others, including Maurras, argued that he was
grateful for the work of *Action française* and its leader on behalf of the
church in France and was opposed to any condemnation. In any
event, Pius X died the same year; and the decree remained in the
drawer, apparently unread and unknown by his successor, Benedict
XV.[37] Whatever sympathies Pius X had for Maurras and *Action
française*, however, they were not shared by Pius XI. He worried
about the impact of the man and the movement among French
Catholics, especially among young Catholics, who identified
Maurras as the figure with the greatest influence in their lives. One
French bishop who shared these worries was Cardinal Paulin-Pierre
Andrieu, the archbishop of Bordeaux, and in 1926 Pius XI prompted
him to make public criticisms of *Action française* and subsequently
confirmed those criticisms in an address of his own.[38] However,
these criticisms came in forms and venues allowing for public debate
and for private maneuvering on all sides.

Maritain became a major figure in the debate. First, he published
Une opinion sur Charles Maurras et le devoir des catholiques, a study actually
written in 1925 and published one year later with additions and
notes required by the supervening events. Here he takes the assessment of Maurras's philosophical and religious thought to have been
settled for Catholics by Andrieu and Pius XI, while leaving open
interpretations of these warnings compatible with practical alle-

[36] *L'Action française et la religion catholique* presents all these rebuttals. See pp. 45 and 58 on the "chair of the syllabus."
[37] Thomas, *L'Action française*, p. 80, and Ann Howard Lindgren, "The Action Française and the Catholic Church: A Study of the Papal Condemnation with Special Reference to the Reactions of Jacques Maritain and Georges Bernanos" (M.A. Thesis: Brown University, 1965), pp. 23–24.
[38] Lindgren, "Action Française," pp. 25–27, and Henri Daniel-Rops, *Un combat pour Dieu* (Paris: Arthène Fayard, 1963), p. 498.

giance to *Action française*.[39] First, he affirms in succession that the truths of metaphysics and *a fortiori* of faith are absolutely superior to those of prudence and political action, that Thomism allows of various practical applications within a particular philosophy of the city, that is, of society and government, and that he himself has never wanted to adhere to any political group.[40] Then, after affirming his personal admiration for Maurras, he takes up one by one the genuine problems raised by his empiricism, his hostility to democracy and liberalism, his slogan of "politics first," and in general his notions of political science and political prudence.[41] In each case, he tries to find acceptable versions while recognizing the hazards. What Maritain proposes is that Catholics form a distinct and coherent group, able to shape itself religiously and morally while uniting with unbelievers for common purposes within the limits of faith and morals.[42] In the last chapter he distinguishes wholesome and unwholesome nationalism, exonerating Maurras from the charges of extreme nationalism and racism.[43]

Within the same year, Pius XI acted still more vigorously; appealing to the lost condemnation of 1914 and to the memory of Pius X, he now not only censured Maurras's writings, but also forbade Catholics under pain of excommunication from belonging to *Action française* or even reading the publications of the movement. The subsequent crisis among French Catholics was immensely more dramatic and more painful than the Modernist crisis two decades earlier, with the most startling development being the resignation in protest of Cardinal Louis Billot, a major figure who had almost certainly contributed to *Pascendi* and had become probably the leading theologian in the church.[44] And Jacques Maritain? He positioned himself as an outspoken defender of the condemnation, participating in two collections, *Pourquoi Rome a parlé* (1927) and *Clairvoyance de Rome* (1929), and also composing his own *Primauté du spirituel* (1927), whose English title, *The Things that are not Caesar's* (1931), involves an interesting shift of images.[45] Gone were the

---

[39] *Une opinion sur Charles Maurras et le devoir des catholiques*, (Paris: Plon, 1926), pp. 7–9.

[40] Ibid., pp. 10–11.　　[41] Ibid., pp. 11–12 and 19–46.　　[42] Ibid., pp. 53–63.

[43] Ibid., pp. 65–75.

[44] Lindgren, "Action Française," pp. 27–28; Thomas, *Action française*, chapter 4.

[45] P. Doncoeur, V. Bernadot, B. Lajeunie, D. Lallemont, F. X. Maquart, and J. Maritain, *Pourquoi Rome a parlé* (Paris: Spes, 1927) and *Clairvoyance de Rome* (Paris: Spes, 1929); Maritain, *Primauté du spirituel* (Paris: Plon, 1927) and *The Things that are not Caesar's* (New York: Charles Scribner's Sons, 1931). Bernard E. Doering's *Jacques Maritain and the French Catholic Intellectuals*

favorable interpretations of Maurras and the *modi vivendi* for Catholics in *Action française*: the volte-face was complete and astounding, and the way in which mind and will were brought so rapidly over to an almost contradictory stance had to puzzle even Pius XI. For Maurras and his followers, Maritain was henceforth "one of the six" (that is, the contributors to *Pourquoi Rome a parlé* and *Clairvoyance de Rome*) and someone whose name could not be evoked without scorn.[46]

In his memorial article, "Il Maestro Reginald Garrigou-Lagrange: 1877–1964," Innocenzo Colosio, a critical disciple and friend, describes his teacher as "conservative and rightist, sympathetic with *Action française* right up to the peremptory and hard condemnation by Pius XI . . ."[47] The words ". . . sympathetic . . . up until . . ." carry much meaning. There would be no resignation in the manner of Billot, the great theologian at the Gregorianum in the years before Garrigou-Lagrange became the great theologian at the Angelicum, but neither would there be any about-face. He published a single essay relating to the condemnation of *Action française*: "Les Exigences divines de la fin dernière en matière politique" in a 1927 issue of *Vie spirituelle*. The article maintains that the church has an indirect power over temporal matters related to the good of souls. Because of this power, the church can take stands on political matters, limit the political activity of its members, and condemn a political party or movement. The faithful must obey even though they believe the condemned movement, whatever its actual faults, good in itself. They may appeal to ecclesiastical authority, but with respect and so as not to produce a scandal. Their task is to find the virtue "in a movement borrowing from the great traditions of the French spirit and enlightened by the Christian faith" while "rectifying without delay the elements which run the risk of deviation." The hurt throughout is all too palpable, and yet he writes without a single reference to *Action française* or to the particular decisions and statements of Andrieu and Pius XI.[48] We can well imagine the discussions at the time among the people around him, particularly

(Notre Dame, Indiana: University of Notre Dame Press, 1983) has been especially helpful for this section and the following one.

[46] Maurras, *Le Bienheureux Pie X: sauveur de la France* (Paris: Plon, 1953), pp. 217–220.

[47] Colosio, "Il Maestro," p. 145.

[48] See "Les Exigences divines de la fin dernière en matière de politique," *Vie spirituelle* 15 (1927), 743–754. On Garrigou-Lagrange's attitude towards *Action française* and the condemnation, see Maritain's *Carnet de notes*, pp. 231–232.

his Dominican confreres, and the considerations behind his public stance of urging acceptance of the papal decree without ever acknowledging the validity of the arguments put forth in it.

Many French Catholics followed neither Maritain nor Garrigou-Lagrange. The words of Daniel O'Connell, "Our faith from Rome. Our policy from Home," proclaimed in the journal *L'Action française* just before the final condemnation, became a slogan of Catholics who could not or would not change their allegiance.[49] For Maurras, Pius XI was a weak man under the sway of Germanophiles at the Vatican and of the Briand government and the religious heirs of Marc Sangnier (mainly Emmanuel Mounier and the intellectuals of *L'Esprit*) at home.[50] The effect of their machinations with the pope, he would always claim, was to weaken French society internally and externally. Numerous people with access in Rome strove to have the ban lifted, but they would have to wait for success until 1939, when Eugenio Pacelli became Pius XII.[51] In any case, the story ended badly for Maurras and for *Action française*. That same year the German war machine overwhelmed the French army and, after the armistice, occupied the northern part of France while allowing a truncated and only semi-autonomous state under Marachal Philippe Pétain at Vichy in the southern part. *Action française* did, in fact, contribute officials to this regime, and Pétain would look to Maurras, who held no office, for steady advice in the construction of a society which could resist the power of Germany and replace the republican "Liberté, Egalité, Fraternité" with the Maurrasian "Travail, Famille, Patrie." Things fell apart for *Action française* as World War II progressed and as the new government lost all independence from the German power so feared and hated by the movement throughout decades. Fresh choices between resistance and collaboration were required. Maurras would always deride the suggestion that he might have collaborated with the "Hitlerians," but, when the war was over, his association with Pétain and Vichy brought him a sentence of life in prison. He rejoined the Catholic Church before his death in 1952, and he never relented in seeing Pius X as having been "the Savior of France" through his opposition to Modernism in general and the *Sillon* in particular and through his protection of

---

[49] Thomas, *L'Action française*, p. 160.
[50] See *Le Bienheureux Pie X*, pp. 26, 32–37, 41–45, 61–63, 69, 95–96, 120, 139, 152, 165 on Sangnier and the *Sillon*; p. 150 on Mounier and *L'Esprit*; and pp. 111–112, 132 on Pius XI.
[51] See *Le Bienheureux Pie X*, pp. 178–181 on Pius XII.

Action française in 1914. How the world might have been different, he mused, if there had been a Pius X on the throne of Peter throughout the 1920s and 1930s.[52]

DIVERGENCE AND CONVERGENCE

Garrigou-Lagrange must have been as nonplused as anyone at his friend's sudden change of heart with respect to *Action française*, but *La Primauté du spirituel* does not seem to <u>have di</u>srupted their relationship in any profound way. In contrast, events in Spain during the 1930s, culminating in the Spanish Civil War of 1936–1939, were to stretch the friendship close to breaking. Supported by a loose coalition of liberals, socialists, communists, anarchists, and separatists, a Popular Front had won the elections of 1936 in Spain with a promise to weaken the power of the old aristocracy and the church. Shortly after this victory, General Francisco Franco had led an army originally based in North Africa against the republican government, thereby inaugurating four years of bloody warfare in Spain and bringing into play auxiliaries from "left" and "right" throughout the Western world. Brutality was rampant on both sides. Because it was a target of the Popular Front and because many of its leaders allied themselves with Franco, the Catholic Church suffered not only an attack on its status and property, but also the violent deaths of thousands of bishops, priests, and religious. One easily understands why large numbers of Catholics, in France as elsewhere, identified with Franco and his nationalists and rationalized away the brutality they inflicted on their opponents. However, the situation was not simple, and Catholics were divided in their views. In their meetings at Meudon, the *Cercle d'Etudes Thomistes* was the scene of many heated debates about Spain and the appropriate attitudes and actions of Catholics with respect to it. Maritain and others refused to make Franco's cause the cause of Christianity, the Catholic Church, and civilization or to excuse nationalist brutalities because of republican brutalities. He was now in league with Catholic literary lights such as François Mauriac and Georges Bernanos, the second of whom had refused to honor the condemnation of *Action française*, and in opposition to others such as Paul Claudel and . . . Garrigou-Lagrange.[53]

---

[52] See Weber, *Action Française*, Part VI, for this story.
[53] See Doering, *Jacques Maritain*, chapter 4, on the debates within the "cercle" on the Spanish Civil War.

Colosio could finish his sentence quoted earlier on the political attitudes of his teacher with the words ". . . he declared himself always favorable to Franco . . ." And, one must add, increasingly distressed at Maritain's public declarations on the Spanish Civil War. In September 1937, after Maritain had published "De la guerre sainte," Garrigou-Lagrange arrived in an extraordinarily bad humor for the annual retreat at Meudon, the best attended retreat ever held there, but one full of tension. How tense things were appears in Maritain's *Carnet de notes*:

Father is extremely angry with me; he goes so far as to reproach me, a convert, for wanting to give lessons in the spirit of Christianity "to us who have been Catholics for three hundred years" . . . It seems that they put the blame on Raïssa and Vera for using their influence to lead me astray. (They're Jewesses aren't they? They who detest these political quarrels and would have been so happy to have me remain aloof from them, if I had not seen in them a witness I had to bear to the truth.) I find myself in a black fit of anger, which I don't hide . . . Father Garrigou would like to forbid me to speak on the philosophy of history and to judge current events and to act on young people in these matters . . . (I know well that he's not the only one in Rome to think like this and to be terrified of the "political Maritain.") Only metaphysics! But he doesn't hesitate to pronounce in favor of Franco and to approve the Civil War in Spain.[54]

It was an unhappy retreat from beginning to end, and the two men would never have the old affection for each other again.

Maritain never stopped writing during this period. Most of the titles from 1931 until 1935 had little evident connection with the contemporary political crises, whether in Spain or elsewhere. We can see the range of his interests by citing just a few: *De la philosophie chrétienne* (1933); *Sept leçons sur l'être et les premiers principes de la métaphysique* (1934); *Frontières de la poésie et autres essais* (1935); *La Philosophie de la nature, essai critique sur les frontières et son objet* (1935); *Science et sagesse, suivi d'éclaircissements sur la philosophie morale* (1935). However, the bibliography for 1935 and after reveals a distinct shift of attention with *Lettre sur l'indépendance* (1935), *Humanisme intégral: problèmes temporels et spirituels d'une nouvelle chrétienté* (1936), *Les Juifs parmi les nations* (1938), *Questions de conscience: essais et allocutions* (1938), and then numerous books and essays during World War II. The most important of these publications for our purposes is *Humanisme intégral*, a volume based on lectures Maritain gave in August 1934 at

---

[54] *Carnets de notes*, p. 232, and Doering, *Jacques Maritain*, p. 114.

the University of Santander in northern Spain; it provides the best idea of the theoretical course of Maritain's thought on the eve of the Civil War in that country. Here he raises the possibility of forming a new Christendom, that is, a Christendom for the modern world, based on the essential truths and values of the Christian faith, but taking a significantly different form from the Christendom of the Middle Ages. "Christendom," he defines as "a certain temporal regime whose formations, in very varying degrees and in varying ways bear the stamp of the Christian conception of life." One can speak of "varying degrees" and "varying ways" because the unity of Christendoms is analogical rather than univocal. Medieval Christendom, as a concrete historical idea, rested on two foundations: "the idea or the myth . . . of force in the service of God . . ." and "the concrete fact that temporal civilization was in some way itself a function of consecrated activity and thus imperatively demanded religious unity." With the Renaissance, the Reformation, and the Enlightenment, the idea of the Middle Ages is no longer concrete and historical, no longer within the possibilities of the Western world. The "holy empire" yielded to a bourgeois humanism, ending in the chaos and exploitation of capitalism, and to a consequent socialist humanism, ending in totalitarian statism.[55]

For Maritain, "Christianity alone seems able to defend at various vital points of Western civilization the vital freedom of the individual and also, in the degree to which it illumines the temporal order, those positive liberties which correspond on the social and political plane to that spiritual freedom." The result, though, will be a new Christendom, because it will have different concrete historical possibilities shaped by the way society and culture have really developed, despite being "founded on the same principles (analogically applied) . . ." It will not have as its goal a consecrated public order, but a secular one, even though inspired by Christian principles. It will be ideologically and institutionally pluralistic; its temporal order will be autonomous and recognized by Christians as an intermediary or "infravalent" end of political action, that is, as a genuine purpose of action although not the supreme purpose; and it will secure the freedom of persons in all areas through respect for their transcendent dignity and not just through fear of civil discord.

[55] See Maritain, *Humanisme intégral* (Paris: Aubier, 1936) and M. R. Adamson's translation, *True Humanism* (London: The Company Press, 1938).

This transcendent dignity, in Maritain's account of the new Christendom, rests on the distinction he establishes between the human being as an individual and the human being as a person. Whereas the individual rooted in matter may be wholly subordinate to the state, the person always has a spiritual dimension giving him/her a finality exceeding the demands of the earthly common good. Although Maritain did not intend *Humanisme intégral* to serve as a political manual, he does endeavor to extract certain practical conclusions for working toward the new Christendom and for living within it. Above all, he regards it as a beacon forever beyond our reach and not as a target to be attained with finality.[56]

Surely Maritain's involvement in the conflicts over *Action française* and over the Spanish Civil War must have led him to expect mixed reviews for *Humanisme intégral* and for the new Christendom laid out both there and in the other political writings of the 1930s. He was, however, probably taken aback by the line of negative criticism these works provoked. For example, the same philosopher who had begun his literary career with a thoroughgoing rejection of Bergsonian evolutionism would find his concept of history traced back to Bergson's theory of creative evolution. Try as he might to escape the trap, "The disciple has not forgotten the master," one critic would say in *La Civiltà Cattolica* in 1956.[57] The most sustained attacks, however, came from Spanish and Latin American Catholics, with Julio Meinvielle, an Argentinian priest, the most determined anti-Maritainist. In the 1945 *De Lamennais a Maritain*, Meinvielle traces the social doctrine of *Humanisme intégral* back to Lamennais and especially to Marc Sangnier and the Sillonists and challenges it as incompatible with the consistent teaching of the Catholic Church. The result of this doctrine was to make a virtue of the laicization of civil society and to undermine the position of Catholic Christianity. Maritain had, then, fallen into the camp of the liberals condemned by Gregory XVI and of the social modernists condemned by Pius X.[58] At the end of *De Lamennais a Maritain*, Meinvielle promised another book in which he would uncover the source of the erroneous social doctrine in Maritain's concept of the human person. He lived

---

[56] Ibid.
[57] A. Messineo, "L'Umanesimo integrale," *La Civiltà Cattolica*, Anno 107, 3 (24 August 1956), 449–463.
[58] Meinvielle, *De Lamennais a Maritain* (Buenos Aires: Ediciones Nuestro Tiempo, 1945). French translation: *De Lamennais à Maritain* (Paris: Cité Catholique, 1956).

up to his promise with his 1948 *Critica de la concepción de Maritain sobre la persona humana*, where he begins directly with the distinction between the human individual and the human person, a distinction that he judges to be both unfaithful to Aquinas and his classical commentators and philosophically untenable. It is because he makes this unfortunate distinction that Maritain can fall into the error of subordinating the common good to the subjective purposes of people taken singly.[59]

Notwithstanding their sharp disagreements about Franco and the Spanish Civil War and then later about Pétain and the Vichy regime, Garrigou-Lagrange provided important support for Maritain throughout the 1930s and 1940s when matters of doctrinal orthodoxy arose in Rome.[60] Most significantly, he provided this support at the very time when he was defining the "Nouvelle Théologie" and ringing the warning-bell about a recurrence of the Modernist threat in the church. Of old, Le Roy had been the villain, but now, Blondel was the unwitting heresiarch through his re-definition of truth as the agreement of thought and life rather than the Aristotelian agreement of thought and reality.[61] Garrigou-Lagrange had remained in Rome, and his role as confessor and counselor to Pius XII bore fruit when the encyclical *Humani generis* (1950) condemned the diverse strains already brought together in a synthesis with "La Nouvelle Théologie, ou va-t-elle?" and many similar articles.[62] Jacques Maritain, in the United States throughout the war and French ambassador to the Vatican afterwards, played no apparent part in the development so worrisome to the pope and his advisor. However, when Meinvielle sought out a response to *De Lamennais a Maritain*, Garrigou-Lagrange gave an answer likely to satisfy neither Maritain nor his accuser.

Meinvielle published the letter in the journal *Balcon*. Garrigou-Lagrange states "that J. M. has not seen where some of his concessions are able to lead logically and that many current events

---

[59] Meinvielle, *Critica de la concepción de Maritain sobre la persona humana* (Buenos Aires: Ediciones Nuestro Tiempo, 1948).

[60] Doering, *Jacques Maritain*, p. 115.

[61] Garrigou-Lagrange, "Vérité et option libre selon M. Maurice Blondel," *Acta Pont. Acad. Rom. S. Thom. Aq.* 2 (1936), 46–69.

[62] See Garrigou-Lagrange, "La Nouvelle Théologie, ou va-t-elle?" originally published in *Angelicum* in 1946 and reprinted in Garrigou-Lagrange, *La Synthèse Thomiste* (Paris: Desclée de Brouwer, 1946), pp. 699–707, and *Humani Generis*: Latin and English Edition (Weston, Massachusetts: Weston College Press, 1951).

ought to show him the danger of these concessions . . ." He reminds Meinvielle "that he has suffered since 1936 from the difference that he finds between the first of his books (where we collaborated in perfect understanding) and the more recent, which have appeared since the bloody revolution in Spain. There is something sad there . . ." But he continues "the title of your book seems excessive to me, for the deviation of which you speak is far from having the proportion of that of Lamennais, who erred more and more on the final purpose of the life of the church, as if it ought to work above all, not to direct men for eternal life, but for the temporal well-being of peoples which ought to be liberated from all servitude." He himself still holds firmly what Meinvielle cites from him in *De Lamennais a Maritain*. Indeed he is all the more confirmed in his position now that he has been reading the works of Donoso Cortés, so different from those of "J. M." In 1850, Cortés had written a long letter for Pius IX precisely on the hazards confronting "peoples separated from Christian and Catholic principles."[63] Maritain's resentment over this correspondence comes out in two letters he sent to his old friend (letters obtained and published by Meinvielle with a commentary intended as a refutation). In them Maritain asks: How could Garrigou-Lagrange have entered into the calumnies of Meinvielle? How could he have passed over the actual situation in Argentina with this correspondence? How could he convert political differences between them into doctrinal differences? When he had gone to the extreme of declaring support for de Gaulle against Pétain a matter of mortal sin, Maritain had never made his theology suspect or accused him of doctrinal deviation. And how could Garrigou-Lagrange have placed works like *Humanisme intégral* in the realm of Lamennais? In these writings, Maritain had been exploring the concrete possibilities of contemporary societies composed of Catholics, Protestants, agnostics, atheists . . . and of the role of Christians and the church in them. In no sense had he ever subscribed to philosophical or theological liberalism or approved the horrors of the French Revolution.[64]

---

63 Meinvielle, "Una Carta del R. P. Garrigou-Lagrange, O. P.," *Balcon* 9 (26 July 1946). The text of the letter is in both Spanish and French.

64 Meinvielle, *Respuesta a dos cartas de Maritain al R. P. Garrigou-Lagrange, O. P.* (Buenos Aires: Ediciones Nuestro Tiempo, 1948), pp. 41–60. To situate Meinvielle in the religious politics of Argentina in the 1930s and 1940s, see Austen Ivereigh, *Catholicism and Politics in Argentina, 1810–1960* (Oxford: St. Martin's Press, 1995).

There is a curious irony in the Meinvielle debate. When *Critica de la concepción de Maritain sobre la persona humana* traced Maritain's social and political thought back to the distinction between the human individual and the human person, Garrigou-Lagrange himself appeared as one of the progenitors of the nefarious distinction.[65] We do not know what either Maritain or Garrigou-Lagrange thought about ending up on the same page, but they arrived at the same last page in another sense. Garrigou-Lagrange finished his work as a major theologian when he systematically went after the "Nouvelle Théologie" as a recurrence of Modernism. He continued writing right up until the eve of the Second Vatican Council, but he was never to have a major impact again on intellectual debates within the Catholic Church. He died in 1964 after a long period, falling under what must have been the effects of Alzheimer's disease; and so we have no evidence of his thoughts on the *aggiornamento* initiated by John XXIII. Maritain, in contrast, lived through the Council and contributed to it through the influence of his past writings on the participants and through his occasional presence. Yet, although he welcomed the changes wrought there, he came to lament many of the intellectual currents which arose in the wake of the Second Vatican Council. Most upsetting for him were the signs of philosophical and theological relativism on the part of some Catholics, particularly in France. Like Garrigou-Lagrange in the face of the "Nouvelle Théologie," he descried a neo-Modernism even more virulent than the one he had confronted after his conversion.[66] So, now widowed and living as a Little Brother of Jesus, he put his worries into writing with *Le Paysan de la Garonne* and for the last time became the center of a controversy between right and left within the Catholic Church.

ELECTIVE AFFINITIES

Goethe used the term *Wahlverwandtschaften* (taken from the chemistry of his day and usually translated as *Elective Affinities*) as the title of a novella about the way in which people form and change relationships (in the novella first the affectionate relationship of a marriage and then an affectionate relationship outside the marriage). As the

[65] See *Critica de la concepción de Maritain sobre la persona humana*, chapter 1.
[66] Maritain, *Le Paysan de la Garonne: un vieux laïc s'interroge à propos du temps present* (Paris: Desclée de Brouwer, 1966), p. 10.

"Captain" explains, people (Eduard and Charlotte and later Eduard and Ottilie) incline this way and that because they have affinity with each other, just as chemicals enter into now one compound and now another, depending on the varying strength of affinities.[67] Something like this process worked for Garrigou-Lagrange and Maritain, not only in the blossoming and declining of their friendship, but also in the interplay between them (together and separately) and the many social networks we call "France," the "Sorbonne," the "Roman Catholic Church," the "Order of Preachers," and the "Action française," each holding together and pulling apart in a pattern of affinities and disaffinities. The affinities themselves are multi-dimensional, embracing not only the seemingly private and intimate aspects of their lives, but also the larger social, cultural, economic, and political realities within which they lived. However, it is important also to stress the element of election, that is, of choice, of *Wahl*, in the shifting of affinities. We humans have at least indirect power to strengthen or weaken, direct or redirect our affinities and in doing so individually help change the possible affinities of an age. Think how things might have been different if Pius X had been less committed to coherence in *Pascendi*, if Garrigou-Lagrange had continued in medical school, if Bloy had been unwilling to receive Jacques and Raïssa, if Maurras had made *Action française* worth a mass, or if Maritain had received its condemnation in 1926 with quiet obedience. Yet not every choice is possible for every person or for every time: to quote Karl Marx, "Men make their own history, but they do not make it just as they please; they do not make it under circumstances chosen by themselves, but under circumstances directly found, given and transmitted from the past."[68]

I want to stand with R. G. Collingwood in maintaining that the historian of ideas must in some measure work on the level of the thinkers he is studying. Of course, one must know the context, but it is also necessary to enter critically into philosophy and theology in order to study the thought of philosophers and theologians: there can be no useful view from the outside and no inside view not already in the process of judging this thought in terms of truth and

---

[67] See Goethe, *Die Wahlverwandtschaften*, in *Goethe Werke* (Frankfurt am Main: Insel Verlag, 1966), chapter 4, and R. J. Hollingdale's translation with introduction, *Elective Affinities* (Harmondsworth: Penguin Books, 1971).

[68] Marx, *The Eighteenth Brumaire of Louis Napoleon* (1852) in Robert Tucker's collection, *The Marx-Engels Reader* (New York: W. W. Norton and Company, 1972), p. 437.

value.[69] Thus the significance of my analysis of Garrigou-Lagrange and Maritain for studying any of the Modernists or anti-Modernists (Blondel, Loisy, Tyrrell, Von Hügel, Pius X . . .) should be that a full understanding of them will necessarily include *both* a deep awareness of their social environment, their individual circumstances, and their personal choices regarding the questions they confronted *and* an informed and judicious assessment of their ideas. Was what they said so, that is, did it square with reality (however changeable or unchangeable reality may be)? Was it said coherently and persuasively? Did saying it bear fruit for their day and perhaps for our day? Not to raise these questions would be to neglect matters of the greatest importance to almost all of these people, Modernists and anti-Modernists alike. If the present article has served its purpose, it has taken one small step toward understanding at least two of them, Reginald Garrigou-Lagrange and Jacques Maritain, as thinkers and actors in history and toward developing a method for similar investigations.

[69] Collingwood, "Human Nature and Human History," *Proceedings of the British Academy* (1936), reprinted in Ronald Nash's collection *Ideas of History* (New York: P. Dutton, 1969), vol. II, pp. 40–43. See also my "Crossing Berger's Fiery Brook: Religious Truth and the Sociology of Knowledge," *The Thomist* 40 (1976), 366–392, and "Truth and the Social Construction of Reality," *Realism: Proceedings of the American Catholic Philosophical Association* (Washington, D.C.: The American Catholic Philosophical Association, 1984), pp. 289–298, for some reflections on the question of truth.

Conclusion

Darrell Jodock

The previous chapters have examined several Modernists and several anti-Modernists. The overall argument of those chapters is that the theological position of neither group should be praised or blamed without first considering the following two questions: Why did the crisis develop when it did? Why did each individual involved in the Modernist crisis take the position that he or she did?

First, why did the crisis develop when it did? If one looks at the writings of the Catholic Tübingen School from the first half of the nineteenth century, it can be seen that the strictly theological issues had not changed very much in 100 years. What had changed was the cultural climate and the socio-political circumstances in which the church found itself. Various facets of that change have been explored in this volume, including the decreased temporal power of the Vatican, the development in France of a state-sponsored system of education which was independent of the church, the separation of church and state, and the declining credibility for many citizens of the church's claims to authority. The Modernists and the anti-Modernists both had to come to terms with these changes. The intensity of the crisis resulted from their radically divergent ways of undertaking the same task: while trying to convey the religious message of Catholic Christianity to the people of their day, the Modernists practiced selective accommodation, while the anti-Modernists practiced selective confrontation. In both instances, the word "selective" is important. Their opponents accused the Modernists of selling out completely to modernity, and the anti-Modernists were accused of rejecting it wholesale. Their respective opponents overlooked the selectivity with which each group responded to modernity.

When viewed in their historical context, both the Modernists and anti-Modernists were dealing with the complex features of

337

modernity – features at once both threatening and inviting. Included under the umbrella of modernity were a differentiation of functions in society, a streamlining (for the sake of efficiency) of social processes, a bureaucratization (built around implementing policies rather than a network of personal loyalties) of social institutions, a respect for the authority of science and whatever is empirically demonstrable, a sense of individual autonomy along with a "leveling" of social authority, and a confidence in the possibility of social reform and improvement. For example, neither the Modernists nor the anti-Modernists could ask the state to settle religio-social disputes; they each had to develop a specifically churchly definition of authority; and their conflicting answers were constructed within the limitations assigned to the church by modern society. Likewise, both the Modernists and the anti-Modernists appealed to history to verify their claims regarding the Scriptures, doctrine, and the church. Such a strategy reflected a specifically modern valuation of history as the appropriate court of appeal.

In retrospect one regrets that the two positions were not allowed to continue to interact, for when contending with modernity Christianity needs a double approach: both selective endorsement and selective resistance. In 1907 papal fiat cut short meaningful debate. Had the mutual critique of these two quite different approaches to modernity been allowed to continue, the importance of a dual response may have become evident, and the complex issues involved in Christianity's relation to modernity may have been identified more swiftly and more clearly.

The second question is why each individual involved in the crisis took the position that he or she did. Each person's story has unique features, of course, but the chapters in this book have amply demonstrated that a combination of non-religious and religious factors were at work. Blondel and von Hügel, for example, both combined a deeply religious awareness with their scholarly endeavors to produce dissimilar positions more or less Modernist. Similarly, for Maritain opposition to Modernism emerged from a combination of religious, scholarly, and political considerations. Looking back, what divided one Modernist from another and one anti-Modernist from another was most often the differing sociopolitical settings in which they found themselves and their differing perceptions of the political developments of the time.

What is fascinating about the Modernists is how deeply involved they were in the issues of their own day. They were concerned about education, revitalizing the piety of Catholic Christians, and the social effects of an economy built around the assumptions of individualism. They exhibited a pastoral concern when dealing with the issues facing the believers of their day. And to a large extent they gave expression to some of those issues. Thus, despite his oft-quoted assertions about the independence of historical investigation, Loisy, prior to his condemnation, was not a narrow academic concerned only with the intricacies of research. He was, as Harvey Hill has shown, interested in involving the church in the moral reform of the nation.

Under other circumstances the Modernists may have been able to add their voices to the diversity of theological expression allowed under the canopy of the Roman Catholic Church, but a form of neo-scholasticism had preceded them that sought not merely to describe and embody Christian teaching but to define it and build around it an authority structure that would insist on the definitions formulated by the neo-scholastics. In other words, the misfortune of the Modernists was that the area under the canopy had been reduced in size. Less room for diversity existed than during some other periods of church history. Under such conditions the creative endeavors of the Modernists were considered subversive of church teaching.

The anti-Modernists were also deeply involved in non-theological issues. They were concerned about the autonomy of the church in the face of modern political movements. They were worried about diplomacy, about the temporal power of the pope, about the existence of religious orders and parochial schools. They may not themselves have wanted to distinguish between the power of the church and its doctrine, but they were worried about theological variation as much because it seemed to threaten the bargaining power of the church vis-à-vis the state as because it undermined specifically doctrinal traditions. Just as much as the Modernists, they were *creating* a new tradition, shaped by their perception of modern culture. Just as much as the Modernists, they were approaching the tradition in a new way.

Because both were shaped by modern culture, neither the Modernists nor the anti-Modernists could have arisen at any other time. Each viewed modernity differently, but they were responding to modernity, not to something else. At bottom both were worried about the delimited role of the church and its integrity in the face of modern culture.

If the theological position of either the Modernists or the anti-Modernists is isolated from their other involvements, an interpreter runs the danger of misconstruing their endeavors. Their theologies cannot be adequately assessed without a clear sense of *what* they were responding to in their historical setting and *how* they were responding to it. Any contemporary appropriation of the theology of either group apart from a recognition of their non-theological involvements de-contextualizes, de-historicizes, and risks distortion.

The final word must be a frank recognition that this volume remains an incomplete undertaking. It is incomplete, first, in the sense that much more is likely to be uncovered about the persons that have been discussed. Still more could be said about the relationship each had to his/her context and about the non-theological factors shaping his/her theological position. The volume is incomplete, secondly, in a more significant way. The investigation needs to be extended into arenas not included here. Similar questions need to be asked about German, Italian, and American Modernists and anti-Modernists, to say nothing of other French and English figures. We hope this volume has demonstrated the value of doing so. And we hope that additional studies will not only enrich our understanding of the people involved in the crisis but also confirm the value of this avenue of study.

The task of clarifying Christianity's relationship to modern culture is not over. Some of the strategies that seemed helpful in 1900 seem less so 100 years later, but for believers and for theologians the relationship still requires sorting out. Greater clarity is needed about the character and consequences of various responses to modernity in the past. From such clarity will come increased wisdom about the role of Christianity today. Discovering that wisdom is yet another part of the unfinished task.

Index

phil is not thought, it is chosen = genealogy method